Encyclopedia of American Holidays and National Days

ENCYCLOPEDIA OF AMERICAN HOLIDAYS AND NATIONAL DAYS

Volume 2

Edited by Len Travers

GREENWOOD PRESS
WESTPORT, CONNECTICUT • LONDON

Library of Congress Cataloging-in-Publication Data

Encyclopedia of American holidays and national days / edited by Len Travers.
     p. cm.
  Includes bibliographical references and index.
    ISBN 0–313–33130–8 (set) — ISBN 0–313–33131–6 (vol. 1) — ISBN 0–313–
33132–4 (vol. 2) 1. Holidays—United States—Encyclopedias. 2. United States—Social
life and customs—Encyclopedias. I. Travers, Len, 1952–
  GT4803.A2E63 2006
  394.26973—dc22   2005036319

British Library Cataloguing in Publication Data is available.

Library of Congress Catalog Card Number: 2005036319

ISBN: 0–313–33130–8 (set)
      0–313–33131–6 (vol. 1)
      0–313–33132–4 (vol. 2)

First published in 2006

Greenwood Press, 88 Post Road West, Westport, CT 06881
An imprint of Greenwood Publishing Group, Inc.
www.greenwood.com

Printed in the United States of America

The paper used in this book complies with the
Permanent Paper Standard issued by the National
Information Standards Organization (Z39.48–1984).

10 9 8 7 6 5 4 3 2 1

CONTENTS

VOLUME 1

VOLUME 2

INDEPENDENCE DAY

Independence Day—the Fourth of July—is by definition America's oldest public holiday. It marks the day, on July 4, 1776, when Congress declared the independence of the new United States from Great Britain during the American Revolution. It is thus, literally, the birthday of the United States.

From the beginning, Americans have used the holiday enthusiastically both to celebrate their nation and to define and shape its meaning. During the American Revolution and the early years of the republic, the Fourth of July functioned as an occasion to help create that which was being celebrated: American national identity and the nation itself. As the festival became firmly established and evolved over decades and centuries, Independence Day would express complicated, sometimes paradoxical, sentiments. It has been solemn and celebratory, politically charged and blissfully apolitical, unifying and divisive, nationally focused and locally based, grandly public and intimately private. Independence Day endures as America's most important public holiday. Too important to be moved in the calendar to form a three-day weekend, it remains anchored firmly on the Fourth of July, when the entire country stops to commemorate the birth of the United States grandly, through parades, pageants, pyrotechnics, picnics, or other simple pleasures.

The American Revolution—which Independence Day generally celebrates and represents—is uniquely popular in American memory. Even in times of controversy and division, virtually all Americans agree that the Revolution was a good thing, worthy of celebration. Such consensus gives the holiday great potential power as a moment to affirm or contest the circumstances or poli-

INDEPENDENCE DAY

- [ ] Independence Day is celebrated on July 4, the day Congress declared independence from Great Britain in 1776.
- [ ] It is America's oldest national holiday, presenting a public opportunity to define and celebrate our nation.
- [ ] Reading of the Declaration of Independence became a fixture in nineteenth-century Fourth of July celebrations, recreating its original proclamation throughout the 13 colonies.
- [ ] Nineteenth-century abolitionists staged annual meetings on July 4 to underline their belief that the Declaration of Independence's assertion that "All men are created equal" applied to African Americans too.
- [ ] In the same spirit, New York and New Jersey announced gradual emancipation for slaves on July 4, 1799 and 1804, respectively.
- [ ] In 1852 perhaps the most powerful challenge to the mindless celebration of Independence Day occurred when the former slave and leading black abolitionist Frederick Douglass, asked, "What, to the Slave, is the Fourth of July?"
- [ ] Advocates for temperance, women's rights, workers' rights, and the plight of children have all used the Fourth of July as a springboard for their campaigns.
- [ ] In the early 1800s workers increasingly used Fourth of July celebrations to assert their independence—often through drunken revelry—from a growing middle class bent on controlling their working and moral lives.
- [ ] Abandoned by white southerners, the Fourth of July became a Republican Party and African American holiday after the Civil War.
- [ ] The Fourth of July developed into a major public festival on Indian reservations despite the holiday's assimilationist goals. While white officials banned Native American rituals they condoned Independence Day gatherings, which could provide cover for continued practice of outlawed Native American religious rites.
- [ ] The delightful meaninglessness of fireworks makes them an apt metaphor for American Independence Day in the twentieth century.
- [ ] In 1908, officials recorded some 5,600 casualties from fireworks, almost half the number killed, wounded, or missing during the American Revolution.

cies of the country. On the Fourth of July, American society and its leaders can be publicly measured by the standards of the Founding Generation and the sacred document adopted on July 4, 1776: the Declaration of Independence. And often, protests have exploded on the Fourth of July like firecrackers to awaken Americans to their shortcomings in realizing the principles articulated or promised in the Declaration. On the other hand, in moments of greater national self-satisfaction, security, or prosperity, the Fourth of July celebrates the United States more implicitly and with less seriousness through escapist, summertime diversions and leisure.

Fourth of July scene on Boston Common from the July 1859 edition of *Ballou's Pictorial*. Courtesy of the Library of Congress.

Identity, citizenship, and the boundaries of American public life are often fundamentally at stake during Independence Day. The Fourth of July presents a public opportunity to define the American nation (expansively or narrowly) as well as celebrate it. Orators, editors, politicians, and public figures have used the occasion to exclude as well as include, declaring who is and who is not legitimately American. Independence Day has functioned as a means to reshape such boundaries, whether defined ethnically or racially, religiously, legally, politically, geographically, socially, or in terms of sex and gender. If some have used the holiday to promote narrow, ethnocentric visions of America, others have proclaimed pluralism as the spirit of the day. Millions of new American citizens have taken their oaths of allegiance to the United States on Independence Day. In the nineteenth century, abolitionists chose the occasion to condemn the hypocrisy of slavery in a land where "all men are created equal." African Americans have employed the Fourth of July to seek true equality; women have similarly claimed equal rights; unions have pushed for greater economic democracy; and American Indians have displayed their own patriotism on Independence Day, sometimes ironically, to assert their own devotion to their homeland and push the United States to fulfill its obligations, based on negotiated treaties and basic human rights.

And the Fourth of July, though not a gift-giving occasion, nonetheless has an economic impact, providing an opportunity for American businesses to promote and sell their products. By the early twenty-first century, for example, home fireworks alone had become a $775 million industry, according to the American Pyrotechnics Association. For well over 100 years, merchants have used the holiday to hawk souvenirs and other items central to its celebration, and each July advertisements for everything from hot dogs to the latest electronics are colored red, white, and blue and festooned with symbolic, sometimes humorous, reminders that Independence Day is near. Such ads are not designed to promote historical understanding or cultivate national feeling, yet they do express and encourage a distinctive American identity, even patriotism, emphasizing Americans' self-image as a prosperous and free people. If Fourth of July holidays are often trivial, light on historical memory and heavy on consumption and pleasure, they still possess the potential for serious political activism, as some Americans occasionally awaken from their summer slumber to call attention their country's shortcomings or to mobilize citizens in the face of new national challenges.

DECLARING INDEPENDENCE

Declaring Independence in 1776 was a revolutionary act. Throughout the war for independence, commemoration of that singular event served the partisan goals of the revolutionary party. Celebration of independence helped

Americans to imagine that they were, in fact, an independent people, a new nation. In a sense, then, revolutionaries did not merely fight to establish the United States but celebrated their new republic into existence.

The mixture of celebration and militant violence, of commemorating an event and establishing it, became clear in New York City in July of 1776. In lower Manhattan, on July 9, following a public reading of the Declaration of Independence, revolutionary soldiers and citizens demolished the city's equestrian statue of King George III, erected only in 1770 by grateful subjects to mark the revocation of the hated Townsend Duties. How quickly King George had fallen from grace. This rambunctious demonstration celebrated a document drafted and formally adopted elsewhere, in Philadelphia, on July 4, yet it also functioned as an unceremonious funeral for the king. It was both a celebration of and a violent if festive act of independence, an event that might contribute to making independence a reality.

The Continental Congress had adopted the Declaration of Independence on July 4 and ordered that it be printed and sent to "the several Assemblies, Conventions & Committees or Councils of Safety and to the several commanding officers of the Continental troops that it be proclaimed in each of the United

Declaration of Independence, an engraving by Waterman L. Ormsby. Courtesy of the Library of Congress.

States & and at the head of the army." The Declaration was written to be read aloud, as Jay Fliegelman has shown. Indeed, it was "publication"—the act of making the Declaration public, through the performance of public readings— and popular acclamation through spontaneous celebrations that gave the Declaration its power. More than text, the Declaration became a form of action and transformation, not merely a document but an event. That event became national in scope, but it was realized locally, as in New York City, and in towns, hamlets, and encampments from Maine to Georgia. It is not surprising, then, that a ritual rereading of the Declaration of Independence would become a fixture in nineteenth-century Fourth of July holiday programs.

Contemplating the historical implications and predicting a grand future, John Adams wrote to his wife Abigail, declaring that "the second of July will be the most memorable epocha in the history of America. I am apt to believe it will be celebrated by succeeding generations as the great Anniversary Festival." In this instance, Adams's prophecy proved true, or nearly so. His national holiday preceded the commonly recognized event by 48 hours, but we might forgive him. July 2 was the day that Congress officially resolved to declare independence. Adams's choice of the word *epocha,* or epoch, reflected his sense that the occasion being celebrated was an extended process—initiated well before July 2 and continuing by necessity in warfare and beyond—not the work of a day. Establishing independence would be a protracted struggle and would require considerable popular support. Looking to the future, Adams offered a catalog of commemoration, "by solemn acts of devotion to God Almighty, solemnized with pomp and parade, shows, games, sports, guns, bells, bonfires, and illuminations, from one end of the continent to the other from this time forward, forever more." Adams mixed apparently frivolous diversions with sober, religious rites. Ironically, such commingling of the sacred and profane imitated traditional celebrations of the king's birthday. As with the destruction of King George's statue in New York, or the removal of the King's Arms from all public places, Americans turned the world upside down by inverting a traditional royal birthday rite in order to represent the death of the king and the birth of their republic, the United States.

Throughout the rebellious colonies, partisans staged impromptu, sometimes massive declarations of joy and revolutionary assent. On July 8 in Philadelphia a representative of the Committee of Safety read the declaration to a mass gathering from a balcony overlooking the State House yard (that is, from the building now known as Independence Hall). That night bonfires lit up the city, as did illuminations in individual houses, where residents placed candles in the windows. In rural as well as urban places, such actions were repeated. Americans read the Declaration publicly and enthusiastically acclaimed and endorsed it, at courthouses, crossroads, public squares, and churches, with processions, musket salutes, "animated shouts," toasts, and even violence against royal symbols or loyalist property. These were local celebrations of a continental event, which was truly national only to the extent that the nation's far-flung constituents endorsed it through virtually simultaneous acts of affirmation.

By contemporary standards, news spread quickly along the eastern seaboard, although it was August before word of the Declaration reached the southernmost colony of Georgia. Committees of safety sent express riders to distant counties; ministers were directed to read the Declaration to their congregations in Massachusetts; in New York, General Washington issued his officers copies and ordered them read to assembled troops with a sober, "audible voice"; and the substance of the Declaration conveyed in letters or quickly-printed broadside copies found their way into private posts. Many would read the Declaration—or have it read to them—from printed versions in American newspapers. Before the month ended the Declaration had appeared in at least 30 American newspapers.

As numerous scholars have recently stressed, the American Revolution developed in the context of an emerging "public sphere," a public arena of communication and interaction that was self-created and autonomous relative to the state. Critical to this process was print, which enlarged the audience for news, information, and ideas; indeed, publication in print increasingly constituted that audience, making it "possible to imagine a people that could act as a people and in distinction from the state," as literary scholar Michael Warner has argued. If, as the political anthropologist Benedict Anderson argues, modern nations are "imagined communities," then a new republican print culture, especially through the dissemination of politically charged festive experience, helped rebellious subjects imagine themselves as citizens of the United States.

But not all Americans imagined themselves equally committed to the new rebel regime, and some were less amenable to celebration of independence. In the years of the Revolutionary War, then, Independence Day was as much political demonstration as celebration. In Philadelphia during the July 4 holiday in 1777, for example, Connecticut representative William Williams reported great expenditures on liquor, powder, and candles for house illuminations. But not all took part, and some houses remained dark, forcing Williams to conclude that "much Tory unilluminated glass will want replacing." A Continental officer in Philadelphia similarly commented on Tory houses, "whose Windows Paid for their Obstinacy." Independence Day demonstrations of joy could thus also function as partisan expressions of intimidation and exclusion. July 4 remained a tool of these partisans, who ceremonially and wishfully declared as fact that which they hoped to accomplish through their war.

Independence Day continued to be celebrated as an anniversary during the military struggle, beginning in 1777, and with the successful completion of the war, marked by the Treaty of Paris in 1783, the United States continued to witness its celebration, with particularly exuberant eruptions of festive and political energy with the ratification of the Constitution in 1788. Although elimination of the defeated Tories transformed the partisan holiday into a universally beloved national fete, July 4 continued to be an occasion of political contention. As historian Len Travers has written, "Because Americans had made the Fourth of July into a Sabbath of self-definition, the rites that defined American identity were prizes worth fighting for." Independence Day thus remained a moment suitable for voicing party interests as well as nationalism. Americans wrapped themselves in the mantle of the Revolution, attempting to sanctify their own positions by constructing them as legitimate legacies of the Revolution. They also increasingly employed the Fourth of July to claim rights promised in the Declaration but unfulfilled in their contemporary United States.

The Independence Day festivals of 1788, for example, displayed both the spontaneous popular joy and the orchestrated political demonstrations that could commingle on or around the Fourth of July. In some cases, they expressed staunch political opposition through street theater and violence. On July 2, 1788, Congress announced officially that the Constitution, drafted in Philadelphia during the previous summer, had attained the approval of the required nine states and had therefore become the new frame of government for the United States (Virginia's ratification on June 25 actually made it 10). On July 4, 1788 in Philadelphia, a carefully planned Grand Federal Procession—the greatest spectacle in the city's history—marked the occasion with pageantry and political education. Some 5,000 marchers formed a line, which stretched a mile and a half and took three hours to pass along the three-mile parade route. Soldiers, horsemen, dignitaries, musical bands, carriages, and great floats thrilled the multitudes. The procession was itself a carefully crafted play, beginning with a chronological pageant of American history, featuring local leaders and elites, and offering as its climax a Constitution float crowned with a 13-foot-high eagle, and the Carpenters' Company float, "The Grand Federal Edifice," featuring a dome supported by 13 Corinthian columns. The procession continued with a marching exhibition of the city's crafts and trades. It ended at Union Green, where some 17,000 people sat down to a banquet. The Federalist organizer, Francis Hopkinson, designed the parade to construe as "truth" the idea that the new federal Constitution represented the legitimate culmination of the American Revolution. Participants—whether as marchers or spectators—were the objects as well as the embodiment of that Federalist lesson.

If Federalists won the battle to appropriate July 4 and have it serve their cause in the 1780s, by the early nineteenth century the tables had turned and Independence Day became a Democratic Republican festival. By then, the Declaration of Independence had assumed its place in July 4 ceremonies as a sacred text. The party of its acknowledged author, Thomas Jefferson, promoted its own partisan purposes. It is in this era that the day and the document assumed a new life, one that few of America's "Founding Fathers" could have anticipated.

Ninteenth-century depiction of Americans celebrating the Fourth of July in Boston. Courtesy of Getty Images / PhotoDisc.

"ALL MEN ARE CREATED EQUAL"

Thomas Jefferson's simple words, approved by the Second Continental Congress and ratified popularly by masses of Americans in 1776, turned out to be as much promise and provocation as declaration. "We hold these Truths to be self-evident, that all Men are created equal, that they are endowed by their Creator with certain unalienable Rights, that among these are Life, Liberty, and the Pursuit of Happiness." What did Jefferson and his colleagues mean? Did "men" mean all mankind—male and female, white and black, newcomers and Natives—or did it mean white men? In a sense, this question was moot from the start. Less important than intention was popular reception—the Declaration meant what the people took it to mean, and how they would construe it and sanctify it in subsequent decades and centuries. The meaning and power of the Declaration's words, in short, were political and thus unstable. After resting in relative obscurity for 15 years, and after its initial use in partisan discourse in the 1790s, the Declaration achieved its present sacred status some 30 years later. By that time, its pronouncements about the legitimacy of separation from Great Britain were increasingly overshadowed by its apparent endorsement of "*the native equality of the human race, as the true foundation of all political, of all human institutions,*" to quote Peleg Sprague's Fourth of July oration in Hallowell, Maine in 1826.

Technically, of course, the Declaration of Independence had finished its work once it proclaimed the new United States' separation from Great Britain, which was the essential function its framers designed it to perform. And, as the historian Pauline Maier has observed, the Declaration was "a peculiar document to be cited by those who championed the cause of equality." Its claims of equality pertained to persons living in a state of nature, not under civil government; many of its contributors, not to mention its author, were lifelong slave-holders, focused in 1776 on severing America's bonds with Britain, not establishing a new political system; and because it was neither a constitution nor a bill of rights, for any state or national government, it had no actual, ongoing legal authority. Yet from the beginning the implications of the Declaration's language garnered attention. Immediately in 1776, for example, a 23-year-old black minuteman from western Massachusetts, Lemuel Haynes, used the Declaration's key lines on equality as an epigraph for an antislavery essay. "I think it not hyperbolical to affirm," Haynes wrote further, "that Even an affrican, has Equally as good a right to his Liberty in common with Englishmen." Such words allowed several slaves to win their freedom in the early 1780s in Massachusetts, where the language of equality was clearly inscribed in the state's bill of rights. Increasingly, the sacred if extralegal status of the Declaration bestowed a unique moral authority to those who invoked it in the cause of increased liberty and equality.

The firm association of the Declaration of Independence with the Fourth of July, and the growing interpretation of the text as an instrument of equality and freedom, infused Independence Day with potential power and meaning as a festival of liberation and reform. In the 1790s, Pennsylvania and Maryland abolition societies began to hold their annual meetings on the sacred day. In New York and New Jersey, gradual emancipation acts took effect on July 4 (in 1799 and 1804, respectively); by 1817, New York required that all slaves born before July 4 in that year be freed no later than Independence Day, 1827. Southern states were equally attuned to the symbolism of the Fourth of July, as

Thomas Jefferson Randolph's 1831 emancipation proposal to the Virginia legislature suggests—the measure, if it had been successful, would have freed slaves born after July 4, 1840. Southerners similarly betrayed their understanding of the power—or the danger—of Independence Day, which could spread the contagions of liberty, when they prohibited slave attendance at white Fourth of July celebrations. Instead, many plantation owners sponsored distracting, nonpolitical midsummer holidays on July 4, featuring relaxation, recreation, and feasting for slaves.

The American Colonization Society—founded in 1816 on the dubious proposition that the solution to America's slavery problem lay in the removal of emancipated slaves (and blacks generally) from the United States and their transportation to colonies in Africa—quickly enlisted Independence Day as the occasion to promote its plans. By the 1830s, however, a more radical Abolitionist movement emerged, and it became increasingly clear that colonization had failed as a viable strategy to end slavery in America. Independence Day, however, continued to be associated with African American liberation. William Lloyd Garrison, among the staunchest of white abolitionists and later publisher of *The Liberator,* criticized the conventional Independence Day celebration of the mid-1830s, ridiculing it as "the time-honored, wine-honored, toast-drinking, powder-wasting, tyrant-killing Fourth of July—consecrated, for the last sixty years to bombast, to falsehood, to impudence, to hypocrisy." Passage of the Kansas-Nebraska Act provoked Garrison on July 4, 1854 to burn copies of the Fugitive Slave Act and the United States Constitution, which he called a "covenant with death," a violation of the Declaration of Independence's sacred truths.

While some African Americans in the North similarly used Independence Day to publicly affirm the principle of equality promised in the Declaration of Independence and to condemn the country's failure to achieve it for millions of slaves, others chose to boycott Independence Day in favor of separate festivals of black freedom. Some African Americans stayed away from white celebrations simply as a matter of safety, given the record of violence committed against blacks who appeared in public streets and squares on such occasions. The Fourth of July received its greatest boost as an African American holiday with the celebration of New York State Abolition Day in 1827, marking the culmination of the state's gradual emancipation process.

For the next eight years, African Americans commemorated the occasion in some 18 separate festivals in five states, often on July 5. While celebrations typically pivoted around church activities—sermons, hymns, and prayers—they increasingly included activities, like those in New York City, staged out-of-doors—parades, gun salutes, banner displays, community banquets, and toasts. Such public exercises consciously presented free blacks as citizens, both to themselves and to whites, as they performed their identity as both African and American.

In 1852, the citizens of Rochester, New York heard perhaps the most powerful challenge ever voiced to the mindless celebration of Independence Day when the city's invited speaker, the former slave and leading black abolitionist Frederick Douglass, asked, "What, to the Slave, is the Fourth of July?" Linking American revolutionaries with Abolitionism, Douglass embraced the principles of Independence Day but rejected the festival's celebration of freedom as premature, hypocritical, even obscene. "Are the great principles of political freedom and of natural justice, embodied in the Declaration of Independence, extended to us?" he asked. "I am not included within the pale of this glorious anniversary! Your high independence only reveals the immeasurable distance between us," Douglass answered. "Fellow citizens, above your national, tumultuous joy I hear the mournful wail of a million! whose chains, heavy and grievous yesterday, are today rendered more intolerable by the jubilee shouts that reach them." Douglass confided, "the character and conduct of this nation never looked blacker to me than on this Fourth of July."

The bitter knowledge that slavery endured in the United States tempered African Americans' joy and inspired some to find a less ambiguous site in the calendar to celebrate freedom. Some black leaders chose July 5—close enough to Independence Day to invoke the principles of the Declaration of Independence and to emphasize African Americans' boycott of a day steeped in hypocrisy. On July 5, black celebrants could avoid confronting white revelers who monopolized public spaces on the Fourth. Sometimes another day in July would serve. Elsewhere, as in New York and Philadelphia, African Americans chose to commemorate January 1—the day in 1808 when the slave-trade ban took effect, and the date of Haitian Independence in 1804. But given persistent violations of the law and the continuation of an internal slave trade, not to mention slavery itself, the January 1 holiday declined, though the date would gain new import as a festival of African American freedom after 1863, when Lincoln's Emancipation Proclamation took effect.

With the emancipation of some 670,000 slaves in the British West Indies in 1834, their day of liberation—August 1—assumed an important place in the African American calendar. August 1 became the most widely commemorated and most enduring of the antebellum freedom holidays in the United States. It remained fundamentally a black festival, a proximate black alternative to the Fourth of July. For northern African Americans, the First of August was unavoidably linked with the Fourth of July, as an alternative, relocated feast of African American freedom. It was a time, like Independence Day, "to preach the DECLARATION OF INDEPENDENCE, till it begins to be put in PRACTICE," according to one orator in 1834. Whether on July 4, July 5, or August 1, such ceremonial moments provided opportunities for political persuasion and mobilization as well as for celebration.

The Union victory in the Civil War and black emancipation, and the sense that African Americans too would finally share the promise of the American Revolution, produced massive black celebrations of Independence Day. Jacob E. Yoder, a teacher in a Freedmen's Bureau school in Lynchburg, Virginia, wrote in his diary on July 4, 1866 that the holiday was finally "a day of rejoicing not only for the white people of this vast country but also for the late slaves of the Southern States. They seem to be generally inclined to select this day as an anniversary day to celebrate their emancipation."

African Americans celebrated their Jubilee of Freedom locally on other occasions after the Civil War, to mark the dates when word of emancipation or southern defeat reached their particular communities. Coincidentally, these local holidays often occurred in the summer, not too far removed from July 4 on the calendar: May 8 (Mississippi), May 22 (Florida), May 28 (Alabama and Georgia), June 19 (Texas), August 4 (Missouri), and August 8 (Kentucky and Tennessee). "Juneteenth" continues to commemorate General Gordon Granger's landing at Galveston, Texas on June 19, 1865 and his reading of General Order Number 3, which proclaimed that "all slaves are free." Word quickly spread throughout east Texas, western Louisiana, southwestern Arkansas, and southern Oklahoma, setting off spontaneous celebrations. But the origins of many of these "Jubilation" festivals are often obscure; celebrants themselves explain simply, on that day their ancestors learned they were free.

The history of these Emancipation Days and their relationship with America's Independence Day is complex, as complicated as the history of African American struggles for equality and civil rights since the Civil War. Some blacks ignored the Fourth of July and favored their own separate celebrations. Others embraced July 4 and abandoned local Emancipation Days when racial integration seemed to hold real promise. Yet the shift toward a multicultural Independence Day, and the decline of particular black celebrations of freedom, has not been steady or uniform. As progress toward racial justice stalled, or as African Americans sought to build community based on a separate collective memory, black Emancipation Days have been nurtured or reborn. In fact, Juneteenth not only persists in the place of its origin, but it has spread throughout the United States, as far afield as Wisconsin and Oregon. Nationally, new holidays—Martin Luther King Jr. Day, for example—have been created, which express African American history, pride, and community. The Fourth of July remains an ambiguous moment for African Americans. In the words of the columnist William Raspberry, it makes blacks feel "like a bastard at a family reunion": "We'd rather be here than not; where else, after all, would we be? And yet we're sure that many of our fellow celebrants see our presence at this American birthday party as faintly embarrassing—as not quite legitimate."

RE-DECLARATIONS OF INDEPENDENCE

Independence Day's celebration of America's first principles invited Americans to contemplate their national origins and judge the country's performance against its sacred values and ideals. Antebellum white reformers consistently found the nation wanting for its failure to fulfill the promises of liberty and equality inscribed in the Declaration of Independence. The slavery question preoccupied abolitionists, but it was not the only national blight that reform-minded Americans considered on the Fourth of July. The nation's birthday served equally well as a moment to confront the evils of drink, irreligion, the plight of children, women's oppression, or worker exploitation.

The Fourth of July represented both a problem and an opportunity for advocates of temperance, the crusade against alcohol, for example. The holiday celebrated the origins of the American republic, dependent on a virtuous citizenry, yet those celebrations traditionally consisted of drunken, disorderly fetes. In response, temperance societies held their own, liquor-free gatherings, at which their adherents and converts might celebrate the day respectably and promote temperance principles. In New York City in 1844, for example, the American Temperance Union banned "the usual public nuisance" of park booths that sold intoxicating liquors. Instead, the park's fountain was cleaned, four tons of ice was added, and citizens were supplied with tin cups and "bountifully refreshed with pure ice-water." Reformers on such occasions declared their independence from King Alcohol. The Washington Temperance Society offered a cold-water toast at its Fourth of July celebration that year, for example, which proclaimed: "The day we celebrate—Our fathers rejoiced on the return of this anniversary, that they were freed from British allegiance—We, as Washingtonians, have greater reason to rejoice that we are freed from the shackles of King Alcohol, 'clothed and in our right minds.'" Another toast declared, "King George 3d and King Alcohol. The first had his armies destroyed by Washington; the latter by Washingtonians."

The Sunday School movement similarly sought to subdue the evils of the traditional, debauching Independence Day and to employ the Fourth of July in the interest of reform. Evangelical Protestants in the early nineteenth century saw Sunday schools as a means to educate working children on Sunday, their only day off. More broadly, Sunday schools represented a more aggressive attempt by evangelicals to challenge the infidelity they perceived around them and to transform the nation into a truly Christian commonwealth. By the 1830s, organizers used Independence Day to instruct, not merely to entertain, while shielding them from the drinking and dissipation of boisterous, boozy celebrations. The Sunday school children's Fourth of July festival thus became a religious and civic institution. In Rockdale, Pennsylvania, for example, the Calvary Sunday School managed to take control of the district's Independence Day event in 1837. At least 600 young scholars and their teachers, and an equal number of spectators, assembled to hail the nation's birthday with "a rational and proper celebration of the day."

Sunday school advocates were less able than abolitionists to quote the language of the Declaration of Independence on behalf of their cause, although they tried to convince the public that America's founders envisioned a fully

Christian republic. Women's Rights supporters faced a language problem as well, stuck as they were with the Declaration's phrase, "all *men* are created equal." Claiming to embody the spirit if not the letter of the Revolution, women simply rewrote the Declaration to assert their "unalienable rights," for example at Seneca Falls in July 1848. Elizabeth Cady Stanton's close revision declared, "We hold these truths to be self-evident: that all men and women are created equal." These sentiments continued, like the Declaration of 1776, in a systematic indictment—of "man," not merely of George III—for the "repeated injuries and usurpations on the part of man toward woman, having in direct object the establishment of an absolute tyranny over her."

Since 1776, women's participation in public celebrations of July 4 had been marginalized. Respectable women were welcome spectators at parades and suitable guests at banquets and balls, but they seldom appeared themselves—as real women, not as allegorical figures—in public processions, as orators, or as toastmasters. Relegated to a domestic world, middle-class women, as republican mothers, were charged with the cultivation of morality among America's citizens. But, as a generation of women's historians have shown, such a responsibility would draw women into public space in the interest of moral reform, as realms beyond individual homes were domesticated by the middle class in the nineteenth century. Women thus became politically active through their devotion to antislavery, temperance, and other moral reform efforts, and they could demonstrate this activism at specialized Independence Day festivals, as we have seen above. It was only a matter of time until such women would discover their own oppression and employ Independence Day, not merely for private enjoyment or benevolent enterprises, but to assert their rights to full citizenship.

For antebellum feminists, the argument and the language of equality came naturally out of their antislavery activism. Women's rights and abolitionism were closely aligned; indeed, the union between these causes—and other reform efforts—both enabled and limited the movement for women's rights. If abolitionism in particular was a training ground for antebellum women activists, it could also direct energy away from women's crusade for their own rights. In years following the Civil War, women reformers continued to maintain a diverse agenda, but they focused more closely on the cause of women's suffrage. On the occasion of the United States' Centennial, the National Woman Suffrage Association used the Fourth of July to issue another "Declaration of Rights for Women." Susan B. Anthony successfully urged that suffragists attend the Independence Day festivities at the Centennial Exposition in Philadelphia and that women throughout the United States "meet in their respective towns and districts on the 4th of July 1876, and ... declare themselves free and independent, no longer bound to obey laws in whose making they have had no voice, and in presence of the assembled nations of the world, gathered on this soil to celebrate our national Centennial, to demand justice for the women of this land." Despite discouragement from centennial organizers, Anthony presented

A crowd watches fireworks in Union Square in New York on the Fourth of July, 1876. Courtesy of the Library of Congress.

a copy of the woman's declaration at the ceremony and read it aloud from a band platform in the shadow of Independence Hall. For Susan B. Anthony and other women's rights advocates, the principles of July 4 were a resource and Independence Day itself an opportunity to promote their cause and reform the United States.

For generations, beginning in the 1790s, the Fourth of July was celebrated as a sort of American Labor Day. If Independence Day was increasingly transformed into a Democratic-Republican festival by the turn of the nineteenth century, in northern urban areas this occurred in large part through the local activities of white workingmen who supported and identified with the party of Jefferson. Independence Day parades consisted largely of marching mechanics and artisans who elaborately displayed themselves and honored their toil as they celebrated the United States' political birth.

In the early nineteenth century, especially after 1820, American cities expanded rapidly, and in the wake of a transportation revolution that linked cities, towns, and hinterlands into a new commercial network, cities such as Philadelphia became centers of manufacturing. Although the shift toward mass production in large factories came gradually, urban workers—even those laboring in workshops and smaller manufactories—saw their lives transformed by the restructuring of work and the application of new values and expectations promoted by an emergent business class. The rapid growth of American industry increasingly eroded traditional crafts, encouraged a shift toward less skilled wage labor, and produced greater social and economic inequality. For many, these unsettling trends seemed to signal the decline, not merely of prosperity or economic "competency," but of independence itself. Moreover, as businessmen developed a new ethos, drawing heavily from evangelical Protestantism, to promote discipline, self-control, and morality among their workers, they clashed with older, preindustrial patterns of male sociability that could be noisy, disorderly, even drunken. For urban workingmen in the first half of the nineteenth century, then, the Fourth of July often assumed a new political meaning. From an uncomplicated, apparently consensual celebration of the new American republic, Independence Day became an occasion to preserve working-class independence or to signal and promote the "unfinished business" of the American Revolution.

In Philadelphia, for example, threats to the craft system, reductions in rates or wages, and increased expectations by employers regarding the quality or quantity of production prodded wage earners to form trade unions and, in the 1830s, to band together into the General Trades' Union of the City and County of Philadelphia. In 1835, a general strike—the first in American history—proved temporarily successful in achieving a 10-hour workday. The strike seemed to demonstrate that more rigid class divisions and a more adversarial relationship had developed, which separated working people from those in the new middle class.

In large part, the new reform activity of the men and women of this class—such as temperance—was directed at working people, particularly men, whose traditional revelry in the public streets and squares on the Independence Day, Christmas, New Year's, and muster days was increasingly defined as uncouth and immoral. Middle-class reformers sought to domesticate public festive sites where working people gathered on Independence Day to celebrate with gusto and feats of drinking. Reformers hoped to tame unruly festivity and impose discipline and order on the metropolis. By the 1820s, authorities banned booths dispensing alcohol, and new, temperate celebrations began to displace traditional ones in public places. Over the course of the nineteenth century, middle-class Americans increasingly privatized their Independence Day celebrations, progressively withdrawing from public spaces to commune and celebrate in countryside retreats or private halls. Laboring people had fewer options for their festivity, and they continued to occupy public streets and squares, where their celebrations attracted greater attention and criticism. For working people beset with new rules of labor and social comportment, the Fourth of July could be a moment to express their independence, simply by ignoring the gospel of employers and reformers and abandoning themselves in the mirth and drunkenness of traditional celebration. Indeed, for some workers, efforts to celebrate the day became radical when employers attempted to force them to work. In such cases, to mark Independence Day required a strike.

By the 1830s, then, the Fourth of July had become a different sort of Independence Day for working people. Its parades, banquets, and festivity became a means, not merely to make merry, but to assert rights, make fresh demands, even to rewrite the Declaration of Independence. In 1834, for example the "Declaration of Rights of the Trades' Union of Boston and Vicinity" offered a liberal paraphrase of the 1776 Declaration, which justified labor association and argued "that labor, being the legitimate and only real source of wealth, and the laboring classes the majority and real strength of every country, their interest and happiness ought to be the principal care of Government." Other workingmen compared their unions to "that *Holy Combination* of that immortal band of *Mechanics*" who dumped tea into Boston Harbor in December 1773.

This resort to the principles and experiences of the Revolution, as interpreted by later generations, persisted. In 1844, New England shoemakers offered their own rewriting of the Declaration of Independence, charging that employers "have robbed us of certain rights," and New England textile workers planned unsuccessfully to stage a general strike for July 4, 1846, which they declared "a second Independence Day." In 1879, Ira Steward's "Second Declaration of Independence" promoted the eight-hour day, the Socialist Labor Party proclaimed a "Declaration of Interdependence" in 1895, and the Continental Congress of Workers and Farmers prepared a "New Declaration of Independence" in 1933.

Labor leaders found object lessons, precedents, and inspiration in the American Revolution, and the Fourth of July continued to serve working people as an occasion to build solidarity and celebrate themselves, while they protested injustice, claimed rights, and asserted their independence. For some labor activists, however, the festivity and principles of Independence Day rang hollow, leading some in the 1880s to invent an alternative vehicle to express their hopes and flex their political muscle—Labor Day. In 1894, the San Francisco Labor Council, for example, refused to participate in the city's official Independence Day celebration because its parade would include military units—federal troops had just been used to break the Pullman strike.

If Independence Day remained a potent event, an occasion that might be used to distinguish one's cause by cloaking it in the mantle of the sacred American Revolution, not all such uses of the holiday were benign. By the 1840s, anti-immigrant feeling in the United States produced a nativist movement that sometimes laid an exclusionary claim to the Fourth of July. In Philadelphia in 1844, for example, the American Republican Party staged a Grand Native American Procession on July 4 to promote its efforts to limit citizenship rights to men of American birth and to curtail Catholic (and Irish) civil rights. This aggressive, reactionary procession nonetheless employed the standard symbols of America's founding moment and claimed a conservative purpose—to protect church and country.

As one historian has shown, increasingly by the late nineteenth century, immigrant communities observed Independence Day separately with other immigrants. Sometimes these celebrations were the only public commemorations held, as the middle classes retreated into private celebrations and left public rites to racial or ethnic minorities in American cities. Each group seemed to use the holiday as much to cultivate its ethnic identity as to assert its American one. Although Independence Day helped make these immigrants Americans, it could nonetheless leave them divided against each other, not only on the Fourth of July, but on election days, work days, and strikes.

SECTION AND NATION ON THE FOURTH OF JULY

The United States was an immense country at its creation, some feared too big to function as a republic. And it continued to grow until its vast dimensions stretched from the Atlantic to the Pacific. The story of this westward expansion is well known and now seems almost inevitable. Yet it was not certain during the early years of the republic that this expansive United States would endure or that western Americans would forge and maintain their connections, as citizens, to the nation. If the integration of the West into the United States now seems foreordained, the disintegration of the Union along a North-South fault line strikes us as equally inevitable in retrospect, given the rupture of the Civil War. Yet, while particular identities and interests increasingly distinguished North from South and colored local and national politics, such regionalism and its connection to nationalism was often ambiguous and complex. We often assume that essential differences divided northerners and southerners from the beginning, and that sectional identity came before national feeling. Yet recently scholars have argued convincingly that United States nationalism worked in tandem with regionalism and that American nationalism created the context for sectionalism.

American nationalism was less a cause than a product of the American Revolution. In declaring independence, Americans severed the one tie they all shared, the one binding them to Great Britain. During and after the Revolution, Americans were forced to follow their destructive act with a constructive one—the forging of a new nation and national identity. The United States' new constitutional order and the developing national public sphere—especially a rapidly expanding print culture—consolidated the nation imaginatively, even as citizens throughout the states and territories expressed their nationalism locally. If nationalism was developed and expressed locally, it is not surprising that such nationalism would take various forms. Indeed, different nationalisms emerged as localized versions emerged regionally, sometimes in protest against the perceived regionalism or sectionalism of other Americans. One region's nationalism could be another region's sectionalism. The South, North, and West discovered themselves as regions, then, as they competed with each other politically to claim the true mantle of nationalism, while they sometimes characterized each other, ungenerously, as sectional and partisan.

Independence Day as a national and nationalist celebration reflected these complicated desires and developments. The holiday promoted national feeling throughout the United States, but it did so in locally specific ways, helping to created various expressions of nationalism in different regions. Ironically, all nationalism was local. The Fourth of July, then, could bind the nation together as citizens celebrated in common, though in far-flung locations; it could express oppositional, regionally informed versions of nationalism; or it could be conspicuously boycotted or celebrated on alternative occasions to protest perceived corruption of the nation elsewhere.

In giving voice to national feeling and identity, Independence Day became a great nationalizing institution. As the famed nineteenth-century orator Daniel Webster put it, "This anniversary animates and gladdens and unites all American hearts. On other days of the year we may be party men, indulging in controversies, more or less important to the public good; we may have our likes and dislikes, and we may maintain our political differences, often with warm, and sometimes angry feelings. But today we are Americans all; and nothing but Americans." Such sentiments were as often expressed in the South as in the North. And in the West, a region unable to claim membership among the 13 original states, inhabitants nonetheless vigorously asserted their American nativity and nationalism in Independence Day ceremonies, attesting to their loyalty and testifying to their worthiness as territories to join the Union as new states.

In the West, Independence Day functioned as a ritual celebration of conquest and incorporation, as well as a means for westerners to forward their claims to equal rights of citizenship and statehood vis-à-vis the East. In 1804, for example, Meriwether Lewis and William Clark embarked on their famous expedition to explore and assert United States control over the vast Louisiana territories recently purchased from France. On July 4, they renamed a nearby watercourse "Independence Creek," or "Fourth of July 1804 Creek … as this creek has no name, and this being the Fourth of July, the day of the Independence of the United States." The creek likely already had a name, but the explorers were concerned, not merely with mapping lands new to them, but with possessing and incorporating them as United States property. Bestowing a new name played a role in their Independence Day celebration, and both promoted a larger imperial project. These naming practices and festive acts would continue, nowhere more monumentally than at Independence Rock along the Oregon Trail in present-day Wyoming. Designated by an early party of pioneers who spent July 4 there, Independence Rock remained a celebration site and natural monument to American westward expansion and nationalism. In claiming and naming the monolith, Americans possessed the country and proved their nationalism to themselves and those in the East. For these westering settlers, who saw not only their personal destiny but that of the United States itself in the West, western regionalism was a form of nationalism to end all sectionalism. Meanwhile, North and South often hoped to replicate their own social, economic, and political patterns in the West, each hoping to see the West as new version of itself. For a time many imagined that the West would be a common expression of an undivided American nationalism, an example of the present and future Union.

Yet the West did not diffuse sectional tensions but aggravated them. When rivalries between the increasingly self-conscious North and South erupted in violence and ruptured the Union, Fourth of July exercises proclaimed an oppositional nationalism in both the South and North. The claim of nationalism came easily to northerners, who remained within the Union. Perhaps surprisingly, such assertions of authentic nationalism came readily to southerners as well. For much of the South, the Declaration of Independence and the Fourth of July had little to say about slavery. Such questions were less important than union and compromise, which abolition, in their view, threatened. Following the Compromise of 1850, one North Carolina toast on July 4 praised "The Declaration of Independence, and the Constitution of the United States— Liberty and Union, now and forever, one and inseparable." As the Civil War approached, southerners debated how Independence Day should be observed. Some favored abandoning the holiday as something belonging "to the history of a union which no longer exists." But others, the Raleigh *State Journal* for example, contended that the South had "as much right to the honors and glories of the first revolution as the North." Southerners were "obligated to assert the right … to … share in that … common heritage." Another southern newspaper editorialized on July 3, 1861, "The conduct of the North in trampling the principles of 1776 under foot and throwing ashes on the memory of its forefathers is no sufficient reason for the failure by the South to recognize and celebrate the Fourth of July as the anniversary of the most glorious human event in the history of mankind."

Nonetheless, the Civil War dampened celebrations of the Fourth of July in the South, and southern observances of the holiday were transformed. White southerners continued to claim the heritage and heroes of the American Revolution—displaying George Washington on the Confederate national seal, for example—but they invested their energy in prosecuting the war and cultivated their alternative nationalism. After the war, some southern editors saw themselves as victims more entitled than northerners to claim the Declaration of Independence and to apply it in a critique of northern tyranny. Southerners, "whose self-respect has not perished with defeat," a Wilmington, North Carolina newspaper claimed, cannot embrace "the Fourth of July with senseless uproar and pretended rejoicing.… To-day, then, should be passed by our people in dignified silence." "Our people," in such a construction, excluded African

Americans, who did celebrate with enthusiasm. "Oh, my, but the Fourth was a big day," recalled Mamie Garvin Fields in her memoir of her Carolina girlhood in the 1890s, "although not for everybody. The old-time [white] Southerners considered the Fourth of July a Yankee holiday and ignored it. So the white people stayed home and the black people 'took over' the Battery [in Charleston, South Carolina] for a day.... I don't think the Battery was ever so alive as on the Fourth." "On the Fourth of July," Mrs. Fields remembered, "many of our parents were actually celebrating their own freedom."

Abandoned, then, by white southerners, the Fourth of July became a Republican Party and African American holiday after the Civil War, a contested nationalist celebration in a divided South. The North Carolina historian Fletcher M. Green could write as late as the 1950s, "today little attention is paid to July Fourth by the people of North Carolina." Celebrations of American Independence Day would return, however, beginning with the Centennial as Reconstruction ended, as the issue of slavery was displaced and the agenda of racial justice abandoned, and as white Americans north and south emphasized sectional reconciliation.

In the years after the Civil War, the West became again a critical site for nationalist expression. Many believed (not the least of whom was the historian Frederick Jackson Turner, who unveiled his "frontier thesis" in 1893) that the West played a critical role in molding American identity and national character. More importantly, inhabitants of the West in the last quarter of the nineteenth century embraced such a notion by placing themselves within the orbit of American political, economic, and social life. In 1864, Nevada entered the troubled Union as the thirty-sixth state. Nine more states—all west of the Mississippi—would join the Union by 1896, having passed their patriotic auditions and achieved the Constitutional requirements for statehood. They were then joined by five more in the twentieth century. In each case, the inhabitants of these places used the Fourth of July to demonstrate their patriotic devotion to the nation.

In these years, the West was the focus of another national concern tied up with nationalism and American identity—the "Indian Problem." The place of Indians in the United States, and in the nation's most sacred public festival—Independence Day—has been problematic and complicated. White Americans asserted their nationalism, identity, and patriotism by conquering the continent's lands and peoples, and the Fourth of July was conventionally an occasion to celebrate their triumph, based on Native dispossession. Pioneers brought dependency or extinction, not independence, to American Indians. We might ask, then, to paraphrase the nineteenth-century black abolitionist Frederick Douglass, what to the Indian is the Fourth of July?

Sacred documents, such as the Declaration of Independence and the Constitution, had little to say to Native Americans, and those Indians who were able sought to avoid the stifling embrace of state and federal governments. Native

American people living east, then west, of the Mississippi River were forced to accommodate the expanding nation in order to survive. Surprisingly, America's great political festival—Independence Day—became a rite of Native American accommodation and survival, as Indians developed their own forms of American patriotism. But how could Indians, often depicted as villains in America's play of political nativity, find anything to celebrate on Independence Day?

In fact, some Indians were themselves veterans of the Revolutionary War or the War of 1812, and they claimed justice based on their service to the glorious cause. The Fourth of July provided a forum for asserting such claims and for appealing more generally to American first principles of liberty, equality, and opportunity. John Wannuaucon Quinney, a Stockbridge Mahican political leader and diplomat, for example, appropriated and challenged Fourth of July traditions, in ways similar to those employed by black abolitionists. Like African Americans, Native Americans could use the holiday to highlight American hypocrisy. Quinney's Independence Day speech at Reidsville, New York in 1854 followed Frederick Douglass's famous oration at Rochester by only two years. At Reidsville, he recalled the heroic traditions of American nationalism but distinguished his own perspective as a disinherited American. "I have been taught in the schools," Quinney observed, "and been able to read your histories and accounts of Europeans, yourselves and the Red Men; which instruct me, that while rejoicings to-day are commemorative of the free birth of the giant nation, they simply convey to my mind, the recollection of a transfer of the miserable weakness and dependence of my race from one great power to another."

Indians did not merely participate in white-sponsored Fourth of July celebrations; some found occasion to stage their own Independence Day events. Alfred Cope, Quaker visitor to the Oneida reservation near Green Bay, Wisconsin in 1849, found the Oneidas' celebration virtually indistinguishable from those of their white neighbors. Other Native American people likewise marked the day, perhaps simply to join "in the general feeling" of the nation, "this being a day of general rejoicing in the land," as an Oklahoma observance was characterized in 1881. Native American people might well have been commemorating survival itself, as their land and livelihood remained endangered. Indian Fourth of July observances were nationalist exercises in a sense, but they were decidedly local, alternative if not explicitly oppositional; they were celebrations less of the American nation than of particular American homelands, Indian nations, communities, and families.

As the last of the Indian wars ended late in the nineteenth century, and Native American people found themselves confined to reservations and subject to intensified programs of assimilation by white officials and reformers, American Independence Day increased in importance among Indians. Of course, many continued to ignore the day. But in reservation communities, and especially in schools both on and off the reservation, white agents and teachers stressed the "civilizing" effects of national ceremonial observances—in the school calendar, from Columbus Day to the Fourth of July—and they foisted these civic ceremonies on their wards.

Independence Day was a cornerstone in this program of civic indoctrination. Surely these efforts, especially in boarding schools, must have had an impact, but Native American people were hardly empty receptacles for patriotic prescriptions. Even the satisfied communications of those encouraging Fourth of July observances in the field betrayed some uncertainty about the nature and content of Indian celebrations. Alice C. Fletcher, for example, among the Nez Percés of Idaho as a special agent, found something unsettling in the tribe's 1890 Independence Day celebration. Some 500 people gathered, a day or two in advance, attired themselves in "citizens' clothes," and conducted a relatively sedate ceremony, complete with religious services, flag waving, singing, and a procession. But something was not quite right. Fletcher did not recognize their song, "We'll stand, Fourth of July," and she found the Nez Percés' salutation odd: "As I walked about I was greeted with a hand-shake, a nod of the head, and smiles, and 'Fourth of July,' much as we say 'Happy New Year.'" A Native American student at Hampton Institute was less ambiguous in his Fourth of July speech in 1887 when he charged, "Then, at the height of this glorious success, a great wrong was done by the American people; this wrong was done to our race.... In the eyes of the law and the eyes of the people whose blood ... was shed for the cause of independence, our race had no protection under the laws of the country.... The white man is the Indian's foe."

On Indian reservations throughout the West, the Fourth of July developed into a major public festival, despite the holiday's assimilationist goals. While white officials banned Native American rituals, they condoned Independence Day gatherings, which could provide cover for continued practice of outlawed Native American religious rites. As one anthropologist studying a Lakota community reported in the early 1930s, "This is the only time the traditional camp circle is now used. This affair comes near the time of the former Sun Dance and arouses much talk of 'old times.'" The Fourth of July became for Lakotas "Ahn-páy-too wah-káhn táhn-ka, the Great Holy Day," according to an Indian agent.

Independence Day could even offer a safe, public means of performing more transgressive acts, expressions of Indian pride and antigovernment dissent, such as the staging of war dances, mock raids, and sham battles. An Indian agent at Klamath in Oregon permitted his charges to engage in such exercises, "dressed in all their barbaric splendor, mounted on fleet horses, filling the welkin with the soul-curdling war whoop." He believed such displays taught schoolboys "the wonderful advancement made in a few years, under reservation training, from active savagery to a position well advanced toward practical civilization." Is this the lesson that Klamaths drew from the demonstration? Did a reenactment of Custer's defeat at Little Bighorn on the Rosebud Reservation in 1900 convey such a "civilizing" message? Indeed, one wonders about the proximity in the calendar between July 4 and June 25, the day in 1876—the United States' Centennial—when Custer and his men were defeated, and whether Cheyennes and Lakotas found a means to merge these two apparently conflicting commemorations.

Not only did Independence Day promote cultural revival and memory within particular Native American communities, it also created opportunities for cultural innovation among Indian peoples more generally and helped forge new, pantribal national identities for Indians. In the last two decades of the nineteenth century, relative peace among plains people and their establishment on reservations denied young men the conventional means of achieving recognition and status. Many turned to art and ceremonial activity—including participation in Indian shows—and with cultural exchanges among tribes new rites emerged that transcended old ethnic and political boundaries and established new, broader ways to be "Indian." Sharing and innovation among Native American people, within and across reservation communities, laid the groundwork for development of the modern American Indian powwow, a festive institution that celebrates Indian life, often on the Fourth of July. Today, annual powwows are staged on Independence Day among the Shoshone-Paiutes at the Duck Valley Reservation in Idaho, the Northern Cheyennes at Lame Deer in Montana, the Yakamas at White Swan in Washington, and in numerous other Native American communities throughout the West.

In today's powwows—whether held on Independence Day or not—the most stately and spectacular event is the Grand Entry, which begins typically with a flag ceremony, honoring the United States flag along with state banners and Indian staffs. Here Native American people celebrate and perpetuate their warrior traditions. United States military veterans (Indians have served in the armed forces at disproportionate levels relative to their population) lead the procession into the dance arena—a considerable honor—wearing war bonnets, dancing regalia, and often military uniforms. In a way that outsiders might find surprising, such acts reflect a deep sense of patriotism among American Indians, which finds expression also in Native American observances of the Fourth of July.

Native American nationalism was hardly blind. It was born of suffering as well as hope, and military service in a wider world exposed Native American people both to new opportunities and fresh prejudices. Fundamentally, Indian patriotism emanated from love of country, veneration literally of the land itself as well as the Native American communities it supports. Independence Day flourished both because the holiday was foisted on Indians and because it offered opportunities for Indians to preserve traditions or invent new ways to survive. It continues to evoke varied responses among Native American people. The Indian Fourth of July exhibits patriotism and particular Native American nationalism; it allows Indians to distinguish themselves from whites by avoiding the holiday's rites; or it offers opportunities for Indians to criticize America's record in upholding its principles and promises.

TWENTIETH-CENTURY FIREWORKS

The Chinese discovered the explosive potential in the mixture of sulfur, charcoal, and saltpeter (potassium nitrate) by the ninth century. By the fourteenth century knowledge of fireworks had reached Europe, where the concoction was soon employed for military purposes. Meanwhile, *feux d'artifice,* or "artificial fire-works," became a fixture of festivity in Europe, even as gunpowder revolutionized warfare and aided colonial expansion. European fireworks displays marked coronations, royal weddings and births, military victories, saints' days, national commemorations, and similar extraordinary occasions, producing real if fleeting pleasure, wonder, and awe. And they did so for centuries before the United States was born in 1776. Yet nothing seems as American as fireworks on the Fourth of July.

The delightful meaninglessness of fireworks makes them an apt metaphor for American Independence Day in the twentieth century. The holiday came to signify everything and nothing. It could be explosive, as some Americans continued to use the occasion to fight for the rights of first-class citizenship, or in time of war to mobilize patriotism. But generally the day is more flash than substance, an opportunity for leisure and pleasure, to avoid politics, not to redefine political identity, challenge historical memory, or claim entitlements.

For most Americans, real problems should not intrude on the Fourth of July. Independence Day reflected the larger trends of the twentieth century—the expansion of the American state, the growth of leisure, mass culture, and consumerism, the rise of experts, professionalism, and regulation, and the advance of an American preference for nostalgia and myth over history.

Middle-class reformers, civic leaders, and government officials early in the twentieth century began to complain that the "Glorious Fourth" was both disordered and dangerous. As fireworks mishaps mounted some dubbed it the "Barbarous Fourth." In 1908, officials recorded some 5,600 casualties, almost half the number killed, wounded, or missing during the American Revolution! In 1903, the *Journal of the American Medical Association* began to compile statistics relating to July 4 deaths and injuries; its 1909 report noted that more Americans were killed or injured celebrating Independence Day that year than suffered similar fates in the Battle of Bunker Hill. Some—mostly "bright, active boys aged from six to eighteen years"—died agonizing deaths, not merely from explosions but from the effects of blood poisoning, or tetanus. "But this annual outrage is not necessary; it is entirely preventable, and the prevention rests with our city governments," the American Medical Association concluded. That year the Playground Association of America advocated a "Safe and Sane Fourth" and proposed alternative programs and activities for the day, which emphasized patriotism and Americanization of immigrants, and which might distract celebrants from dangerous mayhem. Communities across the United States began to plan full-day events and ban the sale of fireworks.

Increasingly municipal governments assumed control of Independence Day festivity in the early twentieth century. As individual neighborhood and ethnic celebrations came under the scrutiny of professional authority, they decried the carnival aspects of these traditional observances. Reformers sought to substitute orderly, uplifting, and instructive festivals for the raucous ones they rejected. Social elites in this era saw occasions such as Independence Day as opportunities for reform and revitalization—not merely of festivity but of American society more broadly. They sought to tame the vulgar exuberance of ethnic minorities and working-class Americans, counteract the drabness of industrial life and the crudeness of commercial amusements, and build a common civic culture, one that reworked genteel traditions, making them more democratic and pluralistic.

Mostly, these reformers failed, but the progressive reform of Independence Day certainly contributed to its transformation into a more organized, official patriotic occasion, at least in its public forms. Private, unofficial celebration of the Fourth of July continued to emphasize recreation and amusement, while public fireworks programs provided apolitical spectacles to complement the light diversions of picnics, concerts, and other popular entertainments.

What about those pyrotechnics? Americans might have become more "safe and sane" in igniting fireworks, but real dangers remain. Perhaps surprisingly, there is little concern today for the perils or environmental impact of fireworks—whether the sorts propelled high in the air officially or fired off popularly. In the summer of 2000, however, the Earth Island Institute, an environmental organization in San Francisco, called attention to the toxic particulates blasted about by patriotic fireworks, which have been linked to lung cancer and heart attacks. Fireworks displays, the institute argued, can generate increased levels of airborne arsenic, cadmium, mercury, lead, copper, zinc, and chromium. In 1976, the United States Environmental Protection Agency studied the effects of a fireworks exhibition in St. Louis, Missouri on the Fourth of July. The EPA found the concentration of fine particulate matter in the air after the fireworks to be about double its morning reading; arsenic levels had been elevated some 28 times those of 12 hours earlier, and the toxic element antimony was found to be about 200 times the previous level. The dangers such elevated pollutants pose is not completely clear, as some scientists reserve judgment while others say unequivocally, "It's a threat." Fireworks makers, of course, defend their products' safety, and most spectators worry little about such hazards.

Still, the horrors of the "Barbarous Fourth" have not been completely eliminated. In 1993, for example, the National Safety Council reported 10 deaths related to fireworks. On July 3, 1996, eight people died in Scottown, Ohio in a blaze of fire, smoke, whizzing rockets, and exploding firecrackers, which had been ignited in a fireworks store filled with customers. A 2000 press release from the United States Consumer Products Safety Commission (CPSC), in anticipation of Independence Day, acknowledged that "fireworks can add fun and excitement to a holiday celebration, but they can also turn a backyard

A modern day fireworks display in Maine. Courtesy of Getty Images / Brand X Pictures.

celebration into a rush to the emergency room." In 1999, hospital emergency rooms treated some 8,500 people for fireworks-related injuries; almost half of the victims were children under the age of 15. These numbers were down from those recorded earlier in the decade, but few imagine that Fourth of July celebrations will ever be fully "safe and sane." Nothing better demonstrates the unconsciousness of consequences in the pursuit of holiday happiness than the simple sparkler, traditionally placed in the hands of young children even though its tip burns at temperatures of 2,000 degrees Fahrenheit. Fireworks sales continue to rise in the early twenty-first century.

Political fireworks can still erupt on the Fourth of July as well, as when the neo-Nazi, white supremacist group, the Aryan Nation, marched in Coeur D'Alene, Idaho in 1997 (attracting more protesters than marchers), but most Americans tolerate only the politics of affirmation on Independence Day—that is, rites that are inclusive and celebratory, not exclusionary and critical. Partisan, electioneering speeches are only grudgingly allowed to intrude on celebrations. More characteristic of public programs are naturalization ceremonies, which welcome new American citizens. During World War I, George Creel's Committee on Public Information saw the Fourth of July as the perfect vehicle for promoting Americanism. On July 4, 1918, Creel staged a media event at Mount Vernon in which immigrants paid homage to the hero Washington. During this period, America experienced the "most strenuous nationalism *and* the most pervasive nativism that the United States had ever known," according to the historian John Higham. Not only were German Americans the victims of antiforeign feelings, but so too were a wide range of immigrant Americans. "100 percent Americanism" demanded loyalty and conformity.

Reformers concerned about the United States' ability to absorb vast numbers of immigrants—even when not questioning their worthiness or loyalty—sought to use patriotic holidays—particularly Independence Day—in their Americanization campaigns. Some even pushed to proclaim the Fourth of July "Americanization Day," and by 1915, cities across the country were using Independence Day as a backdrop for large naturalization ceremonies.

The Independence Day naturalization ritual continued well beyond its origins in the World War I era, as on July 4, 1996, for example, when some 713 immigrants in Detroit, Michigan and 60 in Lincoln, Nebraska publicly took their oaths of citizenship. Seventy-five new citizens participated in a similar ceremony at Thomas Jefferson's home at Monticello in Virginia on the same day, while 4,000 in El Paso, Texas and nearly 200 in Boston did likewise earlier on July 3. On July 4, 1997, more than 5,000 people from over 100 countries became new citizens in a sunny football field ceremony on Long Island in New York. Each Independence Day, a favorite feature in American newspapers across the country is the story or picture of these acts of naturalization, celebrating the country these freshly minted citizens have chosen. Today such rites carry a greater multicultural tone, but they continue unmistakably to celebrate America through these newly chosen people.

If officials choose the Fourth of July to swear in new citizens, native-born Americans similarly have selected the holiday as a natal day in order to affirm the country and their right to belong. In the 1904 musical *Little Johnny Jones,* George M. Cohan proclaimed, "I'm a Yankee Doodle Dandy/ … A real live nephew of my uncle Sam's/ Born on the 4th of July." And the great jazz trumpeter Louis Armstrong, though actually born August 4, 1901, always claimed the Fourth of July, 1900 as his birthday. The Lincoln Center Jazz Orchestra, in deference to Armstrong, thus chose July 4, 2000 to begin the Armstrong Centennial with its performance at the Music and Heritage Festival at Liberty Park in Jersey City, New Jersey. If both the Aryan Nation (and the Ku Klux Klan before them) and the Lincoln Center Jazz Orchestra could use Independence Day to make statements about America at the end of the twentieth century, then the meaning of the Fourth of July is surprisingly complicated and ambiguous. Yet the orchestra's approach to the fete is certainly the one more traditional and more popular today—offering a nonpartisan, inclusive, cultural politics, as opposed to a strident, hate-filled politics of exclusion. And trumpeter Clark Terry's decision to showcase the famous Armstrong number, "Struttin' with Some Barbecue," seemed to capture the spirit of the day.

The Fourth of July today is a time for light fare and to express, inadvertently, complex American identities. Picnic patriots often avoid thinking about politics on Independence Day, but they nonetheless act politically, performing a complicated nationalism. Their lack of seriousness or reverence does not necessarily imply disrespect for American principles derived from the Declaration of Independence, the Constitution, or subsequent sacred documents, such as the Gettysburg Address; indeed it may express a certain confidence and satisfaction.

Some Americans continue to use the Fourth of July strategically to make political claims, to influence policy, or to protest failures to realize American dreams and principles. The New Left activist Jeremy Rifkin and the People's Bicentennial Commission he founded, for example, contested the official observances of 1976, staging demonstrations such as the "Boston Oil Party," which protested the actions of major oil companies. But less criticism emerged than many had expected during the bicentennial, in part because official organizers seemed to employ ambiguity as a strategy to preempt dissent and disruption. Without a central focal site—like Philadelphia at the centennial in 1876—but with some 300 corporate and private sponsors and countless activities across the country, the bicentennial made vagueness a virtue, cultivated national community without consensus, and embraced nearly any version of Americanism, despite internal contradictions. The nation in 1976 was imagined by promoters as an "aggregate of pleasured spectators," according to one sociologist, and maximizing participation—pulling off a successful party—was the point.

Yet some Americans dissented from this "collective effervescence" in 1976. Ron Kovic's memoir, *Born on the Fourth of July*, for example, offered a searing indictment of America's war in Vietnam. "For me it began in 1946 when I was born on the Fourth of July. The whole sky lit up in a tremendous fireworks display and my mother told me the doctor said I was a real firecracker. Every birthday after that was something the whole country celebrated. It was a proud day to be born on." But Kovic's idyllic life was shattered by a barrage of bullets in Vietnam, which he, like many others, came to regard as a senseless war. Returning home permanently disabled, Kovic became an antiwar activist and advocate for veterans. He told his readers, "I am your yankee doodle dandy, … your fourth of july firecracker exploding in the grave."

If such indictments were rare in the last quarter of the twentieth century, Kovic's memoir nonetheless suggests the latent power of Independence Day as a political symbol and as a forum for contesting the status quo as a legitimate embodiment of American ideals. In the early twenty-first century, however, even in the wake of the September 11, 2001 terrorist attack, Americans have done little to tap that critical power. The Fourth of July continues to be, largely, a fete of leisure and American independence from serious political consciousness or action.

FURTHER READING

Cohn, William H. "A National Celebration: The Fourth of July in American History," *Cultures* 3, no. 1 (1976), 141–56.

Dennis, Matthew. *Red, White, and Blue Letter Days: An American Calendar.* Ithaca, N.Y.: Cornell University Press, 2002.

Foner, Philip S., ed. *We, the Other People: Alternative Declarations of Independence by Labor Groups, Farmers, Women's Rights Advocates, Socialists, and Blacks, 1829–1975.* Urbana: University of Illinois Press, 1976.

Hochbruck, Wolfgang. "'I Ask for Justice': Native American Fourth of July Orations." In *The Fourth of July: Political Oratory and Literary Relations, 1776–1876,* ed. Paul Goetsch and Gerd Hurm, 155–65. Tübingen, Germany: G. Narr, 1992.

Maier, Pauline. *American Scripture: Making the Declaration of Independence.* New York: Alfred A. Knopf, 1997.

Newman, Simon P. *Parades and the Politics of the Street: Festive Culture in the Early American Republic.* Philadelphia: University of Pennsylvania Press, 1997.

Spillman, Lyn. *Nation and Commemoration: Creating National Identities in the United States and Australia.* Cambridge: Cambridge University Press, 1997.

Travers, Len. *Celebrating the Fourth: Independence Day and the Rites of Nationalism in the Early Republic.* Amherst: University of Massachusetts Press, 1997.

Waldstreicher, David. *In the Midst of Perpetual Fetes: The Making of American Nationalism, 1776–1820.* Chapel Hill: University of North Carolina Press, 1997.

Warren, Charles. "Fourth of July Myths." *The William and Mary Quarterly,* 3d ser. 2, no. 3 (July 1945), 237–72.

Matthew Dennis

LABOR DAY

- ☐ The first Labor Day in the United States took place in New York City on Tuesday, September 5, 1882.

- ☐ Labor Day emerged from workers' discontent and growing hostility to changes in the workplace brought on by the emergence of industrial capitalism.

- ☐ Early Labor Day events were explicitly designed to demonstrate workers' strength, size, solidarity, and political clout.

- ☐ In 1884 New York's Central Labor Union decided to make the event an annual holiday and changed the date, resolving that they would "observe the first Monday in September of each year as Labor Day."

- ☐ By 1889 unions in more than 400 American cities staged celebrations.

- ☐ Oregon was the first state to legalize Labor Day in 1887. Thirty other states followed suit by the time Congress made it a federal holiday in 1894. By endorsing the labor holiday, the states and the federal government symbolically recognized the value of industrial workers, as well as the growing power of the labor vote.

- ☐ Radical organizations such as the socialists and anarchists were drawn to May Day celebrations while more politically moderate trade unions like the AFL supported Labor Day, mirroring the ideological split in organized labor at the close of the nineteenth century.

- ☐ The twin aims of building working-class unity and recruiting new workers were central features at Labor Day picnics.

- ☐ As time progressed leisure activities such as baseball games, gambling, drinking, and other athletic competitions came to dominate Labor Day festivities.

- ☐ In the early twentieth century progressive reformers sought to strip all references to class and even unions from Labor Day, redefining and making it more inclusive as the civic holiday of American labor.

- ☐ Labor Day celebrations, and labor unions, were revived by the federal government's explicit recognition of the legitimacy of labor's right to organize during the New Deal.

- ☐ Suburbanization, the erosion of the industrial economy, and the weakening of unions during the post–World War II decades diminished Labor Day's initial celebration of the working man and transformed it into a leisure- and consumer-driven three-day weekend signifying the end of the summer season.

"AGITATE, EDUCATE, ORGANIZE": LABOR DAY IN AMERICA

Labor Day was born in 1882, at the peak of the post–Civil War labor movement. It arrived not long after the Great Railroad Strike of 1877, which had demonstrated the promise and perils of class solidarity and opposition to industrial capitalism and had served as a catalyst to labor organizing, leading to growth among the Knights of Labor, trade unions, and socialist and anarchist unions. Not surprisingly, the initial Labor Day articulated a militant critique of industrial capitalism, but this stance had changed by the end of its first decade, reflecting both the suppression of radical unions after the 1886 Haymarket bombing and the American Federation of Labor's (AFL) ascendancy. Labor Day's birth and subsequent history illuminate the trajectory of organized labor in the United States, including its evolving views of capitalism, ideological divisions within the movement, and its successes and failures. Throughout, three things remained consistent: (1) the emphasis on building labor solidarity; (2) the belief in the absolute necessity of unions to achieve workers' betterment; and (3) the celebration of the dignity of labor, its essential significance in the building of the republic, and thus workers' preeminent claim to the status of patriotic Americans. Whatever their ideological divisions, unions invariably emphasized all three on Labor Day.

Like veterans on Memorial Day, union leaders used their holiday to keep workers in the public eye. And like veterans, by the end of the nineteenth century they had succeeded in making political leaders, the press, and business pay at least lip service to their claims to Americanism, primarily because of their potential political power. But this success did not come without a price.

A sketch of the first Labor Day parade, taking place in New York City, 1882. © Culver Pictures.

Unions had to walk a fine line between building the solidarity and militancy necessary to achieve their goals and gaining legitimacy in the eyes of politicians, the press, business, and the public. Labor Day, like Memorial Day, honored a particular group of Americans, albeit a large one. Such holidays run the risk of being perceived solely as special interest days rather than universal American holidays. Attempts to make them more universal may dilute their meaning, but remaining on message tends to limit their appeal. As historian Matthew Dennis has suggested, "Labor Day cannot fully transcend its status as a partisan fete, except when it is divested of its original meanings and political implications." Hence, it has for the most part remained a sort of stepchild in the pantheon of American holidays.

Labor unions have taken varying approaches to this dilemma over the years. For socialists and other radicals, the message of the holiday is everything, and they have maintained a militant stance toward capitalism, which has often put them at odds with other unions. The AFL has proven more willing to compromise to win some degree of legitimacy. In the late nineteenth century it developed a more pragmatic approach to labor organizing that focused on "bread and butter" issues rather than on a broader critique of capitalism, and that concentrated on building and institutionalizing labor unions. It formulated a new understanding of the relationship between capital and labor that posited them not as opposed but as equal partners. The AFL thus continued to insist on the centrality of labor (and unions) while not repudiating capitalism and suggested that workers organized to get their fair share in this partnership. This was a far cry from the original message of Labor Day, however.

"AGITATE, EDUCATE, ORGANIZE": THE ROOTS OF LABOR DAY

The first Labor Day in the United States took place in New York City on Tuesday, September 5, 1882, but it was the culmination of decades of labor organization and protests. Historians have noted the appearance of massed artisans in the federal processions of 1788 that promoted the ratification of the Constitution in Philadelphia, New York, and elsewhere. These workers demonstrated their crafts to showcase both their physical contributions to the new republic and their endorsement of the Constitution, which promised to protect American trades. Printers struck off odes to the Constitution on presses mounted on wagons, barrel makers built a watertight keg they labeled the "New

Marchers take part in a Labor Day parade in New York City, 1909. Courtesy of the Library of Congress.

Constitution," and upholsterers fashioned a "Federal Chair." Artisans thereby proclaimed their centrality to the new republic and their essential American-ism, but they found this link threatened by the antebellum growth of facto-ries and entrepreneurial capitalism, which began to alter workers' relationship with their bosses and spurred the organization of journeymen's political parties, newspapers, and the ancestors of American unions. Journeymen's unions still marched in parades on the Fourth of July and Washington's Birthday, but as historian Sean Wilenz notes, in cities such as New York they increasingly began to hold separate celebrations at which they could articulate their misgivings about the new system and its threat to their republican (and thus American) rights to independence and opportunity, and agitate for improved working conditions, including shorter hours and better pay.

After the Civil War as industrial capitalism took off, workers' declining con-trol over the conditions of their labor, employer intransigence on hours and wages, the increasingly skewed distribution of wealth, and the brutality of the militia and police toward strikers combined to produce stridently anticapital-ist rhetoric and the most violent class conflict in the nation's history. In this climate American workers produced a vibrant labor movement, representing a variety of philosophies ranging from trade unionism and cooperationism to socialism and anarchism. German, Scandinavian, and Czech immigrants, many exiled because of their socialist activities, brought to the United States radical ideologies and a tradition of labor activism, which combined with the increas-ing disillusionment of many native-born workers to form a pungent critique of the emerging industrial system.

Labor leaders recognized that to meet the challenges posed by large-scale industrialization workers had to unite in a common movement. Although indi-vidual unions remained segregated along racial, ethnic, gender, and skill lines, leaders worked to establish national labor organizations after the Civil War. The first of these was the National Labor Union (NLU), which was founded in 1866. Although the NLU did not survive the depression of the 1870s, other national labor organizations succeeded it, most notably the cooperationist Knights of Labor, which rose to prominence after the Great Railroad Strike of 1877, the Socialist Labor Party, and the American Federation of Labor (AFL), organized in 1886 for skilled craftsmen. In addition, local unions united in municipal federations such as Chicago's Trades and Labor Assembly and New York's Central Labor Union.

In an 1876 address to black voters, representatives of Chicago's Labor League proclaimed, "We recognize the existence of but two classes—the robbers and the robbed, the men who labor and the men who live off the products of oth-ers' labor." The Labor League suggested that "the interests of labor demand that all workingmen should be included within its ranks, without regard to race or nationality." African American workers responded by organizing the Colored National Labor Union, whose platform called for "the establishment of cooperative workshops…among our people as a remedy against their exclusion from other workshops on account of color, as a means of furnishing employment, as well as a protection against the aggression of capital."

Such stridently anticapitalist rhetoric and the appeal across racial and ethnic lines typified the postwar labor movement in burgeoning industrial cities. The new unions reflected the diversity of American industrial labor. Most were dominated by skilled craft workers, but the NLU, the Knights, and socialists sought to organize semiskilled and unskilled workers as well. Unions also reflected, more imperfectly, the racial, ethnic, and gender diversity of industrial labor, on a continuum from the least inclusive AFL through the Knights and the most inclusive socialist unions. Although most leaders of the NLU, Knights of Labor, and socialist unions were white, male, and skilled, their working ideology and membership practices defined the American worker in broader terms. The NLU invited the membership of black and immigrant workers, as did the Knights of Labor and socialist unions. The latter organizations also encouraged female workers to join. The AFL, in contrast, restricted its membership to skilled crafts workers. Because a variety of barriers excluded African Americans and women, as well as many immigrants, from most skilled trades, the AFL's definition of the American worker was much more restrictive than that offered by the other unions.

Chief among union demands after the Civil War was the eight-hour workday, for which unions of all stripes agitated. At its first congress in 1866, the National Labor Union proclaimed that the eight-hour law was necessary "to free the labor of this country from capitalistic slavery." As a result of labor agitation, six states, several cities, and Congress had passed eight-hour legislation by 1868. One of those states was Illinois, where the legislature had passed an eight-hour law in 1867. On May 1, the day it was to take effect, 44 Chicago unions staged a procession and mass meeting to celebrate and demand strict adherence to the new law. They followed this celebration with a general strike against those employers who had not implemented the new law. Despite the promise of these early laws, they were rarely enforced and unions continued to fight well into the twentieth century for the eight-hour day. The May Day demonstration, however, provided a blueprint for subsequent labor agitation and, eventually, for the development of a labor holiday.

THE FIRST LABOR DAY

Although both Pittsburgh and Rhode Island held labor celebrations in 1882, historians agree that the first Labor Day celebration took place in New York City in September of that year. It originated in the organizing efforts of New York's Central Labor Union (CLU), a federation dominated by Knights of Labor and socialists. When the Knights of Labor scheduled its national conference in New York City in September 1882, the CLU decided to sponsor a procession and picnic to coincide with the meeting. The main organizers of the "monster labor festival," as the CLU dubbed it, were machinist Mathew Maguire and tailor Robert Blissert, both of whom were socialist trade unionists who belonged to the Knights of Labor and were founders and officers of the CLU. Carpenter Peter J. McGuire, who later, as vice-president of the AFL, claimed sole responsibility for the invention of Labor Day, played a less instrumental role but did attend planning meetings, reviewed the procession, and was one of the day's featured speakers.

The organizers of this festival had a variety of motives. In a public statement two days before the parade typographer and grand marshal William McCabe made clear that the main purpose of the parade was to show capitalists the strength of organized labor by "offer[ing] to monopolists and their tools of both political parties such a sight as will make them think more profoundly than they have ever thought before." In addition, the CLU sought to recruit unorganized workers to union membership. To demonstrate the common bonds that united the city's workers and unify the fragmented labor movement, they invited laborers of all union affiliations, as well as the unaffiliated, to join the celebration. Marching, eating, drinking, and playing together were time-honored ways to build labor solidarity. Maguire, Blissert, and other socialists also hoped to convert the national organization of the Knights to the socialist cause. More pragmatically, they wished to gain financial support for unions. The organizers distributed picnic tickets to participating unions to sell to raise money for their unions; for its part, the CLU hoped to bring in sufficient funds to begin a union newspaper.

The CLU's festival, which became the nation's first Labor Day, drew on a long history of workers' rituals, including artisans' processions, strike parades, and eight-hour demonstrations. The celebration began with a procession through Manhattan on Tuesday, September 5, 1882. Workers marched as members of trade unions and Knights of Labor assemblies, while their families and thousands of unorganized workers watched from the sidelines. Participating unions included those of typographers, machinists, shoemakers, cigar makers, clothing cutters, dress and cloak makers, bricklayers, jewelers, and cabinet makers. Many marchers wore uniforms and emblems that signified their trades, such as the leather aprons and work clothes of the machinists. In addition, members of socialist unions such as the Progressive Cigar-makers wore red sashes or ribbons to denote their politics. Echoing the eighteenth-century federal processions, some unions demonstrated their important contributions to the American economy on their floats. Cigar makers rolled cigars, piano makers showed off their finished product, and printers of a socialist newspaper distributed flyers to the crowd. The typographers announced in a banner, "Labor Built this Republic and Labor shall Rule It." Other unions carried banners expressing support for the eight-hour movement and labor candidates, opposing child labor, and proclaiming the power of labor and unions. Banners declared that "Labor Creates All Wealth," demanded that "The Laborer Must Receive and Enjoy the Full Fruit of His Labor," suggested that "The True Remedy is Organization and the Ballot," and encouraged workers to "Agitate, Educate, Organize."

Estimates of the procession's size ranged widely, from McCabe's conservative 4,000 to the *Irish World*'s 15 to 20 thousand. At Union Square, Knights of Labor head Terence Powderly and other labor leaders reviewed the procession. According to labor lore, it was Robert Price, sitting on the reviewing stand, who coined the term Labor Day as the parade passed by. The marchers wended their way up Fifth Avenue to 42nd Street, where they, their families, and other spectators boarded elevated trains that took them to a picnic at Elm Park. There they listened to four hours worth of speeches from union leaders such as Blissert and McGuire, and labor sympathizers such as John Swinton of the *New York Sun*. One indication of the socialists' role in planning the festivities was the notable absence of politicians and elected officials from both the reviewers' stand and the speakers' podium. One banner warned that "No Capitalists, No Generals, No Lawyers Can Represent Labor." After the oratory, the multiethnic crowd ate picnic lunches, drank German beer, and listened to Irish fiddlers and German singing societies. The evening ended with a fireworks display and dancing to music provided by union bands.

LABOR DAY BECOMES A HOLIDAY

The Central Labor Union made over $200 on the festival. Following this success it sponsored a second Labor Day on the same date in 1883. Without the Knights of Labor national organization in town, socialists more clearly dominated the 1883 celebration. Banners proclaimed "Down with the wage system," "The modern industrial system increases capital and poverty," and "Prepare for the revolution." Maguire and Blissert spoke at the picnic following the parade, and the entertainment again included music, dancing, games, and drinking. In 1884 the union decided to make it an annual holiday and changed the date, resolving that the CLU would "observe the first Monday in September of each year as Labor Day."

Labor Day thus became the nation's first Monday holiday. This change offered industrial workers, few of whom had Saturdays off, the opportunity for a two-day weekend, if they could afford to take the day off without pay. Signaling the appeal of the new holiday to union leaders was the endorsement of Labor Day that year by the national organizations of the Knights of Labor and the Federation of Organized Trades and Labor (predecessor of the AFL). In 1885 the holiday spread outside New York. By 1889 unions in more than 400 cities staged celebrations.

More surprising than its rapid acceptance by workers and unions, given the hostile climate toward organized labor at the time, was the holiday's approval by state legislatures and the federal government. Oregon became the first state to legalize Labor Day in 1887, and 30 other states had followed suit by the time Congress made it a federal holiday in 1894. With their endorsement of the labor holiday, the states and the federal government symbolically recognized the value of industrial workers, as well as the growing power of the labor vote. The legislation, however, contained no provisions for a paid holiday. As the *Chicago Daily Socialist* noted in 1909, "all admit that when a man knocks off work on Labor Day his time is also knocked off the time sheet." Perhaps for this reason, the Ohio Valley Trades and Labor Assembly held Wheeling's Labor Day celebrations on the last Saturday in August until 1900 (many workers by this time worked only a half day on Saturdays). Legislators thus effectively straddled the line between the demands of labor and capital.

Unlike in the rest of the world, May Day never became Labor Day in the United States, in part because the country already had a September Labor Day. Given that the federal government did not approve Labor Day until 1894, however, it is quite possible that the development of May Day and its spread after 1890 played a role in Congress's willingness to endorse the September holiday. May Day began with a one-day strike for the eight-hour day in 1886, which was repeated on an international scale in 1890 and became an annual event thereafter. Although it had initially been supported by unions across the spectrum, the new holiday's international cast and radical tone led the more moderate AFL to back away from it in the 1890s.

On May Day socialists and anarchists condemned capitalism and called for its overthrow, whether by peaceful political means or by revolution. "The spirit of May Day is revolutionary," asserted Ralph Korngold in the *Chicago Daily Socialist* in 1911. "It speaks defiance to the capitalist class." May Day revelers made common cause with workers all over the industrial world. The international character of the day, in an age in which internationalism was a suspect philosophy, and its adoption as an alternative Labor Day by socialists, made May Day suspicious in the eyes of many Americans. The nativism that dogged the socialist movement played a prominent role as well in May Day's failure to catch on in the United States. The dominance of the day by socialists, anarchists, and immigrants made it easy for most Americans to dismiss May Day as a socialist and "foreign" holiday.

Congressional approval of Labor Day, a holiday originated by socialists, suggests that socialist influence over the holiday had declined by 1894, and indeed it had. Socialists, in fact, decried legalization as an emasculation of the holiday. "The original idea of an assertive working class demonstration," the *Chicago Daily Socialist* editorialized in 1903, "has been destroyed by the demagogues who made it a 'legal' holiday." Similarly, the founders of the Industrial Workers of the World in 1905 decided to celebrate May Day as their Labor Day because the latter, they asserted, had "completely lost its class character" since its legalization. Many radicals withdrew from Labor Day festivities or used them to protest trade unions' complicity with capitalism and party politics. Others used Labor Day primarily for recruiting purposes, working the sidelines of holiday processions trying to convince workers to join socialist unions.

The rise of the American Federation of Labor and its commandeering of Labor Day also played an important role in the radicals' criticism of Labor Day. Although the AFL included socialist unions well into the twentieth century, its national leadership made conscious decisions to stay out of politics, accept the permanence of industrial capitalism and work with employers, and focus primarily on pragmatic, "bread and butter" issues for its skilled membership. On Labor Day this translated into celebrating labor while stressing its patriotism and essential Americanism, and prohibiting symbols of radical class consciousness such as the red flag of socialism or the black banner of anarchy.

Socialist and anarchist unions, not surprisingly, offered a clearer message of class identity. They used holiday celebrations to educate workers as well as to recruit them to the cause. They aggressively recruited women, African Americans, immigrants, and unskilled labor. Socialists continued well into the twentieth century to work within the AFL to convert skilled workers to socialism. And while they celebrated May Day as their primary labor holiday by the turn of the century, they took advantage of the amassed workers on Labor Day and made it one of their prime recruiting days.

LABOR DAY TENSIONS

These tensions between pragmatic and radical unionists were evident by the first national Labor Day celebrations in 1885. In Chicago, a stronghold of the revolutionary socialist and anarchist movement, Labor Day from the start could not contain these tensions. The Trades and Labor Assembly, which sponsored the city's inaugural festivities in 1885, prohibited marchers from carrying the red flag of socialism. Socialist and anarchist unions affiliated with Chicago's Central Labor Union consequently decided to boycott the demonstration. In its place they staged a separate Sunday celebration, at which they could wear and wave the red and speak freely of socialist goals. The local Knights of Labor joined the Trades and Labor Assembly's festivities.

The two celebrations provide a study in contrasts that illuminates the ideological tensions between pragmatists and socialists. Whereas the first Labor Day organizers had deliberately excluded capitalists and conventional politicians, the Trades and Labor Assembly invited local businesses to place advertising carts in the parade. One union carried a banner claiming that "Capital and labor should go hand in hand," articulating a conciliatory view at odds with the anticapitalist rhetoric of the postwar labor movement. Capitalists were no longer simply the audience to be persuaded of the validity of workers' demands, they had actually been invited to take an integral part in the demonstration. The day's speakers included the mayor and a judge, who reinforced the message that workers must respect the rights of capital and accept that it was in their interest to work with it. Mayor Carter Harrison told workers that "[l]abor and capital may seem antagonistic, but they are in fact the best of friends." The Trades and Labor Assembly's invitations suggested that its leadership viewed the participation of politicians and businesses, representatives of capital, as legitimizing the celebration and its view of labor's significance.

The radicals, in contrast, saw these invitations as a shocking breach of labor and class solidarity. Banners at the Central Labor Union's parade advocated social revolution and even anarchy, with one warning that "every government is a conspiracy of the rich against the people." The line of march included women workers, as did the line-up of speakers, which featured Lucy Parsons, an ex-slave and radical journalist married to Albert Parsons (who would later be executed for his alleged role in fomenting the Haymarket bombing). Parsons and the other speakers condemned the Trades and Labor Assembly for its subservience to capital, compared the working class to slaves, and called for revolution.

It is tempting to agree with the radicals that the Trades and Labor Assembly's celebration represented a dramatic capitulation to employers' long-term argument that capital and labor were not opposed but had a shared interest. It certainly expressed the evolving position of pragmatic trade unionists regarding industrial capitalism. In the 1880s they began moving away from the outright opposition of the postwar era to a more nuanced acceptance of capitalism. Pragmatic unionists developed in the late nineteenth century an ideology that proclaimed organized labor to be the full partner of capital and articulated the goal of working to improve the condition of workers within this system. It was this ideology that increasingly took center stage on Labor Day.

The second national Labor Day celebrations took place a scant four months after the bombing in Chicago's Haymarket Square and the subsequent attacks on radicalism, which helped to cement the pragmatists' hold on the new holiday. Municipal labor federations, many affiliated with the newly established AFL, used the holiday in 1886 to demonstrate not only labor's significance but its essential Americanism. Carrying the red flag and other signs of socialism were prohibited. In Chicago the Trades and Labor Assembly again sponsored the celebration. Participating unions waved American flags and the red flag was nowhere to be found. The organizers again invited "all manufacturers and business firms to participate and thereby exhibit their productions" in the parade, perhaps hoping that this invitation would lead businesses to agree to the assembly's request that they grant their workers a holiday. Not all unions agreed with the conciliatory message, however. The Pullman Knights of Labor assembly refused to participate because they did not want to march in front of a Pullman car that the company wished to display.

In other cities Labor Day 1886 was similarly dominated by trade unions and Knights of Labor assemblies. Like the Trades and Labor Assembly in Chicago, organizers in New York, Brooklyn, and Cincinnati banned red flags, although the German Typographical Union in Cincinnati was able to get away with carrying a banner that called on spectators to "Read Karl Marx on Political Economy." By the 1890s, however, socialist unions were again participating in Labor Day activities in many cities, although AFL-affiliated unions and federations dominated the holiday's planning. When they participated, socialists often dissented from the antiradical message by defiantly wearing red badges and ribbons. In New York, Chicago, and other industrial centers socialist unions and trade unions sometimes held competing celebrations, so that each could define the holiday in its own way.

The original Labor Day goal of unifying labor suffered other blows as well. As the Knights of Labor declined and the AFL's dominance of the holiday grew, the participants were more and more limited to white male skilled workers. When southern cities adopted the holiday in the 1890s, it was generally segregated. Although white and black miners paraded together in Birmingham, Alabama in 1895, Nashville's separate white and black programs were more typical. The interracial Knights of Labor had been active in Richmond in the 1880s, but that city's first Labor Day celebration in 1890 was restricted to "organized white wage-earners," according to the *Richmond Dispatch*. Even within the ranks of white trade unions, dissension flared. In some cities individual unions opted out of the main celebrations in favor of their own parades or picnics because of inter-union antagonisms. In Chicago, for instance, the stonecutters refused to participate to protest the inclusion of the stonemasons and bricklayers, whom they accused of undercutting their wages and stealing their jobs. In San Francisco in the early twentieth century, the Building Trades Council and the Labor Council similarly staged competing parades because of disputes between the organizations.

THE RITUALS AND MEANING OF LABOR DAY IN THE LATE NINETEENTH CENTURY

Like the 1885 and 1886 exercises, the typical Labor Day celebration in the late nineteenth century followed the pattern laid down by the Central Labor Union in 1882, but the message shifted as AFL-affiliated unions took control of the day's events. Under the aegis of the AFL, Labor Day became an occasion to celebrate the American laborer, who was in partnership with capital rather than opposed to it, who used nonviolent strikes as tactical maneuvers to gain practical benefits, not to attack industrial capitalism, and who prided himself on being a patriotic, flag-waving American who would not tolerate the red flag of radicalism. The AFL sought employers' acknowledgment of the indispensability of (skilled) labor, for which radicals accused it of bowing submissively before capital. The AFL saw the situation differently. Although it accepted the legitimacy of capital, it took the position that labor constituted an equal partner of capital, not a junior or submissive partner. When capitalists or politicians reviewed Labor Day processions, it signified to the AFL acceptance of that equal partnership and of the centrality of labor. In the socialist view, no such partnership was possible. Capital could only be the enemy of labor and, thus, the republic, and, as such, must be eliminated. Radicals insisted on the overthrow of capitalism as the ultimate goal of all workers. To socialists and anarchists, to have capitalists review workers' processions made a mockery of working-class Americanism.

Although pragmatic and radical unionists offered disparate visions of working-class Americanism, their visions did dovetail on several critical points. Both enshrined productive labor as the key to American prosperity and to the very success of the nation, and both claimed to be the true heirs of the American republican tradition. Trade unionists and socialists each sought for workers the rightful fruits of their labor. They agreed that labor unions were necessary to attaining the latter goal, and, despite socialist ideology, both movements were dominated by skilled craftsmen. Perhaps most significantly, both posited unions as the *sine qua non* of working-class identity and solidarity.

The most prominent display of organized labor's power and unity continued to be the parade of the various unions, in uniform and bearing pro-labor banners. Union leaders intended the massed workers to show the strength of organized labor to capitalists and politicians, as well as to the unorganized workers whom they sought to recruit. So important did labor leaders consider the parade that some unions fined members for not participating. In Chicago in 1900, for example, the Building Trades Council threatened to fine members five dollars for not marching in the Labor Day parade. The *Chicago Daily Socialist* explained that unions paraded on Labor Day in order "to show the employers the strength of union labor," and "to encourage the thousands of unorganized laborers who turn out to view the parade, to be part of it the following year." Indeed, socialists often worked the parade route in an effort to recruit workers to the cause. Each year the *Socialist* published a special Labor Day issue and called upon radical workers to purchase and distribute these to marchers and spectators. In 1902 socialists reportedly gave out 40,000 newspapers in Chicago.

In addition to proselytizing socialists, spectators at Labor Day parades encountered a colorful display of union strength. Members of individual unions visually displayed their solidarity by marching as a uniformed group. Painters dressed in the white overalls of their trade, blacksmiths donned their leather aprons, and butchers marched in jaunty red and white checked smocks. The unions demonstrated their utility to the republic as they paraded. Some marchers carried tools of their trade; plumbers bore turnkeys, for instance, while boilermakers shouldered their hammers like muskets. Others showed the products of their labor; cigar makers displayed their cigars and tin, sheet-iron, and cornice workers carried tin umbrellas. Still other unions chose to demonstrate physically the vitality and importance of their trade. Blue-jeaned machinists in one Tucson Labor Day parade operated a lathe on their float, which also included a functioning engine spouting smoke. Not to be outdone, boilermakers noisily riveted a boiler. In other processions, barbers gave shaves, caulkers caulked boats, and bricklayers laid bricks. By demonstrating their crafts, union members in the late nineteenth century, like their eighteenth-century forebears, showcased their contribution to the American republic—the skilled labor that literally made it work. Their holiday floats proclaimed that the printers who kept the presses going, the machinists who kept the industrial machinery turning, the bricklayers who laid the very foundations of American business, were the ones really responsible for American progress. Since the Revolution, America had been defined in terms of useful citizenship, and Labor Day processions asserted that skilled workers were the most useful of citizens and thus the epitome of Americanism.

Although it seemed to undermine their message of labor's importance, unions began to invite businesses to enter advertising floats in Labor Day parades, as Chicago's Trades and Labor Assembly had done in 1885. Although these floats displayed products made by workers, the emphasis had shifted from the process of making the product (the labor) to the object itself, as something to be consumed. In 1886 the assembly explained that the "principal feature" of its Labor Day procession was to be not the union marchers themselves but "a grand industrial parade, to which a cordial invitation is extended to all manufacturers and business firms to participate and thereby exhibit their productions." Although advertising floats remained a relatively minor part of Labor Day processions, they undercut the day's purpose of showcasing the workers who made American goods. If the unions targeted the unorganized workers who watched the parades as potential union members, the businesses who sponsored advertising floats saw both spectators and marchers as potential consumers of their products. The products they displayed grew increasingly divorced from the workers who had made them. Tucson's 1905 procession, for instance, prominently featured the massed display of consumer goods, including furniture, clothing, shoes, and hardware, by a local department store. Socialists and anarchists abhorred such exhibits and refused to share their holiday space with capitalists. To the AFL and its affiliates, however, advertising wagons were just another symbol of the interdependence of capital and labor, the partnership between employers and employees, and capital's implicit endorsement of organized labor.

The banners and flags carried in Labor Day processions, and the music played by union bands, provided additional evidence of the ideological divisions within the labor movement. Whereas socialists favored banners with such revolutionary sentiments as "He who would be free must strike the blow" and "Workers of the World Unite," practical unionists preferred to focus on unionism's compatibility and partnership with capitalism. Their banners bore pro-labor but less controversial slogans such as "Organized Labor is the Bulwark of the Republic." The music played by marching bands similarly defined the unionists' America. At socialist celebrations the air filled with the strains of the French revolutionary hymn, the "Marseillaise," the favored anthem of socialists in the late nineteenth century and a clear indication of the international character of their view of labor. In contrast, at the Labor Day celebrations of the pragmatic unions, such patriotic airs as "America," "Hail Columbia," and the national anthem prevailed. But radicals appropriated American patriotic songs as well, for they continued to believe themselves to be truer to American principles than capitalists were.

The flags carried by unions provided another ideological sign. Displaying the U.S. flag demonstrated that workers were patriotic Americans who contributed to American prosperity. Steamfitters in an 1890 Labor Day parade suggested that patriotism and unionism were indivisible with a red, white, and blue banner bearing the inscription, "We are Union men and carry Union colors." The socialist red flag, in contrast, proclaimed workers' commitment to socialism, the internationalization of the working class, and the continuing belief in the opposition of capital and labor. And the foreign flags sometimes flown by ethnic unions demonstrated their pride in their ethnicity and continued attachment to their homelands.

These flags mingled at early Labor Day parades, but after the Haymarket bombing pragmatic craft unionists embraced the most visible emblem of Americanism and often banned the other flags. The *Chicago Tribune* reported that in the 1893 Labor Day parade "there was but one flag—the Stars and Stripes...There were no black flags [of anarchy] or red flags, no emblems of violence, incendiarism, murder and revolution." When partisans showed such banners, other union men might dispense patriotic justice. For example, at a Labor Day parade in Pittsburgh in 1890 members of the Junior Order of United American Mechanics demanded that the German bakers' union furl its German flag. When the bakers refused, a melee ensued. The Germans lost the fight and watched as the patriotic mob tore the offending flag to shreds, shouting "America for Americans" and "the Stars and Stripes the only banner on our streets." In the wake of the Spanish-American War patriotism even took pride of place over unionism; an 1898 Labor Day banner proclaimed "Our country will ever be first; our union next."

Reacting to this hyperpatriotism, socialists turned more exclusively to the socialist banner at their celebrations. The *Chicago Tribune* complained in 1895 that celebrants at the Socialist Labor Party's Sunday Labor Day picnic "flaunt[ed] a red flag" given to the party by socialist women. City officials, fearing that the socialists would try to parade the banner through city streets, even sent a detachment of police to the picnic grounds "to see that no red flag parade started out from that point."

The pragmatic unions' emphasis on their patriotism was more than a ploy to avoid attacks in the wake of Haymarket or an indication that workers were swept up in the patriotic delirium of the 1890s. They, like socialists, craved acceptance of their unions as an indispensable component of American society and economic progress. One way of acquiring such legitimacy was through the recognition of capitalists and major party politicians. Socialists rejected out of hand the authority of both and thus wanted them only to view socialist celebrations from a distance, with fear and trembling for the future of capitalist America. But to the pragmatic unionists, who accepted capitalism and still sought to work through political channels to achieve their ends, acceptance and even approval were necessary. Thus, whereas the organizers of the first Labor Day had refused to invite representatives of capital or government to their celebration, AFL-affiliated city trade councils invited both to review their Labor Day processions. Rather than viewing this as submission, as socialists did, nonsocialist workers reveled in the power such reviewers imputed to organized labor.

As the potential political power of unions increased, mayors and congressmen found it essential campaign strategy to accept such invitations. By the turn of the century local, state, and even national politicians were reviewing Labor Day parades and speaking afterward. In Richmond in 1900, for example, the mayor and the Virginia attorney general spoke at the holiday exercises, and Tucson's 1905 celebration featured the mayor and city council. In one of the earliest instances of courting the labor vote on the national level, Republican vice-presidential candidate Theodore Roosevelt and Democratic presidential candidate William Jennings Bryan sat together in the reviewing stand on a Chicago Labor Day just two months before the 1900 election.

Socialists, who derided party politicians as agents of capital, refused to invite any but avowed radicals to review their processions, and they steadfastly refused to parade "as slaves before the plutocrats and capitalists." Instead, socialist leaders such as New York journalist John Swinton and Chicago politician and labor leader Thomas J. Morgan reviewed their Labor Day marchers. Socialists fought tooth and nail against plans to have capitalists review joint parades. In 1892, for example, Chicago's Cloakmakers Union vehemently protested the Trades and Labor Assembly's (TLA) plan to parade before "politicians of the capitalistic parties" and withdrew from its Labor Day procession. A violent argument ensued on the floor of the assembly, but the pragmatists won the battle and the TLA president announced that any organization that insulted the flag or the speakers would be barred from the parade. Socialists refused to believe that parading before capitalists could do anything but degrade workers and make a mockery of their holidays. In 1903 the *Chicago Daily Socialist* noted with disgust that at the Building Trades' Labor Day celebration, "an aspirant for governor and a colonel of the militia will orate to the fool workers whose celebration has become a sham."

After the procession on Labor Day, the marchers, their families, and supporters typically headed to a local park for a picnic, which offered workers the opportunity to build social bonds by eating, drinking, gambling, and otherwise playing together. Unions made money by selling tickets to the picnics, and they also received cuts of the proceeds of concessionaires who ran the food, alcohol, cigar, and gambling booths. The twin aims of building working-class unity and recruiting new workers made oratory a central feature at Labor Day picnics. Leaders of local federations and any visiting national or international labor leaders reviewed the procession and spoke at the picnic that followed. Sympathetic politicians and journalists who shared the reviewing stand with labor leaders often shared oratorical duties at the post-parade exercises. Ideological differences showed up in the oratory. At Chicago's 1886 Labor Day exercises, for example, Knights of Labor Grand Lecturer A. A. Carleton shared the rostrum with Congressman Frank Lawler and other politicians sympathetic to the goals of pragmatic unions. Carleton praised the patriotic "industrial army of peace" and asserted that, unlike the anarchists, they sought "not to destroy or tear down, but to build up." The messages of such politicians predictably focused on consensus rather than class conflict. The 1905 speaker in Tucson spoke for many when he said that "capital and labor should not be enemies, but should be on friendly terms." In contrast, radical picnics featured orators such as anarchist Johann Most and Scottish socialist Keir Hardie. The latter told Chicago workers in 1895 that under industrial capitalism, "the property that is produced is stolen from the man who produces it." In response to this theft, radical speakers, according to the *Chicago Daily Socialist,* "told toilers to take all they are entitled to."

Despite the fact that a significant percentage of their members were not native English speakers, the oratory at the celebrations of pragmatic trade unions was typically in English only. In contrast, at radical picnics one was as likely to hear addresses in German, Czech, Norwegian, and a host of other foreign languages as in English. The *Socialist* noted that at the 1910 Labor Day picnic, for example, "addresses were made in all languages." Buffalo's 1895 picnic featured speeches in both English and German. The deliberate use of English might also have been part of the same strategy as the proliferating American flags—to show that workers were just as patriotic and just as American as capitalists. The socialist convention of having speakers in a variety of languages similarly had ideological and strategic functions. It expressed the internationalism of the movement while it also addressed the problem of trying to spread the word to immigrant workers whose grasp of English was often minimal at best.

Whatever their ideological view, the primary purpose of holiday addresses by union leaders was to extol the benefits of union membership, underscoring the day's purpose as a recruiting device. Keir Hardie warned his 1895 audience that any worker who was "not a member of the union of the trade to which he belongs...is practically ranging himself on the side of the millionaire, on the side of the sweater, on the side of every enemy of honest labor." In the South, where unions faced even more hostility than in the rest of the country, this message was particularly important. In his 1905 Labor Day address in Greensboro, North Carolina, printer W. E. Faison asserted that "[o]rganized labor means for the worker shorter hours, larger pay, better conditions, and greater independence." He defended union leaders against the charges of corruption and defended union strategies as peaceful, claiming that hostile businesses and newspapers exaggerated and distorted both the corruption and the violence associated with organized labor. Faison closed with a call to workers to use their vote to elect those who would truly represent the working citizenry of the nation.

Not only union membership but the consumption of union-made products became a test of working-class loyalty and solidarity. At Chicago's Labor Day picnic in 1886, for example, union men attacked and demolished a stand whose proprietor was allegedly selling non-union cigars. The Cigar Makers International Union sponsored a wagon in Detroit's 1894 parade that bore the banner "Smoke Union-Made Cigars." In Wheeling, West Virginia bartenders and musicians who worked at the picnic had to be union members.

LABOR DAY AS RECREATION

Although oratory constituted an essential element of Labor Day picnics in the late nineteenth century, union leaders knew that their audience had no desire to spend an entire afternoon listening to speakers. The picnics therefore featured recreational activities designed to appeal to workers' craving for amusement in their rare free time. Labor Day revelers jammed dance pavilions, wheels of fortune, and beer stands. Sporting events became an increasingly important part of labor holidays, whether within or outside the confines of union celebrations. After watching Boston's 1887 Labor Day procession, woodcarver Charles Adams noted in his diary that he and a friend "went out to see the ball game between the Boston and the Philadelphias." Tucson's 1905 celebration featured both boxing and baseball matches.

As early as 1887, pragmatic unionists bowed to the nonideological nature of the new trade unionism and the realities of the popular taste in amusements. In Chicago that year, the Trades and Labor Assembly and Knights of Labor "decided at the last moment to have no speech-making," as the crowd of 35,000 that filled the picnic grove "was in no mood to listen to vague platitudes about the labor movement." Similarly, in 1890, members of 14 white trade unions united for a Labor Day procession in Richmond, then gathered afterward for food and a baseball game, omitting oratory. The *Nashville Banner* noted in 1892 that fewer addresses were planned because picnic-goers preferred to watch "feats of physical strength and endurance rather than have their minds burdened with some intricate question relative to the solving of the labor problem." Nashville's celebration that year featured a bicycle race along with other athletic contests.

Although the ideological and evangelical nature of socialism all but demanded oratory at holiday picnics, the number of speakers declined even at socialist celebrations. In 1909, for example, the *Chicago Daily Socialist* noted that there would only be one address at the Labor Day picnic, because "picnickers are not much given to listening to speeches." Instead, the socialists of the 22nd ward issued a challenge to any indoor baseball team willing to play against them at the picnic. The following year's Labor Day amusements included dancing, races, a tug of war, and a professional wrestling exhibit.

Union leaders were not untroubled by this development. They had designed Labor Day's rituals, including the parade and oratory, to reinforce the message of labor solidarity and power. They were thus disturbed by the rank and file's apparent lack of interest in these rituals. They viewed Labor Day as sacred, agreeing with Eugene Debs, who wrote in an 1895 article that Labor Day's "supreme

Samuel Gompers participating in a Labor Day parade. © Brown Brothers.

significance… is found in the fact that it is set apart as a day for the discussion of questions vital with interest to all workers" and that the holiday was "intended to stand for something more and superior to physical and mental relaxation, play, and pleasure." In 1912, longtime AFL president Samuel Gompers asserted that "Labor Day is not a time for mere merrymaking and personal enjoyment, but a time for pledging anew our faith to our cause and to each other."

Rank and file workers, however, saw Labor Day less as an occasion to demonstrate union solidarity than as a respite from labor and a victory in the struggle for a shorter work week and more leisure time. For a good many workers, "eight hours for what we will" meant more time for entertainment and play, and they were loathe to devote their holiday from work to marching and listening to speeches. Instead they wanted to enjoy their holiday on their own terms. This might mean spending the day quietly with family and friends, it might mean coming to the picnic and foregoing the parade, or it might mean paying for commercial amusements. In the absence of a labor crisis, many workers chose to exercise their American right to spend their holiday in a manner of their own choosing, disregarding the suggestions of both their unions and their employers. If their unions fined them for not parading, they chose to pay the fine rather than to give up the freedom to spend their holiday as they chose. Indeed, one reason why unions instituted fines for not parading on Labor Day was low participation. Despite the fine threatened by the Building Trades Council in Chicago, for example, only about one-tenth of the membership marched in 1900.

Although union leaders still sought to recruit, educate, and indoctrinate on Labor Day, they found by the early twentieth century that they had to bow to the popular will. Labor unions in many cities dropped both oratory and processions and incorporated more games, sporting events, and other amusements into their holiday celebrations as a result of their members' demands for entertainment. Even on the first Labor Day, the *New York Times* suggested that many union members had skipped the parade because "they preferred to enjoy the day in quiet excursions to Coney Island." In 1895 New York's unions decided "that a parade was not necessary" because there were "no questions to be agitated and no victories to be celebrated." The Central Labor Union instead sponsored an excursion to Coney Island's Sea Beach Palace for its members. Similarly, Richmond's Central Trades and Labor Council decided to drop its parade in 1895, instead urging workers "to regard the day as a day of rest." In 1910 Chicago's AFL-affiliated unions failed to hold a Labor Day procession because only 17 of the 58 member unions had voted in favor of one. Richmond's 1910 Labor Day exercises suggest the extent to which recreation and entertainment had taken over Labor Day. Exercises took place at the fairgrounds, where Richmonders paid a 10-cent admission fee to watch or participate in motorcycle and horse races, a baby show, games and sports, and a balloon ascension. The highlight of the celebration was a reenactment of the Battle of Gettysburg fought by the city's military groups. Similarly, Tucson's Central Labor Council advertised that its 1915 celebration would feature a baseball game, a "grand ball," a band concert, and sports and games, including greased pig and pole-climbing contests, and races for children and both married and single women. Alongside its proclamation that "Unionism means liberty equality justice," the Council assured Tucsonans that at the celebration there would be "Something doing every minute."

Despite such blatant moves to satisfy their members' thirst for amusement over education, unions still saw attendance at Labor Day exercises decline except during times of labor crises such as strikes. For instance, unions across the country passed Labor Day resolutions in 1895 protesting Eugene Debs's imprisonment for his role in the Pullman strike. Atlanta unions revived their parade in 1914 to support striking textile workers, and the Los Angeles parade returned in 1911 to demonstrate solidarity with the McNamara brothers, union leaders on trial for their alleged role in bombing the *Los Angeles Times* building.

The labor movement could lay part of the blame for workers' lack of interest at its own feet. Ira Steward, father of the eight-hour movement after the Civil War, had advocated the shorter work day and increased leisure time as of equal benefit to improving workers' condition, and had suggested that workers would improve their standard of living not by thrift, as their employers proclaimed hypocritically, but by consumer spending. One of Steward's proteges, George Gunton, a radical textile worker turned economist, argued that the eight-hour day would "stimulate consumption, raise the standard of living, and foster elevating desires among the workers." Gunton downplayed class solidarity and suggested that consumer goods and increased leisure time could provide the rewards no longer intrinsic in labor itself. The AFL's pragmatic unionism, by focusing on bread and butter issues, reinforced this message and undermined its efforts to build class solidarity.

Adding to labor leaders' dilemma were the purveyors of commercial entertainment who competed for workers' holiday time on their two-day weekend. They offered workers the opportunity to spend their leisure (and their money) on motion pictures, horse races, baseball games, regattas, amusement parks, and train and boat rides. To compete, many unions moved their celebrations to beaches or amusement parks and incorporated even more entertainment events, including games, sports, baby parades and queen contests, boxing and baseball matches, cakewalks and other dance contests, automobile and motorcycle races, concerts, carnival rides, circus acts, and sham battles.

THE TRIUMPH OF CONSENSUS

In addition to the inroads made by commercial recreation, labor's holiday in the early twentieth century confronted the consensus-building efforts of progressive reformers, who sought to strip all references to class and even unions from Labor Day. They redefined it as the civic holiday of American labor, which was broadly defined so as to include virtually all Americans, and a celebration of American progress, in which capital and labor were partners. In a 1902 article on Labor Day, Toledo mayor Samuel M. Jones decried talk about "the working people," which "seems to carry the idea...that we have a people *who do not work*." In the *Journal of Education* Lee Hanmer asserted that Labor Day should focus on the progress of industry and the dignity of labor, which would aid in ending the "misunderstanding that now exists between employer and employee." A Chicago Labor Day pageant in 1913 depicted this symbolically, with Labor and Capital joining hands to work together for progress. Pageant professionals suggested that Labor Day, along with the Fourth of July and other holidays, was an ideal occasion for building community feeling and patriotism. Pragmatic unions generally went along with these efforts, continuing to downplay class and emphasize the partnership between capital and labor. The AFL also sought to lend religious legitimacy to Labor Day by designating the day before the holiday as Labor Sunday in 1909 and calling for church services to emphasize the spiritual and educational aspects of the labor movement on that day.

At the same time that this Progressive era consensus muted the class dimension of Labor Day, it made the holiday both more universal and more inclusive. Progressive pageant parades showcased immigrants and, to a lesser extent, racial minorities, and Labor Day exercises in this era followed suit. In Los Angeles, for instance, African American, Mexican American, and women's unions participated in holiday parades. Although African Americans had to hold separate holiday celebrations in southern cities at the turn of the century, by 1918 Richmond's labor pageant included "forty-five white orgs...in the main body of the parade...supplemented by...various colored labor organizations." Atlanta's parade also featured a "colored division." In Tucson both Anglo and Mexican unions planned and participated in Labor Day celebrations.

In its September 1902 issue the AFL's journal, the *American Federationist*, published a series of Labor Day commentaries by union leaders and others interested in American labor, including reformers Jacob Riis and Henry George, economist Carroll Wright, and Frank Sargent, the U.S. commissioner of immigration. These comments demonstrated both the broad consensus that was emerging for the holiday and the range of contemporary views on organized labor. Reflecting the educational bent of the Knights of Labor, Terence Powderly maintained that Labor Day was a time to discuss "the history of the day; the causes leading to its establishment...so that young people entering upon their duties as workers may learn of, and appreciate, the struggles of those who preceded them." He also suggested that organized labor might follow the example of veterans who had established the National Soldiers' Home and establish "homes for aged and indigent members of the family of producers."

Max S. Hayes, who represented the socialist viewpoint that still constituted a minority position within the AFL, agreed with Powderly that the holiday should be a time to "encourage and foster education among the workers relative to the history and mission of the labor movement." But he took a dimmer view of cooperation between labor and capital, proclaiming that Labor Day's purpose was "to strengthen the bonds of comradeship, . . . to augment our numbers to overthrow the system that makes exploitation and wage-slavery possible, and to prepare to establish an industrial democracy."

Victor Yarros more closely reflected the mainstream of AFL philosophy, noting that the "quintessence of unionism is concerted action in protecting the rights of labor in a legitimate way" and suggesting that "trades unionism has been one of the great liberating, uplifting and inspiring movements of the last nine or ten decades." M. M. Garland, the former president of the Amalgamated Association of Iron and Steel Workers, the union destroyed by Andrew Carnegie at Homestead in 1892, also saw Labor Day as a time to reflect and remember "the mighty struggles that were required to make possible the time when we could openly celebrate a day set aside for organized labor." He asserted that "Labor Day commemorates the fact that organized labor has won its right to recognition by the people and the government."

If the government's support for organized labor was still shakier than Garland indicated, Frank Sargent's remarks suggested that at least the commissioner of immigration agreed. Claiming that "There is no national holiday when the people should take a deeper interest in its proper observance than on Labor Day," he wrote that workers "should not be regarded lightly when on Labor Day they assemble and demonstrate their numerical strength and proclaim their purpose" by parading as "the army of creation, progression and preservation." Henry George predictably advocated not only organization but the single tax as the solution to labor's woes. Jacob Riis expressed a progressive sympathy for "a living wage" and "decent conditions of working," but warned the worker that to deserve this, he must "consecrate himself to his cause by resolving to be a whole man . . . and do a whole man's duty, and he will find the employer doing his before he knows it." Toledo mayor Samuel Jones praised Labor Day as a time to honor all Americans who work and proposed that the best way to improve the lot of labor was to follow his version of the Golden Rule: "not make it necessary for another to do a kind of work or service that I would not be willing to take a hand at myself or raise a son or daughter for."

In this climate of consensus American businesses increasingly embraced Labor Day as well. If politicians sought to win workers' votes on the holiday, businesses sought their patronage by entering floats and advertising their support of Labor Day and unions. In 1915 the Tucson Ice Cream Company advertised, "Our Ice Creams were indorsed by the Labor Council and will be at the Labor Festival." A candy and cigar store similarly claimed that "There is always a Union Man buying something in Frank's Place." Businesses noted in their advertisements that they would be closed to honor the holiday. A clothing store proclaimed in Tucson's 1919 holiday program: "We sell UNION MADE Merchandise in honor to the vast Army of Bread Winners, will be closed all day Labor Day." In Atlanta a grocery store felt obliged to explain in its holiday advertisement why it was remaining open until noon. Noting that "We are very proud of today's Atlanta Labor Day" and that "it would please us very much to be able to take the day off to play, celebrate and rest," nevertheless, the store explained, "[p]eople must have food" and are "depending on us as their head-quarters" for picnic provisions.

LABOR DAY IN WAR AND PEACE

This Labor Day consensus intensified during World War II. As might be expected, mainstream labor organizations went to great lengths to demonstrate their patriotism and their support of America's entry into the war on Labor Day 1918. Richmond's celebration featured a "monster parade" in which "every labor organization" in the city participated, as did Red Cross workers and members of the YMCA. The unions carried banners demonstrating their loyalty to the cause and exhorting spectators to "Help Win the War" and "Don't Be a Slacker." Machinists proclaimed, "We are the Boys Who Make the Shells." Other banners explained union contributions to the Liberty Loan drives and Red Cross work. After the parade the marchers and their families and friends headed to a picnic with athletic feats, dancing, and oratory by Sen. Robert L. Owen of Oklahoma, who pontificated on the dignity and importance of labor and praised workers for "carrying on this gigantic war for liberty," noting that Americans should be "proud of the spirit shown by labor in support of the republic."

At the same time as the picnic, soldiers training at the fairgrounds across town staged a display of "the great game they are learning" before another 10,000 Richmonders, entertaining them with military drills, a sham battle, a motorcycle race, and a variety of athletic contests. The soldiers also staged a program called "the army at play," which included "tossing the Hun," "bump the Kaiser," and "barrel boxing." Although the mayor attended the labor celebration, Virginia's governor appeared at the military exercises, pledging to buy $500 worth of war savings stamps before going up in one of three fighter planes that thrilled the crowd.

Across the nation the story was similar on the holiday AFL president Samuel Gompers renamed "Win the War For Freedom Day." In New York "soldiers of industry" waved American flags and "shouted victory slogans" as they marched in parade up Fifth Avenue with a military escort and planes overhead. In Connecticut, employees at an engineering plant sent a telegram to Gen. Pershing pledging their patriotism: "To help you win and win soon, we propose to give

Labor Day a meaning true to its name by giving, without compensation, five hours of our time on this national holiday to the building of 155 millimeter guns to shoot the Hun." The *Tucson Citizen* noted that "when so much is dependent upon labor for the winning of the war, an especially hearty celebration of Labor Day will be held." Unions there marched in parade as the mayor, local politicians, and "Red Cross girls" rode in automobiles, and volunteers collected money from the crowd for the "watch fund," to pay for watches for the soldiers going overseas.

Tucson's celebration, unlike the others, did strike a radical note within its patriotism. At the post-parade picnic the marchers and spectators listened to Arizona's former governor, George W. P. Hunt, whom the *Citizen* reviled as a Wobbly and radical, denounce the "autocracy of great wealth" that sought to control his state. Hunt shared his hope that, after bringing triumphant democracy to Europe, American soldiers would come home "and sweep away the power of autocracy" here. The former governor defended himself against charges that he was in league with the antiwar Industrial Workers of the World (known as Wobblies), who had become notorious in Arizona the previous year by leading a strike in the Bisbee copper mines that had resulted in the deportation of more than a thousand strikers to New Mexico. At the same time, Hunt proclaimed his sympathy for the blacklisted strikers, asserted that the blacklist would be swept away with the rest of the autocracy, and opined that "some men of great wealth" would be convicted in the deportation case.

Hunt's criticism of capitalism proved an exception to unions' paeans to their patriotism and loyalty on the wartime Labor Day. After the war, however, it was a different story. Unions that had foregone raises to demonstrate their dedication to the war effort sought their rewards from unwilling employers. In a postwar United States wracked by the ensuing strikes, Labor Day quickly lost its patriotic edge. President Woodrow Wilson used his 1919 holiday address to call for a conference bringing together representatives of capital and labor to open a dialogue aimed at improving their relationship. AFL leaders backed Wilson's proposal, one asserting that the "government should use its influence to emphasize to employers that none can refuse to recognize the right of workers to organize and bargain collectively." The Federated Council of the Churches of Christ in America ordered that Methodist pastors that year observe "Labor Sunday" by discussing with their congregations "the vital industrial and social problems of our country," in the effort to "bring about a new day in our industrial system."

Despite these conciliatory moves, 1919 saw few holiday parades. In New York, the traditional Labor Day opening of new Broadway shows was shut down by a strike by members of Actors' Equity seeking recognition of the union by producers and management. The actors and sympathetic theater unions staged their own counterproductions to entice holiday crowds. This strike and other labor strife led New York's union leaders to cancel that year's parade. Unions in Washington, D.C. similarly omitted the procession in favor of a program of oratory, sports and games, and dancing at a resort outside town. The *Washington Post* noted that the majority of Washingtonians joined the workers and their families in leaving town for the holiday. Foreshadowing Labor Day's transformation into the last three-day weekend of the summer, the paper claimed that "more Washingtonians journeyed out of the city for the three days of rest than at any other holiday period, except Christmas itself."

LABOR'S STRUGGLE TO SURVIVE

Fighting for their lives in the 1920s as the open shop movement gained momentum and businesses instituted welfare capitalism, unions struggled to retain their precarious foothold in America by wooing business, government, and an increasingly conservative public on Labor Day. They toned down the day's militance without giving up their insistence on the necessity of unions. According to historians Michael Kazin and Steven J. Ross, "Labor Day became a more uniform, less vital public occasion" in this era. Toledo's unions, nearly wiped out by local open shop actions, cancelled their parades and oratory in the 1920s. In other cities more unions invited businesses and civic organizations to join in their celebrations. In some places Labor Day parades became almost indistinguishable from other patriotic processions. In Atlanta, for instance, Labor Day was submerged in a festival of urban boosterism. Labor leaders in 1925 agreed to the mayor and chamber of commerce's plan to turn Labor Day into "a great civic 'good will' festival," a day intended to "mak[e] an Atlanta booster out of every visitor to the...celebration." For the first time in its history, Atlanta's Labor Day parade included a division of floats entered by civic groups and businesses, including Christian associations, the League of Women Voters, the Lions Club, the bar association, and even the Chamber of Commerce, and floats included one "showing the Holy Bible as the basis of American civilization." A stunt pilot flew overhead, entertaining the marchers and spectators with loops and twists. Post-parade events that year included a band concert, a field meet, a baseball game, a dance featuring "southern jazz orchestras," and a fireworks display with a climactic "boost Atlanta" piece. The committee judging the parade praised the Atlanta Federation of Trades for "inviting the cooperation of the people of the entire city to participate in a great fall festival" and inspiring a movement to "unite all classes for the upbuilding of the city and state."

Business leaders and the antiunion press viewed this change as a positive one, suggesting that the militant celebrations of old (and unions themselves) were no longer necessary, given the improvement in working conditions. Union leaders agreed, but only to a point. In his Labor Sunday address in New York's Cathedral of St. John the Divine in 1925, AFL president William Green proclaimed that "the forces of capital and labor have passed into a new era, an age of cooperation and reciprocal relationship." But while he disavowed militancy, Green warned that "attempts to prevent organization among the workers must cease." The following day at Detroit exercises he assailed "autocracy in industry and communism as allies in a common purpose of undermining organized labor in America." In St. Petersburg, Florida that same year, AFL secretary Frank Morrison attacked "the open shop advocate as in reality an enemy of organized labor because he 'never concedes the right of his workers to bargain collectively.'" He castigated company unions, group insurance, and employee stock plans as steps to undermine organized labor.

Like Green, other union leaders continued to assert the necessity of labor organizations in Labor Day addresses at picnics, in the press, and on radio. They did so by refining the AFL strategy of asserting both the patriotism and the importance of organized labor. In 1925 union editor Jerome Jones reminded Atlanta workers that "the struggle for national liberty and the establishment of a free government were won on the strength of labor" and that America's wealth came from the efforts of labor. Jones asserted that Labor Day was "not the celebration of an event, but of a movement," which was organized labor, and of "a cause that had its inception in a demand for human rights." He praised the work of the AFL and ended with a typical holiday call to "strive to bring into its ranks every unorganized worker." Historians Kazin and Ross note that the use of radio led the AFL to focus on issues such as the benefits of higher wages and a shorter workweek for both workers and the American economy, rather than on militant demands and class rhetoric, but this was only a continuation and expansion of the AFL's pragmatic message. In the 1930s John L. Lewis, the charismatic president of the United Mine Workers, would perfect this equation of union labor with economic prosperity and help pave the way for a broader acceptance of unions.

LABOR DAY'S NEW DEAL

With the Great Depression in the 1930s threatening both the dignity and livelihoods of American workers, organized labor turned to the government for support and received it. In response to union persistence and the exigencies of the Depression, President Franklin D. Roosevelt's New Deal finally lent government sanction to labor unions. On Labor Day 1933 the Toledo *News-Bee* praised the National Industrial Recovery Act's (NIRA) Section 7A, which guaranteed workers' right to organize unions and bargain collectively, as heralding "Labor's New Day." Although the NIRA was subsequently overturned, the 1935 Wagner Act forced businesses to negotiate with the union winning the majority of workers' votes, undermining the company union tactic that had decimated organized labor in the 1920s. Spurred by this legislation and the organization of the Committee on Industrial Organization within the AFL, union membership soared in the 1930s, from less than 2 million in 1930 to about 10 million by the end of the decade.

As unions stepped up their organizing activities in the mid-1930s, Labor Day processions and programs revived as occasions for building solidarity, recruiting, and legitimizing unions. In Toledo the Labor Day parade returned in 1934, following a major victory by workers at a local plant, who had won recognition of their union after a violent strike. Some 20,000 workers marched, including newly organized locals such as the Waitresses' Union and Agricultural Workers, which reflected a new push to organize unskilled workers. The Agricultural Workers, who were then engaged in a strike against onion growers, headed the line of march and carried a large American flag, which they used to catch contributions to their strike fund tossed by spectators.

The Agricultural Workers' use of the flag suggested a mixed message of patriotism and militancy. With the blessings of the Wagner Act, patriotism now sanctioned union militancy against recalcitrant employers such as the onion growers. Unions now had government support for their long-held position that employers who refused to recognize unions were unpatriotic. Union militancy during the 1930s was aimed squarely at such "unpatriotic" employers who refused to obey the law and who impeded both their workers' and the nation's prosperity by refusing to recognize unions. One float in Toledo's 1935 parade compared the homes of union and nonunion workers, suggesting that union membership brought material prosperity and enabled workers to achieve the "American Standard of Living."

Despite their renewed militancy, the revived Labor Day activities in Toledo and elsewhere continued the early twentieth-century tradition of mixing entertainment with edification, now drawing on icons of the new mass culture. In Los Angeles, union screen stars rode in the parade and performed on floats, while the bands of Count Basie and Louis Armstrong serenaded spectators. The allure of celebrities drew huge crowds to the processions; by the late 1930s they were drawing more than 100,000 spectators. Kazin and Ross suggest that this diluted labor's message by transforming Labor Day activities from "a politically meaningful occasion" into "little more than another form of holiday entertainment," concluding that "[a]musing the public was not the same thing as winning it over." Yet this melding of entertainment and union proselytizing represented more of a continuity with the past than a break from it. Since the late nineteenth century labor unions had been wooing both workers and public opinion by incorporating forms of contemporary popular entertainment and recreation into Labor Day celebrations. Los Angeles's parade in 1937 epitomized this blend, as an actor playing Abraham Lincoln promoted the inclusion of African Americans in unions, while Popeye and the Keystone Cops attacked "scabs."

Communists and socialists, who played a vital role in CIO organizing, found themselves more marginalized in 1930s Labor Day celebrations. At a Toledo parade in 1934, for instance, union leaders segregated radical locals at the end of the line of march. As ideological divisions widened between the CIO and AFL, eventually precipitating a nasty split, they took to staging competing Labor Day celebrations, at which the leaders of each denounced the other organization.

CIO parades in particular showcased the increasing diversity of the labor movement, which now included large numbers of unskilled laborers, such as waitresses and agricultural workers, and workers representing entire industries, such as automobiles and steel. More women now marched, reflecting organizing efforts in the garment and textile industries, and among teachers, clerical workers, and waitresses. The parades became more racially and ethnically diverse as well, as the old barriers to AFL membership fell away under the onslaught of 1930s organizing, and large numbers of African American and immigrant workers joined unions. CIO processions also paid homage to galvanizing moments in the organization's history, such as the auto workers in Detroit who sat down in the midst of the parade route to honor the sit-down strikers who had won recognition for their union.

WORLD WAR II AND THE RED SCARE

During World War II both the AFL and CIO solidified their gains in membership and prestige. Organized labor's partnership with the federal government, forged during World War I and cemented with the New Deal legislation, continued during World War II. Unions in many cities followed the example of the Connecticut engineers in 1918 and voluntarily gave up their holiday during the war years to donate their time to the war effort. Membership soared to 15 million after the war, but organized labor's patriotism again came under attack because of a wave of postwar strikes. In addition, the postwar Red Scare focused attention on leftist connections in many unions, particularly those affiliated with the CIO. In this atmosphere, Congress weakened union protections with the Taft-Hartley Act, passed over President Harry Truman's veto in 1947. The Taft-Hartley Act required union officials to file affidavits that they were not members of the Communist Party; if they failed to do so their unions would lose government protection. Unions responded with a two-pronged attack, by purging communists and other leftists and at the same time using Labor Day to denounce conservative policies and urge repeal of the legislation.

Partially because of conservative politics and partially because of the very success of the union movement, Labor Day activities entered another period of decline in the 1950s. Organized labor's successes made it seem less imperative to recruit new members on Labor Day, and labor leaders increasingly turned to the mass media of radio and television to disseminate their holiday messages. As unions became institutionalized, there also seemed to be less urgency to

A cartoon by Fred Wright dealing with issues surrounding the Taft-Hartley Act in 1947. © Culver Pictures.

create a union culture of solidarity on Labor Day. Moreover, as union workers grew more prosperous and moved to the suburbs, they had even less desire to march in urban parades on Labor Day.

The growing number of union workers in the postwar era did mean that politicians, particularly Democrats, paid increased attention to courting their votes through Labor Day appearances and speeches. Labor Day in fact became the official starting date for presidential campaigns. President Harry Truman kicked off his 1948 campaign with a whistle stop swing through union strongholds Pennsylvania, Ohio, and Michigan over the holiday weekend. Truman met with labor leaders in Grand Rapids, Flint, Toledo, Harrisburg, and other towns, and spoke at five different celebrations in Michigan on Labor Day itself. He told workers in Grand Rapids that their choice on Election Day was between "the Democratic party, which is devoted to the welfare of the little man, and the Republican party, which stands for special interests." In Detroit the president insisted that leaders of the rival AFL and CIO make peace for the day and join him on the platform. A huge audience cheered as the president denounced the Taft-Hartley Act and the "do-nothing 80th Republican congress," and admonished unions that they must get out the vote to sweep the Republicans out of power. (Despite Truman's appearances, Michigan went for his opponent in the election, native son Thomas Dewey.) Detroit, the nation's preeminent union town in the heyday of the American automobile industry, drew a series of Democratic candidates to its massive Labor Day parade in the postwar era, including Adlai Stevenson, John F. Kennedy, and Lyndon Johnson. More recently, Al Gore appeared at a Pittsburgh Labor Day rally in 2000.

LABOR DAY TODAY

For the majority of Americans who do not belong to unions, Labor Day today brings a mixture of apprehension and anticipation completely unrelated to its history. The holiday has come to symbolize the end of summer and the signal for sales marking the imminent start of the school year. Americans make one last pilgrimage to the beach or the mountains, do some last-minute school shopping, or gather for a final summer barbecue.

Although few Americans know the origins of their three-day weekend, unions still regard Labor Day as a sacred day in the civic calendar and use it to reiterate union principles. Historians Michael Kazin and Steven Ross conclude that "What is remarkable about Labor Day over the past 110 years is not how much its celebrations have changed but how much its original purposes and problems have remained the same." The chief message of Labor Day today, as in 1882, is the importance of unions in improving the condition of American workers. Just as in 1882, however, that message remains a hard sell to most Americans, and Labor Day remains symbolic of organized labor's strengths and weaknesses. Unions continue to fight the desires of the rank and file to spend the holiday in nonideological recreation, and their celebrations today, as in the past, most often take the form of picnics, sports, and recreational events, including golf tournaments, road races, baseball games, and car shows.

Aside from a few brief, shining moments between the mid-1930s and the early 1950s, labor's quest for legitimacy on the American stage has proven largely chimerical. Union membership headed into a long, steady decline in the late twentieth century, with the demise of Rust Belt industries, the rise of the Sun Belt with its right-to-work laws and hostility to unions, and increasingly antiunion government policies. Nevertheless, Labor Day retains a militant potential, most often realized during times of crisis. In 1980 Detroit union leaders revived that city's Labor Day parade, which had disappeared in the hard times of the 1970s, and it continues to be one of the few annual processions, despite the decline of the state's auto industry and its unions. Union members paraded in Manhattan, Chicago, San Francisco, and other cities in 1982 to mark Labor Day's centennial and to protest President Ronald Reagan's economic and anti-union policies. Since 1996 the AFL-CIO and the National Interfaith Committee for Worker Justice have sponsored "Labor in the Pulpits" services to fight for social justice on Labor Sunday. As American labor entered the twenty-first century, the Labor Day goal of justice for American workers, which had seemed to be won in the mid-twentieth century, was renewed. Longshoremen marched in 2002 to demand a fair contract for dock workers, and the following year Ohio workers rallied to protest President George W. Bush's economic policies. Ironically, those Ohio workers also used the holiday to demand what the Wagner Act had supposedly guaranteed almost 70 years earlier, the freedom of American workers to join unions without fear of being fired.

FURTHER READING

Borden, Timothy G. "Labor's Day: Public Commemoration and Toledo's Working Class," *Northwest Ohio Quarterly* 70 (Winter/Spring 1998): 4–27.

Kazin, Michael, and Steven J. Ross, "America's Labor Day: The Dilemma of a Workers' Celebration." *Journal of American History* 78, no. 4 (March 1992): 1294–1323.

Litwicki, Ellen M. *America's Public Holidays, 1865–1920.* Washington, D.C.: Smithsonian Instutution Press, 2000.

Smith, Mike. "Celebrating the Worker." *Michigan History Magazine* 85 (September/October 2001): 44–53.

Watts, Theodore F. *The First Labor Day Parade, Tuesday, September 5, 1882: Media Mirrors to Labor's Icons.* Silver Spring, Md.: Phoenix Rising, 1983.

Ellen M. Litwicki

AMERICAN INDIAN DAY

☐ During the early twentieth century American Indians used positive aspects of Indianness found in popular American visions of the past to reform harsh federal Indian policy and alleviate Indian poverty.

☐ In 1911 prominent Indian reformers formed the Society of American Indians to promote Indian citizenship, advancement, self-help, and, a year later, the creation of American Indian Day, which they saw as a vehicle for teaching white Americans a more accurate version of Indian history.

☐ Several states, including New York, Connecticut, and Washington, recognized the holiday over the next 30 years, sponsoring day- and weeklong events focusing on Indian customs and culture.

☐ In 1941 the first of many bills seeking to officially recognize American Indian Day was introduced to Congress. It became a law 42 years later when May 13 was officially declared American Indian Day.

☐ By 1983 most Native Americans had lost interest in promoting their culture to the wider population and had become more interested in political self-determination, undercutting the holiday's value.

AMERICAN INDIAN DAY

[Let us sponsor] a nation-wide holiday (official or otherwise), devoted to the study or recital of Indian lore. Picnics, parades, Indian games, music, ceremonies, dramas, speeches, orations, recitals of history, exercises by schools, clubs, societies, and out-door lovers—see the scheme? Every red-blooded American, whether just born or imported[,] from cradle to dotage, would yell long and loud for American Indian Day. That attention which the red man would command would help him immensely.

—Arthur C. Parker (Seneca), 1912

Beginning in the early part of the twentieth century, American Indian leaders like Arthur Parker began calling for the observance of American Indian Day. They hoped that a national commemoration focusing on Indian culture and history would highlight Indian contributions to American society and help redefine popular perceptions of Native peoples. Furthermore, Indian activists believed that this renewed attention could bolster arguments for Indian civil rights and strengthen efforts to address Indian social problems. In cities across the country, individuals and organizations promoted the holiday and held celebrations, drawing together an eclectic mix of Natives and non-Indians. True to the purposes outlined by Parker, many of these gatherings combined the social, cultural, and political. After World War II, American Indians adopted new strategies and adjusted their goals to reflect their recent experiences and the realities of postwar America. Eventually, American Indian Day became less a vehicle for social and political activism, while remaining an opportunity to educate Americans about Native people and celebrate Indian culture. Non-Indian political leaders came to endorse this incarnation of American Indian

Day and the holiday made headway as a feature of the American calendar. By then Indian activists had invested less in the holiday. Nevertheless, their progress in advancing Indian social issues and improving Indian imagery owes a debt to the American Indian Day that was promoted and celebrated in the first half of the twentieth century.

ORIGINS OF AMERICAN INDIAN DAY

The earliest celebrations of American Indian Day and the promotion of the holiday were a direct response by Indian leaders to both material conditions and public perceptions of Native Americans. The late nineteenth century saw the end of Native American military resistance to U.S. expansion and the hardening of the reservation system. Federal Indian policy steadily eroded the tribal land base, worked to develop natural resources for the benefit of non-Indians, and attacked Indian culture. On reservations, Indians lived under particularly harsh conditions that included crippling deficiencies in health, housing, education, and economic development.

At the same time, public perceptions of American Indians underwent curious changes. The anxieties brought on by industrialization, immigration, and the end of the "frontier" encouraged some Americans to look inward and reevaluate American national identity. Progressive-era reformers saw the Indian experience as an essential precursor to contemporary society and sought to cultivate the "purity" of that earlier era in each person, particularly urban youth and recent immigrants, to teach them the values of America. New organizations like the Boy Scouts and Campfire Girls took up this project by emphasizing the natural environment and developing activities focusing on Indian culture. This fascination, however, was mostly limited to the imagined Indian of old. Contemporary Indians were thought to be corrupted by their long-standing relationship with modern society, poor remnants of their ancestors, and unfit as role models. Some Americans saw Indians as "exotic" and "noble," but only if they provided tourists and scholars with the sense of the past that was expected, unencumbered by the trappings of modern society.

These perceptions, combined with the terrible social conditions that characterized Native communities, encouraged some American Indians to begin working for change. Immersed in the progressive reform movements of the day, they saw links between racist notions of Indians, federal policies, and social and economic conditions. They began to cultivate the positive aspects of Indianness found in the American vision of the past, in an effort to fuel a movement for reform in federal Indian policy and the alleviation of Indian poverty in the present. While they often drew upon the stereotypes of the day, they infused these images with their unique visions of themselves and their communities. American Indian Day emerged as a logical and successful tactic of this effort.

The first stirrings of a movement to create an American Indian Day were connected to the establishment of the Society of American Indians. Meeting in Columbus, Ohio in 1911, six prominent Indian reformers—Charles A. Eastman (Sioux), Carlos Montezuma (Yavapi), Thomas L. Sloan (Omaha), Charles E. Daganett (Peoria), Laura M. Cornelius (Oneida), and Henry Standing Bear (Sioux)—formed the Society as a forum for promoting Indian citizenship, advancement, and self-help. They organized a national conference, which was attended by Indian leaders and the federal Commissioner of Indian Affairs. The following year, the society met again and added the creation of an American Indian Day to its platform. They recommended that the holiday be observed in schools, colleges, churches, and historical and fraternal organizations and be "devoted to the true history of the Indian, his true character and habits before the coming of the white man and to his present social and economic condition today." Arthur Parker, writing in the Society's journal in 1915, repeated the call for an annual weekend of American Indian Day activities in schools, literary and historical societies, and churches. He recommended that observance include a hearty dose of patriotism, including the playing of the Star Spangled Banner, saluting the American flag, and an address on "The Ameri-

The American Indian Day celebration in Omaha, Nebraska, 1898. © Corbis.

can Indian as a Patriot." Moreover, readings from Indian legends and famous Indian speeches, Indian songs, and lectures on the "The Indians of Our State" and "The American Indian in Literature" were to emphasize Indian culture and contributions. Society members continued to promote the holiday through the remainder of the decade.

These efforts and those of local Indian groups interested in American Indian Day quickly bore fruit, as the holiday was recognized and used to bring attention to Indians and their causes. In 1916, schools throughout New York, Connecticut, and Wisconsin held celebrations. The governor of New York State declared the second Saturday in May American Indian Day, then called for recognition of the help that the Iroquois Confederacy had given European settlers and asked that attention be given to the needs of contemporary Indians. In 1919, Washington State endorsed an annual observance and the Illinois legislature set the fourth Friday in September as American Indian Day. The Indian Fellowship League, a group of Indians and non-Indians living in the Chicago area, took up annual sponsorship in Illinois. Through the early 1920s, it held "encampments" at forest preserves around the city that featured displays of Indian culture. Moreover, in 1923, the Indian Fellowship League organized an "American Indian Week" encampment at Cook County Forest Preserve to coincide with the Society of American Indian's annual conference in Chicago.

SPREAD OF THE HOLIDAY

The promotion and celebration of the holiday continued through the next three decades. The Society of American Indians disbanded early in the 1920s, but another Indian group, the Tepee Order, continued to call for recognition of the holiday. The Tepee Order was an adult fraternal organization of Indian and non-Indian members, with chapters in Los Angeles, Chicago, Minneapolis, and Denver. It tended to promote a stereotypical Indian culture, by using an invented system of dating based on suns and moons, and employing official titles such as "Supreme Grand Council Under Great Buffalo Totem Pole," and "Junior Guide of the Forest." Its founder, the Reverend Doctor Red Fox St. James, was almost certainly a non-Indian falsely claiming Indian ancestry. Nevertheless, St. James and the Tepee Order were active in Indian causes, including the movement to establish an American Indian Day. In 1914, St. James completed a 4,000-mile journey by horse from Montana to Washington, D.C. to raise awareness of the holiday, collect gubernatorial support, and seek an audience with President Woodrow Wilson. St. James also promoted American Indian Day through the periodical of the American Indian Association, an offshoot of the Tepee Order. In a 1922 article titled, "Why Nation Should Honor 'Original Landlords': American Indian Day," St. James related accounts of Indians helping early European American communities, documented Indian foods that had made their way into the American diet, cited the bravery of Indian soldiers who fought in the World War and the honors bestowed upon them, called for a process by which American Indians might apply for citizenship, appealed to federal treaty obligations by invoking a 1775 Delaware pact with the Continental Congress, and printed a poem entitled "My Creed," that attested to the "true," "pure," "strong," "brave," and "humble" nature of the American Indian, all in an effort to bolster his calls for celebration of the holiday.

That same year, the Tepee Order sponsored a celebration of American Indian Day in Denver on the last weekend in September. On Friday, St. James and Tepee Order president and Indian reformer Sherman Coolidge (Arapahoe) gave speeches in local schools. Throughout the weekend many stores in the city "displayed in their windows Indian pictures...[and] Indian art...as a special tribute to the American Indians." The highlight of the celebration was the American Indian Day program held on Sunday at the Grace Community Church. After a procession by the Campfire Girls, Boy Scouts, Improved Order of Red Men, Fraternal Order of the Eagles, and Sacagawea Council, there was a prayer to the Great Spirit and a lighting of a ceremonial peace pipe. The Governor of Colorado and the mayor of Denver read tributes and the Campfire Girls sang, "Indian Mother Song." Coolidge closed the proceedings with a keynote address that offered a scathing indictment of Indian-U.S. relations and appealed to Christian ideals in demanding reparation.

Meanwhile, other groups began holding American Indian Day celebrations. In the 1930s, American Indian Day became an annual event in New York City. A multitribal celebration took place on September 30, 1934, in Inwood Hill Park in Manhattan. Featuring speeches, poetry, dancing, and a re-creation of an "Old Indian Encampment," it drew 2,000 people. The following year, the event catered to 3,000 people and included a lighting of a peace pipe and calls for "better understanding" of Indian matters. By 1936, there were multiple celebrations throughout the city. The Inwood Park festivities, now sponsored by the Indian Confederation of America, attracted 3,000 people, featured 50 performing Indians of 25 tribes, and included speeches by the commanders of the Inwood Post of the American Legion and the Catholic War Veterans. In Brooklyn's Prospect Park, members of the United Indian Tribes of America performed dances, gave speeches, and inducted a "paleface" into the "tribe" through a blood-mingling ceremony for 1,000 spectators. The Indian Confederation of America, Inc. celebrated in Queens, in front of a crowd of 200. Rev. Barnabas Skiuhushu (Red Fox St. James under a new name) called for a national observance of American Indian Day and read "commendatory letters" from the bishop of the Episcopal Church and the president of the Boy Scouts of America.

Separate from the other festivities, a monument at the Zion Protestant Episcopal Church in Queens was dedicated to the Matinecoc Indians, where the "last of the tribe" were reburied after a widening of a boulevard disturbed their original place of rest. The ceremonies were attended by descendents of the tribe, members of the church, and a Sioux man named Rosebud Yellow Rose, who sang an "Indian lament." The monument itself was a "split boulder with a young oak growing upward through the rift, symbolic of life over death," with the inscription, "Here Rest the Last of the Matinecocs." In Chicago, sponsorship of American Indian Day shifted to the Indian Council Fire, which held Indian Day exercises throughout the 1930s. As part of the celebration in 1936, the group honored Arthur Parker, the holiday's founder, by bestowing a bronze medal on him in recognition of his achievements as an American Indian. There were also celebrations on Indian reservations. In 1939, the Schaghticoke Indians celebrated on their reservation in Connecticut with festivities sponsored by the Indian Association of America, Inc. Fifty members from a number of eastern tribes attended and "[v]arious Indian ceremonies were held, including a council fire." The guest of honor was the governor of Connecticut, who lauded Native Americans for the way they received the first European settlers.

American Indian Day was also celebrated by Indians on the West Coast. The Wigwam Club, a group organized to raise money for welfare to needy Indians in Los Angeles, sponsored an annual Indian Day Picnic at Sycamore Grove Park, just north of downtown. Beginning in 1928, the event annually drew thousands of Indian and non-Indian attendees who gathered for food, music, dancing, and speeches. The 1929 celebration, for example, included more than 2,500 Indians "from all parts of the United States." As was the case at most of the Indian Day celebrations in Los Angeles, Indian actors working in the motion picture industry supplied much of the entertainment. Among the performers were Chief Big Tree (Seneca), Thundercloud (Cherokee), Little Bear (Mohawk), and Willow Bird (Apache), who contributed "love songs, lullabies, bird calls, and addresses, all in Indian language." By the early 1940s, the sponsorship of the Indian Day Picnic shifted to the California Indian Rights Association, a group interested in Indian political rights and land claims. In 1942, for instance, State Attorney General and future California governor and Chief Justice of the U.S. Supreme Court Earl Warren gave the keynote speech. Indian actors again supplied the entertainment along with students from Sherman Institute, a Bureau of Indian Affairs boarding school in the nearby town of Riverside. Mindful of the ongoing war, the Indian Rights Association asked military post commanders in the vicinity to allow all Indian servicemen to attend and Indian women brought extra box lunches to feed them.

EFFORTS TOWARD A NATIONAL HOLIDAY

During the 1940s the commemoration of American Indian Day also received increasing attention from national politicians and was for the first time seriously considered as a national holiday. In 1941, Bill 1240 was introduced to the U.S. Senate. It made provisions to set aside the fourth Saturday in September as American Indian Day and requested that the president issue an annual procla- mation "inviting the people of the United States to observe such day with cer- emonies, as a memorial to the aborigines of this Nation and their contributions to the establishment and maintenance of this Nation." Moreover, it requested that the president call on the governors of the states "to take such action as they may deem advisable in order to bring about observances of such day."

While under consideration by the Committee on Indian Affairs, several Indian groups wrote expressing their support for the holiday. W. T. Gridley, chairman of the Indian Council Fire and vice chairman of the American Indian Day Committee (created two years prior), noted that Illinois had observed American Indian Day for many years and the Council Fire had been active in promotion through school and radio programs. In a separate letter, he endorsed a national observance and cited the Indian contribution to World War I as jus- tification. Oliver La Farge, of the American Association of Indian Affairs, Inc.,

Native Americans from all over the country gather in New York to urge Congress to adopt American Indian Day as a national holiday, 1929. © Bettmann / Corbis.

New York, favored the bill and stated "that it is only right and proper that the American people should be led as much as possible to give honest consideration to the first Americans." Leda Ferrel Rex, of the American Indians Committee of the National Society of the Daughters of the American Revolution, endorsed the bill and stated that she was "greatly interested in the Indians and what is for their good and pleasure" and that she could be counted upon to be "ever lined up on the side of the Indians and the things for his benefit."

Additional letters argued in favor of the holiday and also revealed how invested local groups had become in their annual celebrations. Following an effort by U.S. Secretary of the Interior Harold Ickes to amend § 1240 so that April 19 would be designated American Indian Day, several appeals were made that the observation stay fixed on either the fourth Friday or Saturday of September. Ickes' suggestion was tied to the founding of the Inter-American Indian Institute, an organization designed to coordinate a Pan-American effort to address indigenous problems. The U.S. groups in favor of American

Secretary of the Interior Harold Ickes signs the Wheeler-Hobard Bill, giving Native Americans self rule, as John S. Collier and chiefs of the Flathead tribe look on, 1935. © AP / Wide World Photos.

Indian Day seemed to have little interest in the Institute and saw the changing of the date as an affront to their regular patterns and motivations for celebration. Arthur Parker, now national chairman of the American Indian Day Committee, endorsed the fourth Friday of September since it was the day that Native organizations, Boy Scouts, and schools celebrated. Parker also noted that the weather that time of year permitted holding pageants and outdoor concerts.

Other Indian groups and individuals supported Parker's arguments. The president of the Rochester, New York, Neighborhood Indian Society noted that their organization, the Six Nations Association of New York, and other organizations in "New York, Brooklyn, Chicago, and elsewhere," had been celebrating in late September for "a number of years" in cooperation with "Boy Scout organizations, prominent citizens, and individual interested in their history." Ben Dwight of the Inter-Tribal Indian Council of Oklahoma City, Oklahoma, stated that Oklahoma Indians were inclined to favor a celebration in late September as well, since "autumnal season traditions are more in [their] minds." W. T. Gridley claimed that the Indian Council Fire had been open to the suggestion of other dates, but that they subsequently conducted a national poll of Indian groups, who in turn responded by voicing their support for the fourth Saturday in September and indicating that an April date made little or no sense in their annual scheme of things. Gridley went on to say that it had taken many years to build support in Illinois for an American Indian Day and that it seemed "only fair" that the Indian groups involved across the nation "should be entitled to this recognition—their own American Indian Day as selected by the groups who have had the interest and stick-to-it-iveness to observe and foster its promotion for years." Clearly, American Indian groups were not willing to give up the traditions that they had worked hard to establish, nor were they willing to exchange local celebrations with nationalist themes for an ill-understood pan-Indian commemoration.

Despite the support for the bill and passage by the Senate on December 9, 1941, it did not get beyond a preliminary reading in the House, most likely because of the nation's sudden shift in attention to mobilizing for World War II. Nevertheless, local groups continued their now time-honored commemorations in New York, Chicago, Los Angeles, and in other urban and reservation Indian communities through the 1950s and 1960s. Increasingly in the postwar period, politicians also came to endorse commemoration of the holiday. Between 1943 and 1981, 35 separate bills to designate an American Indian Day, several of which had multiple co-sponsors, came to the floor of Congress. Often they were accompanied by lengthy speeches nearly identical in terms of the sentiments they conveyed to the speeches given by Indian leaders and speakers at American Indian Day celebrations decades earlier. For example, in 1965 Congressman John V. Tunney of California spoke to the House in favor of a bill establishing an American Indian Day:

The importance [of recognizing American Indian Day] is realized when we glance back through the history of our Republic and observe the contributions made by the Indian people to our heritage and to our present day culture. We can see a proud people who...have emerged as a responsible and patriotic section of our population....We must act to place the national and even world spotlight on the Indian and thus, show our pride toward them. In this way, we can promote better understanding.... We can also help to advance the economic and social welfare of our Indian community.

In 1973, Congressman Mario Biaggi of New York used the occasion of American Indian Day to remind the House of its commitment to American Indians:

[T]omorrow marks the celebration of American Indian Day, a day on which we honor the nobility and rich history of the first Americans, the Indians. Yet it is a hollow celebration in the light of the continuing neglect by the American Government of the problems of Indians... I call upon the President and my colleagues in the Congress to begin this long overdue commitment, so that we can truly celebrate American Indian Day in 1974.

During the 1980s and 1990s, these efforts came to fruition and a number of laws passed providing for an American Indian commemoration. In 1982, Congress passed House Joint Resolution 459, which became Public Law 97–445 and made May 13, 1983, the first federally recognized American Indian Day. In 1986 and 1987, Congress passed laws designating an "American Indian Week." In 1990 a law was passed designating an "American Indian Heritage Month." Influenced by the 500th anniversary of Christopher Columbus's arrival in the Americas, 1992 was designated by Congress to be both "The Year of the American Indian" and the "Year of Reconciliation between American Indians and Non-Indians."

LOSS OF NATIVE AMERICAN SUPPORT

Ironically, as efforts by politicians to recognize American Indian Day moved forward, Indian people themselves came to invest less in the holiday. While continuing to see American Indian Day as a way to recognize and celebrate Indian culture, Indian activists developed new strategies for social and political activism. After World War II, the emphasis of American Indian leaders on gaining the rights of citizenship and adapting to American society—elements firmly embedded in earlier commemorations of American Indian Day—began to give way to the idea of self-determination. Native people came to assert their identities both as Americans and as members of sovereign nations to whom the United States had contractual obligations. Instead of arguing for full inclusion in American society, they began calling for federally funded programs, designed and administered by their members, which would address the specific needs of their communities. Adopting the tactics of civil rights activists and organizations, Native people increasingly used legal means, mass protests, and government programs in pursuit of their goals.

American Indian Day, as early twentieth-century Indian reformers conceived it, was a nationalist holiday that was not designed to support such a redefinition in the nature of U.S.-Indian relations. This is not to say, however, that these reformers would not applaud or approve such changes, or see the need for new tactics in which to address both old and new goals. Despite decades of assimilation policy and rhetoric, early twentieth-century Indian leaders continued to identify themselves as Indians. They found in the promotion and observance of American Indian Day an arena in which to confront the non-Indian world and make Indianness into something that suited their tastes and would work

Derrick Redbird of the Sauk and Fox tribes, dances at the California American Indian Day Commemoration in Fresno, 2003. © AP / Wide World Photos.

to the benefit of their communities. Although over time the holiday weakened in its potential to force a meaningful confrontation, it helped to strengthen the ability of American Indians to forge ahead and find new ways to continue the struggle for the well-being of their people. By the end of the twentieth century, local, state, and federal politicians, in efforts to convince their colleagues that American Indian heritage was a vital part of American culture, echoed the very principles that Indian reformers earlier endorsed.

Moreover, American Indian groups and non-Indians came to study, celebrate, and commemorate American Indian culture and heritage year-round through hundreds of annual powwows, countless county, state and regional fairs, books, films, monuments, museums, and school curriculums. Indeed, American Indian Day is still celebrated in many localities today and continues to showcase Indian culture. At the turn of the twenty-first century, American Indian Day festivities brought Indians and non-Indians together from San Diego, California; to the small town of Blackfoot, Idaho; to the Potawatomi Reservation in Kansas; to Boston, Massachusetts. While Native American people often see less value in using these holidays for social and political activism, their celebrations continue to claim a place for Indians in modern American society. Many Indian people would agree with Shoshone-Bannock tribal member Michelle Hernandez, who said at 1998 celebration, "Indian Day to us is everyday, but for the non-Indians it's something we show them [on American Indian Day] so that they'll know what we're proud of." Most likely, American Indian Day will never become an annual, federally recognized national holiday. It has, however, contributed to a redefinition of ideas about Indians and has helped make the recognition and commemoration of North America's first peoples part of the national consciousness.

FURTHER READING

Deloria, Philip J. *Playing Indian*. New Haven, Conn.: Yale University Press, 1998.
Hertzberg, Hazel H. *The Search for an American Indian Identity: Modern Pan Indian Movements*. Syracuse, N.Y.: Syracuse University Press, 1971.
Patterson, Michelle Wick. "'Real Indian Songs': The Society of American Indians and the Use of Native Culture as a Means of Reform." *American Indian Quarterly* 26, no. 1 (Winter 2002): 44–65.
Quarterly Journal of the Society of American Indians. 1913–1915.

Nicolas G. Rosenthal

COLUMBUS DAY: THE NAVIGATION OF UNCHARTED WATERS

How interesting that our holidays are becoming battlefields or at least boxing rings for the discussion of the meaning of our lives as citizens of the United States and of the world. Christmas is under considerable stress as people debate whether celebrating the holiday as they wish infringes on the freedom of others. Mothers' Day is sometimes at odds with the newly developing images of mothers. But so far, no other holiday has generated the friction and discussion of Columbus Day.

This reaction is dramatic because the arrival of the bold Genoese could be considered one of our drearier holidays. Many yawn at ethnic parades, odes, statues, proclamations, and department store sales. Columbus Day has little to excite children with thrilling anticipation or lost sleep; they only get lectures on perseverance and diligence. Columbus was so long ago. So beside the point. How interesting then that this strange holiday should have the power to excite some to righteous oratory and even violence. This once well-established formal civic ritual has turned into the most contested of holidays, illuminating our divided beliefs over the very meaning of America and the character of Americans.

Columbus Day as a holiday came long after the celebrated event. Although we have good evidence that the day was commemorated on the 300th anniversary in 1792, and the great Columbian Exposition in Chicago took place in 1893 (the ambitious buildings could not be completed in 1892), it was not until 1905 that a government official, the governor of Colorado, asked his people to celebrate the anniversary of Columbus's landfall.

COLUMBUS DAY

- [ ] Columbus Day is observed on the second Monday in October.
- [ ] Columbus Day became a legal federal holiday in 1971.
- [ ] Christopher Columbus never set foot in North America, spending most of his time in the New World in and around the Caribbean Ocean, believing to his dying day he had found Asia.
- [ ] With the colonists' overthrow of British rule in 1776, Columbus fulfilled the desire to find a non-British founder to symbolically cut the origins of America from its mother country, and provide a past that bypassed England.
- [ ] The first known Columbus Day was observed in New York City on October 12, 1792, by the Tammany, or Columbian, Society.
- [ ] In 1791 the new country's capital was named after its founding father, and the spiritual father of the New World: Washington, District of Columbia.
- [ ] In female form, Columbia became a potent eighteenth-century symbol of the dignity and civility of an emerging American civilization.
- [ ] With the establishment of compulsory public education in the early 1800s a regal and paternal, yet progressive and farseeing Columbus was featured in schoolchildren's textbooks, further burnishing the Great Mariner's reputation as a key figure in the founding of America.
- [ ] In the later nineteenth century Catholic immigrants from Italy, Spain, and other countries embraced Columbus to shield themselves from nativist discrimination and affirm their identity as first-class American citizens.
- [ ] Led by the newly founded Knights of Columbus, official recognition of Columbus Day bears fruit as 10 states recognized the holiday by 1909.
- [ ] Elevation of Columbus from the 400th anniversary of his arrival and the 1893 Columbian Fair brings increased scrutiny by historians, who unearth and begin to popularize the mariner's many failings and flaws, for example, introducing Western racism and slavery to the New World.
- [ ] As the darker side of the Columbian legacy came to the fore, in 1992 the 500th anniversary of his westward voyage became a battleground for our entire view of Western culture.
- [ ] Native Americans have mounted the best organized and most militant opposition to Columbus and the celebration of his day.

Still, it was not until 1934 that President Franklin D. Roosevelt sent out a proclamation asking the then 48 states to observe October 12 as a national holiday. And it was not until 1971 that Columbus Day became a federal legal holiday, celebrated on the second Monday in October, closing the schools and halting mail delivery. It is interesting to note that, except for religious holidays, this is the only event that pan-American lands join hands in celebrating.

By the 500th anniversary of Columbus' arrival, however, Columbus Day came under criticism. By then the real event long ago in history was in tension with its interpretation for purposes of celebration. Writing history requires both purposeful remembering and purposeful forgetting, and the history of 1492 is a good example The Columbus story was reshaped to create a Columbus worthy of celebration. As he was turned into a legend in the popular imagination, the perception of the man became as important as the actuality. He was used by Americans to define themselves, but not to universal approval. In the late twentieth century, attitudes changed. The Columbus myth, carefully cultivated to support a national identity, provoked strong reactions, not only for its distortion of historical reality but for the view of the United States it represented.

What happened 500 years ago had receded a long way behind the curtains, leaving a heroic view of the great mariner. Public memory was for many years undivided in a positive assessment of the Italian explorer who became an American hero. He was the center of American history and American myth-making for 200 years after 1792, an obliging symbol whose life could be interpreted in many ways. To understand this situation, we must go back to the actual events of more than 500 years ago.

COLUMBUS AND THE DISCOVERY NARRATIVE

What was Columbus's actual story? One sets off into unknown waters to attempt such a summary. Most facts about Columbus have been challenged, and Columbus himself helped to obscure the actual record. Some of the best-known stories are considered apocryphal, and the facts of one historian are subject to the disapproval of another. Still, here is a brief tentative account.

Born in Genoa in 1451 of a poor but respectable family, young Christopher probably followed his father's trade of wool-comber. He most likely learned to read and write later in life. He probably sighted the New World when he was 41 years old.

The young Columbus spent some years in Portugal where Prince Henry was sending ships down the African coast. Perestrello, a navigator, had been given the governorship of the island of Porto Santo in the Madeira Islands. Columbus married Perestrello's daughter.

Columbus read the exploration accounts of Marco Polo and may have corresponded with Toscanelli, a Florentine physician and amateur geographer, about western lands. He may have gathered ancient predictions from old salts about strange items and bodies washed ashore. In 1475, he sailed to Chios, a Genoese colony in the Levant. Back in Genoa, he joined a fleet attacked by French and Portuguese ships of war. After a fierce battle in which his ship was set aflame, Columbus seized an oar and made his way to land and Lisbon. He may have sailed to Iceland, where he heard of Norse voyages.

In 1477 he was making maps with his brother Bartholomew in Lisbon. He postulated that as the Portuguese were finding new lands by sailing south, he might find land by sailing west. In 1484 he proposed to King John II of Portugal that he provide ships for a western voyage. King John secretly sent out a ship to test this route but was unsuccessful. Columbus, then a widower with a young son, was miffed by this treatment and left Portugal.

In 1485, Columbus, with his five-year-old son Diego, sailed to Palos in Andalusia to offer his "Enterprise of the Indies" to the Spanish monarchs. En route to Huelva, he visited the Franciscan friary of La Rabida, where the monk Antonio de Marchena was intrigued by his story and recommended him to the Duke of Medina Sidonia in Seville, and then to the Duke of Medina-Celi who provided a letter of recommendation to the court at Cordova. While in Cordova, he became involved with Beatriz Enriquez de Harana, an orphan of a peasant family. She bore his second son, Ferdinand, on August 15, 1488.

Ferdinand and Isabella of Spain listened to Columbus and commanded Talavera to convene a commission to consider his proposal. Columbus was summoned to Salamanca in 1486 to meet with the members. In 1490, after five years, the commission advised against the plan.

Retreating to La Rabida, Columbus detailed his woes to Juan Perez, another friendly and interested monk who wrote to Isabella. Spain, which had just conquered Granada, began to see new possibilities. Isabella summoned Columbus back to court, but his demand for recognition as a viceroy and for 10 percent of any income from new lands gave the crowned heads pause. Columbus walked out, but Isabella, fearing a lost opportunity, called him back. He assumed one-eighth of the cost of the venture and was promised titles and profits. He pledged to use his profits to rescue the Holy Sepulchre from the Moslems. Aragon advanced the remainder of the costs. The town of Palos was ordered to fit out two vessels, and Columbus fitted out the third.

The fleet set sail from Palos on August 3, 1492, stopped at the Canary Islands, and proceeded westerly with the trade winds. Columbus expected to encounter Cipangu, or Japan, but as his computations for the size of the globe were too low, he did not find it. He traveled 200 miles further west and then turned southwest. On October 12, 1492, he landed on a low, sandy island which he named San Salvador.

The three ships sailed among the minor islands of the archipelago for 10 days. One ship, commanded by Martin Alonzo Pinzon, broke off to look unsuccess-

Christopher Columbus bidding farewell to the Queen of Spain on his departure for the New World, 1492. Courtesy of the Library of Congress.

fully for gold. Columbus found Haiti, which he named Hispaniola, and accidentally wrecked his ship on the northern side. He established a few men as a colony called La Navidad, using the ship's timbers for a fort. Columbus and the rest of the men embarked for Spain on January 4, 1493, and reached Palos on March 15, after an absence of seven months. His return was greeted with wonder, and the monarchs invited him to sit in their presence and describe his adventures.

This is the factual basis for the great mythic story of Columbus with all its vision, ambition, pride, religion, determination, and perseverance. This is the recognizable heroic Columbus of our national myth. The story should end there, but alas, it does not. Now comes the sorry end of the tale.

On September 25, 1793, Columbus set sail again from Cadiz with 17 vessels and 1,200 people. He sighted land on November 3. La Navidad, the town he had founded, had been destroyed and a new town, Isabella, was laid out to its east. Expeditions for gold were immediately launched, but with little success. The Spaniards got sick, and the natives resisted efforts to mine gold. Twelve

Chromolithograph of Christopher Columbus landing on the island that he named San Salvador and that would be later named Watling Island. Courtesy of the Library of Congress.

ships returned to Spain for supplies. Columbus found Jamaica and Cuba, which he decided were part of the Asian mainland.

When Columbus returned to the settlement of Isabella, he discovered that some men had sailed for Spain to complain of his mismanagement. When the next supply ships arrived, Columbus sent them back with gold samples and a cargo of natives to be converted to Christianity and sold as slaves. He led an expedition into Hispaniola's interior to subdue the natives, who were treated harshly from then on.

When Columbus returned to Spain to defend his record as governor, the monarchs treated him well but delayed his third voyage. He finally set sail in 1498 with six ships. On this voyage he found Trinidad and the northern coast of South America. But back in Hispaniola he found unrest and some Spaniards in revolt. The monarchs dispatched a commissioner to Hispaniola to review the situation and relieve him of authority if necessary. On arrival, Francisco de Bobadilla assumed control of the Crown's property, arrested Columbus and his brother, and sent them back to Spain in chains.

The sovereigns, shocked by the sight of the manacled admiral, offered him whatever he wanted except new power in the islands. He proposed another voyage and set sail on May 9, 1502. He explored the coast of Central America, but he did not break through to find the Pacific Ocean. His searches for gold unsuccessful, the ill Columbus beached two ships at Jamaica and spent a miserable year there. Relieved by Ovando, then governor at Hispaniola, he was nursed until he embarked for Spain on September 12, 1504. Isabella had died and the repeated letters from Columbus to Ferdinand demanding his rights and honors were ignored. Columbus died on May 20, 1506.

This second half of the Columbian story is more what we might expect of swashbuckling gold-seeking adventurers. The Christianity is still there, but much compromised. This is the black legend, the great harshness to native peoples while seeking their treasures, the standard by which most of the Spanish explorers are judged. Columbus gets particularly bad marks because, failing to find enough gold to justify his "Enterprise of the Indies," he instigated the practice of New World slavery.

Even in this brief account we can see the loner Columbus demanding rewards while failing to enlist the loyalty of his men. We see the great wrongheaded mariner losing his health and effectiveness, disgraced while clinging to his demands. This is a man whose single-minded search for fame and fortune overcame his other emotions and values. This is not a new interpretation. Bartolome de Las Casas, a friend and priest who lived in the New World colonies with Columbus, wrote an account of his experiences, putting all this information in the early records. And this second account is in character with the first part of the story.

A telling anecdote shows the pains that Columbus took that his story not be lost. As he returned from his first voyage, his ship encountered a storm of such violence that the men feared they would be lost. At this point, in the teeth of the howling gale, with the ship tossing on the raging seas, Columbus was concerned that his triumph in finding the New World (or Asia, as he thought) should never be known, went to his cabin and wrote an extended account of the voyage and copied it. He wrapped one version in an oiled cloth, enclosed it in a cake of wax, put it into a cask, and threw it into the sea, hoping the account would survive, redeeming his name though the ship and all aboard be lost. The stubborn, unshakeable pride and sense of self that had kept him on his long quest for ships extended to his need that people know what he had done. He would not be robbed of his discoveries.

The letter in the cask did not survive. Neither did the copy made at sea. But, before it was lost, the letter to Luis de Santangel, the keeper of King Ferdinand's funds, as the document is known, was copied by Bartolome de Las Casas and published in Spain in 1493 and became the first reliable account of the journey. Notably the account was by Columbus himself and put the best possible face on his adventures. We know he was great because he tells us so.

THE IMAGE OF COLUMBUS IN THE EARLY AMERICAN REPUBLIC

Although Columbus was mentioned in various published works in the New World, an extended, locally written account including Columbus was not published in what became the United States until 1758 when Samuel Nevill of Perth Amboy, New Jersey, a judge of the New Jersey Supreme Court and the editor of *The New American Magazine* wrote a serial presentation of "A Complete History of the *Northern Continent of America,* from the time of its first Discovery to the present." Nevill, writing from a prerevolutionary point of view, justified the English presence in America by establishing the superiority of the English to the Spanish and the Native Americans. Only the energetic and hard-working English could make good use of the lands, which they had subdued and rendered fit for human use. Nevill considered English appropriation of the land a favor to the natives. Although Columbus had paved the way, John Cabot, who sailed for England, was given credit for first discovering and setting foot on North America. On the eve of the revolution, Columbus was given a part, but not a leading role in the story. He was not needed.

Until the American Revolution, Columbus could have been forgotten or more likely relegated to the group of adventurers like Pizarro and Cortez who despoiled the New World on behalf of Spain. Indeed, he was in that category for almost 300 years. In the early sixteenth century, the New World was named America for someone else. But Columbus did not just remain in his grave. Two histories favorable to him made a great deal of difference. The Abbe Raynal's popular *Philosophical and Political History of the Settlements and Trade of the Europeans in the East and West Indies* was first published in 1770 and in English in 1776. The book painted the mariner as a far-seeing visionary, a brave, mistreated hero who rose above discouragements and difficulties. He was a man of persistence, of genius and courage. The even more significant English historical work was William Robertson's *History of America* (1777). The Scottish historian, Presbyterian minister, and politician conducted extensive research, although the official Spanish archives, which would have been valuable, were closed to him. Discovery and conquest, not colonization, were Robertson's main themes. He acknowledged the blood-stained record of the Spaniards in the New World with their mixed motives of religious enthusiasm and avarice. But he continued to admire their "fortitude and perseverance." Robertson relied heavily on Ferdinand Columbus's biography of his father, recounting much of the mariner's life, his birth and education, his studies, his negotiations at court, his voyages, his efforts, his disgrace, and his death. This biographical treatment became traditional, honoring him for personal experience as well as for his accomplishments, making him much more flexible and durable as a symbol. So he became the driven explorer, combining original thought and action, even as he became the admirable gentleman at court. Robertson presented a Columbus made of finer stuff than the men around him. He was misunderstood and mistreated by his monarchs. He prepared a New World to be providentially populated by British subjects, and he was distanced from other wicked Spanish explorers. His lapses were ignored or explained away.

So when Columbus was needed, he was ready. He was drafted back to service as a symbol for a newly emerging nation, the United States of America, after the Revolutionary War. The 13 little colonies clinging to the eastern seaboard of North America managed to rout the great sea power, England, who had been the mother of them all. The colonies had been founded individually for religious and mercantile purposes and had little loyalty to each other. They were drawn together in their opposition to the English crown by what they considered unfair treatment, distant domination, taxation without a voice in the government, and general disrespect. England could certainly have won the Revolutionary War had she been willing to pay the price, but the cost in money and men, the long-distance supply problems, and the feeling that the colonies were not that valuable helped the poor, ill-supplied local troops to prevail. The irregular colonial troops served under George Washington, who united them and the colonies, forging them into a single nation. The war redirected their vision and their history. They rightly named George Washington the father of the country. He had effected the transformation.

But Washington was of their time, and he represented Virginia. Upon renouncing "Mother England," the new grouping of colonies needed a new history, a joint past. They needed a new tradition to indicate that the new nation was meant to be, that severance from England was a necessary step en route to national greatness. They found that tradition ready-made in the story of Columbus. Washington became the father of the country and Columbus the grandfather, the man who founded the United States of America. No one actually said this, but the new nation quickly appropriated the story of Columbus for these purposes.

This vision had some serious problems. To buy this interpretation required that time be collapsed to make the 1492 voyage a close prelude to American independence in 1776. How could America be discovered when there was no America there? Then, Columbus had spent his time in the West Indies and environs and had never set foot on the mainland of North America. What is more, he believed to his dying day that he had reached Asia. He did not claim, nor did he have any idea, that he had found a world new to the Europeans. His mistaken computations for a smaller earth meant that he could never have reached Asia with his limited supplies; he would have perished at sea if the New World had not been in the way. So there are problems with his magnificent vision and navigation. Another very serious problem, with ongoing ramifications, was that the myth required an empty continent, just waiting for the glorious United States to sprout and grow. That there were already people here with claims to the land, Columbus and later Americans did not recognize. Some character traits were also problematic. Columbus was not the wise and generous hero that some might have wished.

But all that was forgiven. Columbus was needed. He was the man. He had the tradition. He was drafted to be the grandfather of the nation. This is nothing he could have done on his own. Although he could have been defined as a bad influence, he was not. Americans accepted his own account of the discovery and then inflated each virtue and shrank every vice, cheerfully dismissing items less than praiseworthy. Columbus was enshrined in a notable place, providing a past that bypassed England.

All of this led to the first commemoration of Columbus Day in 1792, just after the revolution. This celebration was orchestrated by some patriotic New Yorkers, the members of the Society of Tammany or Columbian Society. The Tammany Society, better known for its political involvement in the next century, had been founded in 1789 as a patriotic, fraternal group. The two patrons of the society were Tammany, the fictive Native American chieftain who represented the New World, and Columbus, the actual but already mythic figure representing the Old World. Both were invoked for ceremonial purposes. As October 12, 1792 neared, John Pintard, a public-spirited New York businessman, proposed a procession and an oration to honor Columbus, as well as a memorial monument. Pintard enlisted his society to commemorate the completion of the third century of the discovery of America. Columbus had been seen in a couple of patriotic processions after the Revolution, but he was a peripheral figure, a point of reference. Pintard's achievement was to make him central.

In Pintard's plans we see the elements that have been used to commemorate Columbus to this day: orations, odes, monuments, parades, toasts. All this was very federalist New York. There was nothing related to the Renaissance court of Ferdinand and Isabella or to the ethnic Spanish and Italian immigrants who have adopted Columbus as their American hero, nothing about the natives Columbus met on the shores of San Salvador. Yet these same celebratory elements have been adopted by thousands of ethnic, patriotic, religious, and school groups, and the same ceremonial aspects have been adapted to commercial traditions as well. The Columbus Day/Thanksgiving parades that introduce the holiday sales are later evolutions of the Tammany Society's original commemorations.

Pintard and company gathered in their clubhouse, known as the Wigwam, for dinner and an oration. Odes were recited, patriotic songs sung, and the patron toasted. In this first ambitious celebration devoted chiefly to Columbus in the New World, the "stately ceremony" of the "Society eclipsed all former efforts in the dignity and pomp displayed," according to the *New York Journal and Patriotic Register.* Pintard created a modest, 15-foot column, which has long since disappeared. The monument resembled black marble but was probably made of cement, ornamented with "transparent devices depicting the events in the career of Columbus." Pintard attempted a "grave and solemn" effort with "a brilliant appearance." Columbus was shown discovering the New World, but also in chains. That face of the monument was entitled "The Ingratitude of Kings," an echo of the way the colonists perceived their king had treated them. Columbus had his multiple faces of hero and victim. He brought the "rights of man," a virtuous man cruelly treated. The celebration spread to an event in Boston and a private monument in Baltimore that same year and was written up in many newspapers.

The society continued to mount special commemorations on or near the anniversary of the first landfall. In 1811, for instance, Tammany and Columbus appeared together in colorful characterization under an oak tree on a float in a procession. Columbus carried the ancient flag of Christendom and Tammany sat on a raised seat. The two smoked the peace pipe as the "Genius of America," a figure who would be called Columbia, fed the flames of liberty on an altar of freedom. Columbus and the female form Columbia achieved a particular potency. Columbia signified the subdued, domesticated space that the nation had become, the United States. Columbia offered the dignity and gentility of an emerging American civilization. She was a perfect symbol for an expanding continental empire. In this procession, neither Columbus nor Tammany participated in the action but looked on approvingly, representing the Old World and the New in harmony. Columbus brought Christianity; the Indians peace; and in their presence, freedom and liberty flourished. The Tammany Society's interest in Columbus waned, but the schools and the historians took on the responsibility for promoting the explorer.

NINETEENTH-CENTURY MAKEOVER

In the early nineteenth century, as textbooks were prepared for the nation's children, the pioneering educators Noah Webster, Caleb Bingham, and Jedidiah Morse included information on Columbus gleaned from the biographical works that were being translated into English. They quoted the account of the mariner's son Ferdinand and information from the Las Casas manuscript via Raynal and Robertson. Aspects of these accounts made their way into children's books. Caleb Bingham wrote in a book published in 1794, in which he said:

> In the life of this remarkable man, there was no deficiency of any quality, which can constitute a great character. He was grave, though courteous in his deportment, circumspect in his words and actions, irreproachable in his morals, and exemplary in all the duties of religion.

One might wonder how Caleb Bingham knew about these virtues. Bingham created a Columbus to serve the purposes of the new nation, the perfect leader, modest, grave, and courteous. Instead of being a rough-and-ready peasant-type adventurer, which might have seemed suitable for a new nation, he is the exemplary courtier. Columbus quietly replaces the British monarch. The many paintings of the mariner in the heroic mode show him in this noble, even royal guise. The rich clothing, the carefully trimmed hair and beard, the elegant props, the noble stance, his elevation above the common seamen and the adoring "savages," even as he is about to leap ashore after months at sea, all this suggests that he is a personage of more than ordinary equipoise and importance. While this is more than an actor playing the role of a glorious leader, everything about these visual and literary images of Columbus is about performance.

Caleb Bingham went beyond virtue and style to accomplishment. He made Columbus the father of American progress. The discovery, he wrote, had "opened to mankind a new region of science, commerce, and enterprize, and stamped with immortality the name of its projector." Columbus could never have orchestrated an inheritance like this. Here in this creation of a founder, an existing leader is appropriated to fill an important role, offering and ascribing to him everything he would need to be a suitable candidate. Writers and orators fell over each other to establish his great worthiness.

Some must have had their doubts. But the public relations machine ground on. The mariner's most significant early American biographer, Washington Irving, in *The Life and Voyages of Christopher Columbus,* made clear that there were often things wrong with the heroes of the ages—and that they did not matter. The following quotation from his book states that historical research should not interfere with reputations.

> There is a certain meddlesome spirit, which, in the garb of learned research, goes prying about the traces of history, casting down its monuments, and marring and mutilating its fairest trophies. Care should be taken to vindicate great names from such pernicious erudition. It defeats one of the most salutary purposes of history, that of furnishing examples of what human genius and laudable enterprise may accomplish.

With that attitude, Irving wrote a worshipful and uncritical book glorifying the Columbus story. A more positive biographer than this accomplished man of letters could not have been found. When Irving included negative aspects of the story, he blamed others rather than Columbus himself. Critics attacked the length of the four-volume book and also Irving himself, saying that the book suffered from the "absence of all manly opinion–that skinless sensitiveness, that shuddering dread of giving offence, by which all the former productions of this writer are marked." But Irving's book furthered the Columbian reputation. The nineteenth century showed steady progress for the mariner. Beginning with school books and expanding through the Chicago Columbian Exposition in 1893, the Columbian legend grew.

Undated portrait of Washington Irving. Courtesy of the Library of Congress.

COLUMBUS IN THE CAPITOL

Anyone who would like to see this developing legend in one place, beautifully preserved and showing development and expansion from year to year should visit the Capitol Building of the United States of America, created and preserved as the nation's classroom for patriotic veneration. The decoration of this space occurred during the elevation of the Admiral of the Ocean Seas. The building itself is a tribute to the father of the nation George Washington, who is represented in about 30 works of art. But second to him is the treatment of that national grandfather Christopher Columbus, who can be seen in about 10 versions. Numbers are inexact because some works have been destroyed by fire, and others have been withdrawn. These two great founders were often paired; our nation's capital is named for them. The commissioners who named the new capital city sent a letter to designer Major Pierre-Charles L'Enfant, dated from Georgetown on September 9, 1791. "We have agreed that the federal district shall be called 'The Territory of Columbia,' and the Federal City, 'The City of Washington': the title of the map, will, therefore, be 'A Map of the City of Washington, in the Territory of Columbia.'" By the time the Capitol was being

A statue of Christopher Columbus. Courtesy of Getty Images / PhotoDisc.

erected, Columbus was already the spiritual father of the New World, a creation of the American imagination. The rising Capitol provided visiting citizens with a patriotic altar and Columbus worked perfectly to invoke that mythic meaning.

The Columbus legend can be seen to best advantage in the Capitol Rotunda. Visitors to the United States Capitol symbolically enter by way of the experience of Columbus, through the huge and heavy bronze double doors that depict the story of the admiral. Designed by Randolph Rogers, the doors, 19 feet high by 9 feet wide, tell the best Columbus stories in nine scenes. Again we have his whole life story rather than just the discovery. Who knows anything of the youth of Pizarro and Cortez?

Once through the doors, the visitor stands in the great Rotunda. A guidebook of the late 1860s described the planned decoration as depicting the gradual progress of the continent "from the depths of barbarism to the height of civilization," from the wild state of the hunter tribes, through the "advance of the white and retreat of the red races." The massive Rotunda features eight huge paintings, each 12 by 18 feet. Visitors can almost step into these paintings, symbolically experiencing the action of the picture. Included are four on the Revolutionary War, one of De Soto discovering the Mississippi River, one of the Pilgrims, and another of the baptism of Pocahontas, who is honored as she leaves her Native American ways. The last is John Vanderlyn's *The Landing of Columbus*. These paintings all represent the triumph of America—over the British, over enemies of Christianity, over the New World itself. Columbus could have been interpreted as part of the old order over which the genius of America triumphed. Instead he is part of the American system. Vanderlyn's painting, showing Columbus bringing Christianity to the natives, includes a Franciscan monk, although none was present on the occasion. Again we have Columbus as the European nobleman; he has slipped below decks to don a rich velvet outfit and unsheathe his naked sword for the occasion. An anonymous account of the painting, slightly paraphrased from Washington Irving's biography, praises his navigational powers.

> The bold Genoese launched his frail barks upon the trackless waters, and pursued his mysterious voyage, with no cloud by day, no pillar of fire by night, to guide his path through the wilderness of waves.

The Vanderlyn painting dates from 1844, the bronze doors from 1863. There are several other Columbian effigies in the room and the building, but I will note just one more in the Rotunda dating from 1878. This one, in a massive frieze more than 8 feet high and 300 feet long, circles the Rotunda ceiling 58 feet above the floor. Constantino Brumidi, who did much of the Capitol's decoration, tells the history of the nation in classic episodes. The first scene is a general "America in History" depiction. The second features the imperial Columbus, gazing into heaven as he descends a gangplank. He wears his rich clothes and carries a flag. All, mostly Native

Americans, kneel in homage before him. The message here, as with other works of art in the Capitol is the imperialistic power of the United States, the Manifest Destiny that would extend her powers across the continent, in effect conquering the natives who appear to welcome the Christian invaders as superior beings.

A HERO FOR THE DESPISED

Other groups adopted Columbus as a personal hero. He served as an important leader for immigrants, of whom he could be classed as one of our first. Italians and Spaniards and Catholics from all countries adopted him. He was useful to them against the nativism they faced. His combination of faith and perseverance was compelling for new citizens finding their way in the New World, seeking to escape discrimination and to achieve legitimacy as first-class citizens. Americans moving from an agricultural to an industrial economy also found hope in the Columbus story as had the white Americans forging a post-colonial national identity against Britain. All these people were casting off into the unknown, seeking new opportunities, hoping for success. Columbus continued to figure prominently when other ethnic, racial, class, and gender groups sought liberation and definition. All who seized the mariner for their own purposes invested heavily in their symbolic Columbus. To challenge any of these constructed Columbuses threatened the constructors who opposed changes in interpretation that questioned their identity as Americans.

A major theme of New York's 400th anniversary commemoration was the importance of Columbus as a Catholic leader, an identity related to but superseding his identity as an Italian. Catholic groups were closely involved in all celebrations, and several specifically Catholic events were scheduled. In honoring Columbus, the United Catholic Societies and the Catholic Historical Society, as well as parish and school groups, demonstrated their impressive organization and numbers. Catholic participation formed the backbone of events everywhere that year.

This participation illustrated a well-organized American nationalism that could be called Columbianism, a movement both militantly Catholic and proudly American. The mariner has been a powerful talisman for Catholics and other ethnic Americans for more than 100 years. He had lent his name to more places in the United States than anyone but George Washington as a source of ethnic pride. As Columbus had sailed for a Catholic queen and had established Catholic Christianity in the New World, the nineteenth-century American Catholics could read their own presence in America as the direct fulfillment of prophecy, the answer to prayer. One lasting fruit of the movement was the organization of the Knights of Columbus, founded in 1881 by a young Irish, not even an Italian, priest. The group organized for social, religious, and fraternal purposes to meet the needs of Catholic families. Before the Catholics took hold, no holiday honored Columbus. The Knights of Columbus began the organized effort to have him recognized, and by the end of 1909, they had succeeded in 10 states.

THE COLUMBIAN EXHIBITION OF 1892

The nation fastened onto the 400th anniversary of the first landfall of Columbus in the New World as an opportunity to commemorate America's success and basic goodness. Surely a magnificent exposition using Columbus as justification to demonstrate how the present was turning into the future should be held. Cities vied for the privilege to host the fair, greatly upgraded to compete with the 1889 third Paris Nationale which featured the Eiffel Tower. New York was thrust aside by Chicago, which won out by pledging 10 million dollars and by showing the same desperate perseverance as Columbus himself.

The fabulous and gorgeous results of Chicago's Columbian Exposition are well known as was its purpose: to show off American progress. The fruits of the chosen land were displayed. Artistic excellence, technological superiority, and natural resources were gathered to cast favorable light on Chicago, the "Garden City of the West, the Queen City of that continent." The 28 stately edifices built of glass and snowy white stucco constituted a "city in the clouds." Columbus in name and effigy, in symbol and in armor, majestically surveyed it all.

The 400th anniversary in 1892 was the last uncontested celebration of Columbus, and even that was contested at one level. The elevation of Columbus invited revisionist thinking, tempering some of the accolades. Historian Hubert Howe Bancroft summed him up more coolly than national pride, religious sympathy, and hero worship had formerly permitted. "As a mariner and discoverer Columbus had no superior; as a colonist and governor he proved himself a failure. Had he been less pretentious and grasping, his latter days would have been more peaceful. Discovery was his infatuation; but he lacked practical judgment, and he brought upon himself a series of calamities." Bancroft acknowledged Columbus's virtues but showed that his failures were his own fault. Rather than the helpless victim of thankless monarchs and jealous courtiers, he brought trouble on himself. But this evaluation, circulating between historians, did not reach the general public, still in the thrall of Washington Irving's vision.

CHALLENGES TO COLUMBUS'S IMAGE

The most blistering and telling summation of the admiral was the work of Justin Winsor, the learned librarian who in 1891 assembled and critiqued the scholarship and current thinking on the Columbian questions for an educated audience. He evaluated the sources, steering through the conflicting accounts. Winsor considered Irving's charming book insidious. In his effort to "create a hero," Irving had glorified what was heroic, palliated what was not, and minimized the doubtful aspects of Columbus's character. Irving had excused Columbus from Spanish excesses.

Winsor suspected that Columbus had intended to enslave the natives from the beginning. His first description suggested the natives were "well-fitted to be governed." During his second voyage, Columbus suggested to his sovereigns exchanging Carib natives for livestock. The sovereigns hesitated and asked for further thoughts, sending their reply in a little supply fleet. Into these ships for a return voyage, Columbus packed 500 natives to be sold in Seville as slaves. Winsor did not defend him. "The act was a long step in the miserable degradation which Columbus put upon those poor creatures whose existence he had made known to the world." In his policies of repartimientos and encomiendas, he bound the natives to the land, allowing every colonist absolute power over the natives entitled to him by his rank and position. Las Casas, the contemporary of Columbus, had also referred to the "reeking passions of the enslaver," canceling out the excuse that Columbus was only a man of his time. Winsor laid the Admiral of the Ocean Seas to rest thus:

> We have seen a pitiable man meet a pitiable death. Hardly a name in profane history is more August than his. Hardly another character in the world's record has made so little of its opportunities. His discovery was a blunder; his blunder was a new world; the New World is his monument! Its discoverer might have been its father; he proved to be its despoiler. He might have given its young days such a benignity as the world likes to associate with a maker; he left it a legacy of devastation and crime. He might have been an unselfish promoter of geographical science; he proved a rabid seeker for gold and a viceroyalty. He might have won converts to the fold of Christ by the kindness of his spirit; he gained the execrations of the good angels. He might, like Las Casas, have rebuked the fiendishness of his contemporaries; he set them an example of perverted belief. The triumph of Barcelona led down to the ignominy of Valladolid, with every step in the degradation palpable and resultant.

These stark words, fierce in their denunciation, were generated from the librarian's study as he sifted through the old documents. Outside in the streets, the world prepared a celebration of gratitude for the 400th anniversary of the voyages of Christopher Columbus and for the great good and progress that had resulted from them. The speakers eulogized him, the paraders marched, the monuments were raised and dedicated, the crowds cheered.

MONUMENTALIZING THE MAN

Part of New York's grand celebration of the 400th anniversary in 1892 was the dedication of the major Italian contribution, the Columbus monument at 59th Street and Broadway and Eighth Avenue on the West Side. This was the gift of

Italians and Italian-Americans. Attended by Benjamin Harrison, president of the United States, and Roswell P. Flower, governor of New York, the monument was blessed by New York's Catholic Archbishop Corrigan. Also present were the Italian minister, consuls, and vice-consuls of Italian societies and the officers of an Italian cruiser. Italian bands played and the artillery fired a salute. Annie Barsotti, daughter of the monument committee's president, unveiled the monument created by Italian sculptor Gaitano Russo.

The monument was part of a much larger debate about public art provided by private sources. Some citizens, concerned by the city's indiscriminate acceptance of public statuary and the installation of these works in prime locations, had organized to "ensure united action by the art societies and to foster and protect the artistic interest of the community." Two proposals to install statues of Christopher Columbus, one from the Italian-Americans and another from the Spanish Americans, had been turned down. Both had wanted Fifth Avenue and 59th Street on the East Side. The Italians were offered the West Side location, the Spanish Americans the location at Mt. Morris at 120th Street and Fifth Avenue, which they rejected as a "second-class place." They never executed their project.

But the Italians' monument, erected in an unimportant place, took on great importance. The little statue became a secular shrine for immigrants. Although derided by the upper crust, who put up their own lesser-known Columbus statue in the Mall of Central Park in 1894, a little late, the Italians' very ordinary statue of Columbus, placed so high on a granite pillar that it cannot even be seen, came to identify its neighborhood and to be adopted by the public at large while still serving as a hallowed Italian place. At this writing, the area is undergoing an expensive transformation and will soon feature streams of water, walking paths, and benches for the rest and relaxation of the citizenry, an oasis encircled by traffic.

As the images of Italian artists decorated the U.S. Capitol, so sculptures created by their countrymen began to dot the countryside. After the major celebrations of the 400th anniversary, the Catholic Church and the Knights of Columbus guarded the admiral's legacy. Italian groups steadily erected additional effigies of him in ever smaller cities in the United States. The inscription on a statue of Columbus dedicated in Worcester, Massachusetts in 1979, in the presence of 1,000 citizens, tells the story as it came to be understood: poetic, heroic, and inspired, compressing 300 years at a single stroke. Note the similarities to the description of the Vanderlyn painting paraphrasing Washington Irving quoted above:

> Not even the mountainous waves of the mighty Atlantic could halt the progress of the Nina, Pinta, and Santa Maria under the guidance of the great navigator inspired by the Lord to go forth, search for and find these United States of America. The nation had existed in ghost-like form from the beginning.

A SYMBOL OF ANOTHER SORT: THE CONTESTED QUINCENTENARY

By the time the 500th anniversary approached, there was opposition. Changes had taken place. The very pillars of the structure that had held the mariner up to public view began to crumble. The reasons he was honored were questioned. Groups contested the assumptions about the purpose and meaning of the United States of America and the identity of Americans.

Columbus's very perseverance and indomitable courage were criticized. If only he had let well enough alone, revisionists reasoned. He and his relentless "Sail on! Sail on!" If he had just failed to reach the enchanted isles. Then the native tribes, who have taken on a mythic heroism and grandeur of their own, might have managed to live on in their peaceful splendor. But we all know that if it had not been Columbus, there would have been some other intrepid explorer who braved the Atlantic and claimed the New World in the name of a European maritime power. The New World could not have remained pristine and untouched by the influences of Europe. It was just a matter of time, and very little time. Would someone else have treated the local inhabitants more gently? The English settlers, meaning to do better, did not manage to. The Native Americans, for all our current respect, sympathy, treaties, and subsidies, were a conquered and decimated people. The American landscape was steadily Columbianized (that is, Americanized) as it was cleared of Indians.

The other charges of twentieth-century critics were many. That Columbus had ignored, and worse, mistreated a large segment of the New World's population was certain. And there is no question that the whole myth of America has been flawed by picturing an empty, virgin continent, hidden from the eyes of the European world. Using Columbus as the first chapter of the history of the United States had falsified the record and disregarded a whole civilization.

Even worse, the treatment displays a woeful record of racism on the part of Columbus and his voyagers and on the part of the European exploring nations, and of the United States' perceived vision of itself. The paintings and sculptures of Columbus with cowering and adoring natives kneeling about his feet display an unfortunate imperialism. This differentiation, never justified, has been increasingly attacked. Coupled with the evidence of Columbus's subjugation of island people, along with their torture and mutilation, the eventual wiping out of the Taino tribe, and the traffic in slavery, any worshiping of the white Italian "god" seems forced.

On the other hand, some people act as if this were all Columbus's doing. Though less than an ideal man, he was long dead before he was drafted as America's hero, and he has continued quite dead throughout. We sometimes see him gazing down from the clouds on the great nation for which he is supposedly responsible. But Columbus did not manage his ascendancy and, much as he would have liked this notoriety and considered himself worthy of it, he was not responsible for it. He was picked up and was rehabilitated to serve a specific purpose. For the most part, he has served very well. And he has been of immense value to many aspects of our body politic—to children as a role model, to immigrants as a forerunner who made good, to patriots as a strong, steady leader and as an excuse for conquest, to seekers and strivers as a man who never gave up, and to religious leaders as the messenger of Christianity. Columbus remains useful to all those and to many more factions who do not want to let him go. And it seems likely that Columbus, having failed, risen, and failed, may yet rise again.

What is the lesson to be learned here? Holidays remain public arenas in which American identity, principles, promises, policy, and history are debated. Holidays focus the attention of special interests, providing a place and time for discussion and showing the impact of pluralism in American life. Columbus Day has been useful in defining and expanding the limits of citizenship in the United States. Columbus helped many claim first-class citizenship. Those excluded could complain and enlist critics of their own marginalization. For just as the holiday has embraced belonging, it has emphasized exclusion, identifying regional and sectional fault lines. Identities, local and national, unified or conflicted, have molded and expressed ethnicity, religion, region, or class as legitimately American.

The 500th anniversary of the first landfall negotiated yet more uncharted waters. Stephen J. Summerhill and John Alexander Williams, academicians involved in the celebration, told the tale of the evolution of the commemoration from awe of the great admiral to the wish that he had never darkened western shores. The celebration, they write, was upgraded from "an innocuous ethnic celebration" to a "battleground for our entire view of Western culture."

The authors describe the commemorative plans in considerable detail. John Alexander Williams was the director, for two years, of the Christopher Columbus Quincentenary Jubilee Commission of the United States with its ethnic conflicts, sparse funding, and conflicts of interest. He and Summerhill describe plans for the 1992 Chicago World's Fair, which supporters had hoped would equal the Columbian Exposition of 1893. Ethnic and party tension and conflict between the old guard and the ethnic neighborhood ended that plan. In other places, Spain spent lavishly; Italy had a traditional celebration. The Dominican Republic, where Columbus actually landed, was enthusiastic, but underfunded; Mexico was subdued.

The authors conclude that these celebrations, old-fashioned and ineffectual, failed. Traditional commemorative events could not ignite the public. But, in the triumph of revisionism, the celebration was not so much disregarded as redirected. "Truths" about Columbus were reinterpreted in new frameworks, recognizing the imperialist ethnocentrism that oppressed native peoples during European colonization. Traditional Columbian programs, insensitive to indigenous people, were shipwrecked on populist shores. The ground shifted under the program planners.

Columbus, who had benefited so much from selective memory, was demonized. He was blamed and condemned for old, but newly discovered, faults. Columbus had been forgiven much because he was gallant and brave, a poor boy who succeeded, a devout Christian, and because he was needed to begin the American story. Now the story has other first chapters.

Columbus's discovery has been redefined as an encounter, an expedition, an exploration, and as the exchange of people, plants, and diseases. Whether Columbus was the first to arrive on the continent no longer matters. Columbus was like a bee fertilizing the flowers from which it stole. The white man invaded and exchanged food stuffs, diseases, and traditions. The mariner himself was largely beside the point. Columbus, however, had achieved a public relations coup. As Summerhill and Williams note, he returned to Europe, held a press conference, and got government funding to return.

Some successful 500th anniversary activities took place in his name. The "Honeymoon Project," a symbolic "wedding of worlds" of the Statue of Liberty and Columbus, for which Miss Liberty's immense trousseau was displayed in Las Vegas, had a certain resonance. Two Washington, D.C. exhibitions, "Circa 1492" at the National Gallery and "Seeds of Change" at the Smithsonian got high marks. Neither said much about the Admiral of the Ocean Seas. Expo '92 in Seville was a success. The tour of reproduction caravels was admired, although only one proved seaworthy.

Aside from these limited successes, Summerhill and Williams argue that the official and traditional quincentenary succeeded because it failed, becoming a celebration of the *other*. Columbus was dismissed, but he was still central in disgrace, having provided the context for debating diversity and tolerance, myth and history. In the mirror of Columbus much of the world reevaluated the meaning of the past 500 years. Hoards of people were energized and invigorated. Columbus reemerged reinterpreted, enhanced, and diminished as the world debated the future meaning of the past. Although the events of 1492 were then 500 years old and supposedly unalterable, Americans continued to refashion history. Their disgust with the mariner was another celebration of his enduring myth, the great admiral led home in chains. And even those who wrote negative and dismissive books and who poured blood on his statues were surely commemorating him.

COLUMBUS DAY TODAY, AND ITS FUTURE

Columbus Day, since the 500th anniversary, although much less an event than in 1992, continues to be commemorated and contested. Columbus is now seen more as a villain than in the past, but less as a war criminal. Columbus's

Mayor Michael Bloomberg attends the Columbus Day parade in New York, 2005. © AP / Wide World Photos.

multiple personalities are feted and decried, and he is considered less responsible for all the good and evil of the last 500 years. Columbus Day has become a venue to assert the legitimacy of ethnicity and to acknowledge American pluralism.

President George W. Bush's 2003 Columbus Day proclamation carefully praised what could still be defended, that Columbus had "launched an era of discovery" that continued "through exploration of land, sea, and space," to the present day. He said that Columbus had led millions of Italian immigrants to these shores making "America stronger and better." He noted that we admire his "courage and vision," sketched a little history about the celebration of the holiday, and called upon the people of the United States to "observe this day with appropriate ceremonies and activities." Bush acknowledged that Columbus has been praised for some things offensive to the feelings of others. As Native American Vine Deloria Jr. noted, "When asked by an anthropologist what the Indians called America before the white man came, an Indian said simply, 'Ours.'" John Mohawk, a Seneca, wrote in 1992 that "Christopher Columbus is a symbol, not of a man, but of imperialism," and that the things that happened then were still happening today. Jimmie Durham, a Cherokee, in his often published poem "Columbus Day," notes "In school I learned of heroic discoveries / Made by liars and crooks."

The Native Americans have mounted the best organized and most militant opposition to Columbus and the celebration of his day, and they receive a great deal of respect for their opposition. Most would now cede that they had a right to complain. But more than complaining, they have an agenda, opposing the perpetuation of racist assumptions, condemning the educational and social system that has taught a disregard for Native American civilizations. The American Indian Movement proposes stripping Columbus of his national honors and replacing his day by a more inclusive event reflective of the cultural and racial richness of all Americans. They further advocate the removal of anti-Indian icons throughout the country. All statues, street names, and public parks honoring the devastators of Indian peoples should be removed or have their names changed. In a position statement on behalf of the American Indian Movement of Colorado in 1991, Russell Means and Glenn Morris proposed that all statues, street names, and public parks honoring the devastators of Indian peoples be removed. American Indian activists loudly ask, "Why should we celebrate a power-hungry man, no better than Hitler?" They suggest that Columbus be indicted for "Grand Theft, Genocide, Racism, Initiating the Destruction of a Culture, Rape, Torture, and Maiming of Indigenous People." A proposed petition to the U.S. Congress and other elected officials notes that "Columbus Day" is "deeply insulting to American Indians and many native-born Americans of all cultures" as well as incorrect and Euro-centric. The petition proposes a name change for the holiday to bring a sense of pride and togetherness to all Americans. "First Americans Day" would instill pride and be meaningful to all Americans, they say. Costa Rica has acted and now celebrates *Dia de la Raza,* Race Day, to celebrate all of the peoples who constitute the country's cultural base.

Changing the holiday name, however, would be a mistake. To celebrate "Columbus and Race Day" or "Indigenous People's Day" or "Indian Heritage Day" requires too much explanation. In addition, to eliminate the admiral altogether removes a valuable target for Native American demonstration. They should fight him, in all his mythic manifestations, not ignore him. They make news when they make trouble. If protestors confront only the real human Columbus, whose narrow shoulders cannot carry all the ills of Western civilization—capitalism, imperialism, racism, sexism, environmental degradation—they lose the drama of their fight against their own sinister Columbus. Native American opposition to the Columbian encounter, an invasion of America, should, and probably will, continue. The protean admiral makes a very useful target, a neat center for future debate.

FURTHER READING

Badger, Reid. *The Great American Fair: The World's Columbian Exposition and American Culture.* Chicago: Nelson Hall, 1979.

Bushman, Claudia L. *America Discovers Columbus: How An Italian Explorer Became An American Hero.* Hanover, N.H.: University Press of New England, 1992.

Dennis, Matthew. *Red, White, and Blue Letter Days: An American Calendar.* Ithaca, N.Y.: Cornell University Press, 2002.

Irving, Washington. *The Life and Voyages of Christopher Columbus.* 2 vols. New York: George P. Putnam, 1850.

Summerhill, Stephen J., and John Alexander Williams, *Sinking Columbus: Contested History, Cultural Politics, and Mythmaking during the Quincentenary.* Gainesville: University Press of Florida, 2000.

Winsor, Justin. *Christopher Columbus and How He Received and Imparted the Spirit of Discovery.* Boston: Houghton, Mifflin and Company, 1891.

Claudia L. Bushman

HALLOWEEN

- Halloween is celebrated on October 31.

- Our modern Halloween descends from the pagan Celtic feast Samhain, which on November 1 marked the first day of winter, and the new year.

- During Samhain, food and drink were left out for the souls of the previous year's dead, who, it was believed, crossed into the otherworld on this transitional day.

- Similar days of the dead, like All Soul's Day and eventually Hallowe'en, continued to be observed after Ireland's conversion to Christianity. They also became associated with Hell and demons.

- Irish immigrants brought Halloween and its customs to America.

- Ritual door-to-door begging, or "mumming," was one imported Halloween custom.

- Trick-or-treating is thought to have begun in the 1930s as a way to deflect youthful Halloween pranks, and it caught on nationally after World War II when suburbanization took off.

- In recent years adults have reclaimed Halloween as a time of carnivalesque inversion and license.

HALLOWEEN

Halloween is celebrated on October 31, the eve of All Saints Day in the Christian Church calendar. It can be traced historically to a pre-Christian Celtic feast known as Samhain (pronounced "Sahwen"). In the United States today the celebration has become massively popular, generating consumer sales second only to Christmas and providing the occasions for public masquerading and processions of many different kinds and involving many different age-groups.

EUROPEAN ORIGINS

Historically, the contemporary Halloween is most often said to descend from the Celtic feast of Samhain, one of the four great Quarter days in the ancient Celtic calendar. The Celts were the ancestors of the contemporary Irish, Scottish, and Welsh nations among others. Samhain, celebrated on November 1 in the Roman calendar, was in fact the greatest of the Quarter days; it was the first day of winter and the first day of the new year. While little is known directly of Samhain in pre-Christian Ireland, the sagas that were written down by monks centuries after the conversion (circa 300 C.E.) indicate that Samhain occupied a central position in the temporal organization of that society. As a turning point, both of a new season (or quarter) of the year, and of the year itself, many beliefs and rituals accrued to the festival. Traditionally there were bonfires, and there was a general belief that during this time of transition the barriers that separated the world of the living from that of the dead were permeable. The souls of those who had died during the year traveled to the otherworld during this period. Offerings of food and drink were left for these traveling spirits.

As Ireland converted to Christianity, the older celebrations and feast days were replaced with the official holy days of the church. Nevertheless, the pre-Christian traditions were maintained, often in an uneasy relationship with Christian doctrine. For instance, the mythology of the fairy world is thought by many scholars to be an adaptation of older Celtic myth to the new conditions. November 1 was celebrated as All Saints Day or All Hallows Day beginning in the seventh century, and November 2 became All Souls Day in the tenth century. These days of the dead may have been intended to redirect the

All Hallows Eve. © Brown Brothers.

pre-Christian spirituality toward church-approved devotions to all the saints who did not otherwise enjoy their own feast day, and to praying for the souls of those who had died during the previous year. However, this strategy also allowed for the continuation of many of the older beliefs and practices. The Eve of All Hallows, known by many names, including Halleve, Holy Eve, and Hallowe'en, became (or continued as) an important annual festival of family, both living and deceased.

Halloween remains an important holiday in Ireland today. In some rural areas, people might leave a fire burning in the hearth for the returning spirits—members of their family now said to be traveling from Purgatory to Heaven. The belief in Purgatory as a place where lesser sins are temporarily punished is Roman Catholic. Among Protestants, spiritual apparitions are thought to be diabolical or evil in nature, since the souls of the dead are thought to be in either Heaven (which they would not leave) or Hell. With Christian dualism came the identification of the Otherworld with the concepts of Heaven and Hell. No longer was November 1 concerned solely with death. Now it also became associated with evil, as manifested by various demons or the Devil himself.

Most Roman Catholics, however, welcome the returning members of their extended family. Candles might be left in the windows for them. More generally, Halloween bonfires are built by members of all faiths, and none. In Northern Ireland, these are joined by fireworks displays at home and in town centers. Officially, since explosives are banned in Northern Ireland, homemade firework displays are illegal. This law is loosely enforced at Halloween, however.

Halloween in Ireland is also a time for family reunions and feasts. It is similar to the American Thanksgiving in this regard. The Irish equivalent to trick-or-treating, Halloween rhyming, is done in the weeks prior to Halloween, leaving the night itself open to family get-togethers. Due to its perceived origins in ancient Celtic traditions, and its position as one of the four great Quarter days, Halloween remains a major festival in contemporary Ireland.

HALLOWEEN COMES TO THE UNITED STATES

It is said that when millions of Irish people immigrated to the United States in the nineteenth century, fleeing the potato famine, they brought their Halloween traditions with them. Earlier Irish immigrants, including the Ulster Protestants who had helped colonize North America, had already introduced Halloween to the New World, but in the nineteenth century the holiday took hold as a day for parties and games, much as it had been at home. "Dunkin'" for apples, burning nuts on the hearth to predict whether a couple would have a good relationship, trying to bite an apple suspended from a string ("snapapple") and other games and divination beliefs were joined by traditional pranks and tricks. The spirits of the dead were joined by living mischief-makers who were given license to make noise, harass homeowners, and overturn outhouses. Perhaps because of its origin as a transitional point in the old calendar, Halloween is a time out of time—a liminal period when the dead join the living; marginal creatures such as ghosts and witches roam; the future can be determined, and people are allowed to break the rules of order.

Halloween rhyming in Ireland is directly descended from earlier mumming practices. "Mumming" involves dressing in traditional disguise and processing from home to home, where a performance of some sort is rewarded with a gift of food or drink. The American analogue, trick-or-treating, is clearly influ-

A group of children in costume ready for trick-or-treating. Courtesy of Corbis.

enced by the Irish model, as well as the many ritual begging customs of other peoples who came to the United States. Thought to have begun in the 1930s as a way to deflect the ever-spiraling pranking of youngsters, trick-or-treating caught on nationally after World War II, as urbanization and suburbanization grew rapidly. By the 1950s, it had all but displaced domestic parties as the primary custom of Halloween (pranking continued apace in more rural areas), and Halloween became known as a children's holiday. However, within two decades, Halloween was appropriated by college and university students as a festival of public costuming as well as of excess. Further, in major cities such as New York, the holiday was appealing to great numbers of adults. For some time, Halloween had been utilized by groups of gay people as an occasion to publicly parade their otherwise forbidden identity. In Boston, gay men dressed as women and paraded annually, as they did in New York. Eventually the New York Halloween parade became a kind of performance art festival, joined by people of many backgrounds. Likewise, in cities throughout the country adults reclaimed Halloween as an occasion of masquerading and festivity. Many cities now are home to more than one such street festival: Washington, D.C. features one such carnivalesque occasion in the Georgetown section, comprised largely of students from the nearby university, while families with children promenade in costume along East Capitol Street on Capitol Hill.

With the growing involvement of an older generation has come the inevitable consumerism. As trick-or-treating became established, store-bought sweets gradually replaced the homemade treats such as apples and doughnuts. Store-bought costumes replaced the old clothes and rags scoured from drawers at home. Today, these commercial efforts have been joined by "trick-or-treating at the mall" and among merchants, efforts that are often blatantly commercial in nature. Other Halloween customs have quickly been capitalized upon, as well. For instance, along with the street festivals, people have begun to decorate their homes extensively with assemblages of symbolic objects such as dummies, ghosts, corn stalks, and so forth. Mass-produced versions of these usually homemade objects are now found in the department stores, along with electric outdoor display lights similar to those used at Christmas.

Nevertheless, despite its increasing importance economically, Halloween remains a popular celebration that allows for inversion and political satire. Images of politicians and celebrities have joined the traditional costumes of ghouls and other evil, malevolent folk. I have seen groups of people disguised as atomic waste—this and other contemporary plagues, such as consumer goods that have been tampered with, are all part of the parade of taboos publicly paraded at Halloween. It remains a time of danger, as attested by the legends of poisoned treats and razor blades in apples, all of which have proven untrue. If people once feared demons and vampires, today we are more likely to fear the neighbor we do not know, or the stranger who just might be an axe murderer. For all its corporatization, Halloween remains a night of festive inversion, a

An assortment of Halloween candy overflows from a trick-or-treat pumpkin. Courtesy of Corbis.

time when people partake in age-old customs, not because they have to, but because they want to.

FURTHER READING

Rogers, Nicolas. *Halloween: From Pagan Ritual to Party Night.* New York: Oxford University Press, 2002.

Santino, Jack. *All Around the Year: Holidays and Celebrations in American Life.* Urbana and Champaign: University of Illinois Press, 1994.

———. *The Hallowed Eve: Dimensions of Culture in a Calendar Festival in Northern Ireland.* Lexington: University Press of Kentucky. 1998.

———, ed. *Halloween and Other Festivals of Death and Life.* Knoxville: University of Tennessee Press, 1996.

Jack Santino

Election Day

Does America need a new holiday—Election Day?

The national elections of 2000 and 2004 dramatically highlighted issues of voter registration, access to the polls, and voter turnout. Despite the somewhat larger turnout of 2004, and overall defeat for the Democratic Party, Democrats in early 2005 introduced legislation for voting reform aimed at increasing voter participation. Included in the plan was a proposal to create a new federal holiday, Election Day, to stimulate voters. Backing for an Election Day holiday is not limited to any one political party, however. Supporters claim that such a measure would help remedy some serious concerns regarding voter access and turnout: despite the fact that it has become steadily easier to register over the past four decades, fewer and fewer Americans are casting ballots.

Voter turnout statistics show disturbing trends. Since 1970, the percentage of eligible voters casting ballots for the House of Representatives has ranged between 33 and 45 percent. Americans are more likely to turn out to vote during presidential election years; nevertheless the 1996 presidential election turnout fell below 50 percent for the first time since the 1920s, and that of 2000 was only slightly better. Clear biases of education in turnout have also become apparent. Since 1966 turnout rates have plummeted for people with lower levels of education. From 1966 to 1994, turnout among Americans with only high school degrees dropped from 60 to 41 percent, while participation of those lacking a high school diploma fell from 47 to a mere 26 percent. Even those with college degrees have become less likely to vote: over the same three decades described above, the presence of college-educated Americans at the polls has declined, from 71 to 64 percent.

Age is also a major factor in voter turnout rates. Young voters have consistently demonstrated the lowest participation, which may be one of the reasons there was so little resistance to lowering the voting age to 18 in the early 1970s.

In the 1994 congressional elections, for example, a paltry 17 percent of eligible voters between 18 and 20 actually cast ballots, and only 5 percent more of their slightly older colleagues (21 to 24) showed up. In stark contrast, more than three times that percentage of Americans over 45 cast ballots. Gone, apparently, are the days when advancing age led to a decline in turnout among the over-60 age group. Issues of vital interest to these Americans, such as Medicare and Social Security, have seen to that.

For millions of Americans, elections have become a chore, a frustration, inconvenient, and boring. Political conventions once received broad television coverage; today they are easily trumped by sporting events. In response to abysmal convention coverage ratings, television networks have drastically abridged their reporting of these events. The rapid expansion of available TV channels over the past decades has exacerbated the problem, as has, paradoxically, the expansion of Web news and political sites. Instead of balanced news coverage and analysis, viewers can select channels and sites that most appeal to their current biases, or even avoid public-affairs news altogether. Critics fear that the result will be an ever-increasing inequality of political knowledge and critical thinking, with "political junkies" becoming ever more knowledgeable, "while the rest of the public slips deeper into political apathy."

So would an Election Day holiday stimulate and help broaden voter turnout, and reverse some of the more worrisome and embarrassing voter trends in America?

Definitely, argue supporters. The day established by law in 1872 for national elections—the first Tuesday after the first Monday in November—is awkward and inconvenient for voters, falling as it does on a regular workday. There is no standard national polling schedule, and workers are not guaranteed time off to vote. According to the United States Census, in 2000 more than 20 percent of eligible voters who did not vote (the proportions were even higher among Asian Americans and Latinos) failed to do so due to scheduling conflicts, or inconvenient polling times and procedures. Voting rights advocates argue that one obvious way to improve this is to set aside an entire day. An ordinary act of Congress placed Election Day where it is today, and a similar act could move it, some advocate, to a Saturday, giving more people a whole day to vote. Saturday, however, is still a sabbath for Jews and Muslims, so the alternative would be to make Election Day a national holiday. The United States, supporters argue, is among the few Western democracies that do not schedule elections for weekends or a designated holiday, and they point out that other nations that do so enjoy higher voter turnouts. There is evidence of this even closer to home: Puerto Rico makes Election Day a holiday and in 2000 had 82 percent turnout—far more than any state in the union.

Opponents of the proposed change, however, predict more harm than good. First, some argue, there is no pressing need for action: if Americans do not vote, they may in fact be signaling a general satisfaction with their government. Employers maintain that giving up another whole day of profits would be damaging to business and pointless. Motivated voters always manage to vote anyway, they insist, and polls are open long after regular work hours for this purpose. Many, perhaps most, nonvoters will still not vote, but simply take another (paid?) day off. And David Morris, political commentator for the American Voice 2004 project, finds no explicit link between higher voter turnout in other countries and Election Day as holiday: there may be other, cultural factors at work.

Proponents of a new Election Day hope to make the occasion a kind of civic revival: as with Independence Day, the new holiday would awaken and focus Americans' awareness of themselves as part of an expansive, unified polity. Rob Richie, executive director of the Center for Voting and Democracy, imagines a federal Election Day as an occasion for people to "all come together for the common good." Ultimately, he contends, an Election Day holiday would be an opportunity for "a festive, politically exciting event" that would generate "a whole different sensibility" about voting. Working against this vision is the growing practice of allowing voters to cast ballots days or even weeks early; the significance of a single voting day is increasingly diluted. In 2004, the majority of states permitted unrestricted early or absentee voting. But supporters of Election Day counter that early voting does not of itself increase voter turnout, and that early or absentee voting is largely the response to the inconveniences of holding elections in the midst of a work week—which a federal holiday would make moot. Tova Wang, a fellow at the Century Foundation, adds that early voting erodes the opportunity for people to vote "together as an American community and as individual communities."

In response to the controversial presidential election of 2000, the National Commission on Federal Election Reform, headed by former presidents Jimmy Carter and Gerald Ford, recommended merging Election Day with Veterans Day to create a *de facto* Election Day holiday. The proposal has obvious advantages. It would combine two, often underappreciated, occasions into a kind of "super-patriotic" holiday emphasizing civic duty and sacrifice. Since Veterans Day is already a federal holiday, businessmen and employers would lose no additional revenues. Lastly, citing the chronic shortages of poll workers on current Election Days, the new holiday would "increase availability of poll workers and...make voting easier for some workers." Acting on the recommendations of the commission, several bills have come forth in Congress calling for an Election Day holiday, but there is as yet no broad support, either in Congress or among the general population.

Curtis Gans of the Committee for the Study of the American Electorate, a nonprofit think tank, believes that pinning hopes on a holiday to increase voter turnout ignores the larger, more systemic factors behind waning American voter participation. "The problem of...voter participation in America is a problem of motivation...people are much more likely to go fishing than voting if they're given a day off." Thus, he concludes, tying voting to the work-week cycle is better than tying it to a day of rest. Making Election Day a holiday would nullify the effects of "certain instruments of mobilization, like shop stewards, employers, teachers, etc." According to this argument, holding elections during the workday is in many ways favorable to turnout, as colleagues and coworkers provide encouragement to vote. The relatively small community of the workplace is much more familiar, and important, to the potential voter than is the "imagined community" of millions of anonymous Americans and what they are doing that day.

An Election Day holiday, however conceived, may go a long way toward making voting more convenient for Americans and solve some of the perennial problems surrounding national elections in America. But as journalist Michelle Chen observes, "if people would elect to go fishing over voting, they probably need more than convenience. The hard part of voting may not be the act itself, but the challenge of seeing why it matters."

POPE'S DAY/GUY FAWKES DAY

- ☐ Pope's Day, or Guy Fawkes Day, was celebrated on November 5 of each year.

- ☐ The holiday originated in England to commemorate the thwarting of Catholic militant Guy Fawkes attempt to assassinate King James I by blowing up the House of Commons in 1605.

- ☐ Brought to North America by British settlers but resisted by Puritans, observance of the anti-Catholic Pope's Day was decreed by King Charles II in 1665.

- ☐ The event was marked by fireworks and bonfires, upon which effigies of Guy Fawkes and the pope were burned.

- ☐ Early celebrations expressed a key, socially shared value in the heavily Protestant American colonies: extreme suspicion of Catholics and Catholic-influenced government.

- ☐ Symbolically the holiday affirmed political allegiance to the British Crown. Accordingly, widespread observance of Guy Fawkes day in the colonies ended during the Revolutionary War.

- ☐ Pope's Day was celebrated in several northern New England seaport towns up until about 1920.

POPE'S DAY/
GUY FAWKES DAY

A visitor to eighteenth-century Newburyport, Massachusetts arriving around November 5 would have witnessed a sight as alien and bizarre to modern Americans as it was normal to them. As the day progressed, the visitor would have noticed more and more young boys cruising the seaport's streets dragging little wagons of their own construction. On these carts rested grotesquely decorated miniature effigies of the pope that they rolled about the town on their wagons, a politicized foreshadowing of "trick or treat" practices. At night, the same boys, assisted by the community's young men, dragged a large and complex stage bearing large effigies of the pope, monks, and Satan through the streets before destroying them all in a large bonfire normally attended by a raucous crowd. The same sort of bonfires burning similar effigies would have been visible in most if not all of the major port towns on November 5 in British America in the eighteenth century.

The participants were celebrating Pope's Day, also know as Gunpowder Day and Guy Fawkes Day, the anniversary of the discovery of a purported plot led by a Catholic militant to blow up King James I and the English House of Commons in 1605. Quickly made an annual celebration by that king, in eighteenth-century America Pope's Day was one of 26 days linked to the history and life cycle of Britain's monarchs that expressed an intense loyalty to those rulers and a shared imperial identity. Along with the king's birthday and Coronation Day, Pope's Day was the leading holiday in a calendar of annual celebrations that defined political life in royal America.

A bonfire is built in celebration of Pope's Day. Courtesy of Getty Images / PhotoDisc.

The holiday celebrated James I's foiling of the purported plot, but it was memory of England's own tumultuous and haphazard reformations as well as the sporadic warfare between the island nation and Europe's Catholic powers that had helped cement this anti-Catholic holiday in English national culture. Indeed, November 5 was not the first anti-Catholic holiday of the English nation; Pope's Day supplanted November 17, Queen Elizabeth I's coronation day. November 5 thus gave symbolic form and release to the ferocious paranoia against Catholics that developed across the late sixteenth and seventeenth centuries. In a deeper sense, these hyper-Protestant holidays supplanted November 1, All Saints Day on the Catholic calendar, as well as substituting for harvest festivals with folk origins.

HOLIDAY BY DECREE

The holiday's official character is the key to understanding its appearance and spread in England's American colonies. It was royal authority and an expanding print culture, to a large degree controlled by the state, rather than oral traditions or informal plebeian celebrations, that firmly established Pope's Day in the provinces. Puritans were hostile to cyclical rituals, yet by the 1660s

A depiction of the capture of Guy Fawkes. © Culver Pictures.

November 5 was a yearly anniversary holiday in the northern colonies. It was the restored power of the Stuart monarchy that planted Pope's Day in America in the face of Calvinist resistance. As early as 1662, November 5 was declared "a day of Public thanksgiving" in Charlestown, across the Charles River from Boston. Royal pressure to celebrate the holiday culminated in Charles II issuing a decree to the Massachusetts General Court in May 1665, ordering the Bay Colony's government to "kept the 5th of November" as a day of thanksgiving for "the miraculous preservation of our King & country from the gunpowder treason." In 1667, Massachusetts's legislature declared November 5 a day of

public thanksgiving, making it an annual holiday. The Puritan elite continued unofficial resistance to the holiday until after the Glorious Revolution of
1688–89, when William III and Mary II, whose claim to the English throne
was based on their Protestantism, legitimated Pope's Day as a way of normal-
izing their own rule. Gunpowder Day, as the holiday was also known, was then
embraced in the colonies, allowing the population a ritualistic release for their
intense anti-Catholic feelings.

By 1700, the celebration of Protestant monarchy on November 5 was becoming common in British America's port towns along the entire eastern seaboard.
In all these areas, instructions sent to imperial governors and other officials
played the key role in establishing this holiday as well as the other official
rites of the first British empire in America. Immigrants and sailors also carried
knowledge of Pope's Day practices to America, but it was royal authority that
normalized the holidays.

The rapid expansion of provincial print culture in the late seventeenth century amplified the impact of the Pope's Day rites and encouraged their spread.
As early as the seventeenth century, New England almanacs, the period's pulp
literature, recorded the "Powder Plot, 1605," on their calendars. Southern
almanacs also promoted the holiday. In the eighteenth century *The Virginia
Almanac* recorded "Nov. 5 Powder Plot," and the other eighteenth-century
almanacs from the region routinely recalled the salvation of the English nation
from popish intrigue. These publications often situated the custom historically
and provided instruction on how to perform its rituals. Nathaniel Ames's *An
Astronomical Diary, or, AN ALMANACK For the Year of Our Lord Christ....
1737,* printed in Boston, provided instructions, in the form of a poem, for
Pope's Day celebrants. On the calendar's November leaf, Ames wrote "Ere you
pretend/ to burn the Pope/Secure the papists/with a Rope." Thus by royal proclamation, and print, a politicized understanding of this central imperial holiday
spread throughout the colonies, and the reporting of the celebrations by the
colonial newspapers carried the November 5 rites' emotional power beyond the
larger towns' horizons.

The southern colonies began celebrating Pope's Day in one form or another
by 1700, and again it seems to have been institutional action that established
the holiday. Certainly, by the 1740s, imperial encouragement had planted it
in Georgia, Virginia, and South Carolina. The College of William and Mary
spurred the celebration of November 5 in Virginia for reasons very specific to
its primary patrons. Because William III had landed at Torbay on the east coast
of England on November 5, 1688 on his way to depose Mary's father James II,
that day (which was also celebrated as William III's birthday) became a triple
holiday at the school. In Georgia, the government established the holiday soon
after the colony was founded. On November 5, 1743 Georgia Governor William Stephens remembered "one of our annual Rejoycing days," by hoisting
the British flag, ordering the firing of the guns at Savannah's fortifications, and

leading an assembled group in "the drinking a few Glasses of Wine with the usual healths [to the royal family]."

The custom was also established in the mid-Atlantic region in the same period. As early as November 5, 1689, Jacob Leisler recorded a pope burning during the unrest in New York that came to bear his name. In 1700, the town's government supplied alcohol and wood for bonfires to the town's population. The degree to which the holiday was celebrated in New Jersey and Pennsylvania in this period is unclear, and it may be that religious and cultural scruples inhibited its initial establishment in those colonies.

ANTI-CATHOLIC RALLY IN A GROWING EMPIRE

Over the course of the eighteenth century the way the holiday was celebrated changed. These changes reflected growth in the size of towns, overall population growth, and the course of events in the continuing struggle of the British empire against the Catholic powers of Europe, especially France. In late seventeenth-century New England, Pope's Day was marked by daytime sermons and celebrated in the evening around bonfires, usually on the edge of towns on common land. Notified by officials, crowds gathered, consumed alcohol (often provided by the authorities or leading men) and invariably an effigy of the pope would be burned or even blown up. The practice of creating pope's effigies was almost certainly derived from England, where numerous such effigies were burned on November 5 during the Popish Plot hysteria and Exclusion Crisis of the late 1670s and early 1680s. In 1689, Jacob Leisler reported the burning of just such a "pope" during the anniversary's celebration in strife-torn New York City. Immediately after 1688, then, the holiday was focused exclusively on the pope effigy and the providential defense of Protestantism against popery generally, paralleling the broader political culture's embrace of William III as a defender of pan-European Protestantism.

The constant tensions between England and Europe's Catholic powers assured that November 5 would continue as an important holiday in the eighteenth century. The celebration's imperialization, its overt linkage to dynastic issues, and its visible use to educate provincial populations about the continuing Catholic threat, began around 1700. Observances came to comprise the inclusion of imperial themes in the yearly sermons, the custom of artisans parading through the major ports' streets on November 5, and the infusion of new effigies associated with the dynastic struggle against the Catholic branch of the Stuart family (deposed in 1688 by William and Mary) in those processions.

The development of parading is chronologically connected to the holiday's imperialization and to the port town's growth. While early celebrations seem to have been fixed in their location immediately after 1688, by the beginning of the new century yearly processions on November 5 became commonplace

417

in the major port towns. Who initially thought of organizing these parades is uncertain, and thus it is difficult to say what exactly motivated them. They may have had knowledge of similar parading in London and other parts of Britain and Europe. Its chronological development further suggests a reaction to the growth of the towns, which had become larger and had begun developing distinctive neighborhoods or districts. Parading asserted a commonly held value in a society grown larger than the familiar.

The small changes that occurred in the processional iconography between 1690 and 1740 speak to changing political perceptions related to developments in the empire. What began as a public expression of the provincials' fierce anti-Catholicism gradually evolved toward a more complex rendering of colonial concerns and imperial perceptions. The early processions were centered on the large pope effigy, mounted on a pole or lashed to a cart, which was paraded and then invariable burned in the evening of November 5. This sort of thing was occurring in Boston by 1700 and may have existed there a decade earlier. The pope's figure and the ferocious anti-Catholicism it represented remained a part of the processions through the eighteenth century. It expressed a key, socially shared value: extreme suspicion of Catholics and Catholic-influenced govern-

Children build an effigy of Guy Fawkes in preparation of the November 5 celebration. © Culver Pictures.

ment. But in the eighteenth century, processional iconography began to evolve, shaped by new provincial concerns about the empire and colonial society.

This evolution was visible in Boston as early as 1702, when the effigy of the Stuart Pretender (the claimant to the throne from the deposed House of Stuart) was added to a stage that carried the pope's figure. This iconography soon spread to other port towns. The pretender's image was a potent anti-Catholic symbol, but it was a specifically British image, designed to express the empire's political unity against a deposed dynasty believed to be Catholic absolutists allied with France. The processions thus legitimated the Dutch and later German rulers who sat on the British throne by virtue of their Protestantism.

The processional iconography became more elaborate over time and reflected imperial developments. The base iconography at Boston by the 1740s consisted of the devil, "with a pitchfork in his hands covered in tar and feathers," his supernatural assistants, the pope, "dressed in gorgeous attire with a large white wig on, over which was an enormous gold-laced hat," and the Stuart Pretender's effigy, mounted on a mobile stage and presented in a manner that suggested Satan's ultimate control over the deposed House of Stuart. At New York, a similar composition of effigies was used. "The Pope, the Pretender and the D—l" one newspaper reported, after having been carried through the streets, "were Burnt…in the Commons near this City," by a large crowd. Similar celebrations occurred in other northern port towns, and evidence suggests that this base iconography was used as far south as Charleston, South Carolina. Of course, there were variants on these themes. At Newburyport, Massachusetts, the processional cart contained monks and friars, and no doubt other local renditions of the cosmopolitan themes existed.

In the 1740s, provincial concerns over the continued warfare between France and Britain began to alter the iconography and the behavior in the processions, particularly at Boston and New York. In the former port, "Admiral Bing [who had been court marshaled and shot in England for allegedly refusing to fight during a naval conflict against the French in the Seven Years' War] hanging from a gallows," was added to the moving stage, positioned between the devil and the pope. At New York, a Pope's Day procession stopped before a home where a captured French general was imprisoned in 1755; the revelers threatened to tear the house down, only to have the general, familiar with holiday mobs in France, send down silver coins to his tormentors, to which the processioners responded with cheers.

Around 1740, female figures began to be added to the processional carts in New England, particularly in Boston. They acknowledge contemporary concerns over morality in a society at war. Known as Pope Joan and Nancy Dawson, they embodied the moral corruption of the Catholic, anti-Hanoverian forces arrayed against the first British empire. Pope Joan was believed to be a medieval, cross-dressing woman who became pope and then gave birth during a procession honoring St. John, and thus an emblem of Catholic hypocrisy.

By constructing sexual immorality as Catholic and female, the Boston procession makers sought to confine sexual expression in their own community to the appropriate channels, a task no doubt increasingly difficult in a port town awash in soldiers, sailors, and prostitutes.

REVOLUTIONARY AGITATION ON POPE'S DAY

While reflecting one of the first British empire's core values, mainly the hatred of Catholics and fear of what was called popish, arbitrary government, Pope's Day processions encouraged considerable popular participation and initiative in the creation and destruction of effigies, thus separating it from other imperial holidays that were more tightly controlled and involved militia parading. Artisans, apprentices, sailors, and others routinely became involved in a holiday designed so that "the Wonderful deliverance the Protestants met with on Nov. 5th" would never be forgotten. The participation of the "lower orders" was seen as a way of educating those outside the formal power structure and permitted a controlled release of political energy. The parading of multiple effigies in towns reflected this and neighborhood rivalries as well, which were especially evident in Boston, where the North End and South End artisans fought annually on November 5 on Boston Common to capture the other's "pope." While there are numerous ways to understand the artisans' behavior, and participation had different meanings in different contexts, the most obvious understanding—that people enjoyed the holiday and accepted/embraced its meaning—seems to be logical. It allowed provincials to publicly proclaim their loyalty to the monarchy, and, more generally, to the emerging monarch-centered imperial culture. Its establishment reveals how imperial perceptions were extended to the provincial population as a whole over time. And it suggests the interconnection of so-called popular beliefs with the culture of power.

So completely did provincials accept the holiday that the outbreak of the Stamp Act crisis brought not a repudiation of it but rather its adaptation to imperial protest. At Boston, New York, and Savannah, Georgia, crowds used either the processions of November 5 or aspects of the behaviors common to Pope's Day to protest the Stamp Act, which went into effect November 1, 1765. A rapid adaptation of the November 5 rites to imperial protest followed. One correspondent reported he saw three popes and effigies of "Ld. North, Gov. Hutchinson [Thomas Hutchinson, the vilified last royal governor of Massachusetts Bay] & General Gage [commander of British forces in North America]" paraded and burned in Newport, Rhode Island in 1774. Such usages were by then common up and down the Atlantic seaboard. The outbreak of fighting and the hope of an alliance with Catholic France curtailed the celebrations in many areas, although Boston crowds apparently still drew on practices and figures from the celebrations to punish Tories during the Revolution.

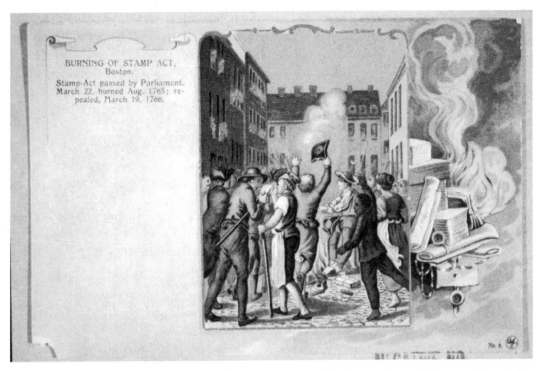

People used behaviors common to Pope's Day to protest the Stamp Act, which went into effect November 1, 1765. Courtesy of the Library of Congress.

Scholars have generally believed that Pope's Day died out in America after 1776, and certainly it passed from historical view. However, local records from northern New England's coastal region suggest that this is not entirely the case. At least at Newburyport and Marblehead in Massachusetts and at Portsmouth in New Hampshire boys and young men continued to mark the holiday into the early twentieth century. Apparently, these groups had no knowledge of the holiday's historical origins or connections to British royalty; they simply maintained the custom and some of its forms as they had received them. They may have retained some anti-Catholic connotations, although that is unclear from the accounts of them. Some of the celebrants' practices, like the carrying of pumpkin lanterns, suggest a convergence with or an influence over Halloween customs as it became the major holiday of the late fall. As nearly as can be determined, the custom died out some time around World War I, for reasons that are unclear. With its end in northern New England, Pope's Day was extinguished in America, although it has continued to be celebrated in Northern Ireland and parts of Britain until today as Guy Fawkes Day. There it retains the echoes of its original usage, as a celebration of British identity, and perhaps, anti-Catholicism.

The royal political culture of which Pope's Day was a key part dominated public life in America between the Glorious Revolution and American independence. Those rites were part of an intellectual and social machinery that produced a very different kind of American, that being a subject and a monarchical provincial loyal to a distant ruler. So completely was the memory of them wiped away by the Revolution and the society's subsequent democratization that it is difficult now to imagine their centrality to public life in early America. Yet that centrality is obvious in the records of the period and the behavior of provincials living in British America.

FURTHER READING

Cressy, David. *Bonfires and Bells: National Memory and the Protestant Calendar in Elizabethan and Stuart England.* Berkeley: University of California Press, 1989.

Forbes, Esther. *Paul Revere and The World He Lived In.* Boston: Houghton Mifflin, 1942.

McConville, Brendan. "Pope's Day Revisited, 'Popular' Culture Reconsidered." In *Explorations in Early American Culture* 4 (2000): 258–80.

Shaw, Peter. *American Patriots and the Rituals of Revolution.* Cambridge, Mass.: Harvard University Press, 1981.

Shea, John Gilmary. "Pope-Day in America," Unpublished paper read before the United States Catholic Historical Society, January 19, 1888, stored in Library of Congress Broadsides.

Brendan McConville

VETERANS DAY

Almost every major American war has produced a holiday—some of the most important include the Fourth of July and Memorial Day. But other holidays were observed for only a short time and then interest in them faded. After the American Revolution, New Yorkers celebrated Evacuation Day—November 25—to mark the anniversary of the departure of British forces from their city in 1783, but in the early twentieth century interest in this holiday faded as the city became a major metropolis. For a few years after the Spanish-American War, some Americans tried to inaugurate Dewey Day in honor of the admiral who defeated the Spanish fleet in Manila Bay, but this holiday never gained momentum. Initially, Veterans Day emerged as Armistice Day, honoring the service of those who fought in World War I. Celebrated on the eleventh day of November, Armistice Day marked the official anniversary of the end of World War I. After World War II and the Korean War, this holiday became Veterans Day and honored the service of all veterans who served in time of war.

MOBILIZING AMERICANS FOR WORLD WAR I

World War I deeply divided American society, and these divisions would play an important role in shaping how Americans celebrated the Armistice Day holiday and why it eventually would be renamed as Veterans Day. In August 1914, when fighting broke out in Europe, few Americans expected they would enter this conflict, especially since most expected the war would not be a long

VETERANS DAY

- ☐ Veterans Day is observed on November 11 of each year and is an official federal holiday.

- ☐ Known originally as Armistice Day, the holiday was created to commemorate American servicemen who served and died in World War I (1917–18).

- ☐ Congress made Armistice Day an official federal holiday in 1938, but many Americans observed November 11 in the 1920s and 1930s by pausing for two minutes of silence on the eleventh hour.

- ☐ World War I veterans group the American Legion played a pivotal role cultivating and pressing for Armistice Day observations.

- ☐ On November 11, 1922, President Warren Harding traveled to Arlington National Cemetery and laid a wreath at the Tomb of the Unknown Soldier, inaugurating a custom his successors would follow.

- ☐ In 1954 Congress renamed November 11 Veterans Day, after American participation in World War II (1941–45) and the Korean War (1950–53) made Armistice Day an anachronistic holiday in need of recasting to keep its relevance for Americans.

- ☐ In 1968 Congress acknowledged the growing commercialism of the American holiday calendar and passed the Monday Holiday Act, mandating that several civic holidays, including Presidents' Day, Memorial Day, and Veterans Day, be observed on a Monday instead of their traditional dates.

- ☐ Under the Monday Holiday Act, Veterans Day was then observed on the fourth Monday of October.

- ☐ Veterans groups successfully lobbied Congress to return Veterans Day observations to November 11, in 1978.

one. Initially, President Woodrow Wilson proclaimed an official policy of neutrality, but the United States would soon protest the German sinking of British and French passenger and merchant ships. Wilson denounced these actions as a violation of international law and demanded that German submarines only sink merchant ships after a suitable warning and that they refrain from attacking passenger vessels.

Many Americans, led by such prominent leaders as former President Theodore Roosevelt, actively crusaded for America's entrance into the conflict. They portrayed Germans as a barbaric people that sought to despoil Western civilization. Those supporting entrance into the war also expressed great sympathy for Germany's enemies—especially, France, Great Britain, and Belgium. But other Americans disagreed, especially German Americans and the small, but influential, peace movement. Many German Americans criticized Britain for violating international law in the way it blockaded German ports. Irish Americans had no desire to aid Britain, given the refusal of this imperial power to give up control of Ireland. Supporters of the peace movement argued that the United States should further the cause of peace by serving as a neutral mediator and staying above the fray.

In the election of 1916, Woodrow Wilson barely won reelection to a second term as president under the slogan "He Kept Us Out of War." After Germany embarked on a campaign of unrestricted submarine warfare in April 1917, Wilson asked for a declaration of war from the U.S. Congress. In taking America to war, Wilson proclaimed that the United States went to war not only to punish Germany for violating neutral rights on the high seas, but in order to make the "world safe for democracy." Wilson viewed Germany as a threat to Western civilization and portrayed this struggle as messianic to ensure the triumph of freedom.

Entering World War I required an unprecedented mobilization of American society. To raise an army, the United States abandoned the volunteer system and established conscription. The federal government allocated much of the nation's industrial capacity and labor supply to meet the need for munitions and other military supplies. It also developed a systematic propaganda campaign, encouraging Americans to support the war effort. Americans were encouraged to buy Liberty Bonds, display the American flag, voluntarily contribute to the American Red Cross, and conserve scarce foods and materials.

What type of war did America enter? By March 1917 the major combatants were at the point of exhaustion. All sides suffered staggering casualties that numbered in the millions and threatened to bankrupt all the major belligerents. On the eastern front, the German armies inflicted a series of defeats on the Russian Empire that provoked the collapse of the czarist government of Nicholas II. In place of autocracy, a new liberal democratic regime came to power under Alexander Kerensky determined to keep Russia in the war. On western fronts both sides were stalemated. Although France and Britain halted the German attacks of 1914, they proved unable to launch a successful offensive to end the trench warfare that characterized the fighting since late 1915.

Even after Congress declared war, there remained a significant number of Americans who opposed American involvement. Several hundred Americans were imprisoned by the federal government for their public wartime opposition. Thousands of young men refused to fight and did not register for the federal draft. Despite the strength of this antiwar opposition, America succeeded in raising an army over two million strong and dispatched it to France. Late to enter the war, most American forces did not experience combat until 1918. Nonetheless, the "doughboy" played an important role in both halting the German spring offensives and in launching a series of Allied counterattacks in the summer and fall. American forces arrived in France in just enough time to decisively tip the balance against Germany.

On the morning of November 11, 1918 the German government signed an armistice with Britain and France that called for the end of the war on the eleventh hour. In the morning, the war continued, but at 11:00 P.M. the guns fell silent. For the victors—especially in the United States, France, Belgium, Great Britain, Canada, Australia, and New Zealand—wild celebration broke out among both soldiers and civilians. On the still battlefield soldiers emerged from their trenches and celebrated with food and drink. Civilians poured into the streets of New York, London, Paris, and in countless smaller communities to celebrate not just victory, but also the end of a conflict that cost both victors and the vanquished millions in killed and wounded. In many places in America, the celebrations were raucous, even dangerous. Citizens in Tucson, Arizona celebrated the end of war and the coming of peace by shooting firearms into the air. In the case of Newport News, Virginia soldiers and sailors flocked into town and went on rampages requiring authorities to call out the National Guard to suppress the lawless celebration.

ARMISTICE DAY IN AMERICA

The anniversary of the end of World War I—Armistice Day—would be widely observed not only in the United States, but also in a number of other countries. Armistice Day celebrations around the world incorporated ceremonies that called upon the living to remember the war dead. In 1919, President Woodrow Wilson issued a proclamation calling on Americans to observe the anniversary of the armistice. Although Congress did not make Armistice Day an official federal holiday until 1938, many Americans observed November 11 in the 1920s and 1930s by pausing for two minutes of silence on the eleventh hour. Parents recalled children who went off to France and never came home, veterans remembered fallen comrades, soldiers and communities honored those who had answered the call of arms.

Even though Armistice Day struck a responsive chord with many Americans, it might not have become a national holiday without the patronage of the American Legion. Founded in Paris, France, in 1919, the American Legion emerged during the interwar years as the preeminent organization for World War I veterans. Although the majority of those veterans never joined the Legion, this organization played a decisive role in shaping observances surrounding Armistice Day in communities across the nation. Founded to preserve the ties of comradeship forged during the war and to honor the memory of the fallen, the Legion believed it was essential for the veterans of World War I to protect the nation from new dangers. The Legion recalled how it fought against Prussian militarism during World War I and determined in the postwar period to counter what they perceived to be the dangerous influence of Bolsheviks and other left-wing radicals within the United States.

The American Legion had the support of national leaders in promoting the observance of Armistice Day in the United States. Shortly after the war ended, federal lawmakers created an important national symbol—The Tomb of the Unknown Soldier—that figured prominently in Armistice Day observances beginning in 1921. Although the Tomb of the Unknown Soldier was built by the federal government in a national military cemetery—Arlington National Cemetery—the American Legion viewed their organization as the proper custodians of this memorial.

Americans were not the only people to make Armistice Day into a holiday, nor was the United States the only country to honor an Unknown Soldier. To a large degree, the emergence of the Unknown Soldier as an important symbol stemmed from the changing ways nations fighting World War I viewed the war dead. All the major combatants, including the United States, built massive cemeteries for the war dead. In these official cemeteries, the gravestones, the landscaping, the chapels, and the monuments stressed the heroic sacrifice of the fallen to the nation. Although the American, British, and French armies created an elaborate system to mark the graves of those killed in battle, there remained a myriad of unidentified soldiers. In other cases, the bodies of many soldiers who were killed were never recovered. Great Britain and France began the practice of pressing the bodies of unidentified soldiers into further service to the nation. These governments selected an unknown soldier killed in their nation's service and gave him a state funeral. In the case of Great Britain, the Unknown Warrior for the British Empire was buried in a cenotaph outside of Westminster Abbey. France entombed its Unknown Soldier under the Arc de Triomphe.

In the United States, Representative Hamilton Fish of New York initiated the idea of honoring an American Unknown Soldier to embody the sacrifice of all those Americans killed in World War I. Fish's proposal quickly gained the support of both the outgoing Wilson administration and the incoming administration of Warren G. Harding. The bipartisan political support for creating a

Tomb of the Unknown Soldier envisioned this memorial as not only symbolizing the sacrifice of those who died in military service during the war, but also to emphasize a vision of American national unity. The Unknown Soldier would serve to promote a vision of nationalism that stood above divisions of class, ethnicity, region, and religion.

Once the decision had been made to select an Unknown Soldier, army officials in France went about the grim task of assembling the bodies of several soldiers killed in the war who could not be identified. With great ceremony, one of these was selected and placed on a war ship for a journey from Europe back to America. Upon arriving in the United States, the body of the Unknown Soldier received an honor normally bestowed on statesmen and presidents—lying in state in the Capitol rotunda. President Warren Harding, congressional leaders, the diplomatic corps, military leaders, and prominent civic leaders visited the coffin of the Unknown and paid their respects. For several days, thousands of average Americans streamed past the coffin of the Unknown in hushed silence.

On November 11, 1921, a procession carried the body of the Unknown Soldier from the Capitol across the Potomac River for a funeral and entombment at the Memorial Amphitheater at Arlington National Cemetery. Clergy from several denominations offered prayers on behalf of the Unknown Soldier and the nation. The Unknown Soldier received several posthumous medals for bravery, including the Congressional Medal of Honor. With all official Washington in attendance, mourners listened to President Warren G. Harding eulogize the valor and bravery of the Unknown Soldier. The young man, Harding speculated, could have been born rich or poor, northerner or southerner, native-born or an immigrant, but whatever his exact background, he was a representative American in his courage and willingness to sacrifice on behalf of the nation. Before the grave was sealed, Crow leader Plenty Coups offered a traditional Indian blessing for the soul of the Unknown.

Millions of Americans who could not attend the ceremonies at the Tomb of the Unknown Soldier could still learn about them from newspaper reports and newsreels. Holding the ceremonies for the Unknown Soldier on Armistice Day served to cement this day as a national holiday. Were there other days that could have been selected? Memorial Day, the holiday dedicated to the remembrance of the Civil War dead, remained an obvious candidate. But veterans of World War I, especially those belonging to the American Legion, wanted their own, unique holiday to commemorate what they believed had been a "war to end all wars." Nor did the American Legion seek to supplant Memorial Day—in fact, the American Legion joined the older Grand Army of the Republic to support the observance of this day commemorating the fallen of the Civil War. American Legionnaires gladly marched in Memorial Day parades with the steadily shrinking number of Civil War veterans.

On November 11, 1922, President Harding returned to Arlington National Cemetery and laid a wreath at the Tomb of the Unknown Soldier, inaugurating a custom that his successors would follow. On Armistice Day (later renamed Veterans Day), presidents customarily visit the Unknown Soldier and lay a wreath at his tomb and often participate in ceremonies organized by the American Legion. Moreover, presidents often use Armistice Day to make speeches centered on themes related to issues of war, peace, and diplomacy. Franklin D. Roosevelt—the first president to make widespread use of radio to reach the American people—made several addresses to the American people on November 11.

As with all national holidays, the federal government could not dictate how different states and communities observed this day. As a result, there remained considerable variations on how different communities commemorated the occasion. In most places, the American Legion and other veterans' organizations took the lead in organizing ceremonies to mark the day. Typically, World War I veterans paraded through the downtown business districts and ended their march in front of a local memorial dedicated to World War I where ceremonies were held, featuring speeches by prominent politicians or military leaders. For instance, New York City's Armistice Day parades ended at Madison Square Park, where veterans joined city dignitaries in ceremonies before a memorial known as the Eternal Light. Besides parading, many veterans gathered together for special luncheons or dinners. Churches often marked the day by holding special memorial services that honored those who fought and died in their nation's service.

Several state governments did make Armistice Day an official holiday in the 1920s, and in some places schools, local governments, and banks were closed. In 1926, Congress passed a resolution calling on the president to issue an annual proclamation calling for the observance of Armistice Day. But, since Armistice Day was not a federal holiday until 1938, federal offices, banks, and most businesses remained open for the day. The majority of business executives and merchants rejected the wish of many veterans that businesses close in observance of Armistice Day. But one custom was widely observed by many Americans even if they toiled on the day—the two minutes of silence at the eleventh hour. It is difficult to determine the exact number of Americans who followed the custom, but it was widespread even in major cities. In New York City, the subways halted service for two minutes at the eleventh hour, and the New York Stock Exchange halted trading.

Armistice Day ceremonies typically emphasized the virtues of military service. Veterans paraded in their old uniforms and proudly displayed their decorations, often joined by units of the active-duty military. Martial tunes were the standard for most bands that participated in Armistice Day ceremonies and other programs. Orators delivering Armistice Day speeches, especially if speaking under the auspices of the American Legion, stressed the need for military preparedness in order to prevent future wars.

Despite the emphasis placed on promoting and honoring military service by those who fought in World War I, and encouraging a strong military, Armistice Day ceremonies were seldom jingoistic. Orators on Armistice Day and newspaper editorials often stressed the inhumanity of modern warfare, and the deadly destruction caused by chemical weapons, machine guns, high-explosive artillery, tanks, and fighter planes. Many of the poems read and hymns sung at Armistice Day ceremonies had a mournful air.

Some peace activists sought to focus Armistice Day ceremonies and symbols on the promotion of peace. On the first anniversary of the entombment of the Unknown Soldier—November 11, 1922—several hundred protesters in Washington, D.C. marched on the White House demanding pardons for draft resisters convicted during the war. Some sought to co-opt Armistice Day and the Tomb of the Unknown Soldier and convert them to antiwar symbols. John Haynes Holmes, pacifist minister in New York City, wrote a play during the interwar era that portrayed the Unknown Soldier condemning war from the grave.

By focusing public attention on World War I, Armistice Day served to renew debates within American society over the legacy of the war. Should the United States embrace internationalism or should American involvement in World War I be considered an aberration? In 1919, at the end of World War I, President Woodrow Wilson wanted the United States to join a new international organization—the League of Nations—in order to prevent future wars. His efforts failed, and voters decisively rejected Wilson's call to make the election of 1920 a referendum on joining the League of Nations. Still, there remained significant support for internationalism in the 1920s and 1930s. Internationalists stressed the need for the United States to take a more activist role in world affairs and embrace the League of Nations, saying that otherwise the victory achieved and commemorated on Armistice Day would be lost. After Woodrow Wilson's death in 1924, supporters of his vision of internationalism regularly gathered in Washington's National Cathedral on Armistice Day for a memorial service.

Not all Americans were convinced that the gains of World War I would be lost by failure to join the League of Nations. In the late 1920s and early 1930s, Armistice Day ceremonies conveyed optimism that World War I constituted a decisive turning point in American and even world history. Peace prevailed in Europe, and Germany had a functioning democracy under the Weimar Constitution. Although the United States had not joined the League, it did support disarmament and played a leading role in negotiating a series of treaties limiting naval forces. Newspaper editorials on Armistice Day often spoke of the progress made toward creating a peaceful world order. But this optimism would be dealt a severe blow by world events.

FROM ARMISTICE DAY TO VETERANS DAY

Over the course of the late 1930s it became increasingly apparent to observers that World War I had not been the "war to end all wars" nor had it paved the way for a more democratic world order. In 1933, the German Republic ended in the dictatorship of Adolf Hitler and the Nazi Party. By the end of the decade Hitler had reoccupied the demilitarized Rhineland, seized Austria, and successfully pressured Britain and France to allow him to seize a significant portion of the Sudetenland from Czechoslovakia. In March 1939, Hitler annexed the rest of Czechoslovakia, provoking Britain and France to affirm their opposition to any further German aggression. In the summer of 1939, Hitler threatened Poland with war. In contrast to their inaction regarding Austria and Czechoslovakia, Britain and France affirmed their commitment to defend Polish sovereignty. When Hitler's army invaded Poland on September 1, 1939, Britain and France declared war on Germany, beginning World War II.

The outbreak of World War II required that the meaning of Armistice Day be reassessed. Americans continued to pause on the eleventh hour in memory of those killed, but World War I soon came to be viewed as the harbinger of World War II. The armistice signified not the beginnings of a lasting peace, but simply a temporary truce between Germany and the Western powers.

Would America enter World War II? Initially, the American Legion voted against supporting intervention in another European war. Several prominent World War I veterans—Congressman Hamilton Fish, Chicago newspaper publisher Robert R. McCormack, and General Hugh Johnson—emerged as outspoken isolationists. In the view of many isolationists, the United States had saved Europe once but should not do it again. Others saw continuity between the struggle against German militarism in 1917 and the threat posed by Nazi Germany in 1939.

The question of American neutrality was settled on December 7, 1941 as a result of the Japanese attack on Pearl Harbor. In contrast to the situation in World War I, the Japanese decision to resolve their differences with the United States by striking directly at the U.S. military base sparked unprecedented unity within American society. Moreover, three days after the Japanese attacked American forces, Germany honored the Axis Pact with Japan and declared war on the United States. Fighting a global war required the United States to undertake a mobilization of American society that surpassed World War I in terms of the men and women under arms—over 15 million ultimately served in the armed forces. In contrast to 1917, the United States in World War II more effectively mobilized industry and labor to serve as an enormous arsenal of democracy, supplying not only the American military, but also meeting many of the needs of its Allies—Great Britain and the Soviet Union.

Why did World War II fail to produce a distinctive holiday supplanting Armistice Day? More Americans were killed in World War II, and they fought longer, and the United States along with its Allies forced the unconditional surrender of both Germany and later Japan. On hearing the news of Germany's surrender on May 8, 1945 (VE Day), joyous crowds gathered at New

York's Times Square and in countless other communities to celebrate the victory. But celebrations of this victory were subdued; most businesses and factories remained open because of the continuing struggle against the Japanese in the Pacific. Victory against Japan (VJ Day) led to celebrations that rivaled those that took place during Armistice Day a generation earlier. Although two states—Arkansas and Rhode Island—eventually made VJ Day into state holidays, there existed little support in Congress to make the day into a national holiday, this despite the fact that American involvement in World War II far overshadowed U.S. involvement in World War I.

Armistice Day might have faded as a holiday if the American Legion had closed its membership to World War II veterans. In contrast to the Grand Army of the Republic, which limited membership to Civil War veterans and thus doomed the organization to eventual extinction, the Legion ensured its survival for future generations by inviting World War II veterans to join. Not only did the American Legion welcome recent veterans into the fold, but even during the fighting overseas it lobbied Congress on their behalf and played an instrumental role in the passage of the G.I. Bill of Rights in 1944. Although most veterans of World War II never joined a veterans' organization, most of those who did affiliate became members of either the American Legion or the Veterans of Foreign Wars. Although there emerged several veterans' organizations founded by World War II veterans, most notably the more liberal American Veterans Committee, these groups never attracted a mass following among those who fought in World War II.

Even though the American Legion welcomed World War II veterans to their organization, its leadership in the 1940s and early 1950s was dominated by veterans of World War I. The American Legion wanted to preserve Armistice Day as a day of special significance tied to World War I. The same applied to both the senior civilian and military leadership of World War II who had been junior leaders in World War I. Franklin D. Roosevelt had been an Assistant Secretary of the Navy in 1917, and his wartime successor, Harry S. Truman, had served in an artillery unit in France. George Marshall, Dwight D. Eisenhower, Douglas MacArthur, George Patton, and a host of other senior officers had begun their careers prior to World War I. During one presidential press conference, former general Eisenhower mused about the special meaning Armistice Day had for his generation.

After the Armistice of 1918, the threat of war seemed distant. Following the pattern of earlier conflicts, the United States had demobilized, and the size of the armed forces shrank dramatically. This pattern did not recur after World War II, as by 1947 the United States viewed the Soviet Union, and all Communist ideology, as imminent threats to American national security. The Cold War quickly followed World War II and as a result the United States never fully demobilized from a wartime footing in the 1940s. Although the United States dramatically reduced the size of its armed forces after VJ Day, it invested heavily in the development of atomic weapons and air power to counter the Soviet conventional strength. After North Korea attacked South Korea in 1950, the United States engaged in a limited war in order to halt Communist aggression. The Korean War, coming only five years after VJ Day, ended any illusion for Americans that either World War I or II had led to an era of lasting peace. In many ways, Korea made Armistice Day an even more anachronistic holiday that needed to be recast in order to remain relevant for Americans.

In 1954 Congress, with the support of the American Legion and other veterans' groups, changed the official name of Armistice Day to Veterans Day. No longer would the holiday officially commemorate U.S. participation in World War I; it also honored the veterans of both world wars and Korea. Moreover, the recasting of Armistice Day into Veterans Day served to diminish the rituals of mourning associated with this holiday. Presidents or their representatives continued to lay wreaths at the Tomb of the Unknown Soldier, and memorial services continued to be held at the Arlington National Cemetery on this holiday. But fewer Americans paused at the eleventh hour of the day to mark the signing of the Armistice in 1918. Instead of focusing on the fallen of World War I, Veterans Day oratory and rituals honored the living veterans of the wars of the twentieth century.

In order to help further the new role of Veterans Day as a holiday honoring living veterans, the Eisenhower administration bolstered the connection of Memorial Day as time to remember the fallen servicemen and women of all wars, not simply those killed during the Civil War. In 1958, the Tomb of the Unknown Soldier—a memorial associated with World War I—became the Tomb of the Unknowns. Unknown Soldiers from both World War II and the Korean War were entombed next to the Unknown Soldier from World War I in ceremonies reminiscent of those held in 1921. Instead of entombing these Unknown Soldiers on Veterans Days, however, these ceremonies were held on Memorial Day.

VETERANS DAY AS HOLIDAY

Even with the remaking of Armistice Day into a holiday focused on veterans, there remained a marked decline in public ceremonies observing the day. In many communities the ranks of both marchers and participants thinned as Americans moved into suburbs and left behind the central cities. Television and leisure travel diminished public interest in commemorating Veterans Day, and a whole host of civic holidays. Many Americans given Veterans Day off from work often used it take an excursion out of town. Retailers viewed Veterans Day, like most holidays, as an opportunity to bolster profits by luring shoppers with holiday sales. Of course, this pattern is not unique to the post-1945 period. In the late nineteenth century, Civil War veterans bemoaned the widespread popularity of picnicking and other leisure activities on Memorial Day, and the failure of citizens to use the day to visit and place flowers on soldiers' graves. But the commercialism of Veterans Day and other holidays was accelerated by the affluence of post-1945 American Society that encouraged consumerism.

In 1968, Congress acknowledged the growing commercialism of the American holiday calendar by changing the day of the week when many holidays were observed. The Monday Holiday Act mandated that several civic holidays, including Presidents' Day, Memorial Day, and Veterans Day, be observed on a Monday instead of their traditional dates. In the case of Veterans Day, Congress directed that the holiday be commemorated on the fourth Monday of October instead of November 11. Supporters of the Monday holiday bill dominated the debate. In their view, Monday holidays would grant Americans more leisure time and encourage travel. It would benefit employees, especially those of the federal government, by diminishing the absenteeism that emerged when holidays were observed midweek. Critics complained that the shift to Monday holidays challenged tradition and argued that holidays—especially Memorial Day and Veterans Day—should stand above narrow commercialism and represent more enduring values.

After the Monday Holiday Act took effect, the American Legion, joined by other veterans' organizations, lobbied Congress to restore Veterans Day to November 11. In 1975, Congress acceded to this campaign and restored Veterans Day to its traditional date in 1978. Despite this return to tradition, memories of World War I continued to fade throughout the 1970s as the World War I generation—then in their seventies and eighties—died in increasing numbers. At the same time a new generation of veterans, who fought in America's longest war—the Vietnam War—were trying to come to grips with their own experiences.

Do rituals matter? In contrast to their World War I counterparts, most Vietnam Veterans had little interest in joining such established veterans' organizations as the American Legion or the Veterans of Foreign Wars. Vietnam Veterans of America and other groups established by Vietnam veterans never attracted a significant following among servicemen and women who served in Southeast Asia. Most Vietnam veterans went off to war not with an established unit, but as individual replacements. They came home from war when their tour of duty ended, and few received a welcome-home parade or other rituals to mark their return. Some efforts to create rituals and symbols proved unsuccessful. For instance, an Unknown Soldier from Vietnam was entombed in the Tomb of the Unknowns. In contrast to their counterparts from World War I, most Vietnam Veterans did not find the Tomb of the Unknowns an important symbol of remembrance for them. Moreover, advances in forensics led to the eventual identification of the Unknown Soldier from Vietnam, calling into question the viability of entombing Unknown Soldiers in future wars.

In a sense, Vietnam veterans wanted rituals and symbols to affirm their service. Many responded favorably in the 1980s when a number of communities staged belated welcome-home parades. In 1980 Vietnam veterans successfully lobbied Congress to authorize the construction of memorials in Washington, D.C. to memorialize their comrades who died in the conflict. The national Vietnam Memorial, known unofficially as The Wall and built entirely with private funds, was dedicated during Veterans Day weekend in 1982. Vietnam veterans from all over the country gathered in Washington, D.C. to participate in the memorial's dedication. Since 1982, the national Vietnam memorial has served as an important place for Vietnam veterans to gather, especially on Veterans Day. During the Congressional debate over changing the name of Armistice Day to Veterans Day, one Congressman observed that there were too many wars for the United States to be able to create official holidays for all of them. The ending of the Cold War in 1991 did not mean the end of American involvement in overseas wars. In 1991, the United States fought the first of two wars with Iraq. In 2003, the United States again went to war with Iraq in order to topple the government of Saddam Hussein. The recasting of Armistice Day into Veterans Day in 1954 proved prescient and recognized the reality of the country's continuing need for men and women to serve in the armed forces in times of war. In a real sense, the original vision of Armistice Day—the eradication of war—remains very distant for American society in the new century.

FURTHER READING

Dennis, Matthew. *Red, White, and Blue Letter Days: An American Calendar.* Ithaca, N.Y.: Cornell University Press, 2002.

Hatch, Jane M., ed., *The American Book of Days*, 3d ed. New York: H. W. Wilson and Company, 1978.

Litwicki, Ellen M. *America's Public Holidays, 1865–1920.* Washington, D.C.: Smithsonian Institution Press, 2000.

Pencak, William. *For God and Country: The American Legion, 1919–1941.* Boston: Northeastern University Press, 1989.

Piehler, G. Kurt. *Remembering War the American Way.* Washington, D.C.: Smithsonian Institution Press, 1995.

Schauffler, Robert Haven, ed. *The Days We Celebrate.* New York: Dodd, Mead, 1940.

G. Kurt Piehler

THANKSGIVING

- [ ] Thanksgiving is observed on the fourth Thursday in November.
- [ ] Thanksgiving days (and fasting days) originated in the turmoil of the English Reformation as the Puritans sought to eradicate the lingering practices of Catholicism in the Anglican Church.
- [ ] The Puritans brought to America the Sabbath, days of humiliation and fasting, and days of thanksgiving.
- [ ] By the end of the seventeenth century a new tradition of regular if unfixed springtime fasts and autumnal thanksgivings existed in parallel to the original practice of declaring special holidays in response to providential events.
- [ ] The fall thanksgiving became standard practice first in Connecticut by 1650 and in the other colonies by the end of the century, while spring fasts were regularized about a decade later in the same fashion.
- [ ] Henry Laurens, president of the Continental Congress, proclaimed the first national day of thanksgiving for the new United States for Thursday, December 18, 1777.
- [ ] George Washington declared his first thanksgiving as president on October 3 for Thursday, November 11, 1789, and a second national thanksgiving for Thursday, February 19, 1795.
- [ ] Thanksgiving at the beginning of the nineteenth century was an unselfconscious part of contemporary life and focused on the immediate basics of New England life: church, household, food, and domestic leisure.
- [ ] Before the Civil War (1861–65) Thanksgiving was thought of as an early winter rather than fall event and, in New England, a substitute for Christmas.
- [ ] The Pilgrims' 1621 First Thanksgiving did not exist in the popular imagination before 1841, when Rev. Alexander Young first identified the Plymouth harvest celebration as the "first New England thanksgiving" in his *Chronicles of the Pilgrim Fathers.*
- [ ] The revival of national Thanksgivings may have even begun in the Confederacy with a Thanksgiving appointed by President Davis and the Confederate Congress throughout the South on Sunday, July 28, 1861. The Union had its turn when President Lincoln declared a national Thanksgiving on Sunday, April 13, 1862.
- [ ] On October 3, 1863 Lincoln declared a general New England–style holiday for the last Thursday in November. It is this second Thanksgiving that initiated our modern series of national Thanksgivings.
- [ ] Football games became popular Thanksgiving events in the 1870s; parades entered holiday lore in the 1920s as department stores used the holiday to announce the start of the Christmas shopping season.
- [ ] By the post–World War II period, Thanksgiving was the primary focus of the Pilgrim story in popular culture.
- [ ] In 1970, the United American Indians of New England and the local Wampanoag community instituted the National Day of Mourning, an annual "counter-holiday" in answer to Thanksgiving.

THANKSGIVING

The popular perception of America's Thanksgiving holiday might be summed up as "it all began with the Pilgrims." After a successful harvest, so the story goes, Governor William Bradford declared an official thanksgiving day in November 1621 to which Massasoit, the principal sachem of the Wampanoag, was invited. The 50 or so Pilgrims who had survived the lethal "First Winter" of 1620/21, together with Massasoit and with a royal retinue of 90 men, sat down to a huge outdoor feast prepared by the Pilgrim women. The pièce de résistance was of course turkey, but every local foodstuff imaginable was included as well, thus initiating a Thanksgiving tradition of culinary excess that has continued to this day. Like similar legends, the "First Thanksgiving" has a factual basis in history. The meal, or something like it, did occur, and the attending Indian guests did join the colonists at dinner and in "recreations" over a three-day period. However, those few facts have been so embellished through art, literature, and commerce that it is the symbolic connotation of Thanksgiving, not its historical particulars, that shape our understanding of the American holiday.

MYTH OF THE "FIRST THANKSGIVING"

The "First Thanksgiving" is an etiologic tale, a story told to explain and define the holiday through an account of its supposed origins. The New England Thanksgiving is thought to have originated in 1621 with the Pilgrims, so it is fitting that the modern holiday adopt the hospitable Pilgrims and their Native

An oil painting of "The First Thanksgiving," created around 1932. Courtesy of the Library of Congress.

American guests as its symbolic patrons. Generations of artists and writers have used their stylized images to represent the holiday. Whenever we see a be-buckled Pilgrim and his natural prey, the turkey, or a generic American Indian amid the fruits of the harvest season, we are immediately put in mind of Thanksgiving. They have become an indelible part of the ideographic holiday cycle that includes babies with numerical banners, pink hearts and cupids, leprechauns and shamrocks, Easter lilies and fancy hats, Uncle Sam and fireworks, black cats and witches, Pilgrims, turkeys, Indians, and Santa Claus. In addition, the imagery of the harvest season—pumpkins, corn, autumn foliage, and the ubiquitous turkey—indelibly marks the holiday's essential seasonality. Thanksgiving plays a significant role in our civic religion as the embodiment of the virtues attributed to the early colonists (or alternately nowadays, their Native American neighbors) and as the modern equivalent to the agrarian harvest celebration.

The problem is that historically, the New England Thanksgiving evolved without any association with Pilgrim dinners, Indian guests, or harvest celebrations. The Pilgrims' 1621 First Thanksgiving did not exist in the popular imagination before 1841, when Rev. Alexander Young first identified the Plymouth harvest celebration as the "first New England thanksgiving" in his *Chronicles of the Pilgrim Fathers*. The sole account of the famous three-day celebration, described in an epistle by Pilgrim Edward Winslow, was first published in a small edition in 1622, and soon forgotten. No copy was accessible to American scholars until one was discovered in Philadelphia in 1819. Until then, all that was available was an abridged version in Samuel Purchas's *Hakluytus Posthumus or Purchas His Pilgrimes* (1625), which omitted the harvest celebration description.

Furthermore, identifying the famous Plymouth harvest festival as a thanksgiving, let alone *the* "First Thanksgiving" is problematic in that it meets none of the qualifications for a legitimate Calvinist thanksgiving. It is only after the holiday had evolved into a sentimental secular occasion in the nineteenth century that the 1621 event could be seen to resemble a New England Thanksgiving in retrospect. As historian DeLoss Love argued in 1895, "It was not a thanksgiving at all, judged by their Puritan customs, which they kept in 1621; but as we look back upon it after nearly three centuries, it seems so wonderfully like the day we love that we claim it as the progenitor of our harvest feasts." The successful 1621 harvest was indeed a matter for giving thanks, and we may assume the colonists did so in the context of their regular Sabbaths and family devotions. There is no indication in primary sources, however, that the participants considered the 1621 events a formal thanksgiving. More importantly, the very nature of a celebration, extending over several days or a week with secular "recreations" and non-Christian guests, is what pious Calvinists such as the Pilgrims would be first to declare had no place in any Christian holy day.

Far from initiating a tradition or influencing the actual evolution of the New England Thanksgiving, the 1621 harvest celebration was a unique event that had no effect on history until it was recast as a myth of Victorian invention. The American Thanksgiving holiday evolved out of English Calvinist practices quite independently of Pilgrims and harvest festivals. In fact, before the Civil War, Thanksgiving was always thought of as an early winter rather than fall event and, in New England, a substitute for Christmas. The iconography of the holiday was dominated by snowy scenes of early winter in New England with contemporary family reunions, cozy indoor dinners at ancestral homesteads, and turkey dinners. Earlier images of sleigh rides to grandfather's house and snowy farm scenes were only gradually supplanted by our familiar impression of Thanksgiving as an autumnal harvest event toward the end of the nineteenth century, at about the same time the Pilgrims were cemented in their association with the holiday.

Yet there is no denying that the story of the Pilgrims and their First Thanksgiving has played a critical role in the shaping of the modern Thanksgiving holiday. It just did not happen in quite the way that is commonly assumed. Two parallel processes are at work in the history of the American Thanksgiving holiday: the evolution of a providential Puritan holy day into a modern semi-secular American holiday, and the development of a legendary 1621 Plymouth harvest festival, to which the "First Thanksgiving" significance was assigned by posterity. When these two developments came together, our modern holiday was born—but not before.

A familiar scene of a typical American family sitting down to Thanksgiving dinner. Courtesy of Corbis.

TRANSATLANTIC ORIGINS

It is quite correct to identify the origins of today's Thanksgiving with New England. The American holiday originated in the Puritan communities of the northeast and spread from there across the nation. Memories of gathering at the meetinghouse, followed by family reunions around the festive table, were treasured by generations of expatriate Yankees and shared with their new neighbors throughout the rest of the country. To comprehend the true origins of the holiday, however, we must look first across the Atlantic. Thanksgiving may have developed most fully in the New World, but it was not born in America. It came from England as a part of the mental baggage of every Puritan colonist. Thanksgiving's origins were rooted in the early Puritan practices of providential holy days, and the holiday—with its dour twin, Fast Day—was fully mature before the English settlers supposedly stepped on Plymouth Rock.

Thanksgiving days originated in the turmoil of the English Reformation as the Puritans sought to eradicate the lingering practices of Catholicism in the Anglican Church. One of the many complaints about medieval Christianity during the Reformation was the inordinate number of holidays that had been introduced over the centuries. Until Henry VIII began the work of reform, there were, including Sundays, 147 religious holidays each year. They included not only the Christological cycle of Christmas, Easter, Whitsuntide, and the feasts of the Virgin, but an ever-increasing number of saints' days. No work was allowed on these days, even at crucial times of the agricultural year such as planting or harvest. Not only could people earn nothing during their holidays, but the traditional celebrations were costly in food and drink, decorations for churches, processions, and the like. The medieval world of wakes, guild celebrations, church-ales, and bride-ales (an "ale" being a sort of drinking party celebrating an event or acting as a fund-raiser in support of some cause) had become more of a burden than a blessing. These festivals also contributed to the "beery buffoonery, bawdiness, idleness and profanity" of a susceptible portion of the populace. It was pragmatism as well as piety that influenced the reformers to limit the holidays that threatened people's livelihoods, stopped craft production, endangered the food supply, and encouraged drunkenness and violent behavior.

Henry VIII's 1536 reforms reduced the number of holidays to the Sabbath and a more manageable 27 festival days a year. The old "evens" or evenings preceding holidays were transformed into times of fasting rather than carousing, a reform that was brought to New England. In addition, the harvest season of July 1 through September 29 (Michaelmas) was set aside as a time when work took precedence over church and tavern. This solved the practical problems while leaving plenty of time for religious and social needs. However, the growing numbers of Puritans in England were not satisfied. They questioned the fundamental justification for the holidays, declaring them to be "Popish inventions" that were not only unsupported by scripture but of obvious pagan origin. The Puritan faction first demanded that the number of festivals be reduced to the primary celebrations of Christ's life and the Sabbath, and no more. When this did not happen, the reformers became more radical after the example of John Calvin of Geneva, who had gradually arrived at the opinion that only the Sabbath was permissible. Reformers sought to abolish all of the remaining old holidays including Christmas and Easter. However, there was another influence at work that would eventually modify this extreme constraint.

There arose a custom among the Reformed churches of declaring special days in response to God's providence whenever unexpected disasters or special benefits to society occurred. The English Church declared such days on a national basis from time to time so that appropriate observations might be held in each parish, or as was customary, people from several parishes gathered at officially sanctioned central assemblies. The assembled faithful were treated to pertinent sermons, communion, and admonitions to wrongdoers, whereupon the entire company might close the day with an evening community meal (fast days officially extended from afternoon to afternoon, so an evening meal on the day itself was quite acceptable). In addition to nationwide observances, fast and thanksgivings days might be observed by individual congregations or even by private families, depending on the nature of the providential event. Fasting became a regular practice not only in response to providence, but in preparation for any important decision or momentous occurrence. As good Protestants they wanted to avoid the "empty practice" or mechanical observance of the Roman Church, where corporal abstinence might not be accompanied by earnest spiritual activity, so not only abstinence and prayers, but psalms, preaching, and even "prophesy" (informal commenting on theological matters) soon slipped into the mix.

Authorities announced fasts whenever it was felt that God had visited some unusually threatening or dangerous "judgment" on His people. Similarly, these same authorities declared thanksgivings to celebrate some impressive "mercy" awarded by God to his grateful flock. Consequently, fasts were held in response to drought in 1611, floods in 1613, and the plague in 1604 and 1625, while thanksgivings were declared for the victory over the Spanish Armada in 1588 and for the queen's safe deliverance in 1605. These special observances were normally included as part of the usual church services on Sunday, Wednesday, or Friday, and had appropriate services in the *Book of Common Prayer* and the orthodox Anglican liturgy. There were exceptions to the rule, as in case of the Fifth of November, a special day set apart to give thanks for the deliverance of King James and his government in 1605. The Fifth of November—popularly called "Gunpowder Plot" "Guy Fawkes Day," or (in America) "Pope's Day"— was an anomaly in that it became an annual thanksgiving and was adopted by the Puritan faction as their most significant national commemoration. Ironically, there was no biblical support for an annual thanksgiving of this sort, a fact that some Anglicans were pleased to point out. An essential quality of God's special providences was that they were unique and unpredictable. Having an annual thanksgiving flew in the face of Puritan theory by presuming to predict or take for granted God's unrevealed will.

The Puritan holidays also served as a regulatory device whereby the nation, community, or family adjusted its behavior so as to stay aligned with God's will and remain in divine favor. Thanksgivings praised God for his goodness and made sure that his people's gratitude was made evident. Providential "mercies" were seen as signs that he was pleased with his people while "judgments" with their attendant calamities were believed to be sent by God to mark his displeasure with the way things were going. Days of humiliation or fasts were used to identify the reasons for God's displeasure and to put the community back on track when it strayed from the path of righteousness. They served the Puritan establishment as a means of controlling the behavior of the community in God's name, and maintaining the rule of the godly against its enemies and malcontents. If unregenerate individuals were guilty of grievous sins and flouting God's commandments, he would punish the whole community. It became the responsibility of the godly therefore to see that these sinners were discovered and punished so that the community's relationship with God could be repaired. This allowed the Puritan leaders considerable discretion in rooting out and punishing wrongdoers, and insuring that their neighbors conformed to their stringent system of law and morality. It was this tradition of providential holidays, in which fasts and thanksgivings were key elements in maintaining God's presumed will on Earth, that the Puritan migrations carried to New England.

The Puritans brought to America the Sabbath, days of humiliation and fasting, and days of thanksgiving. The Sabbath set the basic pattern of how religious days were observed. The faithful were commanded to prepare for the Sabbath on the "eve" or Saturday afternoon at 3:00 (the hour of Christ's death) with family devotions and prayers. The Massachusetts Bay Company's directors sent specific instructions to Governor John Endicott in April 1629: "And to the end the Sabbath may be celebrated in a religious manner, we appoint that all that inhabit the Plantation, both for the general and particular employments, may surcease their labor every Saturday throughout the year at three of the clock in the afternoon; and that they spend the rest of that day in catechizing and preparation for the Sabbath, as the ministers shall direct." They made sure that meals and other necessary labors such as feeding livestock were so arranged as to involve the least amount of effort on the day itself. On Sunday morning, they went to church at around 8:30 A.M. and remained there the whole day, with a short break at midday, listening to sermons, singing psalms, listening to exhortations to live more godly lives, and participating in other uplifting spiritual exercises. Fast days and thanksgivings, which were similarly observed, were two sides of the same providential coin. Normal work was forbidden, as were sports and other worldly pastimes.

PROVIDENTIAL HOLIDAYS IN EARLY NEW ENGLAND

The first documented providential holiday in New England was a fast day declared during a serious drought in Plymouth Colony in the summer of 1623. When the colonists began planting their fields in April, the weather was favorable and seasonable. Six weeks after the final sowing, however, drought threatened both the crops and the very existence of the little settlement. Edward Winslow, one of the settlers, recalled:

> But it pleased God, for our further chastisement, to send a great drought; insomuch as in six weeks after the latter setting there scarce fell any rain; so that the stalk of that [which] was first set, began to send forth the ear before it came to half growth; and that which was later [set], not likely to yield us any [corn] at all, both the blade and the stalk hanging the head in such a manner as we judged it utterly dead. Our beans also ran not up, according to their wonted manner, but stood at a stay; many being parched away, as though they had been scorched

before the fire. Now were our hopes overthrown; and we discouraged: our joy being turned into mourning.

The previous year's harvest had not been good. If the approaching harvest failed as well, Plymouth Colony might not survive another year. The colonists met in hope that by humbling themselves before God, they would gain his mercy and be able to carry on in New England for "his glory and our good." The day of fasting and humiliation—"appointed by public authority, and set apart from all other employments"—was held on a Wednesday, most probably July 16, 1623.

The skies were clear when they gathered for public worship. They spent eight or nine hours together in the meetinghouse, praying, singing psalms, and listening to sermons and exhortations. When they came out, they were gratified to see that it had clouded over. The next morning "soft, sweet and moderate showers" began, which continued off and on for the next two weeks. The wilted corn and their drooping spirits were revived, and the crops saved. The Indians noticed the providential rescue of the crops. Hobbomock was a Wampanoag *Pniese* (superior warrior and counselor) who lived near the English settlement. As Winslow related, Hobbomock noticed that the colonists were having a religious service in midweek only three days after their previous one and asked a boy why they were doing so. When the gentle and effective rains came the very next day, Hobbomock told the neighboring Indians about the impressive power of the white man's god who had "wrought so great a change in so short a time."

The Plymouth colonists were no less impressed by this providential mercy. Having so dramatic an example of God's favor and acceptance, they felt they should do something substantial to show their gratitude and not "smother up the same" or "content ourselves with private thanksgiving for that which by private prayer could not be obtained." They therefore declared that another solemn day be set apart and appointed for the glory, honor, and praise, with all thankfulness, to God. This first recorded Plymouth thanksgiving probably occurred on Wednesday, July 30, the day before the *Anne* arrived in Plymouth with friends from England and Holland.

In this single two-week period we have the first examples of the Puritan providential holidays in New England. Even Puritans needed some ritual in their lives. One question that might arise is why they waited until 1623 to declare a fast and a thanksgiving when there had been plenty of earlier events that could have justified such observations. The simple answer is that we do not know that they didn't have earlier fasts or thanksgivings. But if they did, no reliable record of them has survived. However, the very early years are recorded in sufficient detail by Bradford and Winslow that it is quite unlikely that an official proposal for a public thanksgiving has been omitted.

The Massachusetts Bay colonists brought the same tradition of providential holidays as their Plymouth compatriots. During the 1629 emigration they held two fast days at sea, a thing that the sailors said that they had never heard of before. The first was close to the beginning of the voyage on Thursday, May

21. After weeks of contrary winds they had finally cleared the English Channel and were well at sea. Following the practice of having a fast to ask God to look favorably on their momentous enterprise, they observed a day of humiliation. One of the passengers, Rev. Francis Higginson, reported:

> Thursday, there being two ministers in the ship, Mr. Smith and myself, we endeavored, together with others, to consecrate the day as a solemn fasting and humiliation to Almighty God, as a furtherance of our present work. And it pleased God the ship was becalmed all day, so we were freed from any encumbrance. And as soon as we had done prayers (see and behold the goodness of God) about seven o'clock at night the wind turned to north-east, and we had a fair gale that night as manifest evidence of the Lord's hearing our prayers.

The passengers held a second fast for favorable winds on Tuesday, June 2, which they believed met with immediate results. After they arrived, they observed a third fast on Thursday, August 6, preceding their choice and ordination of elders and deacons for the new church.

This pattern recurred with the larger Winthrop fleet in 1630, when the passengers held fasts five times: Friday, April 2; Friday, April 23 (St. George's Day); Friday, May 21 (with regard to the weather); Friday, June 4; and Monday, June 7 (when they caught some very welcome fresh fish). They had their first thanksgiving on Thursday, July 8, 1630, following the arrival of the last straggling ship. Interestingly, the Winthrop company selected Friday, the orthodox Anglican day for fasting, while the Higginson and Plymouth groups chose Wednesday and Thursday dates.

When colonists from Dorchester settled Connecticut in 1635 (pushing out traders from Plymouth who had gotten there first) and New Haven in 1637, the tradition of providential holidays also came to the new colonies. The first occasion for a providential holiday in Connecticut was the successful conclusion (from a colonial point of view) of the Pequot War in 1637. The war and the terrible massacre at the Mystic village was the result of events stirred up by Massachusetts Bay and its Connecticut settlements for which the unfortunate Pequots got the blame. The Puritan colonies were immensely heartened by the "victory" and declared a day of thanksgiving and praise for October 12, 1637, which was observed in Massachusetts, and in Scituate in Plymouth Colony as well. This event has sometimes been misidentified as the "first New England thanksgiving" by modern critics of the early colonists. It was the first Connecticut thanksgiving, however, and was followed by other fast and thanksgiving days after the manner of the other Puritan colonies.

We know about the Plymouth colony celebration of the 1637 thanksgiving at Scituate through Rev. John Lothrop's church records for Scituate and Barnstable (where Lothrop and his congregation moved in 1639). These brief records shed valuable light on how fasts and thanksgivings might be declared by an individual congregation, as opposed to "public" providential days commanded for the entire colony by the civil magistrates. The Lothrop records also provide a unique glimpse of what took place at the earliest New England thanksgivings.

Lothrop's records begin in 1634 before the Scituate church had been formally covenanted. The potential congregation met for a fast on November 6, 1634 at James Cudworth's house, and had another fast on Christmas day before they were joined in a covenant on January 8—during yet another fast. Altogether, the church observed 34 days of humiliation and fasting but only nine thanksgivings days between 1634 and 1653. The first Scituate thanksgiving was on December 22, 1636,

> in ye Meetinghouse, beginning some halfe an houre before nine & continued untill after twelve a clocke, ye day beeing very cold, beginning with a short prayer, then a psalme sang, then more large in prayer, after that an other Psaleme, & then the Word taught, after that prayer—& the[n] a psalme,—Then makeing merry to the creatures, the poorer sort beeing invited of the richer.

The next thanksgiving on October 12, 1637 was

> performed much in the same manner aforesaid, mainly for these tow particulars. 1. Ffor the victory over the pequouts, ye 2. Ffor Reconciliation betwixt Mr. Cotton and the other ministers.

The third thanksgiving was the congregation's first at Barnstable on December 11, 1639:

> att Mr. Hull's house, for Gods exceeding mercye in bringing us hither Safely keeping us healthy & well in o[u]r weake beginnings & in our church Estate. The day beeing very cold o[u]r praises to God in publicke being ended, wee devided into 3 companies to feast togeather, some att Mr. Hulls, some att Mr [Mayo's], some att Brother Lumberds senior.

These brief descriptions are the only Plymouth Colony examples of how thanksgiving feasts were conducted in the early seventeenth century.

By 1640, the Puritan holidays were established in every New England colony except Rhode Island. Providential holidays might be declared both by the churches and by civic officials, and Plymouth, Massachusetts, Connecticut, New Haven, and New Hampshire passed laws determining the responsibility of civic authorities to declare public fasts and thanksgivings. There was an apparent aversion to *official* colony-wide fasts and thanksgivings in Rhode Island, and the only examples on record are those that the colony was obliged to observe during the period of the Dominion of New England (1686–1689) when Sir Edmund Andros commanded thanksgivings and fasts for all of the colonies, starting with a thanksgiving on Thursday, December 1, 1687. Andros's subsequent two thanksgivings were on Sundays in the Anglican tradition, which was a bitter pill for the New Englanders. After Andros was deposed in 1689, the colonies returned to their earlier practices, and Rhode Island lapsed back into avoiding colony-wide providential days altogether.

Second and third generation New Englanders, who had no personal memories of the old holiday calendar of Christmas, Easter, and saint's days, grew up with fasts and thanksgivings as familiar parts of their lives, and this familiarity eventually led to modifications in practice. By the end of the seventeenth century a new tradition of regular springtime fasts and autumnal thanksgivings existed in parallel to the original practice of declaring special holidays in response to providential events. The New Englanders made scheduled regularity the basis for seasonal celebrations. Orthodox Puritans such as Samuel Sewell objected to the liberties being taken with the old providential rules ("T'was not fit upon meer Generals as the Mercies of the year to com[m]and a thanksgiving"), but they were overruled by the majority.

The new regular thanksgivings and fast days did not begin in one colony and spread to the others but rather evolved simultaneously throughout the region. There was no single "First Annual Thanksgiving" or "First Annual Fast Day" that started an unbroken tradition for succeeding generations. According to DeLoss Love, the fall thanksgiving became standard practice first in Connecticut by 1650 and in the other colonies by the end of the century, while spring fasts were regularized about a decade later in the same fashion. Although the vernal fast generally occurred between February and May and the autumnal thanksgiving between October and December, the precise days were not legally established events like our modern holidays. People still waited for the exact dates to be announced each year. There might be no thanksgiving at all in years when conditions were as grim as they were during King Philip's War, but otherwise the annual holidays might be confidently anticipated in their seasons each year.

Eighteenth-century practice combined the old occasional holidays with the new seasonal ones in such a manner as to make it seem that it had always been done that way. By the middle of the century, New Englanders were so used to annual days that they tended to believe that such days had been customary throughout the history of the colonies. Colonial historian and royal governor of Massachusetts Thomas Hutchinson wrote that the early settlers" constantly, every spring, appointed a day for fasting and prayer to implore the divine blessings upon their affairs in the ensuing year, and in the fall, a day of thanksgiving and public acknowledgement of the favors conferred upon them in the year past. … It has continued without interruption, I suppose, in any one instance, down to this day." De Loss Love notes that Hutchinson was wrong about the interruptions, and that he had not carefully examined the evidence. Oral tradition minimized the irregular observances and doctrinal disputes that the holidays had undergone in becoming annual, presenting an idealized past that contributed to later belief that there had always been a November thanksgiving.

FEAST AND FAST IN THE EARLY REPUBLIC

Providential holidays were not limited to the more puritanical colonies. During the eighteenth century, Rhode Island and Vermont also appointed fasts and thanksgivings, while New York, Pennsylvania, New Jersey, Delaware, and even Virginia had their own occasional fasts or thanksgivings. The American Revolution brought the observance of the providential holidays to a national level when Congress declared fasts and thanksgivings for the entire 13 colonies. On June 12, 1775, the president of the Continental Congress, John Hancock, declared a fast day in the United Colonies for Thursday, July 20. Hancock announced another all-colony fast for Friday, May 17, 1776. Henry Laurens, subsequent president of the Continental Congress, proclaimed the first thanksgiving for the new United States for Thursday, December 18, 1777. This thanksgiving followed the New England model, with its Thursday date and Puritan-style admonition in the proclamation:

> And it is further recommended, That servile Labor, and such Recreation, as, though at other Times innocent, may be unbecoming the Purpose of this Appointment, be omitted on so solemn an Occasion.

There were 12 additional providential holidays declared by the Continental Congress for the nation by the end of the war.

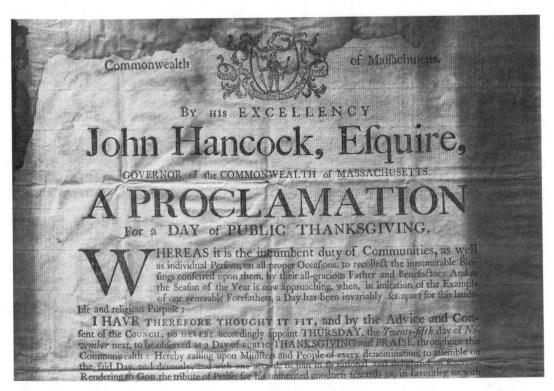

A detail of a historic document, dating from 1790, of John Hancock proclaiming Thursday, November 25, "to be observed as a Day of Public Thanksgiving and Praise." © AP / Wide World Photos.

George Washington declared his first thanksgiving as president on October 3 for Thursday, November 11, 1789, and a second national thanksgiving for Thursday, February 19, 1795. John Adams declared no thanksgivings during his term, but announced two fast days; Wednesday May 9, 1798, and Thursday April 25, 1799. James Madison proclaimed wartime fast days for Thursday August 20, 1812; Thursday September 9, 1813; and Thursday, January 12, 1815. Madison also declared the last national providential holiday before the Civil War: a thanksgiving for the conclusion of the War of 1812 on Thursday April 13, 1815. In between the national holidays, the New England states continued holding their regular spring, fall, and occasional providential days. In the years that followed 1815, all of the New England states including Rhode Island, Vermont (after 1777) and Maine (after 1820) maintained the spring fast and fall thanksgiving tradition.

In the early nineteenth century, the annual fast day receded in importance even as the autumn thanksgiving gained in popularity. As the New England Puritans became Yankees during the eighteenth century, the rigors of daylong services and four- or five-hour sermons diminished until a single two-hour morning service sufficed in many churches. Austere Calvinist religion, and the days of fasting and humiliation that embodied that view to the fullest, held few attractions for Americans in the emerging age of sentimentality. Providential fasts in response to dramatic calamities such as assassinations or disasters were declared from time to time into the twentieth century, but the annual fast was sustained more by custom than public enthusiasm. Many people avoided the church services and enjoyed a day off from work for their own secular purposes. Henry Ward Beecher observed in *Norwood or Village Life in New England* (1867) that "while starved Fast-day, like a consumptive moon, grew pale, and thin, and wasted away, every year dying, and yet clinging tenaciously to life, the well-fed Thanksgiving-day, like a new moon, grew bright and round, and lay upon the year's horizon like a joyful pumpkin upon the ridges of a Yankee corn field."

In Massachusetts, the annual fast was traditionally held on or about the nineteenth of April before it was abolished in 1894, and April 19 became Patriot's Day. Maine replaced Fast Day with Patriot's Day in 1907. The New Hampshire annual fast day lasted until 1991 when it became "Civil Rights Day." In 1999, this compromise holiday was joined with Martin Luther King Jr. Day on the third Monday in January, with the stipulation that the new holiday has "the same status as Fast Day." The annual fast was combined with the observance of Good Friday in Connecticut in 1795, where it is still observed today, the last of the New England states to do so.

After the national thanksgivings ceased in 1815, annual thanksgivings proclaimed by the individual states maintained the holiday tradition. There was still no fixed date for these annual events, a holdover from Puritan providentialism, but most were scheduled in late November or early December. Each year, the date was announced by civil authority. The state governor "advised" the churches by official proclamation of the date when they should observe the holiday. By the 1850s virtually every state and territory observed an annual thanksgiving.

The inhabitants of the states of course anticipated the announcement of their particular Thursday in November or December. Once the proclamation had been published and read in the churches, the flurry of preparation began. Housewives made pies days—even weeks—in advance, depending on cool seasonal temperatures for their safe preservation. On the evening before the day itself, all chores that could be done in advance were taken care of to make possible a day of relative leisure. On the farms (and the majority of New Englanders were still farmers) animals were foddered, the house cleaned, and fowls plucked for the next day's cooking. In town, householders visited the market to bargain for the necessary ingredients of the feast.

A brief supper ("a sort of 'picked-up' dinner") was provided the evening before for the family and guests who had arrived earlier. The holiday was a time of gathering as family, friends and neighbors met at church and in the homes of the community, just as they had in Scituate almost two centuries earlier. However, there was seldom any discouragement of secular entertainment, especially if it did not occur during the morning of the day itself. Thanksgiving balls were quite a popular addition to the holiday. Another custom found on the North Shore of Massachusetts was the Thanksgiving Eve visit by poor people (especially Revolutionary War veterans) to more well-off households to ask for charity, which were met with gifts of food supplies such as flour, rice, or the like. Children used the occasion to dress up in ragged clothes and pretend to be needy petitioners as a prank.

Thanksgiving Day itself began with the household getting up at dawn, which at that time of year meant they arrived for breakfast rather later than they would on a work day. After breakfast, the cooking of the dinner was begun and family members prepared for meeting (one went to "meeting," not to "church," in New England). Not everyone went to meeting, however, as someone had to oversee the preparations for the feast, and the youngest children were not expected to attend the service. The sheer amount of labor involved in preparing the huge dinner for family and assorted guests was a burden to housewives and servants alike, as Mrs. Anne Lyman noted in a rare departure from the generally rosy reminiscences of the old-time holiday in 1840:

> We got through Thanksgiving as usual,—after a great struggle on my part—with fifteen at the table, who seemed to enjoy themselves highly—I did not. I am sure, however, that I have much to rejoice in … But the reflections connected with the past most always make these annual festivals, to people who are as advanced as I am, to be days of sad retrospection.

The meetinghouse bell began to ring at ten o'clock and soon after the congregation arrived and sorted themselves into family pews. Attendance varied from year to year depending on the weather and the enthusiasm of the meeting-goers. In 1800, although meeting attendance was still expected of any respectable citizen, only one in 15 Americans was an actual member of a congregation. Most churches had only a "forenoon" meeting, with the standard order of service. Thanksgiving sermons were often political or topical in nature; the sermon's length being determined by the aspirations of the minister and the expectations of his audience. Although organs were still a rarity, instrumental music was very popular at the beginning of the nineteenth century. In addition, the meeting's choir and congregation sang psalms and hymns. An important part of the Thanksgiving service was the collection for the poor—which might have been begun the week before—with the proceeds given to the less well-off families to ensure that they too would have a proper dinner. The conventional charity of the season also included gifts of prepared food sent to poor relations and neighbors not included in the household gathering.

When the morning service was over at noon or one o'clock, families and guests returned to their homes to await dinner, which was usually served at two or three o'clock. Predictably, turkey was the foundation of the feast, but it also included chicken pie, roast beef, the various vegetables available to New Englanders in November or December, pies and puddings, and ended with dried fruits and nuts. Cider (which was always alcoholic) and wine were commonly served before the temperance movement organized its challenge to this custom. Children in some families might eat separately from the adults. Thanksgiving was not a child's holiday, as much as they might enjoy it, but one in which adult activities such as games and dancing included the younger members of the family. After dinner, the company gathered for various pastimes such as games, conversation, songs, story telling or visits to other households. There was a supper later on, if desired. The more pious households kept up the older tradition of a discussion of the sermon followed by fireside prayers, and most families had some sort of prayer at the end of the short late-autumn evening. Schools were often closed for the entire week, and the following Friday was sometimes enjoyed as a day off from work as well.

The most significant characteristic of Thanksgiving at the beginning of the nineteenth century, however, was that it was still an unselfconscious part of contemporary life. Holiday traditions were simple and unpretentious, focusing on the immediate basics of New England life: church, household, food, and domestic leisure. It was a time to review the current year, reminisce about one's personal past, and recall family members and friends who were no longer among the guests by reason of distance or death. Most importantly, it carried no suggestion of commemoration. The holiday was not perceived as an evocation of olden times or invested with sentimental significance beyond its gathering of clans and family reminiscences, when "conversations run backwards" as Plymouth author Abby Morton Diaz said. Rather, it was simply unquestioned tradition, the accepted thing to do at each year's end.

After 1820, New England society shifted from intellectual Calvinism to emotional evangelicalism, from living on farms to life in factory towns, and replacing homespun virtue with commercial consumption. As historian John R. Gillis wrote about the succeeding generations who made Thanksgiving their own, "The Victorians—or more specifically, the Protestant middle classes—were the first to experience the pastness of the past." The example of the passing Revolutionary generation now became the touchstone for appropriate holiday behavior, and nostalgia began to suffuse Thanksgiving sentiments. The rising generations would soon locate the archetypal Thanksgiving in an idyllic and unrecoverable past, evoking the celebrations of the colonial and early national era to give the holiday a sentimental historical atmosphere quite unlike the immediacy it had enjoyed earlier.

The adoption of the above-described Thanksgiving customs outside of New England was in part a result of the great Yankee exodus that occurred after the American Revolution. The war had brought debilitating debt and inflation to the small New England farmers and shopkeepers, a burden compounded by high state taxes by which local governments tried to recover from the same problems. A steady flow of Yankee emigrants passed into northern New York, the Northwest Territory, and beyond, bringing with them all of the particular attitudes and traditions of their old home region. In new states with large numbers of Yankee expatriates (such as Michigan or Wisconsin), annual Thanksgivings were soon introduced. By mid-century the Thanksgiving holiday was observed in most states and territories, even southern ones, although southerners might follow the older Anglican practice of Sunday thanksgiving services instead of the Yankee custom of the Thursday observation. Thursday had been the day that Plymouth Colony and Massachusetts Bay traditionally held thanksgivings. In both Boston and Plymouth, Thursday was both market day and "Lecture day," when a special sermon might be delivered in churches on some topic of current interest.

CREATING A NATIONAL HOLIDAY

The revival of national Thanksgivings may have even begun in the Confederacy. The heartening victory at Bull Run in 1861 was celebrated with a Thanksgiving appointed by President Davis and the Confederate Congress throughout the South on Sunday, July 28. The northern states had little to celebrate in 1861, although the individual states and territories declared customary November Thanksgivings. The Union had its turn when President Lincoln declared a national Thanksgiving on Sunday, April 13, 1862 (on the 47th anniversary of the 1815 event) for the victories at Forts Henry and Donelson and at Shiloh. The South had a second and final Thanksgiving on Sunday, September 28, 1862 after the second battle of Bull Run. In 1863, the Union celebrated *two* national

Thanksgivings, one on Thursday, August 6 following the victory at Gettysburg, and on October 3 Lincoln declared a second, general New England–style holiday for the last Thursday in November. It is this second Thanksgiving that initiated our modern series of national Thanksgivings.

Perhaps the 1863 November Thanksgiving was due in part to the efforts of Sarah Josepha Hale, editor of the influential *Godey's Lady's Book* magazine. Mrs. Hale, a loyal New Englander despite having moved to Philadelphia, had lobbied hard for an annual national thanksgiving since 1837. She wrote editorials and other notices in favor of this idea (sometimes twice in a year) and tried to rally all the states to observe the holiday. In 1854 she stated that her objective was a nationwide observance:

> from Maine to Mexico, from Plymouth Rock to Sunset Sea, the hymn of thanksgiving should be simultaneously raised, as the pledge of brotherhood in the enjoyment of God's blessings during the year. How this national festival can be made sure, we must leave to those who have the guidance of public affairs; but we do earnestly desire to see the *last Thursday in November* become the fixed time for this American jubilee.

Although Mrs. Hale continued to extol the annual appearance of the holiday tradition, she also wanted Thanksgiving to be established once and for all by the U.S. government, a dream best expressed by her editorial in *Godey's* in 1871:

> We have long endeavored to secure the celebration of this great festival upon the same day in every American State and Territory, so that it might be a National Holiday. In 1863 the Southern States could not be reached. Application was made to President Lincoln, who issued a proclamation, the first since that of Washington from the representative of the nation, and appointing the same day, the last Thursday of November. His example has been yearly followed by his successors. But one thing is wanting. It is eminently fit that this National Holiday shall rest upon the same legal basis as its companions, the Twenty-second of February [George Washington's birthday] and the Fourth of July. As things now stand, our Thanksgiving is exposed to the chances of the time. Unless the President or the Governor of the State in office happens to see fit, no day is appointed for its observance. Is not this a state of things which calls for instant remedy? Should not our festival be assured to us by law?

By the end of the century, the custom of holding Thanksgiving on the last Thursday in November was well established, but the legal mandate that Mrs. Hale so desired did not arrive until long after her death. In 1939, the last Thursday in November was also the last day of the month. A Thanksgiving this close to Christmas would considerably shorten the customary shopping season. President Roosevelt was petitioned by merchants to declare an earlier date for Thanksgiving to insure the commercial success of the crucial holiday shopping season. On October 31, the president proclaimed Thursday, November 23, as the national day of Thanksgiving. The result was a storm of protest.

A majority of Americans were dismayed by the apparent victory of commerce over tradition—not to mention the confusion that this change had on college football schedules. Some governors and mayors followed the president's lead while others chose to keep the 30th as Thanksgiving in protest. In the end, 23 states had Thanksgiving on the 23rd, 23 held out for the 30th, and two (Texas and Colorado) celebrated two Thanksgivings that year. A similar division occurred in 1940 when many states kept their holiday on November 28 despite the fact that Roosevelt had declared the 21st as Thanksgiving. In the spring of 1941, the president admitted that the effort had been a mistake (and a failure as well—there had been no improvement in Christmas sales, perhaps due to the confusion) and announced that Thanksgiving would revert to its traditional date in 1942. It was too late for 1941, calendars and schedules already having been prepared. In November 1941, Congress passed a law mandating the fourth Thursday in November as the permanent date for the Thanksgiving holiday. This was a compromise between the old "last Thursday" custom and the recent "Franksgiving" observances. After the few holdouts gave up their attempts to observe the day on the last Thursday regardless of legal date, the Thanksgiving holiday quietly assumed its place in the regular round of American holidays. The holiday was at last as Mrs. Hale had wished, nationally guaranteed and legally sanctified.

SPORTS AND PARADES

Entertainment had always been an important part of the holiday tradition, either as family activities or with community-wide participation. Even before the Civil War, the firemen of New York had held "public reviews" and militia companies conducted parades and turkey shoots, followed by the very popular Thanksgiving balls. But while the firm hand of tradition kept the basic essentials of the holiday true to their nostalgic roots, new elements were introduced as well, the most important being the annual college football game.

In the 1870s stories and illustrations of football games joined stories about family dinners in the popular press each November as Thanksgiving embraced its new sporting tradition. Just as the earlier winter associations were being replaced with idyllic harvest scenes, the spectator sport of college football supplanted earlier hunting expeditions or turkey shoots. Colleges had played casual soccer-style football since the 1860s, but the beginning of the modern American game came in 1876, when Harvard adopted rugby football rules in games against McGill. Also in that year, the student-run Intercollegiate Football Association initiated annual Thanksgiving Day games between the year's two leading college football teams. The "showdown" games became wildly popular; in 1891 *Harper's Weekly* could report that

There may be some who like family dinners; and there are other wicked ones who sympathize with the young woman who assented to having a family dinner by saying, 'Yes, and let us have any other family but our own.' It may not be so everywhere, but around New York city, ... a great and powerful and fascinating rival has come to take the place of the Thanksgiving day

The cover of a 1949 issue of *The New Yorker* depicts a family sitting down to Thanksgiving dinner, all intently watching football on television. Courtesy of the Library of Congress.

dinner[:] the Thanksgiving Day Game. And now everyone goes out to see Princeton and Yale decide the football championship instead of boring each other around the dinner table.

The next important holiday event emerged in the 1920s: the Thanksgiving Day parade. Strictly speaking, Thanksgiving parades are not about Thanksgiving at all but about Christmas, but they do provide a Thanksgiving Day activity that is enjoyed by millions of Americans in person or on television. Initiated by downtown department stores to signal the "official" start of the Christmas shopping season, the parades became a family-oriented event that were very popular in those cities that supported them. There had been earlier parades on Thanksgiving in the nineteenth century, but these were the informal marches by groups of "Anticks" or "Fantastics" who also paraded at Christmas, New Years, Washington's Birthday, and the Fourth of July. Historian Elizabeth Pleck discovered that

> In New York City and Philadelphia, the Fantastics held elaborate parades, enlisting other groups and marching bands. In the late nineteenth century in lower Manhattan the event began at the call of a horn. Costumed men staggered out of sallons where they had been given free drinks. They mounted horses and carts for their parade. Along the way they would stop briefly to blow a horn into the ears of women spectators crowded along the sidewalks. At the end of the parade they feasted on turkey and drink at an afternoon picnic, where fistfights often broke out. The evening ball that followed went on until the early morning.

These parades were accompanied by children dressed in crude costumes who begged for money in the manner of those of North Shore Massachusetts.

The first modern Thanksgiving parade was put on by Gimbel Brothers Department Store in Philadelphia on November 25, 1920. It consisted of 50 people, 15 cars, and a fireman dressed as Santa Claus who marched in the parade and then entered Gimbel's toy department by a ladder. The central feature of the Gimbel's Thanksgiving Parade was the "official arrival of Santa Claus" in his most marketable guise as patron saint of holiday commerce. The theme of children and toys was central to the early Thanksgiving parades, with many of the floats and costumed characters designed to represent nursery rhyme and fairy tale settings. The Thanksgiving parade instituted by J. L. Hudson's Department Store in Detroit in 1924 was based on nursery rhyme and fairy tale themes with floats featuring The Old Lady Who Lived in a Shoe and Mother Goose herself. The most famous Thanksgiving parade of all also began in 1924, when the employees of Macy's Department Store volunteered to conduct a parade of costumed characters in New York. Now billed as "America's Parade," the Macy's parade has grown over the years into a spectacular media event and a continually changing mirror of popular culture. The first Macy's parade, in which the predominantly immigrant employees marched six miles down Manhattan from 145th Street to 34th Street, featured Santa Claus and Mother Goose, 35 clowns, and animals borrowed from the Central Park Zoo. It finished as the Gimbel's parade had with Santa, entering the toy department via a ladder.

The way in which Americans observed the Thanksgiving holiday changed little after the Civil War except for the inclusion of football and parades. What did change was the way in which the holiday's symbolic significance was interpreted in popular culture. Thanksgiving was joined with other holidays in the school-year cycle in the 1890s. Concerned progressives seized the opportunity to use holidays as a means to inculcate American values in the socialization of

Macy's Thanksgiving Day Parade in New York City, 2004. © AP / Wide World Photos.

the young and of immigrants. In 1907, an anthology of Thanksgiving literature for use in schools was published in the Robert H. Schauffler series of American holidays with a historical essay by May Lowe on the "First" and subsequent thanksgivings, and the appropriate chapter from the popular novel *Standish of Standish* was reprinted. As Elizabeth Pleck cogently observes,

School teachers recognized that they had to develop an emotional bond between the immigrant and the nation, a love of country. Immigrant children could be taught American history and learn about the holidays, but the home was where the deepest feelings of patriotism were conveyed.... A feast around a common table represented an acceptance of American customs and history by the new comers and their recognition that they would do their part in encouraging their child's budding patriotism. Schoolchildren acted as cultural conduits, bringing home ideas about celebration, national history and cultural symbols learned at school.

The modern Thanksgiving myth was now fully realized, at least for children.

THANKSGIVING ADOPTS THE PILGRIMS

How did the Pilgrims fit in all this? For a century and a half following the 1620 landing, the Plymouth colonists were not recognized as anything more than the first wave in the great New England Puritan emigration. They were honored by New England historians such as Nathaniel Morton, Cotton Mather, and Thomas Prince for their role in establishing the Puritan commonwealth, but the anniversary of their arrival in 1720 passed unobserved. The first effort at commemoration did not occur until 1769, when the Old Colony Club of Plymouth instituted a celebration (Old Colony Day, subsequently Forefathers Day) on the anniversary of the date the exploratory expedition from the *Mayflower* first set foot on the shore of Plymouth harbor. By a tradition dating to 1741, the mainland landing had taken place on or near a singular boulder on the Plymouth waterfront on December 11, 1620, Old Style. As the old Julian calendar had been discarded in favor of the Gregorian model only 17 years earlier, the clubmen decided to adjust the anniversary by the 11 extra days that had been added to the calendar in 1752. This made the anniversary December 22, which became the established date for "Forefathers Day," the original Pilgrim holiday.

In 1774, the rock identified with the forefathers landing was levered from its bed, and, the upper half splitting off, that was dragged up to the Town Square and placed at the foot of a liberty pole. Thus began the process by which the humble Plymouth colonists became the symbolic founders of New England, and by extension the new United States as well. Their voluntary separation from the Old World to establish a new Christian commonwealth in America was seized upon as historical sanction for the American separation from England, and their high ideals and simple way of life were extolled as a model for all Americans. In contrast to the sordid history of early Virginia or the authoritarian nature of Massachusetts Bay, the Plymouth story was refreshingly virtuous and unexceptionable. The Pilgrim Fathers were anachronistically credited with Enlightenment values such as tolerance, a love of liberty, public education, and a reverence for law in addition to their deep religious faith. Also, it did not hurt that New England writers had a virtual monopoly on interpreting American history at the time and were able to promote its own forebears as the true founders of the nation. The Plymouth Forefathers were ideal candidates for the eighteenth-century Founding Fathers' own "founding fathers."

The Pilgrims' legend blossomed despite (or perhaps because of) the relative lack of original accounts. Governor Bradford's manuscript history of the colony had disappeared during the British occupation of Boston, leaving historians dependant on Nathaniel Morton's *New England's Memorial* (1669), a simplified version of his uncle William Bradford's chronicle. The detailed account of Plymouth's first year, familiarly known as "*Mourt's Relation*" (1622), was only available in an abridged version published by Samuel Purchase in 1625, and Bradford's history was not rediscovered until 1856. However, the basic components of the of the Plymouth Pilgrims' history were sufficiently well known to support the central story of courage, suffering, and perseverance without these additional resources.

Just as the American thanksgiving tradition had its own well-developed associations and customs, the Pilgrim Story was firmly focused on the 1620 landing and Longfellow's *Courtship of Myles Standish* (1858). That the Thanksgiving holiday had originated among the New England Puritans was widely acknowledged, but it was usually represented in a generic and diffused manner as one of the many legacies from the colonial era along with blue laws, excessive sobriety, and humorlessness. There were isolated references to the Pilgrims' First Thanksgiving after 1841, but none of any significance. Historian Diana Applebaum discovered isolated references to the Pilgrims in a proclamation from Iowa in 1844 and another in Utah in 1851. There are few references to the Pilgrim event in Mrs. Hale's *Godey's* editorials, even after 1865 when she expressly credited the Pilgrim event as initiating the holiday. In fact, the most common representation of Thanksgiving's colonial roots in this period drew on tropes of violence and racial tension.

Thanksgiving was most commonly presented from a contemporary rather than historic perspective in stories and verse during the nineteenth century. Thanksgiving meant attendance at church, return to the old homestead, and the reunion of the extended family in a private communion with tradition. The turkey, the New England homestead, soldiers or cowboys in camp, and occasionally insulting representations of African Americans dominated Victorian representations of the holiday. An interesting Thanksgiving cartoon by Thomas Nast that appeared in *Harper's Weekly* on November 20, 1869 entitled "Uncle Sam's Thanksgiving Dinner" shows an optimistic view of the Thanksgiving holiday as a metaphor for the peaceful diversity of the nation. Beneath the portraits of Lincoln, Washington, and President Grant and a view of Castle Garden (Ellis Island), Uncle Sam carves a fat turkey for his assembled guests representing the many nationalities that made up America. Seated between Chinese and African American families at the far end of the table, Columbia (the United States) acts as hostess.

A survey of Thanksgiving illustrations and articles in the popular *Harper's Weekly* and *Frank Leslie's Illustrated* newspapers turns up only a few isolated references to the 1621 event. An engraving entitled "Thanksgiving Day Among the Puritan Fathers in New England" that appeared in the December 3, 1870 issue of *Harper's Weekly* presents a unique representation of the 1621 celebration. The scene is an interior where a group of colonists are arrayed around a dinner table and six Indians stand on the sidelines before the meal begins. A similar interior representation painted at about the same time by Edwin White (who was also responsible for other Pilgrim scenes) depicts a New England household interior with a single Indian standing as a witness.

Another Plymouth Thanksgiving representation, C. S. Reinhart's "Thanksgiving Week—1621," which appeared in the December 1, 1894 issue of *Harper's Weekly,* is quite different. The scene is not a dinner, but rather a contest between an Indian man with a bow and a colonist with a musket. They are shooting at a target of a scarecrow made from English clothing. This event, suggested by a reference to weapons exercises at the 1621 feast in *Mourt's Relation,* presents a more uneasy message than the now-familiar outdoor feast, in which tension between the two cultures was closer to an armed standoff than a friendly dinner party. The Reinhart image reflects a far more popular Victorian conceptualization of early New England Thanksgivings, characterized by a climate of violence and tension between the New England colonists and Native Americans. This is particularly well represented in a dramatic scene and commentary published in *Frank Leslie's Illustrated,* November 27, 1869. Titled "Thanksgiving Day in New England two hundred years Ago," the anonymous engraving depicts a New England family interrupted at their Thanksgiving dinner by an attack by an invisible Indian enemy. The arrival of a warning messenger coincides with a hail of arrows flying through the open door, as the family arises from the table in alarm, one man reaching for a musket hung on the wall. The accompanying commentary reinforces the idea that the threat of attack from "an implacable enemy" was central to the colonial—and contemporary frontier—experience. Racial violence was a perennial theme in representations of colonial Thanksgivings in the illustrated newspapers, periodical cover art, and in cartoons in the old *Life Magazine* (1883–1936). Like most stereotypes, the theme survived longest in humorous contexts, remaining a popular theme well into the twentieth century.

The violent Thanksgiving trope began to give ground to our modern peaceful dinner image at the end of the nineteenth century. In 1889, Jane G. Austin (the American author, not her more famous English namesake) published *Standish of Standish: A Story of the Pilgrims,* the first and most popular of several titles dealing with the Pilgrim saga. It was an immediate success, going through at least 28 imprints and a dramatization in 1919. In *Standish of Standish,* Austin includes a fictional and sentimental account of the "First Thanksgiving," which appears to have had an important influence on the Thanksgiving myth. Austin's embellishment of the 1621 harvest celebration led to a new appreciation of the origins of the Thanksgiving holiday. In the 1897 November issue of the *Ladies' Home Journal,* Clifford Howard drew heavily on Austin's fictional account for an ostensibly historical description of the First Thanksgiving. Accompanying Howard's article was "The First Thanksgiving Dinner with Portraits of the Pilgrim Fathers" by W. L. Taylor. This is the first recognizable illustration of the now familiar autumnal outdoor feast commonly associated in popular culture with the Pilgrim Thanksgiving. Another contemporary "First Thanksgiving" account appeared in *The Story Hour: A Book for the Home and the Kindergarten* (1890). Written by Kate Douglas Wiggin and Nora A. Smith, this collection of stories went through a number of printings and editions. Smith's "The First Thanksgiving Day" is a largely accurate retelling for children of the 1621 Plymouth event. The 1920 Tercentenary of the Pilgrims also inspired new versions of their story, such as the unabashedly romanticized version in an elementary textbook called *The Land of the Pilgrims* (1925).

The new version of the First Thanksgiving story struck a resonant chord with the American public. It fulfilled the cultural desire for a romantic origin for the holiday and also provided the Pilgrims with a new role as tolerant American peacemakers. The cessation of the Indian Wars in the West and a widespread sentimental interest in Native American culture made it possible for a reassessment of Thanksgiving's colonial roots. It was now not only feasible but also fashionable to think of welcoming the Native Americans to the table. Another factor was the progressive mindset at the turn of the twentieth century that sought to bring reform and a rational order to American society. It was now time to create unity out of diversity and invite others to join together at the national table, as Thomas Nast's prescient cartoon had suggested in 1869.

The image of the Pilgrims and their Native neighbors dining in dignified harmony was an appropriate symbol of the peaceful assimilation and Americanization the reformers sought. Two influential historical paintings depicting the 1621 feast, J.L.G. Ferris's "The First Thanksgiving (ca. 1912) and Jennie A. Brownscombe's "The First Thanksgiving at Plymouth" (1914) established the dominant motif for future depictions of the event. Both show an open-air feast derived from the Austin description in which Pilgrim hosts and Native guests dine together in a dignified manner on the autumnal bounty. Despite various inaccuracies such as log cabins and western Native costumes, these images faithfully reflected the brief moment in 1621 when the two cultures met in the relative harmony described by Edward Winslow.

The 1621 First Thanksgiving had yet to achieve hegemonic status. The postcard fad that flourished between 1905 and 1912 produced a large number of Thanksgiving Day images, many of which employed colonists, Indians, and turkeys in various combinations, but illustrations of the famous dinner are noticeably absent. A survey of standard primary school textbooks from 1900 to 1940 shows that references to the Pilgrims often omitted any mention of the 1621 Thanksgiving. The "First Thanksgiving" was not even represented in either of Plymouth's two major historical pageants, Margaret M. Eager's "Old Plymouth Days and Ways" (1896–97) or George P. Baker's "The Pilgrim Spirit"

(1921). Nevertheless, there was sufficient awareness of the 1621 myth among the American public to prepare the nation for a widespread acceptance of the "First Thanksgiving" by World War II. In 1937 the famed historian Samuel Eliot Morison captured the prevailing consensus when he observed that "the Pilgrims in a sense have become the spiritual ancestors of all Americans, whatever their stock, race or creed." The First Thanksgiving began to edge out the *Mayflower*, Plymouth Rock, and the "Courtship" as the Pilgrims' fundamental contribution to the American Way of Life. The Pilgrim Story now had a romantic, happy ending, with all parties gathered together on an eternal golden autumn afternoon around a table laden with the fruits of the first New England harvest. The 1621 feast found its way onto calendars and into magazine advertising and cover art while the old, violent images were buried in library vaults. An increasing number of children's books brought the story to younger generations, each adding its own fictional gloss to the picture. Greeting cards and schoolroom decorations left no uncertainty that the Pilgrims were at the core of the Thanksgiving tradition.

By the post–World War II period, Thanksgiving was the primary focus of the Pilgrim story in popular culture. The association of the popular holiday with its supposed Pilgrim origin had become a self-evident historical truth—the world had been sold on the "Pilgrim" brand of Thanksgiving. The First Thanksgiving myth was supported by the social consensus that reigned from the late nineteenth century to the mid-1960s because it effectively mirrored the values and beliefs of that society. It was only after the turmoil of the 1960s brought traditional authority and its beliefs into question that the questionable canonical status of Thanksgiving (and many other cultural icons) became generally apparent. The recognition that something was wrong with the way in which American society portrayed its own past became clear, but identifying exactly where the truth lay amid the fallacies and myths was far more difficult.

THANKSGIVING MYTH IN THE "CULTURE WARS"

Conscientious scholars sought to exorcise the First Thanksgiving myth by painstakingly exposing its various historical inaccuracies and anachronisms. The American public was told repeatedly that there were flaws in their conception of the First Thanksgiving, that the Pilgrim did not eat cranberry sauce, that buckles and huge white collars were not a Plymouth fashion, and that turkeys are not mentioned in the more important of the two references to the event. Yet these very iconic elements continued to turn up in classrooms and popular culture every November. To attempt to explode a myth by carping about the minute details of its narrative was to attack the symptoms, not the disease. Myth is not a rational but an expressive understanding of history, a matter of unconscious belief rather than intellectual conviction, and it is all but immune to objective criticism.

On one hand, the conservative evangelical community has waged a spirited defense of the classic First Thanksgiving story and the traditional significance of the Pilgrims in American society. At the other extreme, the Native American community and its allies understood that the optimistic portrayal of Native-Colonial relations embodied in the holiday stereotype has obscured the tragedies that have afflicted their culture for over 300 years. In 1970, the United American Indians of New England and the local Wampanoag community instituted the National Day of Mourning, an annual "counter-holiday" in answer to Thanksgiving to address the other side of the symbolic coin. Turning Morison's observation on its head, the new perspective proposed that it was the Native Peoples who are the true "spiritual ancestors" of the American people, and that the American Thanksgiving holiday should rightly celebrate Native American traditions of giving thanks rather than continue to focus on what is portrayed as a dishonest and unworthy Puritan Thanksgiving tradition. The 1621 Plymouth celebration was recast as an event at which the local Wampanoag were the hosts and suppliers of most of the food to an inept and treacherous colonial community whose survival depended solely on the aid as well as the forbearance of the Native population. This alternative view sometimes asserts that the actual "first" New England thanksgiving was declared in 1637 after the bloodthirsty Pilgrims returned from massacring the Pequot community at Mystic, Connecticut. As historical interpretation, this revision is largely rhetorical nonsense, but it is a potent basis for new myth.

Much of the new Thanksgiving myth can be found on the World Wide Web. The identification of the 1637 Thanksgiving following the Pequot War (in which, incidentally, the Plymouth Colonists had no role, having postponed their involvement until after the cessation of hostilities) as the real First Thanksgiving can be found in the Web site by Moonanum James and Mahtowin Munro, "Thanksgiving: A National Day of Mourning for Indians." Julia Armstrong Murphy identified the 1676 proclamation as the official first proclamation of Thanksgiving in her Web essay, "Thanksgiving from an Indigenous Point of View." Perhaps it is because it is the earliest surviving example of a *printed* proclamation that some believe it to be the first. The actual first (oral) proclamation of Thanksgiving in Plymouth Colony was of course in the summer of 1623, and the first in Massachusetts was in 1630 following the arrival of the "Winthrop Fleet." Neither concerned the Native population. Another idea, that the Wampanoag supplied most of the food for the 1621 feast, and similar inventions, can be found in a Web essay by Chuck Larsen et al., "Teaching About Thanksgiving."

The new Thanksgiving myth fights fire with fire. It seeks not so much to debunk as to supplant earlier beliefs. The revisionist Thanksgiving story has found a receptive audience among segments of the American public eager to expose old hypocrisies and redress the wrongs of the past. In general, the new myth has been successful in gaining converts insofar as it speaks to individual hopes and fears, but the inroads it has made in American life have so far been scattered and numerically insignificant. Neither the conservative defenders nor the reformist opposition have had much influence beyond their own partisans and sympathizers. The general public remains unconcerned with the failings of the traditional Thanksgiving story. They continue to enjoy their decorative be-buckled Pilgrims and war-bonneted Indians while consuming turkey and cranberry sauce in the perfect confidence that they are maintaining a tradition begun in 1620. They may be aware of the cultural battles surrounding Thanksgiving and give intellectual allegiance to one version or the other, but as with the contest between Santa Claus and Christ's Nativity, this cognitive dissonance has no effect on habitual practices and tastes.

The current effort to substitute a more satisfying myth for the older tradition is no answer to the problem. It simply puts the injustice on a different footing and does not honestly confront the real problem, which is that popular history continues to oversimplify the American past in all of its lights and shadows. As permanent residents in Thanksgiving Land, the Native Americans, be they the aboriginal heroes or mere straightmen for the Pilgrims, can never transcend the limitations that stereotypes impose. The ideal solution might be to institute an entirely separate holiday that is focused on their real heroes and escape as far as possible from the confines of the Thanksgiving table. After all, if the First Thanksgiving was in fact not a thanksgiving at all, should they accept a Phyrric victory that mythically binds them to this event?

The benefit of a release from the Thanksgiving table would perhaps be even greater for the Plymouth colonists. It is not always appreciated that the burden of a favorable stereotype can have as harmful consequences, historically speaking, as a negative one. In the case of the Pilgrims, they have been turned into mythical figures, the Ghosts of Thanksgiving Past. Their predetermined role is restricted to a brief, strictly scripted appearance each fall before lapsing into irrelevancy during the rest of the year, at least outside of Plymouth, Massachusetts. The Plymouth colonists would greatly benefit if they could once again be seen as real people rather than historical May[flower] flies who sprang to life, had their brief bright moment of glory, then disappeared off the stage of history in an autumnal haze.

FURTHER READING

Applebaum, Diana Karter. *Thanksgiving: An American Holiday, An American History.* New York: Facts on File, 1984.

Gildrie, Richard P. "The Ceremonial Puritan Days of Humiliation and Thanksgiving." *New England Historical and Genealogical Register* 136 (Jan. 1982): 3–16.

Love, William DeLoss. *Fast and Thanksgiving Days of New England.* Boston: Houghton, Mifflin, 1895.

Pleck, Elizabeth. *Celebrating the Family: Ethnicity, Consumer Culture, and Family Rituals.* Cambridge, Mass.: Harvard University Press, 2000.

Pope, S.W. *Patriotic Games: Sporting Traditions in the American Imagination, 1876–1926.* New York: Oxford University Press, 1997.

Young, Alexander. *Chronicles of the Pilgrim Fathers of the Colony of Plymouth.* Boston: Charles C. Little and James Brown, 1841.

James W. Baker

HANUKKAH IN AMERICA

- [ ] The first evening of Hanukkah starts after sunset of the 24th day of the Hebrew month of *Kislev,* and the holiday is celebrated for eight days. On the Gregorian calendar Hanukkah begins anywhere between late November and late December.

- [ ] In the Jewish religious calendar Hanukkah is a minor holiday that has assumed greater significance to American Jews because of its proximity to Christmas.

- [ ] Hanukkah emerged in the second century B.C.E. when the Jewish Maccabees rebelled against the forced imposition of the Hellenistic Seleucids' religion and culture in Judea.

- [ ] Hanukkah, meaning "dedication," commemorates the Maccabees's reclaiming of the Temple of Jerusalem.

- [ ] The Maccabees decreed a celebration of the Temple's rededication annually on the twenty-fifth of the Hebrew month Kislev, with eight days of "gladness and joy."

- [ ] Rabbis declare Hanukkah a minor observance following the spread of the Jewish diaspora after Rome's conquest of Judea in the second century C.E., signally a spiritual shift away from Temple sacrifices toward sacred texts and local communities.

- [ ] The eight-branched *hanukiyah* reminds Jews of the seven-branched *menorah* that stood in the Jerusalem Temple, its added light reminding them of the sacred oil's eight-day miracle.

- [ ] For centuries, Hanukkah's candles, its message of God's protection, and its games encouraged Jews to hope for a better world.

- [ ] In the nineteenth century Hanukkah and the story of the Maccabean revolt were used by Reform and Orthodox rabbis to convince Jews to rededicate themselves to Judaism and examine their relation to American culture.

- [ ] Hanukkah advocates among both traditionalists and reformers agreed that Jewish children needed festive Hanukkah experiences to shield them from the influence of Christmas.

- [ ] By the 1890s Hanukkah festivities became a staple within the Jewish community as Jews worked to counter the notion that Christmas was an American holiday among new Jewish immigrants as well as among their own children.

HANUKKAH IN AMERICA

"[No one is] so well fitted to cause a reaction in Israel as…mothers."
Dr. H. A. Henry, San Francisco, 1864

Today, Hanukkah (also spelled Chanukah) is a winter festival familiar to most Americans. Its blue and silver colors adorn wrapping paper, cards, and holiday decorations. Greeting card companies market their Hanukkah products alongside Christmas cards in addition to the more than 440,000 Internet sites for purchasing Hanukkah greeting cards. Newspapers around the country advertise the concerts, candle-lighting ceremonies, museum exhibits, and fairs arranged especially to celebrate the holiday. Barney, the big purple dinosaur beloved by American children, recently sang a Hanukkah song on his popular television show, and the RugRats cartoon characters appeared in special books and videos for the holiday. In many cities, gigantic Hanukkah candelabra, called *hanukiyot* (sing. *hanukiyah*) or Hanukkah *menorahs,* are lit in public spaces. These activities make Hanukkah more publicly visible than any other Jewish sacred time, suggesting to many non-Jews that it is a major holiday, perhaps the most important one of the Jewish calendar. Yet, according to Judaism, Hanukkah is ranked a minor festival.

The annual gala we know today is largely the creation of American Jews, despite nearly 3,000 years of Jewish religious life. In 1990, more than three-fourths of American Jews reported performing Hanukkah's central ritual, the lighting and blessing of special candles at home. Children view Hanukkah cartoons in movie theaters, on television and video, and play Hanukkah music from CDs that are widely available. The United States Library of Congress owns more than 800 Hanukkah items, including song sheets and recorded music, holiday guide books and story books for children and adults, and original dramas usually performed by children in religious or Jewish cultural schools, or by adults in religious or social clubs. Most items were written, composed, or created in the United States. Some were brought to this country by Jewish immigrants or travelers as they elaborated upon a holiday that grew increasingly important to them. American Jews turned to these prayer books, published sermons, songs, stories, ritual manuals, and plays each December to find ancient reflections of their own experience in confronting a compelling but alien religious culture, that of Christian America, in the season of its greatest attractiveness—the Christmas season. They looked to the ancient tale that explained Hanukkah for inspiration, for reassurance, and for fun to carry them through America's annual Christmas frenzy in safety and in style. This essay will explore the American origins of one now commonplace Hanukkah activity, the communal children's Hanukkah celebration. Often, these are held in religious schools and today five professional education journals advise teachers and the parents who assist them in creating Hanukkah festivities.

This was not the first time Hanukkah was remade to serve the needs of Jews confronting a different religious life. In fact, a similar confrontation set the stage for Hanukkah to emerge.

HANUKKAH'S ORIGINS

Hanukkah emerged in the second century before the Common Era when Jews confronted Hellenic religion and culture. For centuries, Jewish Temple priests had performed their duties according to rules set down in the biblical books of Exodus, Leviticus, Numbers, and Deuteronomy, confident that they were fulfilling their religious obligations to provide forgiveness and worship to Jews in the manner dictated by holy writ. When Alexander the Great won control of Judea in 332 B.C.E., he planted Hellenic culture there. Jews began to speak Greek in addition to Hebrew or Aramaic, and Greek became the language of business and government. Over the next 300 years, some Jews, especially wealthier individuals living in urban areas, adopted Greek fashions and delved into Greek literature and its world view, sparking new ideas and new literary styles. For example, the biblical book Qoheleth (Ecclesiastes) offers a Hellenic attitude about the meaning of life different from earlier biblical texts.

After Alexander's death his generals divided his kingdom and Judea came under the control of the family known as the Seleucids. In an effort to unify his territories and concentrate his armies against Egypt's military and political power, Antiochus IV of that family demanded that Jews adopt his own version of Hellenic religious culture. He forbade rites central to Judaism, including circumcision and observance of the Sabbath, and required Jews to adopt his own cult, which focused on a statue of Zeus carved with his own features, which he had installed in the Jerusalem Temple. Accounts of Antiochus's brutality in enforcing his decrees appear in the four Books of the Maccabees written in Greek or Hebrew between 124 B.C.E. and 70 C.E. Some modern historians argue that those extreme measures to control Judea prove his mental instability, while others claim that the military threats posed by formerly competing generals and their families compelled him to take drastic measures to unify his kingdom. If he could make Judea and its center, Jerusalem, fully Greek, Antiochus may have reasoned, its political status and wealth would increase and he need not worry about a revolt. He could use all his soldiers against outside threats to his kingdom.

To ensure that Jews worship Greek gods even in the Jerusalem Temple, Antiochus replaced Onias III, the legitimate High Priest, with Onias's brother Jason, who purchased the office. Antiochus also sold a priestly office to Meneleus, whose family was not authorized to fulfill priestly duties. Jason and Meneleus supported Antiochus's actions and established Greek gymnasiums in Jerusalem, where sporting events dedicated to Greek gods were conducted in the nude, contradicting Jewish monotheism and standards for modesty. His changes turned the Temple into a place where Jews would be forced to worship a god other than the God of the Bible, thereby committing the most terrible of sins according to Judaism, and to sacrifice and eat pigs, an animal forbidden to Jews by biblical law.

Antiochus's demands created an uproar and divided Jews. Priestly corruption in the Jerusalem Temple especially outraged some rural priestly Jewish families. The revolt against Antiochus IV and the Jerusalem priesthood erupted in 167 B.C.E. in Modein, a small town northwest of Jerusalem, where a family of priests called Hasmoneans lived. Begun by the elderly father, Mattityahu, the rebellion soon came under the leadership of his five sons, Judah, Jonathan, Simon, John, and Eleazar. Judah led the military actions; Jonathan and especially Simon later took over governmental duties. Together, the band came to be known as the Maccabees. Maccabeus could have been a nickname for Judah, famed for military prowess, because it is similar to the Hebrew word *makevet,* meaning 'hammer.' In 165 B.C.E., three years after Antiochus IV took over the Jerusalem Temple, Judah and his men reclaimed it and rededicated it to their God. Hanukkah, meaning "dedication," commemorates that event. The revolt did not end there, however, and Judah ultimately died in battle before Antiochus and his generals were completely defeated. After Judah, his brothers and their descendants led both the revolt and the government that was established after its successful outcome.

The Maccabees laid the foundation for today's Hanukkah festival. Judah, his brothers, and the men with them decreed a celebration of the Temple's rededication annually on the twenty-fifth of the Hebrew month Kislev, with eight days of "gladness and joy." They cleaned out the Temple, repaired and rebuilt the lamp stand, altar, and table, and restored the interior courtyards. They made an incense offering and relit the lamps. Their own celebration began with thanksgiving hymns accompanied by harps, lutes, and cymbals. People prostrated themselves in worship. They rejoiced for eight days with various offerings to God. The "garland(s)...and flowering branches...(and) palm fronds" in their festivities were reminiscent of Sukkot, an autumn harvest holiday delayed because the Temple had remained in Antiochus's control. Judah and his men had celebrated Sukkot in the mountains while they conducted war.

The Maccabean revolt gave the Hasmonean family political power. For the next 130 years the Hasmonean dynasty governed Judea, expanding its own priestly power, engaging the country in repeated warfare, and subjecting it to a succession of difficult alliances with foreign countries. But ultimately, those alliances entrapped Judea in Rome's thrall. Rome later installed a puppet king, Herod, who eliminated Hasmonean rule. A Jewish uprising against Rome ended when Rome destroyed the Jerusalem Temple in 70 C.E. Rome soon implemented more direct governance over the area and removed much of the Jewish population from its land. After a second, failed revolt in 135 C.E., Rome further centralized its control of Judea, and as the Jewish polity failed, organized Judaism fell apart. Centuries of Jewish religious life that had centered on priestly sacrifices came to an end, and any normative Jewish ideological system collapsed in Judea. Centers of Jewish life shifted away from Judea, but everywhere, Jews now lived under the control of non-Jews. Diaspora Jews across the Mediterranean basin, many among them artisans and merchants, fared better than the Jewish peasants of the eastern Mediterranean in and around Judea. Jews explained this realignment theologically as exile. This exile brought dramatic changes to Jewish religious practices.

REWRITING HANUKKAH

Jews now faced a different sort of religious and cultural conflict than the Maccabees had confronted. Scholars of religious texts and law, called rabbis, now salvaged Judaism by replacing priestly sacrifices with their own approach to religious life, which centered on mastering the Torah (first five books of the Bible) and applying its rules to daily life based upon an oral tradition that adapted the law to changing historical conditions. Maccabees had fought to restore the Temple, but rabbis understood the Temple-centered religious life to be over. The rabbis set new rules about Hanukkah's rites and determined it a minor festival. The Hebrew Bible includes many accounts in which military actions determine political and priestly power, but the early rabbis chose not to include the Maccabees' story in the Jewish canon, which they set around 90 C.E. They may have assigned Hanukkah a lesser status because they disagreed with the way that the Hasmoneans handled their power, which ended in civil war about 130 years after the Maccabean revolt. Or, they may have been especially concerned to prevent any more uprisings after the failed later rebellion in 135 c.e. left Judea with even less ability to govern its own affairs. Those rabbis may have believed that Jews now living without a country of their own and without any recourse to military defense needed to avoid armed insurrection and to trust completely in God. Perhaps they also felt that sacrificial cults, such as those that had been performed in the ancient Temple and in temples to other gods throughout the region, too often provoked conflict between Jews and their conquerors and should disappear from Jewish religious practices.

Rabbis wrote down their legal discussions about Jewish law and life, sharing them with fellow rabbis in distant lands and with future generations. With that rabbinical correspondence, Jews in many different countries refocused their religious lives on their local communities and on their sacred texts, rather than upon sacrifices performed by priests. Over the next several hundred years, rabbis collected their discussions, adapting biblical law to Jews' new historical situations. Between 200 b.c.e. and 500 c.e., rabbis compiled those discussions in two multivolume works collectively called the Talmud. Their work created today's Judaism.

In the Talmud, rabbis explained the Maccabean victory as a miraculous event that evidenced God's continuing protection. In their celebration, Hanukkah honored God's power. In the daily prayers rabbis compiled, still used today, Jews at Hanukkah thank God for delivering the strong into the hands of the weak. In synagogues, Psalms 113–118, collectively called the Hallel, are recited. On the Sabbath that falls during Hanukkah, a special reading from the prophet Zekharia including the phrase, "not by might, nor by power, but by my spirit, saith the Lord," is recited after the Torah portion for that day. Together they seem to completely deny Maccabean effectiveness. One Talmud tractate tells of a miracle of a small flask of pure oil prepared by the High Priests for Temple use that survived Antiochus's desecration. After the Maccabees reclaimed the Temple, it says, there was only enough oil to keep the sacred flame, representing God's presence, lit for one day, yet the flame lasted eight days until new oil was prepared. Through that miracle, the rabbis taught, God conveyed to the victorious Jews that divine power had fought with them. The eight-branched *hanukiyah* reminds Jews of the seven-branched *menorah* that stood in the Jerusalem Temple, its added light reminding them of the sacred oil's eight-day miracle.

Other Talmud tractates advise on the correct blessing to be recited when lighting the lamp. Jews light the *hanukiyah* at home each evening of Hanukkah, using small candles and reciting two blessings praising God for miracles performed at this season in ancient days. On the first night a third prayer thanks God for sustaining those lighting the candles and bringing them to this special occasion. Each Hanukkah evening an additional candle is placed in the *hanukiyah*, ascending from right to left; they are lit from left to right by means of an

A child in New York lights the candles of the menorah. Courtesy of Corbis.

additional ninth candle. Talmud also instructs Jews to place the lighted meno-rah in public view to advertise the miracle, and for women to join in lighting the lamp. Women must do so, the Talmud says, because Antiochus's governors demanded sexual relations with Jewish brides on their wedding nights, much as medieval lords sometimes did among their peasants in Europe. The miracle, as the Talmud calls the Maccabean uprising, rescued those women. A poem from the Maccabean era described "every bride...mourning in her bridal chamber." The Fourth Book of Maccabees describes young women who had just entered the bridal chamber being "carried away unveiled," and "raising a lament...as they were torn by the harsh treatment of the heathen." Rabbis concluded that Antiochus IV or his representatives claimed wedding night rights to every Jewish bride.

Although Hanukkah's rites say little about the Maccabees, Jews remained curious about them. In tenth century Italy, a new popular Jewish history called the *Josippon* included an account of the Maccabean revolt and stirred widespread interest. A Hebrew edition was published in Mantua, Italy in 1476 and a 1558 English translation roused curiosity about Jews among

Rabbi Yekutiel Feldman says a prayer over the Hanukkah lights at the Chabad house in New York, 2003. © AP / Wide World Photos.

Christians in England. By 1661, a version with illustrations appeared in Yiddish, then the daily language of most Jews throughout central and eastern Europe.

For many centuries, Hanukkah folklore voiced Jewish hopes for liberation like the sort the Maccabees ultimately achieved. European Jews suffering economic and political disenfranchisement, libels, ghettoization, or violence found occasions for hope in Hanukkah's story. Jewish folklore gave the Hasmoneans superhuman strength and made them "swifter than eagles and stronger than lions." In one Hanukkah tale, divine power caused the angels protecting enemy nations to turn their soldiers' arrows against themselves. In that tale, Maccabees fought not only the Hellenized Syrians, but 70 nations combined, collectively called Greeks. By implication, the Hasmonean victory defeated the forebears of Jews' contemporary oppressors along with the ancient Hellenized Syrians. For those European Jews, Hanukkah offered a yearly promise that God might again protect them from their oppressors.

By the late middle ages, Hanukkah's promise inspired new poetry and songs. A thirteenth-century Jewish poet penned a five-stanza poem, *Maoz Tzur* (Hebrew: Sheltering Rock) recounting past instances of divine deliverance. Set to the tune of a popular German folk melody two centuries later, the song became the customary finale to Hanukkah's candle-lighting ceremony among Jews in central and eastern Europe. In the sixteenth century, during a time of persecutions and expulsions, an unknown poet added a sixth stanza. It asks God to avenge Jews' sufferings and swiftly return them to their homeland. *Maoz Tzur* became a standard addition to the Hanukkah ritual as families sang it after lighting and blessing the holiday candles.

New customs for celebrating Hanukkah also developed. Because Hanukkah lights commemorate a miracle, they cannot be used for practical purposes. No work can be done while the slender candles burn, and Jews used that time, usually about 30 minutes, for festivities. Spinning tops had been used for gambling in the ancient world, but today's most popular Hanukkah game developed in Europe. In the 1500s, central European Jews adapted a widely popular game of chance to Hanukkah. The Hanukkah top is called a dreidel (Yiddish for spinner) or a *sevivon* (Hebrew). Letters inscribed on its four sides indicate the game's rules, but Jews reinterpreted them to mean "A Great Miracle Happened There." Most rabbis frowned upon gambling, but after Jews modified the game to recall Hanukkah's story, rabbis quieted their objections.

Gambling seems to underscore Hanukkah's message. Through dreidel games fortune is overturned again and again in concrete actions that seem to make miraculous rescues plausible. Anthropologist Victor Turner views occasions like the time marked by the lit Hanukkah candles to be outside ordinary, everyday time. These moments offer a threshold to new possibilities, to a new social order that can be seen only during the ritual. Judaism's holidays often separate sacred time from ordinary time to create occasions for imagining events in Jews' ancient past and contact with the divine. For centuries, Hanukkah's candles, its message of God's protection, and its games, encouraged Jews to hope for a better world.

Hanukkah foods also recall miracles. In some places it became customary to eat foods cooked in oil to recall the oil that miraculously was said to burn for eight days. In eastern Europe, Jews often fried pancakes in oil. In southern Europe and the Middle East, some Jews ate Hanukkah doughnuts. By the nineteenth century, eastern European parents customarily gave their children small coins, or *gelt,* on Hanukkah, expecting the children to give at least part of this *gelt* to charity or to their teachers. Through special songs, games, foods, and gifts, Jews created a convivial holiday that cheered them with the promise of divine protection amid family festivities.

Beginning in the late eighteenth century, western European Jews slowly integrated into predominantly Christian societies. There, Jewish emancipation required new laws and as they were debated, old prejudices and hatreds sparked new anti-Jewish violence. Hanukkah domestic celebrations continued largely

Gold chocolate coins are often a part of Hanukkah celebrations. Courtesy of Corbis.

unchanged even as Jews' legal rights in Europe underwent reform. For nineteenth-century Jews in small towns in Alsace, for example, Hanukkah meant visiting each other's homes for holiday meals, games, and small entertainments. Emancipation's early days did little to change Jews' appreciation for Hanukkah miracles.

When some European Jews did encounter modern Western culture it enhanced their own knowledge of Maccabean history. Jews who obtained a classical education read works by ancient historian Josephus Flavius, whose *Antiquities of the Jews* (written about 93 C.E.). included the revolt against Antiochus IV. Born Joseph son of Mattatiah, Josephus commanded a Jewish force in a first-century battle against Rome before he fled to Rome and took a Roman name. His many volumes defended Judean religion and culture. It was his *Antiquities* that the *Jossipon* condensed and mixed with folklore. In the mid-nineteenth century, university-trained German Jewish historian Heinrich Graetz compiled an 11-volume history of the Jews that incorporated Maccabean exploits into a modern history of Jewish life. By the end of that century, Graetz condensed that work into three volumes widely read in many languages on both sides of the Atlantic.

Reading in classrooms or alone, some Jews learned of more Hanukkah history because Christian tradition preserved ancient accounts of Maccabean exploits. Greek versions of Jews' Hebrew scripture began to appear after the third century B.C.E. to make the Bible accessible to the many Greek-speaking Jews living throughout the Greek empire. By the first century C.E., they included portions of all four Books of the Maccabees, but only the first two books passed into Roman Catholic Bibles in the collection called the Apocrypha. Roman Catholic tradition identifies all Jews who protested Antiochus's rule as Maccabees. A painting now in Rome's Basilica of Saint Pietro in Vincoli (Chains) depicts martyrdom by the sons of an unnamed mother and her ultimate suicide, calling it "seven Maccabee brothers with mother." Greek Orthodox Christians celebrate her as St. Solomnis and many early Christian Greek Bible manuscripts included the Fourth Book of the Maccabees where her story is elaborated. Rabbis had forbidden all Christian sacred texts to Jews, but when modernity weakened clerical power, modern liberal rabbis culled these Maccabee stories for Hanukkah sermons and inspirational fiction. Liberal rabbis in Germanic lands who gathered in 1869 to harmonize the religious changes taking place among modernizing Jews recommended that Hanukkah festivities be made more elaborate. Looking back on that era from his 1960 vantage point, one American rabbi suggested that when modernity cast its skeptical eye upon Hanukkah's tale of miraculous oil, it encouraged Jews to read books formerly banned by rabbis, including the Books of the Maccabees Christians held sacred. In reading those books, Jews learned a new appreciation for the Maccabean revolt, seeing it as the "first fight in history...(for) religious freedom."

JEWS ENCOUNTER AMERICA

In America, Jews integrated as nowhere else. No ghettoes separated them from non-Jews, no laws banned them from occupations or demanded their clothing mark their religious identity. Yet, comprising no more than 1 percent of the American population, nineteenth-century Jews did not always enjoy true equality. Some states limited Jews' rights by insisting that legal oaths be sworn on a Christian Bible, keeping Jews from political office and from witnessing in court. But because the Constitution did not allow the government to support any religious authority and banned restrictions on practicing religion, American Jews could argue for and win legal rights. When New Hampshire granted Jews equal rights in 1877, it was the last state to do so. Jews in America confronted an alien religious culture in a far more complex manner than they had ever faced.

Despite those limitations, Jews felt America was different. As early as 1790, Virginian Rebecca Samuel wrote from her home in St. Petersburg to tell her mother in Hamburg, Germany that she could "not know what a wonderful country this is...everyone lives here peacefully." Thirty years later Charleston, South Carolina poet Penina Moise penned similar confidence in America, urging those "whose pilgrimage from Palestine we trace...[to] brave the Atlantic," promising "a western sun will gild thy future day." By the end of that century a poem by the gifted New York writer, Emma Lazarus, urged Europe's "huddled masses yearning to breathe free" to look to America. Americans endorsed her sentiments by inscribing them on the base of the Statue of Liberty. Lazarus drew her inspiration from the impoverished Jewish immigrants then living in lower Manhattan, part of an immigration of more than two million eastern European Jews who came to the United States between 1881 and 1924.

Yet America's freedoms presented Jews with a new conundrum. Despite her praise for Virginia, Samuel soon relocated to Charleston and its larger, 300-strong Jewish community where she could more easily raise her children as Jews. In St. Petersburg, Jews had no Torah scroll and no kosher meat. But Charleston also presented dilemmas. Soon after Moise penned her paean to America's freedoms, her synagogue there split apart over attempts to dramatically transform its worship rites. Especially before the late nineteenth century, only adventurous Jews were likely to relocate to America. They knew they would not find the strong religious, educational, and cultural supports long sustained by Europe's larger Jewish communities. But those strong communities constrained change. Without them, and with religious freedoms unknown in Europe, American Jews created the religious institutions they most desired. Some advocated streamlining Jewish religious life to fit both the time limitations American life placed upon religious activities and adopting the popular Protestant philosophical perspectives that deemed ritual less important than belief. These Jews shortened religious services, translated many prayers into everyday languages like German or English, sometimes abandoned dietary laws like those forbidding pork or shellfish, and often prayed without head coverings and did not separate men from women in synagogue worship. By 1875 they established a seminary to train liberal rabbis in this new style of Judaism. Others felt that American Jews needed to build their own strong traditional educational, religious, and cultural institutions to live fully Jewish lives in the United States. They especially strove to educate American Jews about the meaning of traditional Jewish religious practices. Debates about these different perspectives sometimes grew acrimonious. By the time Emma Lazarus wrote, American Jews practiced a wide variety of worship styles.

Few personal letters written by American Jews before the Civil War mention Hanukkah rites being performed in homes, although the Sabbath, Passover, Yom Kippur, and Sukkot holidays are commonly noted. When a reforming group broke away from Charleston's sole congregation in 1824, they omitted Hanukkah prayers from the new prayer book they compiled. Instead, Hanukkah, along with Purim, another winter festival, became an occasion for gala charity balls in many nineteenth-century American Jewish communities.

AMERICAN RABBIS REMAKE HANUKKAH

Fiery debates between religious reformers and traditionalists agitated American rabbis for many decades, but both camps drew upon Hanukkah's story for inspirational sermons that could convince American Jews to rededicate themselves to Judaism. In 1846 reformer Max Lilienthal (1815–1882) asked Jewish parents in Augusta, Georgia to model their concern for their children's religious educations upon the ancient mother who encouraged her seven sons to withstand fatal torture rather than violate holy law. "Mothers," he asked the women in his audience, "do you feel what [that mother] did for the Jewish religion" by instructing her children in it? Lilienthal, an emigré from Bavaria, settled in Cincinnati where leading reformer Isaac Mayer Wise (1819–1900) led a nearby synagogue. Both men believed that Hanukkah's story could inspire Jews to greater devotion. These men believed they offered a route back to Judaism for Jews who felt unable to fit Judaism's traditional practices into modern life. Those feelings seemed to be more common among Jews in small towns like Augusta, Georgia. Jewish fathers ought to teach by example, Lilienthal said, and urged them to "show by your life how Jewish faith ennobles you." God is with us, he assured them. The Hanukkah story proves that "Israel...is never forsaken"; therefore, "never apostasy!" Always "confide in the Lord" in times of weakness or despair. Finally, Lilienthal hoped the congregation would "live in peace and harmony with one another." The Maccabees were victorious because they did not quarrel among themselves, he told them.

Lilienthal sent his sermon in a letter to the Augusta congregation, but many religious debates ran in the nearly 60 magazines published by and for American Jews in the nineteenth century. Holidays often occasioned inspirational sermons, admonitions to live more religious lives, and instructions for ritual observances. Wise regularly included Hanukkah editorials in his *Israelite* after it appeared in 1854. A prolific author, Wise himself wrote much of the material that appeared in his newspaper. In 1860, he penned an original romantic version of the Maccabean story that he serialized over 39 weeks. Ten years later, the Maccabees had become a Hanukkah fixture in most American Jewish periodicals.

Wise's biographer claimed that the rabbi opposed lighting Hanukkah candles because the holiday is not mentioned in the Bible, which most reformers prized over Talmud. Yet Wise often wrote about Hanukkah in his *Israelite* and adapted the most popular print vehicle in secular culture, the serialized novella, to imbue American Jews with the Maccabean spirit. Wise called his tale "The First of the Maccabees," but few readers knew that there were four original books of the Maccabees, or that Wise drew much of his story from the first book. Years later, he claimed to have written his novels to simply fill the space allotted for them in his magazine, sending them immediately to the press without any editing or revision. By that account, he wrote them quickly and without a second thought. Yet, such easily written pieces probably expressed his own real views. Wise had worked tirelessly on a scholarly history of the Jewish people that found few readers. His historical romances popularized an approach to Jewish history he had struggled to convey. Like most Jewish reformers in the United States and Europe, he believed that a historical understanding of Judaism would help contemporary Jews appreciate their tradition.

In Wise's hands the Maccabean story looked like other popular fiction in the Victorian era. Victorians expected to find religious virtues, patriotism, and strong gender distinctions in their literary romances, and Wise delivered. Wise's Judah and his brothers were brave and noble, self-sacrificing and heroic. In Wise's narrative, Jewish men became exemplars of contemporary American masculine values, explaining they fought for liberty, justice, truth, and manliness itself. One figure explains, "death is not the greatest evil... [it is] ... sacrific[ing] truth, justice and liberty." Wise's colleague Lilienthal edited a magazine for Jewish children in which he conveyed a similar message. He wrote to his young readers, "Like our American Patrick Henry, [Matathaias] said; "Give me liberty or Give me death!" By mining American history to illustrate Hanukkah's lessons of bravery and patriotism, Lilienthal encouraged Jewish children to see loyalty to Judaism as important as loyalty to their country, to see their own religious tradition as exciting as the American Revolution, and to see Hanukkah within American culture.

Women made up much of the readership for American magazines and fiction, and Wise's romance of the Maccabean revolt provided novel female characters who motivate soldiers and help to secure victories. Wise helped his readers to imagine that ancient Jewish women, like their men, also embodied the personal attributes esteemed by Victorian Americans. Wise added a female character, Miriam, mother to Judah and his brothers, who depicted a Victorian maternal ideal. At her husband's deathbed, she explains her faith in his eternal life, hearing angels singing as God receives him and grants him "eternal bliss." In the original ancient Books of the Maccabees, Judah's father instructs his sons to continue the revolt. In Wise's story, mother Miriam does so. "I dedicate my five sons to thy service, O God of Israel," she says. She tells her sons as they kneel at her husband's deathbed, "Rise...and join hands over the remains of your heroic father [and]...promise to...drive the invaders from this holy land, and restore Israel's sanctuary...rights and liberties." It was the sort of deathbed scene popular in Victorian fiction. The scene's emotional intensity is expressed by a woman although shared by men. The resolution of those emotions moves the story in new directions. For American Jews whose tradition-minded parents and older family members had remained in Europe, a character like Miriam, an elderly mother who monitored her grown sons' religious commitments, would have carried emotional power. Miriam instructs her sons throughout the story, keeping them committed to victory.

Wise also added lovely young Iphegine, love interest for a younger Maccabee brother, Jonathan. Iphegine's spy missions among the invaders, dangerous encounters, and repeated rescues by Jonathan enhance the story's drama. Her women friends discuss their trials under foreign rule, as their husbands, lovers, brothers, and fathers leave to fight or are murdered by their enemies. Iphegine's father is Meneleus, a traitor, but she casts her lot with the Jewish resistance. Iphigine expresses the conundrum of many American Jews who adopted much of general American culture, practiced little Judaism, yet considered themselves loyal Jews. She explains that although she acts like a gentile, she believes in Judaism. "I worship no gods besides the God of Israel, "she begins. "I love beauty and chastity, therefore I am a devotee of...Venus.... But I worship only the God of heaven and earth." Presenting these ideas as the views of a young woman undermined them and made them easy to correct by a hero, Jonathan, who rebukes her, urging Iphegine to dedicate herself to Jewish traditions. "These imaginary deities...corrupt...(you)," he said. Wise expected some of his readers to see themselves in Iphegine, a young person attracted to the style and form of non-Jewish culture. Jews who read this story learned that respectable American values matched Jewish values and that Jewish men and women who remained loyal to Judaism could embody them.

Countering reformers, Philadelphia's Isaac Leeser (1806–1868) and other traditionalists argued that because God had ordained Judaism's practices they were not subject to the "whims of the age." Traditionalists believed reforms would provide a route out of Judaism for too many Jews, not a road back into Judaism for those who had already abandoned some Jewish practices, as reformers claimed. Unless Jews disavowed the Bible and their own ancient history, Leeser and traditionalists argued, Jews must recognize God's commandments. For them, both Hanukkah's miracles and Maccabean victories justified their trust in God and their traditions. Leeser's *Occident and American Jewish Advocate* regularly criticized efforts to reform Judaism. Yet, although Lilienthal worked to reform Judaism, Leeser printed his Hanukkah sermon in *The Occident* because the speech itself lauded traditional Jewish commitments. Usually, Leeser only printed reformers' ideas to refute them. Wise complained that Leeser forced him to "cringe and bow low" in order to publish in *The Occident*. But Leeser himself also mined that story for similar purposes.

Hanukkah occasioned some of the most pointed attacks between reformers and traditionalists. Wise called the holiday a "monument to liberty" and argued that although the holiday's message is to resist pressures from outside forces, that only applied to Judaism's "essence, doctrines, and theories," not its rituals. In response, Leeser sought to portray reformers as a fringe movement lacking both widespread appeal and authority. He publicized special events and rituals from congregations around the country to back up his view that most Jews accepted tradition's authority and only needed the resources to assist them in fulfilling their duties—not a change in Judaism itself. He praised a Cleveland congregation's Hanukkah dedication of its new building and noted that benevolent societies in both Cleveland and Baltimore hosted annual Hanukkah banquets. Hanukkah, he felt, refuted reformers because the Maccabees insisted on maintaining some of the Jewish "prohibitions" that reformers cancelled, like dietary laws. Leeser scoffed at a reform leader in San Francisco who told his congregation that Hanukkah's meaning was simply to keep "the light of religion in our hearts," and that Jews need not light the Hanukkah lamps. That synagogue's lamps remained dark. "Is this...progress?" Leeser asked his readers. He insisted that many San Franciscans lit Hanukkah lamps in their homes and contended that the dark synagogue prompted members to leave and to found another congregation under more traditional principles. Leeser opposed both the reforms and the discord they engendered. In his mind, both were wrong.

San Franciscan traditionalist Rev. Dr. Henry A. Henry agreed with Leeser, insisting that reformers who reshape their synagogues to conform to American culture mimicked the ancient Jewish Hellenists who betrayed the Temple and Judaism under Antiochus's rule. Then gymnasiums shared buildings with sanctuaries and female voices sang in choirs at worship—both innovations that marked leading Reform congregations. These changes, Henry said, made Jews into Hellenists, not Maccabees. Hanukkah, he argued, meant resisting those temptations. Henry hoped to see "true champions who will fight the battles of the lord," appear in his own day. He began his plea for a Jewish champion with military imagery and reminders of Judah Maccabee, but soon asked women for their aid. American men of all religions seemed absorbed by labor, so religious organizations often asked women for support. Yet first, rabbis needed to convince women that they had an important role to play. "In all ages of our...history, the women of Israel...boldly stood forward in defense of their religion," Henry began.

He discussed Judith, heroine of a story written about the same time as the Books of the Maccabees. The *Shulchan Aruch* (the Set Table) a sixteenth-century code of religious laws that became standard for Jews, mentions Judith's story in its section on Hanukkah. Although few American Jewish women were familiar with the *Shulchan Aruch,* Judith's tale enlivened Jewish folklore. Judith's story is set 400 years before the Maccabean revolt, at the time of the siege of the first Jerusalem Temple by Babylonia, but it is told at Hanukkah because it recounts a similar tale of Jews overcoming a more powerful foreign culture that attacked both their spiritual and physical existence. In her story, Judith is a pious and beautiful widow who seduces the enemy's general and decapitates him while he is drunk, thus preventing his planned attack against her town. Its structure recalls other Hellenic romances of its time. Judith's name is a female version of Judah, hero of the Maccabean tale, meaning "Jew." Her story offers women a courageous and daring Hanukkah heroine. Henry then listed biblical Jael, Esther, and female judges and prophets who led Jews in obedience to God. Today, he said, no one is "so well fitted to cause a reaction in Israel as...mothers." Yet Jewish women, just as men, enjoyed American culture and often labored alongside men in family businesses. In Europe and in America, articles in the Jewish presses blamed Jewish women for adopting what critics believed to be too many elements of gentile culture, and, like those critics, Henry urged them to devote themselves to religious traditions. Urging them to choose Judaism over economic success, he said, "Set aside...your love of worldly pleasures...[because]...on you depends the progress of Society." His message echoed that of many other religious leaders who hoped their influence over women could translate into influencing men as well. "Draw your husbands to a religious...life, and...your children will follow in your footsteps." Henry hoped to convince American Jewish women that they held the keys to Judaism's future.

All Jewish clergy seemed scandalized by Jewish families who disregarded Hanukkah but enjoyed domestic Christmas festivities. Even such leading Jews as Mordecai Manual Noah, who organized an island of refuge for Jews on Grand Island in New York State, put up Christmas stockings for his children each December. American women's magazines praised the German custom of erecting and decorating a tree and exchanging gifts at Christmas and the most popular magazine, *Godey's Lady's Book,* instructed its readers in accomplishing a similar result. Christmas festivities seemed to advertise not only items to buy and trees to decorate, but Christianity itself. *American Hebrew* editors told young readers to "respectfully tell (your parents) no" when they talk about giving you a Christmas tree, promising that "[y]our Christian friends will think more of you for doing so." The *Jewish Messenger* asked its readers to make

Hanukkah appealing to children so that they would not "look forward with anticipation to festivities of another faith." One Jewish woman called Hanukkah the "Jewish Cinderella" who should be put on an equal level with its "richly adorned" Christian sister.

In New York, *The Jewish Messenger's* editor, Rev. Samuel Isaacs, assumed that Jewish girls attending fashionable French style schools would be the first to bring Christmas trees into their homes. Jewish clergy worried that Jewish girls left without a religious education might not be satisfied with the simple *hanukiyah* and its small candles. Reformers and traditionalists alike mobilized to wean such Jews, men and women, from Christmas. In the 1860s essays discussing this problem ran in *The Israelite, The Occident,* and the *Jewish Messenger.* Although Wise later claimed he "always treated the Christian religion and its founder with respect," he published several articles designed to make Christmas less appealing to Jews. He pointed out that no one really knows Jesus's birthday, in order to undercut Christmas's historicity, and lessen its legitimacy. American Protestants who did not celebrate Christmas argued similarly, and Wise in no way felt he was denouncing Christianity—only the domestic Christmas customs that many Jews found appealing. By contrast, the Maccabean revolt had an undisputed date and historical authenticity. Compared to Hanukkah, Wise implied, Christmas carried little credibility.

HANUKKAH TO SAVE THE CHILDREN

Late nineteenth-century American middle-class families embraced a new attitude toward children. These smaller families sought to understand the personalities of each individual child, and few children in these homes labored for wages or shouldered many of the burdens of housework. These parents believed their primary duties were to protect their children and to educate them. When Christmas advertising beguiled Jewish children, Jewish parents faced a dilemma: Should they fulfill their youngsters' requests?

Hanukkah advocates among both traditionalists and reformers agreed that Jewish children needed festive Hanukkah experiences to shield them from Christianity's festival and from evangelists who acted like "sneak thieves," stealing Jewish children during the few weeks preceding Christmas. Jewish children themselves might ask for Christmas trees and gifts simply because their Christian friends enjoyed them. Herman Baar, rabbi at New York's Hebrew Orphan Asylum wrote that, sadly, Jews had done so little to "glorify" their own victory over darkness that their children envied their Christian playmates. Reform leader Kaufmann Kohler argued that it was time to "invest our Hanukkah with the…charm and captivating beauty" of Christmas. "We are passing a crisis" Kohler said, much like the one faced by the Hasmoneans. Religious institutions are "sapped" by criticism, cosmopolitanism, and skepticism. Jews lack self-respect in the face of an overwhelming and alien religious culture. To counter those problems, Hanukkah must be made more "radiant with joy," love, and charity. Kohler suggested that the talmudic tale of the miracle of the oil actually symbolized the Jews themselves, whom many people expected to disappear but who continued alive to their faith. A Louisville, Kentucky writer praised "teachers in our Jewish Sabbath school [who] make the feasts of Chanukah and Purim...feasts of joy...to which both teachers and children...look forward with longing and delight." Editors of the *American Hebrew* believed Jewish children would need these "fond recollections" of Jewish life when they are adults to be capable of answering "the demands the future may make" upon them.

Lilienthal proposed a plan for transforming Hanukkah, assuring his readers that the occasion could be "celebrated to delight young and old." He explained, "Chanukah is entirely neglected in so many of our Jewish families [but] we [should] celebrate it publicly in our temples. [It] should be celebrated in every congregation [so that] the children...shall have it as a day of rejoicing [in] our religion." Many Christian Sunday schools customarily held special Christmas festivals with hymns, decorations, and pageants, and Lilienthal was among the first to adapt those events to Hanukkah. At his own congregation, Lilienthal organized a festival attended by over 200 children who answered to the holiday blessings in a chorus and enjoyed ice cream and other sweets, all in a room festively decorated by the "ladies of the congregation" who had worked "with a will." His magazine, the *Hebrew Sabbath School Visitor* explained it to his readers.

Beginning with a simple program, Lilienthal offered a prayer and oversaw the lighting of candles. Members of the school committee gave addresses, the choir supplied music, school children presented gifts to their teachers and enjoyed "eatables" before going home. After their celebration, an entertainment "planned by the ladies of the congregation" for adults lasted "far into the night." Wise's congregation hosted a similar festival for 250 pupils. There, the congregation's reader lit the candles and led the hymn singing before Wise's address. Children recited grace and enjoyed light refreshments. Other congregations soon adopted the custom.

By 1870 Reform Jewish Sunday schools began hosting festive Hanukkah celebrations for children. Lilienthal's Cincinnati congregation may have been the first. Such festivities always featured the Hanukkah candle-lighting ceremony, but *tableaux,* dramatic readings, plays, balls, poetry, and Chanukah hymn singing often expanded the program. Most often, women called these events "entertainments" rather than religious celebrations and strove to create the same light-hearted atmosphere for Hanukkah that Christmas had recently achieved. Nonetheless, women usually worked with rabbis who explained the holiday's importance or lit Hanukkah candles in an opening or closing ceremony. St. Louis women held their Hanukkah celebration in a synagogue and assisted their rabbi throughout the children's performances. Afterward, youngsters enjoyed dancing, singing, recitations, dialogues, and supper. Children usually ate ice cream, cake, candy, and fruit, at these Hanukkah events, but according to historian Kenneth White, Reform congregants sometimes feasted on turkey, duck, or even oysters. Potato pancakes fried in oil did not become popular at Reform festivals until after the massive immigration of Jews from eastern Europe made that tradition commonplace. Rabbis delivered special Hanukkah sermons in their synagogues and choruses performed. Some synagogues and Jewish Sunday schools framed Hanukkah candle-lighting ceremonies and the singing of some English translation of *Maoz Tsur* with secular amusements like magic-lantern exhibitions of "A Trip to the World's Fair," scenes of the holy land, or moments in Jewish history, Punch and Judy shows, or piano or violin musical solos. Entertainments like these had previously been staged at Purim, a late-winter holiday long noted for carnivalesque festivities. Now they were marshaled to create a more joyous Hanukkah.

In creating these new communal festivals Jews drew on several different sources. Hanukkah's rites and traditions supplied the candle-lighting ceremony, hymn singing, and the religious meaning explained in speeches at many, but not all, communal celebrations. From Christian Sunday schools Jews adapted the Sunday school locale and the active role played by female teachers, just as Jewish Sunday schools themselves had been adapted from Christian schools when the first such Jewish school opened in Philadelphia in 1838 under the leadership of Jewish women there. Many Jewish congregations adapted the custom of lay theatricals from Purim to their communal Hanukkah celebrations. Since mid-century, Jews in Philadelphia and New York staged gala masked balls at Purim to raise funds for local Jewish charities, and the custom spread to many other communities. In Rochester, New York and Bloomington, Indiana children presented a Purim play at their Hanukkah festival. Some Hanukkah dramatics were entirely secular, however; students in Detroit, Michigan staged an operetta, "Red Riding Hood's Rescue." Hanukkah also became an occasion to enjoy the entertainments beloved by many American children of all religions, including stereopticon exhibitions, jugglery, and marionettes. Communal Hanukkah festivals also expressed local values, interests, and abilities. In northern New Jersey, for example, women operating a Jewish Sabbath School cooked a Hanukkah feast for local families. Most unusual was an 1890 Denver, Colorado festival where 28 girls performed a broom drill and 40 boys a sword drill, which reviewers claimed "would have done genuine soldiers…proud."

In both traditionalist and reformist circles, women arranging new Hanukkah festivals also drew upon Christmas's dominant image, evergreens. In 1878, women of Philadelphia's traditionalist Beth El Emeth congregation trimmed refreshment tables with arches of evergreens. Chicago's Reform Sinai Congregation decorated its temple with a "Chanukah Tree brilliantly illuminated with wax candles." The next year, at New York's Reform Temple Emanu-El, amid a profusion of evergreens, Rabbi Gustav Gottheil explained the meaning of the holiday, two women recited poems, and children sang songs. Bloomington, Illinois, women organized a festival for children and their families in a B'nai B'rith hall that they decorated with candles framed by evergreens and a "Merry Chanukah" banner. Yet many Jews felt uncomfortable borrowing the Christmas decor for their holiday. When one child at Temple Emanu-El remarked that the decorated room "looked just like Christmas," a male instructor retorted that Christmas "was not an event that should interest you."

All sorts of Hanukkah festivities required women's energy. In 1879, New York's Young Men's Hebrew Association organized an elaborate pageant called the Grand National Revival of Hanukkah, where hundreds of young women and men posed in and provided costumes for the Revival's six *tableaux vivants*. When Baltimore's YMHA mounted a similar event the following year, a young woman read an "explanatory address" specially written by Henrietta Szold, who later became a decisive figure in twentieth-century Jewish life. A second young woman read a poem by Minnie Desau Louis, an important philanthropist soon to organize a free industrial school for New York's Jewish children. That poem, "Hannah and Her Seven Sons," told of the mother who saw her children tortured to death for refusing to eat a pig sacrificed to Epiphanes/Zeus.

A woodcut depicting the Hanukkah celebration by the Young Men's Hebrew Association at the Academy of Music in New York, 1880. Courtesy of the Library of Congress.

Women who created communal Hanukkah festivals were "loudly praised and cheered for their good will and motherly love." Such praise motivated many women to marshal local talent and resources to amuse and educate children and to raise funds for their charities. In Philadelphia young women invited local rabbi Marcus Jastrow to speak at their entertainment to benefit the Jewish Foster Home. Charitable women who helped to support an industrial school in New York instituted annual Hanukkah celebrations there. Afterwards, the women distributed garments, books, and various prizes to the children. Women who aided New York's Hebrew Orphan Asylum preferred simply to amuse children. No matter the program, these festivities customarily concluded with refreshments, usually ice cream and cake, candy, nuts and fruit, and sometimes, a dinner.

THE NEW HANUKKAH TRADITION INSTITUTIONALIZED

When the *American Hebrew* and *Hebrew Sabbath School Visitor* published accounts of Hanukkah festivals around the country they displayed both the ways American Jews fit their Hanukkah entertainments to local tastes as well as an emerging national Jewish culture. In Atlanta, Georgia, a United States flag was wrapped around a Torah scroll in a Hanukkah celebration whose theme was American patriotism. But in Las Vegas, Memphis, Boston, Baltimore, and Milwaukee, the similarity of Hanukkah celebrations in religious schools, halls, and synagogues reflected the Jewish press's national influence. In cities like Philadelphia, Cincinnati, and St. Louis, Hanukkah festivities were similar to those in New York. Hundreds of poorer Jewish children often were specially invited to Hanukkah celebrations in larger synagogues. But in smaller towns like Dayton, Ohio or Utica, New York, competing events, like the building of a new synagogue, might preempt a communal Hanukkah festival. Although Philip Cowen, editor of the *American Hebrew* for 27 years, disagreed with Lilienthal and Wise on many points about Judaism, these men encouraged American Jews to create joyful communal Hanukkah festivities, and their community reports provided examples for others to follow.

Some Hanukkah festivals were organized in B'nai B'rith halls. B'nai B'rith (Sons of the Covenant), a Jewish men's club founded in New York in 1843, counted lodges in towns throughout the country by late century. These groups sought to unite Jews for local charitable and social purposes and to counter the reformist versus traditionalist battles and ethnic diversity dividing American Jews. A Hanukkah entertainment held in a B'nai B'rith Hall might bring more Jews together than a synagogue festival. In these halls too, women mixed entertainment with religion, feasting, and charity. In Bloomington, Indiana, they recounted the tale of the martyred mother and sons, arranged a patriotic

Students from the Greater Washington Yeshiva dance in celebration during the National Chanukah Menorah Lighting Ceremony, December 7, 2004, on the Ellipse in Washington, D.C. © Win McNamee / Getty Images.

American tune, and enjoyed flute and piano solos. Supper was provided for the children who in turn donated funds to the Cleveland Orphan Asylum, the nearest such institution for Jewish children

Young Jewish women and girls often took leading roles in Hanukkah entertainments. In many locales, Jews looked to Sabbath schools to create Hanukkah festivals, and Jewish girls were more likely to attend a Sabbath school than boys. Such schools were a novelty in Jewish education and parents were more willing to experiment with their daughters' education than with their sons'. Girls did not become bar mitzvah, as boys might, and so did not require a traditional education in Hebrew reading to prepare them for the rite. Sunday schools' largely female faculty seemed to many parents to mark them as best suited to girls. For example, girls' performances dominated the 1887 Sabbath School Hanukkah entertainment in Detroit, where the program included a juvenile operetta based on the story of Little Red Riding Hood. In Evansville and Quincy, Illinois, too, girls performed most of the Hanukkah songs and orchestral pieces.

The number of Hanukkah celebrations steadily increased. "To judge from the number of Chanuka entertainments, grand, petty, and mediocre, the lessons of the [Grand National Revival of Chanukah] were broadly and amply enforced not only in New York but in the smallest town all over the union," remarked the *American Hebrew* in 1881. Reports of these festivities multiplied each year, in part due to a rise in the number of communal organizations that sponsored them. Across the country, older organizations like synagogues, fraternal associations, and women's clubs organized new charitable efforts that provided expanded religious school activities, industrial schools, penny lunches, orphan asylums, kindergartens, free libraries, mission schools, settlement houses, and medical aid to new Jewish immigrants and especially to their children. By the end of the decade the *American Hebrew* claimed that 10,000 people participated in these events in New York alone and concluded that they led to increasing numbers of domestic Hanukkah celebrations as well. Hanukkah's advocates felt they had accomplished their goal; they were sure Jewish children now "longed for" communal Hanukkah celebrations as they had once done for Christmas trees.

By the 1890s Hanukkah festivities became a staple of Jewish orphanages, settlement houses, and organizations catering to immigrants, as well as the Sunday schools of Reform congregations. In all venues, Jews worked to counter the notion that Christmas was an American holiday among new Jewish immigrants as well as among their own children. Historian Kenneth White wrote that "after the firm establishment of the Chanukah festival the newspapers began to lessen the amount of coverage about them. Upon Wise's death in 1900 the editorial policy of the *Israelite* almost eliminated all but the least mention of them in published articles. Attention switched to more social news." The Sunday school festival had become a fixture and editors no longer considered it newsworthy. These festivals for children flourished in Jewish congregations throughout the twentieth century and across all Jewish denominations.

The new Hanukkah festival tradition established in the nineteenth century became even more an institution in the twentieth century. When the National Federation of Temple Sisterhoods linked women volunteers in congregations identifying themselves as Reform in 1913, it began a century of providing assistance to women supporting congregational Hanukkah festivals nationwide. Fourteen years later, Deborah Melamed's *The Three Pillars,* providing advice to more tradition-minded women about Jewish observance, and including a separate chapter on Hanukkah, was distributed by the Women's League for Conservative Judaism. Reissued in new editions through 1958, it guided Jewish women in, among other things, creating Hanukkah celebrations at home or in a communal site like a synagogue or hall.

In the second half of the nineteenth century, Reform's changes had influenced so many congregations that many American Jews concluded that it would become the "wave of the future." To their surprise, the more than 2.3 million Jewish immigrants from eastern Europe who arrived in America between 1881 and 1924 turned that tide. By the time of Wise's death, the Union of American

Hebrew Congregations, the Reform union, represented only about 40,000 of America's one million Jews. But nineteenth-century reformers as well as traditionalists wrote and sermonized to instruct American Jews about what to *keep* while adapting Judaism to America. For all of these leaders, Hanukkah provided lessons about the courage to be different and the value of Jewish tradition. This holiday that had long been counted as a minor festival grew increasingly meaningful in the Christmas season. As Jews increasingly defined themselves as Americans, it seemed to illustrate their contemporary dilemma and to ask them, will you adopt a foreign religion or will you maintain Judaism?

FURTHER READING

Ashton, Dianne, and Rebecca Gratz. *Women and Judaism in Antebellum America.* Detroit, Mich.: Wayne State University Press, 1997.

Eisen, Arnold M. *Rethinking Modern Judaism.* Chicago: University of Chicago Press, 1998.

Sarna, Jonathan. *American Judaism.* New Haven, Conn.: Yale University Press, 2004.

Silverstein, Alan. *Alternatives to Assimilation: The Response of Reform Judaism to American Culture, 1840–1930.* Hanover, N.H.: Brandeis University Press, 1994.

Wolfson, Ron. *Hanukkah: The Family Guide to Spiritual Celebration,* 2nd ed. Woodstock, Vt.: Jewish Lights Publishing, 2002.

Dianne Ashton

FOREFATHERS DAY

A GENTEEL COMMEMORATION

In January 1769, in Plymouth, Massachusetts, seven young men from the town's leading families met to establish a private club that would avoid "the many disadvantages and inconveniences that arise from intermixing with the company at the taverns in this town of Plymouth." They called their new organization the "Old Colony Club," after the popular name for the part of southeastern Massachusetts that had once been the independent Plymouth Colony. They decided that the anniversary of the legendary landing on Plymouth Rock in December 1620 should be the date of their annual meeting. According to a 1621 account, the exploratory party from the *Mayflower* (which initially anchored at Cape Cod) had first arrived at Clark's Island in Plymouth harbor aboard a shallop—a large work boat—on December 8, 1620, and by tradition had landed on Plymouth Rock on Monday, December 11. The term "Pilgrim" referring to the Plymouth colonists had not yet come into use, and they were still just the "Forefathers" of the Plymouth community rather than the symbolic Pilgrim progenitors of all New England. This anniversary, first referred to as "Old Colony Day" and later known as "Forefathers Day," was first observed on December 22, 1769, according to a town historian, in the following manner:

> On the morning of the said day (Dec. 22, 1769), after discharging a cannon, was hoisted upon the hall [Old Colony Hall, in the center of town] an elegant silk flag, with the follow-

FOREFATHERS DAY

- ☐ In 1769 seven well-heeled young men in the town of Plymouth founded the Old Colony Club and first observed Forefathers Day on December 22 of that year to commemorate the day Pilgrims landed on Plymouth Rock in 1620.

- ☐ Local, simply prepared produce, meat, and seafood, meant to recreate the original settlers' dining fare, made up the banquet's menu.

- ☐ In 1798 Forefathers Day was observed in Boston for the first time, and the term "Pilgrim" came to designate the original Plymouth colonists.

- ☐ Expatriate New Englanders carried Forefathers Day commemorations West and Southward during the early nineteenth century and helped establish commemorations in Philadelphia, New York, Charleston, St. Louis, San Francisco, Chicago, and many other cities, making it a national event.

- ☐ As transplanted New Englanders faded away so did the holiday's popularity. By the 1920s the day was observed in only a few East coast cities; by the 1950s it was observed only in Plymouth.

Nineteenth-century lithograph of the landing of the Pilgrims on Plymouth Rock in 1620. Courtesy of the Library of Congress.

ing inscription, 'OLD COLONY, 1620'. At eleven o'clock, A.M. the members of the club appeared at the hall, and from thence proceeded to the house of Mr. Howland, inn-holder, which is erected on the spot where the first licensed house in the Old Colony formerly stood, at half after two a decent repast was served, which consisted of the following dishes, viz. 1, a large baked Indian whortleberry pudding; 2, a dish of sauquetash; 3, a dish of clams; 4, a dish of oysters and a dish of codfish; 5, a haunch of venison, roasted by the first Jack brought to the colony; 6, a dish of seafowl; 7, a dish of frost fish and eels; 8, an apple pie; 9, a course of cranberry tarts, and cheese made in the Old Colony.

By creating a specific anniversary for the landing of the shallop at Plymouth Rock (the *Mayflower* arrived in Plymouth harbor five days later), the Old Colony Club made that event pivotal in the Forefathers' story, and provided a focus for much of the Pilgrim symbolism that was to follow. The dinner itself incorporated a number of emblematic elements to emphasize the significance of the event. The food selected was intrinsically native and "dressed in the plainest manner (all appearance of luxury and extravagance being avoided, in imitation of our ancestors, whose memory we shall ever respect)." The president sat in a chair that had belonged to Governor William Bradford and called for a dozen toasts to honor the memory of their ancestors, and to give assent to the desire for liberty and prosperity. After the toasts, the evening was spent "recapitulating and conversing upon the many and various advantages of our forefathers in the first settlement of this country, and the growth and increase of the same,—at eleven o'clock in the evening a cannon was again fired, three cheers given, and the club and company withdrew."

The December 22 date was chosen to adjust for the discrepancy between the Julian or "Old Style" and the Gregorian or "New Style" calendars. When many Catholic nations adopted the corrected Gregorian system in the 1580s, Protestant England ignored the change because of religious and political ramifications. When England and her colonies finally did accept the new system in 1752, 11 days had to be added to make the adjustment. With this recent event in mind, the Old Colony Club converted the Landing anniversary to December 22 by adding 11 days. In this they miscalculated; actually it was only necessary to add *10* days to adjust an early seventeenth-century date, since the two calendars then had not yet diverged by an 11-day interval. The adjustment would also result in odd juxtapositions in later history books, where the Forefathers would arrive at Cape Cod and sign the Compact on November 11 (using Old Style dating), but make their famous Landing on December 22, 1620 (using New Style)!

The next year, 1770, Forefathers Day was celebrated on Monday, December 24 in order to avoid the eve of the Sabbath. This time the observances extended beyond the club's membership. Youths paraded the streets of the town at daybreak firing off a cannon and small arms. The club members assembled at ten A.M. and were joined by many of the leading citizens by invitation. Once again there was an entertainment at which "the history of emigrant colonies and the constitution and declension of empires, ancient and modern" was discussed over a meal "foreign from all kinds of luxury, and consisting of fish, flesh, and vegetables, the natural produce of this colony." The company marched to Old Colony Hall accompanied by the local militia, where they were met by a well-disciplined group of schoolboys and their master, and Rev. Chandler Robbins of the First Church. Edward Winslow Jr., one of the club's founders, delivered a speech reciting the usual remembrance of the Forefathers, closing with a thinly-veiled reference to the strained relations between Britain and her American colonies: "if we, their sons, act from the same principles, and conduct with the same noble firmness and resolution, when our holy religion or our civil liberties are invaded, we may expect a reward proportionate."

Traditionally, the commemoration of any New England event was made from the pulpit, but three Forefathers Day observations went by before this was suggested. In 1772, Rev. Robbins duly provided the club and its guests with an appropriate sermon. By that time news of the annual celebration reached beyond the Old Colony and was becoming recognized for its potentially radical message of separation from the mother country. The celebration was noted by Samuel Adams of Boston, who congratulated the Plymouth Committee of Correspondence (Plymouth being the first town to respond to the call for the establishment of such committees that year) "on the return of that great Anniversary, the landing of the first Settlers at Plymouth," without which England would not have had its restless American colonies.

AN EVENT FOR THE YOUNG REPUBLIC

In 1773 the revolutionary Plymouth Committee of Correspondence met with the Old Colony Club—there was some overlap in membership—and rather presumptuously informed the Club that they were determined to recognize Forefathers Day in their own way and requested that the club "join with and conform thereto." Not surprisingly, the conservative members of the club resented this unsolicited invasion of their territory and disruption of existing plans. The conservative members of the club voted to observe the holiday privately, which they did, after which the club, which had already lost its patriot members, disbanded. The Town of Plymouth carried on the Forefathers Day tradition in 1774, when inflamed partisan passions led to the following report of the celebration in the *Boston Gazette* (Jan. 2, 1775, pp. 2–3): "We the Posterity of those of those illustrious Heroes are now suffering under the galling pressure of that power, an emancipation from which, was the one grand object they had in view, in the settlement of this Western World.... But, wonderful as it may seem, a pitiful number, who bear the names, and descended from the loins of these ever-to-be-revered Patriots, by their infernal intrigues, and persevering obstinacy, have involved their native Country, enriched with the Blood of their Fathers, in accumulated Calamities and Distresses." The Town sponsored six more such public celebrations before observations were suspended between 1781 and 1792.

By the end of the century, the observance of Forefathers Day had spread to Boston. In 1772, a correspondent ("Philadelphus") had written to the *Boston Gazette* commenting favorably on the Forefathers celebration in Plymouth that year and hinting that Salem, as the initial settlement in Massachusetts, should do (or perhaps did; the meaning is unclear) likewise. However, the first reported public Forefathers anniversary celebrated in Boston was on the Plymouth anniversary of December 22, 1798. The event was sponsored by a club or group called "The Sons of the Pilgrims" and chiefly commemorated the Plymouth colonists, to which the term "Pilgrim" was now attached. The first toast of the evening was to "The Pilgrims of Leyden: May the Empire which has sprung from their labours be permanent as the rock of their landing," and an ode by Robert Treat Paine Jr. contained the lines "The pilgrim man, so long oppress'd, / Had found his promis'd place of rest" and "Heirs of Pilgrims, now renew, / The oath your fathers swore for you." Perhaps the fact that the Plymouth Forefathers were not the actual ancestors of the Boston contingent inclined them to select the more general term "Pilgrim," which had been used to refer to the early Massachusetts colonists since the 1760s.

The Forefathers dinner in Boston received the nickname "The Feast of Shells," ostensibly in recognition of the symbolic humble clam that had long represented the "simple fare" of the New England forefathers. However, historian Albert Matthews in 1915 noted that "It should be pointed out that...the expressions 'the shells of feast,' 'the shells of joy,' 'the feast of shells,' occur in the Ossianic poems; Macpherson explaining, 'To rejoice in the shell, is a phrase for feasting sumptuously.'" In 1799, the organizers of the Boston celebration borrowed an enormous 200-pound oyster shell from the Museum of Natural history to grace their table. It held about a bushel, and was filled with the traditional succotash for the company. A further reason for the adoption of a shell as a symbol was suggested by the association of the famous scallop shell symbol carried by medieval pilgrims who had been to the shrine of St. James Compostella in Spain. The scallop shell rather than the original New England clamshell eventually became the shell associated with the American Pilgrims.

Just as Plymouth Rock came to symbolize the heroic and providential nature of the *Mayflower* voyage, an icon was required to celebrate the Plymouth colonists' courageous perseverance through their suffering and deprivation. A symbol of colonial want and fortitude that grew out of the Forefathers Day celebrations was the "five kernels of corn." Their appearance is first recorded at the 1820 Forefathers Day dinner when five symbolic parched corn kernels were placed on each plate to remind the diners of "the time in 1623, when that was the proportion allowed to each individual on account of scarcity." The General Society of Mayflower Descendants, in a small pamphlet published on the topic in the 1950s, relates the tradition:

> After the corn planting in the spring of 1623, the scant supply remaining until the following harvest, when pooled and divided, permitted a ration, according to tradition, of only five kernels of corn per day per person. Nevertheless, still other demands arose and even this slender supply became exhausted before the next harvest. Thus came about the memorable 'starving time.' The suffering became intense. Strong men fell exhausted at their work. However, it is recorded that not one succombed [sic]. Their great faith, and indomitable will to survive, carried them through to the next harvest, and the well-earned years of plenty ahead.

The story was related by writers such as Joseph Banvard, *Plymouth and the Pilgrims* (1851) and Frances Baylies, *An Historical Memoir of the Colony of New Plymouth* (1866), but there is no mention of the suppositious ration in any contemporary sources such as William Bradford's history of the colony, rediscovered in 1856. As J.A. Goodwin in *The Pilgrim Republic* (1888) observed concerning the tradition, "the story rests on no foundation, and is opposed to common-sense." There is no reason to believe that the colonial leaders would actually issue a daily corn ration of five kernels, which was not enough to be of any nutritional benefit. Instead, they simply ran out at the end of the spring season in April when they planted what they had put aside as seed. However, the custom of placing five kernels of corn (often in a small scallop shell) still occurs at Mayflower Society dinners and similar events.

Pilgrims dealing out five kernels of corn per family member during the starving days. © Culver Pictures.

The occasion in Plymouth had originally been a nonpartisan event, but public Forefathers Day celebrations in the 1790s in both Plymouth and Boston were soon identified with conservative interests. The revival of the celebrations came at a time when political factionalism was emerging from the consensus of the Revolution. The development of the Federalist and the Anti-Federalist or Republican parties broke down the earlier New England unity, much to the indignation of both sides, and the Federalists appear to have adopted the Plymouth Forefathers as the patrons of their faction. The celebrations in Boston sponsored by the Sons of the Pilgrims featured partisan toasts and sentiments that excited the ire of the Anti-Federalists. "The doings of some Federalists of the *modern* stamp *after* Dinner, is a melancholy discovery that in Plymouth as well as Boston, there are too many of [the Pilgrims'] Posterity who dishonor them by their sentiments and practices, and are melancholy evidences that they are indeed the DEGENERATE *Plants of a* NOBLE VINE" (*Independent Chronicle,* Jan. 5, 1799). The supporters of the Pilgrims were then attacked for their snobbery, which was not the last time that the Pilgrims became identified in the popular mind with elitism.

Criticism of the sentiments at Forefathers dinners became a common theme as Federalists and Republicans fought over the former's pro-British policies and declining popular support. The 1799 Boston celebration roused the indignation of a correspondent to the *Independent Chronicle* (December 31, 1799, p. 2), signing himself "Propriety": "Strange it was that the managers of that feast, should imagine that those Heavenly Pilgrims could approve of the practice of toasting, to which they were so much adverse on earth." The contesting political parties helped to make the Pilgrims a symbol worth fighting for, as both claimed to be the true heirs of the first settlers' values and character.

Forefathers Day celebrations in Plymouth attracted some of the most celebrated orators of the early republic. John Quincy Adams gave a significant address in 1802 in which he identified the Mayflower Compact as a formative influence on the American Constitution, an assertion that had a lasting impact on the perception of the Pilgrim contribution to the new nation. The newly founded Pilgrim Society celebrated the 1820 bicentennial of the Pilgrim landing at Plymouth with an outstanding Forefathers oration by Daniel Webster. Among the eminent speakers that followed Adams and Webster in Plymouth and at Boston were Edward Everett (1824), Lyman Beecher (1827), Richard Yeadon of Charleston, South Carolina (1853), Charles Sumner (1853) and William H. Seward (1855), who would later compose Abraham Lincoln's famous 1863 Thanksgiving proclamation.

THE NEW ENGLAND SOCIETIES AND THE SPREAD OF FOREFATHERS DAY

What had begun as a local commemoration was about to become an event with national appeal, a celebration of the history and traditions of New England, with the Plymouth Pilgrims as its symbolic basis. Expatriate New Englanders founded "New England Societies" in cities in America and abroad, first as benevolent societies for the charity and mutual assistance of members (generally business and professional men) and later as convivial clubs for elite men of Yankee origin or descent. While ostensibly honoring the example and achievements of their colonial forebears, New England Society gatherings tended to focus on the membership's nostalgic memories for New England scenes and their own family origins.

In 1805, the first Forefathers Day celebration in New York was reported in the Boston *Independent Chronicle* as an elegant occasion in which "150 gentlemen of the society, forgetting all differences of party and opinion, united to celebrate the occasion with an affectionate remembrance of their common origin and in the true spirit of a society, the objects of which are friendship, charity and mutual assistance." This celebration was held by the New England Society of New York, founded in New York City on May 6, 1805 following a meeting of interested expatriate New Englanders residing there. A second New England Society was founded in Charleston, South Carolina (which had had ties of trade and family relationships with Plymouth since the seventeenth century) in 1819, and the annual celebration of Forefathers Day was instituted there as well.

The New England Societies mobilized the widest support for the holiday. Before the Civil War autonomous branches were founded in Philadelphia, Augusta (Georgia), Louisville, New Orleans; San Francisco; Detroit, Chicago, Cincinnati, Cleveland, and even in Montreal and Quebec. Additional ones were established later in Wisconsin and New Jersey; in St. Louis, Olympia in the Washington Territory, and in Washington, D.C. With the exception of the more prestigious societies such as those in New York, Brooklyn, Philadelphia, and Charleston, few New England Societies flourished for any length of time, but they were for a period a "power in the land," as a writer for the *Magazine of American History* observed in 1884. They were (with one exception in Michigan) exclusive bastions of male privilege, and most if not all celebrated Forefathers Day with lavish dinners, orations, and convivial songs. The earlier toasts sometimes gave way before the challenge of temperance advocates, but both substantial speeches and humorous after-dinner remarks (by Mark Twain among others) were perennial attractions.

The other association that particularly promoted the observation of Forefathers Day during the nineteenth century was the Congregational Church. Like the expatriate Yankees who founded the New England Societies, the American Congregational Church adopted the Plymouth Pilgrims as their symbolic progenitors and celebrated this heritage in the observation of Forefathers Day by Congregational Clubs and similar church-related organizations in Detroit, Grand Rapids, Omaha, Atchison, Portland (Oregon), and elsewhere. By adopting Forefathers Day, these two organizations also promoted the symbolic significance of the Pilgrims long before the Plymouth colonists were in any way associated with the Thanksgiving holiday, as they are today. Local newspapers reported Forefathers Day sermons, speeches, and sentiments at length and helped popularize the Pilgrim story and establish it as a key element in America's founding myth.

The New England Societies were at their apogee at the turn of the twentieth century. Their Forefathers activities received considerable attention in the press and aroused interest among historically and patriotically minded citizens before World War I. Yet it was not long before both the New England Societies and Forefathers Day itself began to disappear from the American landscape. Only a few societies, such as those of New York and Charleston, survived the 1920s, and Forefathers Day was soon largely forgotten. By the mid-twentieth century, the celebration of Forefathers Day had receded back to Plymouth where it had begun, enjoying a modest revival there in the 1950s:

> During the first half of the twentieth century, the day was observed by a simple service in the First Church and a business meeting in Pilgrim Hall [a museum built in 1820 to house Pilgrim-related artifacts]. After the mammoth celebrations of the 19th century, this form of observance seemed rather tame. Consequently, in 1953, Warren P. Strong, then Secretary, Librarian and Cabinet Keeper of the Society, determined that it was possible and desirable to reinstitute the Forefather Day Dinner in the lower hall.

Since that time the celebration has outgrown the capacity of Pilgrim Hall itself, and the traditional dinner, complete with the de rigueur accompaniment of the ceremonial "Plymouth succotash" (a traditional dish), has been held in local halls, churches, and hotels each December 21.

The change in dates was the outcome of the discrepancy in the calendrical adjustment of the anniversary date, which was a matter of debate for half a century. In 1850, a committee of the Pilgrim Society of Plymouth published a report on the problem and judged that the addition of 10 days was the correct solution, concluding that "the celebration in future of the Landing of the Pilgrims at Plymouth be held on the *twentyfirst* day of December." The weight of tradition was not so easily shifted, however, and the society did not adopt the new date until 1870. Then in 1882, *The Nation* (July 6) reported that the Pilgrim Society had again changed course, declaring

> That while we recognize the historical fact that the passengers on the shallop of the *Mayflower* landed on Plymouth Rock on the 11th of December, 1620, and that the 21st of the new style corresponds to the day of the landing, yet, in view of the fact that the 22nd has been hallowed by an observance during a period of over one hundred years, and consecrated by the words of Winslow, Webster, Everett, Adams, Seward and other eminent orators of our land, it is hereby resolved that hereafter the 22nd of December be observed by the Pilgrim Society as the Anniversary of the Landing.

The Pilgrim Society eventually adopted the reformed date, but the traditional 22nd of December date was retained elsewhere, even in Plymouth itself. In 1875, the revived Old Colony Club of Plymouth chose to have its annual meeting on the 22nd just as the original organization had done a century before, and it still holds its annual celebration on that day.

A feature of the original eighteenth-century Old Colony Club celebrations of Forefathers Day was a dawn march marked with the firing of a cannon, guns, and cheers. Club Historian L. J. Bradbury revived this event during his terms as president. On December 22, 1956, the members of the Old Colony Club gathered at the club house early in the morning. At six o'clock, with flags and music, and wearing tall hats, they marched across the street to the court house lawn. There President Bradbury paid verbal respects to the Pilgrim Forefathers. After firing a small signal cannon and shouting hurrahs, they marched down Main Street to Town Square (site of the original settlement) and back to the club house, where they partook of a breakfast comprised of cranberry juice, ham and eggs, muffins, doughnuts, and coffee. After breakfast, the members gathered at the flagpole on the club house lawn, raised the American flag, and gave their pledge of allegiance. This has since become a unique Plymouth custom, and regardless of the weather on Forefathers Day, club members have unfailingly performed their 6:00 A.M. march ever since (complete with a small band), much to the amazement of new residents in the downtown area. In the evening the club reassembles for a business meeting followed by a traditional Plymouth succotash dinner and after-dinner speech.

Today Forefathers Day revolves largely around the preparation and serving of a traditional local food dish. Plymouth succotash is a descendant of a primary Indian meal in the southeastern New England area, a hulled-corn and bean soup made with various meats or fish. Ever since the first Forefathers Day dinner in 1769, this succotash has been prepared each December with much fanfare. Plymouth succotash can actually take two forms: a boiled dinner consisting of corned beef, fowl, and salt pork served with white turnip, potato, hulled corn (whole hominy) and boiled white navy beans in broth; or a thick soup containing these ingredients. Only the Old Colony Club maintains the method of service in which the meats are served separately, with pieces cut for each guest, while the vegetables are presented in the broth in which the meat was cooked. Elsewhere the ingredients are made directly into a rich soup, which is how leftovers were originally served the following day. The correct composition of this dish is as serious an undertaking as is making a proper chili in Texas, and a modern vegetarian version of lima beans and sweet corn (known locally as "summer succotash") is entirely out of the question for traditionalists. The preparation of succotash was an annual rite among old Plymouth families, and for many years it was prepared and sold by local restaurants, although this custom has now largely disappeared.

THE RETURN TO A LOCAL EVENT

There were a number of factors behind the precipitous decline of Forefathers Day outside of Plymouth. First, the pool of native New England emigrants from which the membership of the New England Societies was drawn had dwindled away, and the popularity of small independent benevolent societies and private men's clubs waned. Unlike the large nationally organized sodalities such as the Freemasons, Elks, Moose, and similar benevolent groups, the autonomous New

England Societies lacked any supportive network to sustain them or redefine their mission. Service clubs such as the Rotary (1905), Kiwanis (1915), and Lions (1917) attracted the businessmen who had previously given their time to such local clubs. Second, the attraction of the Pilgrim connection was drawn off by the new genealogical societies such as the General Society of Mayflower Descendants (which not only admitted but greatly depended on its women members) and the increasing popular association of the Pilgrims with Thanksgiving. This had begun only in 1841 when the account of the "First Thanksgiving" was rediscovered. Until then Thanksgiving was regarded as a generic New England holiday and the sole Pilgrim holiday was Forefathers Day. By 1900, the Plymouth colonists had become closely associated with Thanksgiving and would soon become that far more significant holiday's primary symbol, thus competing with Forefathers Day for this particular historic appeal. Third, the holiday's awkward mid-December date naturally conflicted with the expand-

Undated portrait of Charles Ives. © Brown Brothers.

ing Christmas season. Even the New England Society of New York, which still flourishes today, has all but dropped the observance of Forefathers Day, and one suspects this was the reason. The final factor that dampened popular participation and mass appeal of the holiday was that Forefathers Day had largely been an elite, male-dominated event.

Generally, the occasion of Forefathers Day had no artistic or cultural influence worthy of note, with one exception. American composer Charles Ives actually composed a suite for Forefathers Day. His "Holidays Symphony" (also known as *A Symphony: New England Holidays*) consists of four movements: Washington's Birthday (Winter), Decoration Day (Spring), The Fourth of July (Summer), and Thanksgiving and Forefathers Day (Autumn). "Thanksgiving and Forefathers Day" was the first of the four movements that Ives composed around 1903 and 1904 and was dedicated to Ives' brother-in-law Edward Carrington Twichell.

While Forefathers Day had been observed on occasion in schools and by Yankee families in its heyday, it was never a civic holiday outside of New England. Even in Massachusetts it did not become a public occasion. As an event primarily celebrated within private organizations, there was little opportunity for participation by anyone who was not directly connected with these groups, a circumstance that could not engender much enthusiasm among the general public. Outside of its occasional inclusion in lists of American holidays or in grammar-school anthologies of seasonal observances, Forefathers Day was not recognized in popular art, or by commercial exploitation that enabled newer holidays such as Memorial Day, Labor Day, and Mother's Day to gain national prominence and achieve popular acceptance. What popularity the holiday had was mainly due to the Pilgrim symbolism and the interest of the local news media in the activities of their influential citizens. When the New England and Congregational societies ceased to celebrate Forefathers Day, and the holiday's association with the Pilgrims and their story was absorbed by Thanksgiving, it marked the end of Forefathers Day's national existence.

FURTHER READING

Matthews, Albert. "The Term 'Pilgrim Fathers' and Early Celebrations of Forefathers' Day." *Transactions of the Colonial Society of Massachusetts* 17 (1915): 292–391.

"Records of the Old Colony Club." *Proceedings of the Massachusetts Historical Society* 3 (1888): 382–444.

Vartanian, Pershing. "The Puritan as Symbol in American Thought: A Study of the New England Societies 1820–1920." Ph.D. Diss, University of Michigan, 1971.

Way, William. *History of the New England Society of Charleston, South Carolina, 1819–1919.* Charleston, S.C.: Published by the Society, 1920.

James W. Baker

CHRISTMAS

- Christmas is celebrated every December 25 and was declared a national holiday in 1870.

- Jesus's exact date of birth is mentioned nowhere in the Bible, nor is there any other reliable evidence when he was born.

- The Roman Catholic Church declared December 25 as the Feast of the Nativity in the third century C.E.; the first known Feast was held in 336 C.E.

- The Feast of the Nativity was created to counter popular Roman pagan winter solstice celebrations.

- In Norman England the Feast of the Nativity was marked by feasting, gambling, dancing, and games—activities frowned upon at other times of the year.

- Calvinist Puritans and Cromwell's Puritan Commonwealth condemned Christmas in the mid-1600s as a Popish holiday. Older, bawdier customs persisted nonetheless.

- English colonists brought Christmas customs with them to the New World in the early seventeenth century.

- The Massachusetts Bay General Court banned the keeping of Christmas in 1659. King James II forced the Court to lift the ban in 1681.

- Christmastime rowdiness peaked in the early nineteenth century when packs of mischief-making young men would wander city streets, drinking and fighting, banging and blowing on homemade instruments, and enter the homes of the elite for food and drink.

- By the mid-1800s an emerging middle class popularized new Christmas customs, including Santa Claus, the family dinner, and decorated trees, which domesticated the holiday and resolved complicated interrelationships between faith, market, community, and family.

- Santa Claus was popularized by Clement Clarke Moore, whose 1822 poem "An Account of a Visit from St. Nicholas," was reprinted in newspapers around Christmastime.

- The custom of keeping a decorated evergreen tree in the household during Christmastime arrived in America via Germany and the Nordic countries around the mid-1800s.

- Sending Christmas cards became popular in the late 1800s after German immigrant Charles Prang perfected multicolor lithography.

- Santa's credibility as an American folk hero depends on his role as a highly successful manufacturer and distributor of toys, placing him in the pantheon of America's captains of industry.

- New York City was the first to erect a Christmas tree in a public square, in 1912. In 1923 President Calvin Coolidge began the tradition of an annual National Christmas Tree lighting ceremony.

- In 1939, Montgomery Ward distributed free to its customers nearly two and a half million copies of *Rudolph the Red-Nosed Reindeer,* a story written by its ad department.

- In 1998, Americans spent more than $160 billion on presents, about $700 per person.

CHRISTMAS

Should one say "Merry Christmas?" Or is it more polite and inclusive to say "Happy Holidays?" Is Christmas a religious holiday or a national festival? Is it sacred or secular? Can only Christians celebrate it? Or can anyone have the "Christmas spirit?" Throughout its history Christmas has functioned both as a religious holiday and a secular one, joining together sometimes quite opposite expressions that satisfy a broad spectrum of cultural needs, from spiritual to worldly. This is particularly so in America, where Christmas enfolds a core expression of Christian belief, the solvency of local and national economies, the unity of extended family, and the psychological strains of anticipation and disappointment. In short, the holiday, perhaps America's most important one, is a window on American experience, revealing much about the contradictions and ambiguities of our national character.

THE EARLY CHRISTMAS CELEBRATION

Christmas began in Europe as the Roman Catholic Church established itself at the center of Western Christianity. The earliest Christians gave little attention to Jesus's birth. They expected the Second Coming soon and in any case viewed birthday celebrations as heathen. As the hope of Jesus's imminent return faded, the faithful began to search for evidence of the day or even season of Jesus's birth. They found no clues in the Gospels, nor anywhere else in the

Bible. Nor could they locate any other reliable sources to pinpoint the date of his nativity.

Sometime in the fourth century, the Roman Catholic Church began to celebrate a Feast of the Nativity (the first known reference to the Feast is 336 C.E.). A variety of issues influenced the decision. Rome's pagan winter celebrations, which culminated on December 25, the winter solstice according to the Julian calendar, had become more and more raucous, and its increasing focus on Mithras, the Invincible Sun, offered significant competition to the Church. Making matters worse, some within the Church contended Jesus was mortal, not divine. Striking at both internal and external challenges, the Church created a new holy day, a Feast of the Nativity, to be observed on December 25.

The overlapping of the Roman holiday, Saturnalia, and the Feast of the Nativity set the terms of future debate over the Christmas festival, framing the holiday's enduring duality of sacred and profane. Christmas's Christian aspects, at least in their most intense form, emphasized heavenly afterlife. The heathen elements absorbed into the festival affirmed earthly life and exalted its annual renewal. The Church made no clear separations between the two perspectives. It sustained the hope that sacred would eventually overtake profane, and that converts would eventually abandon their pagan revels.

Over the next thousand years, Christmas observance followed the expanding community of Christianity. By 380, Christians in Constantinople celebrated the holiday; and by 432, Egyptians. By the end of the sixth century, Christianity had taken it into Norse culture, where it fused with the pagan Yule. Around the time of the Norman incursion, England joined the celebration, where it quickly acquired associations with feasting, dancing, singing, card playing, and gambling—pleasures discouraged during the remainder of the year. Philip Stubbes's *Anatomy of Abuses* (1583), for example, described its celebrants as "hel hounds" in a "Deville's daunce" of merriment. By the seventeenth century, the holiday's excesses had grown to magnificent proportions featuring extravagant dinners, expensive plays, and elaborate games.

It fell to Puritan reformers to put a stop to the unholy English fun and to bend arguments over the proper keeping of Christmas into an older and more basic one—whether there should even be a Christmas. The Bible, they argued, expressly commanded keeping only the Sabbath. The rise of Oliver Cromwell's Puritan Commonwealth dealt a sharper blow to the country's indulgent Christmas celebrations. Among other measures, Parliament purposely met every Christmas from 1644 to 1652, and in 1652, it "strongly prohibited" Christmas observance. The economic and social upheaval of the late sixteenth and early seventeenth centuries further altered the English Christmas. As the holiday returned with the Restoration, it increasingly came to symbolize a time for charity toward the poor and the maintenance of the older social order, when times had been more prosperous and when the different levels of society had understood their relationship toward one another.

AMERICAN COLONIAL CHRISTMASES

It was within the particularly turbulent years just before and during the Puritan Revolution that settlers carried English Christmas customs to Virginia and New England. Most welcomed it as a day of respite from the routines of work and hardship. Some observed it, at least in part, as a holy day. On Christmas, 1608, Captain John Smith, having endured for "six or seven dayes the extreame winde, rayne, frost and snow" as he and his men traveled through Virginia colony, reported that they "were never more merry, nor fed on more plentie of good Oysters, Fish, Flesh, Wild-foule, and good bread; nor never had better fires in England." In New England, Puritans and Pilgrims tried to ignore the holiday. The Plymouth settlers of 1620 spent Christmas constructing buildings. The following Christmas, however, non-Separatist newcomers "excused them selves and said it wente against their consciences to work on that day." Governor William Bradford allowed the "lusty yonge" Englishmen to rest but emphasized "ther should be no gameing or revelling in the streets."

As the first settlements grew into more established communities, new patterns of Christmas celebration appeared. Geographic separation from European homelands, the diversity of religious and ethnic groups living close to each other, and the hardship of new beginnings disrupted old habits and holidays. Pennsylvania Quakers scorned Christmas as adamantly as Puritans did. The colony's Huguenots, Moravians, Dutch Reformed, and Anglicans, however, each kept Christmas in their own ways. Elizabeth Drinker, herself a Quaker, divided Philadelphians into three categories. There were Quakers, who "make no more account of it [Christmas] than another day," those who were religious, and the rest who "spend it in riot and dissipation."

"The rest" referred to by Drinker were often mummers or masqueraders who, during the Christmas season, disguised themselves, sometimes dressing as animals, or wearing clothes of the opposite sex. They played crude tricks on one another, or roved from house to house and entered without permission. An informal code dictated that the householder ask the uninvited guests "into the house and regale them with mulled cider, or small beer, and home made cakes," or "give the leading mummers a few pence as a dole, which . . . they would 'pool,' and buy cakes and beer." In return, the visitors might dance, sing, beg food, and act "a rude drama," mocking propriety and challenging the social order. One never "address[ed] or otherwise recognize[d] the mummer by any other name than the name of the character he was assuming." Such antics, drawn from folk customs in England, Sweden, and Germany were especially prominent in the Middle Colonies, but their affronts to propriety could be found throughout the British settlements.

Southerners marked Christmas as a season of visiting and pleasure. Virginians, Carolinians, and Marylanders enjoyed dancing, card playing, cock fighting, nine pins, and horse racing. "All over the [Virginia] Colony, a universal

Hospitality reigns," *London Magazine* reported in 1746; "full Tables and open Doors, the kind salute, the generous Detention, speak somewhat like the old Roast-beef Ages of our Fore-fathers. ... Strangers are sought after with Greediness, as they pass the Country, to be invited." In 1773, Philip Vickers Fithian, a tutor at one of the wealthiest Tidewater plantations, described a southern Christmas season. "Nothing is now to be heard of in conversation, but the *Balls,* the *Fox-hunts,* the fine *entertainments,* and the good fellowship," Fithian wrote. Anglicanism, the established religion in most of the southern planting colonies, did not pressure its members into sacred observance. The family attended church on December 26, reported Fithian, to listen to a 15-minute sermon on "For unto us a child is Born &c."

This broadly permissive (and not very religious) approach to Christmas contrasted sharply with New England Puritans' struggle to dampen the holiday, especially as orthodoxy waned and the proportion of non-Puritans grew substantially. At first, Puritans tried to quell Christmas with "informal pressure of like minded co-religionists." In 1659, in an atmosphere of tension over Anglicanism and British authority, the Massachusetts Bay General Court banned outright the keeping of Christmas by "forebearing of labour, feasting, or any other way." The law aimed to prevent the recurrence of further, unspecified "disorders" that had apparently arisen in "seurerall places ... by reason of some still observing such Festiualls," and provided that "whosoever shall be found observing any such day as Xmas or the like" would be fined.

Although compelled by Charles II to lift the ban in 1681, the Puritan battle against Christmas persisted. Congregational ministers routinely ordered fasts on Christmas Day and preached that the celebration of Jesus's birth was "Popery and prelatic tyranny, a destroyer of consciences." Yet secular frivolity continued. In 1711, Cotton Mather recorded in his diary, "I hear a Number of people of both Sexes, belonging, many of them to my Flock, who have had on Christmas-night, this last Week, a Frolick, a revelling Feast, and Ball, which discovers their Corruption, and has a Tendency to corrupt them yett more, and provoke the Holy One to give them up into eternal Hardness of Heart."

Although Mather viewed the merrymaking as an "affront unto the grace of God," he tacitly understood that his belief would not prevail. Heterogeneous populations and requirements of social harmony throughout the colonies shaped and encouraged Christmas celebrations. Yet its status as a holiday remained haphazard. Like the colonies in general on the eve of the Revolution, regions and communities were as notable for their different approaches to the holiday as for their commonalities. Thus, Christmas, although widely celebrated, retained little importance in society as a whole precisely because of religious and cultural diversity. It would take the project of nation-building in the wake of the Revolution to begin to define an American conception of Christmas.

A NEW DOMESTIC HOLIDAY

Americans celebrated relatively few holidays before independence and even fewer after. Besides revoking all official British holidays, the new states did not replace them, nor did they consolidate their many calendars into a single, national one that encoded republican and democratic values. National holidays simply did not exist. Moreover, disestablishment insured that no specifically religious holidays would receive state sanction. The spare American calendar seemed even more problematic given that special religious and civic days could temporarily release celebrants from the everydayness of life to renew social, spiritual, and civic commitments. In short, they characterize and reflect the nature and needs of a society; they are essential to the formation of a cultural identity. Young, dynamic America though, increasingly criss-crossed with linguistic, ethnic, and regional differences, had yet to define itself as a nation.

A few thoughtful Americans voiced concern over the nation's sparse and ragtag calendar. Some faulted religion. "Our Protestant Faith affords no religious holidays & processions like the Catholics," John Pintard remarked in 1823. The English, "Jews…Heathens…Greeks & Romans, the Celts, Druids, even our Indians all had & have their religious Festivals.… [B]ut with us, we have only Independence Christmas & New Year, 3 solitary days." Washington Irving faulted modernity. As a character in one of his stories remarked: "One of the least pleasing effects of modern refinement is the havoc it has made among the hearty old holiday customs."

While Irving looked nostalgically to some earlier, better holiday time, remnants of European customs persisted, albeit in new, urban contexts. In traditional, smaller, and more familiar communities, mumming harmlessly reaffirmed the social order by temporarily overturning it. However, early in the nineteenth century, young men had begun wandering the northern cities in packs at Christmas time, drinking in taverns and fighting on street corners, banging and blowing on homemade instruments, and entering the homes of the elite, intent on creating mischief to match their noise. Philadelphia's *Daily Chronicle* reported on Christmas Eve, 1833, that "riot…and uproar prevailed, uncontrolled and uninterrupted in many of our central and most orderly streets. Gangs of boys and young men howled and shouted as if possessed by the demon of disorder." The saturnalian behavior of these so-called Callithumpian bands alarmed "respectable" city dwellers not only because of their destructiveness, but also because they were almost invariably strangers over whom merchants and homeowners could exert little control.

Such public (and primarily male) Christmas mayhem contrasted strikingly with the civility of city dwellers enjoying the new wealth of commercial expansion. Only a decade after the publication of *Bracebridge Hall* (1819), in which Washington Irving mourned the passing of Christmas, New York City, along with Boston, Philadelphia, and other (mostly northern) cities, was reinventing the holiday season. New York's stores began staying open until midnight during the Christmas season. Bright gas lights illuminated "[w]hole rows of confectionery stores and toy shops, fancifully, and often splendidly, decorated with festoons of bright silk drapery, interspersed with flowers and evergreens," wrote Gabriel Furman. "[V]isitors of both sexes and all ages" filled the streets, "some selecting toys and fruit for holiday presents; others merely lounging from shop to shop to enjoy the varied scene." The day after Christmas in 1842, Isaac Mickle "walked up and down Chestnut Street [Philadelphia] with some friends. I never saw so many people turned out to celebrate Christmas," he wrote. "The main streets were literally jammed."

Changed times meant changed holidays, and the emergent Christmas centered on the urban middle class, which had experienced perhaps most keenly, because of their new status and surroundings, the absence of stabilizing religious and folk traditions. In particular, they wished to preserve those ideals that best promoted the moral values they espoused for society as a whole, and to create new ways and manners to help knit society into modern fabric. "At present time," wrote Lydia Maria Child in 1842, "indications are numerous that the human mind is tired out in the gymnasium of controversy, and asks earnestly for repose, protection, mystery, and undoubting faith." For middle-class city folk, sobriety, gentility, moral living, prosperity, and a well-ordered civic existence became ideals for the entire nation. Drawing on their repertoire of Christian experience and belief, these Americans relocated the emphases of Protestant faith within home's walls. There they guarded and embellished traditional Christian values and reinstituted the order, cohesion, and moral authority that churches had once exercised over the larger community. In this sphere of domesticity, women played a unique and central role as wife, mother, and keeper of hearth and faith as she worked to make house and household a place of "rest from the stormy strife of a selfish world," a place where children were honored and Jesus venerated.

Christmas became a perfect medium for transporting religion and religious feeling into the home and for righting the excesses and failures of the public world. Its rituals and icons—gift-giving and family dinner, Santa Claus and evergreen tree—symbolically bridged the widening gap between rich and poor. It rejuvenated the weakening bonds between church and family and channeled the immoderation of the marketplace into charitable goodwill, all the while reflecting the complicated interrelationships between faith, market, community, and family that attended the dawning modern age. It also provided the essential element of ceremonial structure and symbolic ornamentation. Antebellum wives and mothers began to create in their home a texture of ritual detail generally eschewed by Protestant theology and practice. In this way, they established a sense of sacred time and sacred space that set home distinctly apart from the profane outer world.

SANTA CLAUS

At the center of this new domestic holiday stood Santa Claus, who, laden with small toys and treats, called on more and more American children each year. This stealthy saint traced his lineage back to a human Saint Nicholas, born in Turkey, possibly in 280 C.E. and reincarnated in later European folk figures. He first traveled to America only in the early nineteenth century. Santa Claus owed his modern incarnation to the imagination of three New Yorkers. Following the Revolution, New York City's boosters, in their efforts to promote the rising commercial and political importance of their city, had renewed investment in their history as a Dutch colony. John Pintard, a city merchant, fostered a particular fascination with the old Dutch St. Nicholas and successfully promoted him as a suitable symbol of the city. At about the same time, his friend Washington Irving published *Knickerbocker's History of New York* (1809), replete with references to St. Nicholas as the city's patron. The characters in this quasi-history provided the first descriptive outlines of what was to become

A classic illustration of Santa and his sleigh by Clement Clarke Moore. © Brown Brothers.

the American Santa. One passage, for example, recounted a dream in which "the good St. Nicholas came riding over the tops of the trees, in that self-same wagon wherein he brings his yearly presents to children."

The third inventor of an American Saint Nick was Clement Clarke Moore, an acquaintance of both Irving and Pintard. In 1822, he wrote "An Account of a Visit from St. Nicholas" to amuse his three daughters. In it, a "right jolly old elf" arrived amid much noise in a sleigh pulled by flying reindeer, then slid down the chimney to deliver toys. A newspaper printed the poem the following year and afterwards "A Visit from St. Nicholas" appeared sporadically but seasonally in newspapers throughout the nation. As a news carrier's holiday gift to customers, its circulation widened a common imagery for Santa Claus and his deeds.

In an era of growing material prosperity and a loosening of child discipline, this urban saint functioned as a conduit of parental authority and love, and, not incidentally, consumerism and faith. Put to work in the domestic sphere, he rewarded good behavior. "About the first of December," one writer recalled, "I was duly told that if I was not a good boy my stockings in the big fireplace would get little or no recognition." Always testing, children hung their stockings "with care, in hopes that St. Nicholas soon would be there." Elizabeth Cady Stanton pinned hers "on a broomstick, laid across two chairs in front of the fireplace." On the plantation where Susan Dabney Smedes grew up, everyone hung up a "sock or stocking" along the staircase. The next step—waiting—usually proved more difficult. Many "listened for the jingling of his sleigh bells" all through the long night. If lucky enough, children found oranges, candies, nuts, toys, or other such trifles tucked in their stockings the next morning.

As more parents arranged for Santa Claus's visits, he became a more open-handed and forgiving soul. He tended to reward more often than discipline. His visits allowed parents to indulge their children's material wishes (and their own) without compromising other virtues such as frugality and the value of earning what one received. Moreover, the fantastic appearance of Santa's gifts in the night removed them from the profane context of money and work that charted consumer cravings.

Associated with dollars, good fortune, and children, as well as generosity and good nature, Santa Claus seemed a natural for Americans. Children who expected gifts from him learned from an early age "to take and to receive," a custom that at least one folklorist believed "important training" for life in a capitalist society. Yet he also embodied the miraculous realities of the invisible world. As believers in Santa, children were "simply taught to believe in a supernatural being with magical powers and omniscience—a belief supported by the whole society, demanding moral behavior, involving prayer, public ritual, and every element of religious faith." Santa had, in fact, become part of a nascent national folklore, a full-fledged product of American humor and naive optimism. However, unlike such heroes as John Henry or Davy Crockett, Santa seemed to prefer the city, where he mediated the often disparate worlds of market and hearth, reality and miracle.

GIFT-GIVING

Perhaps more than any other element, the rise of commerce and consumerism, and the availability of goods as a key feature of the American economy determined the customs of Christmas gift-giving. Like Santa Claus, the idea of giving Christmas gifts, for most Americans, was a fairly recent one. Early Christians refrained from gift-giving because it reminded them of the Roman Saturnalia. During the sixteenth and seventeenth centuries, the English revived the custom, but generally at New Year's. Not surprisingly, Puritans strongly opposed giving gifts, regarding the custom as yet another diabolical pagan rite countenanced by the Anglican Church. Quakers and Separatists likewise declined. In fact, few colonists, north or south, regardless of religion, commemorated either Christmas or New Year's with presents.

By the nineteenth century, gift-giving had become more prevalent, and some reciprocal giving could be found. In most cases, though, giving tended to be one-way, a reflection of status relationships. Those of higher rank gave gifts to those of lower status; servants, and sometimes children, most often benefited. In the South, masters and house slaves played a game of surprise at Christmas that reinforced status lines. Whoever was the first to greet another with the phrase "Christmas gift" received a gift. Nearly always the master took the role of the good loser and presented a small token kept ready for the occasion. Similar rituals existed elsewhere. Workers often chose New Year's to remind patrons of status obligations, and newspaper carriers presented their subscribers with "a New Year's Address," a short poem for which they expected, and got, "a douceur." Givers were rewarded in another way. "I love to make a cheerful heart," noted Thomas Cope of Philadelphia. "The awkward scrape of the leg, the smile of satisfaction & the thankee sir, thankee, are a rich regard for the trifle bestowed."

As American social and economic structure began to change during the antebellum period, so too did patterns of gift-giving, yielding to exchanges among family, friends, and neighbors. Also, Christmas, rather than New Year's, became the primary gift occasion. Stores and shops throughout the nation offered the consumer an ever-growing feast of choices, nearly any of which might be made a gift. These could be anything from "silver slop basin," marbles, and knives to a "beautiful box with writing materials of all kinds" or "pair of boots worth seven Dollars." The ideal gift combined an appreciation for the monetary worth of an object with values loftier than the money that purchased it. Consequently, in addition to brooches and other finery, items such as Bibles and lavishly bound books served as lucrative mainstays of the gift trade.

The marketplace, blessed with an unprecedented abundance of goods and eager customers to buy them, played a crucial part in broadening the appeal of giving gifts. "Our shops," wrote a Bostonian in 1842, "are so filled at this season with every kind of tasteful article to attract one that it is hard to refrain." (About the same time, a woman visiting New Orleans noted that "the streets and shops display the most attractive & beautiful articles," adding, "—how little do I want.") Indeed, the notion that money and commerce might taint the holiday was significantly absent. This was in part because Protestantism itself used financial success as an indicator of faith. The Rev. Dr. Dewey of New York, for example, published a series of sermons in 1838 that, to his mind, illustrated that "there is an object, in the accumulation of wealth, beyond success; . . . and that is virtue." A cornucopia of goods available in stores, "virtuous" money to buy them, and the ways in which gifts reinforced domestic ideals insured that commerce and values of home intertwined to encourage consumption—for oneself and to give to others.

Gifts and the act of giving fit well into the concept of Protestant home religion as well, joining ideals of family and religion together. In the context of religion, a gift symbolized God's gift of Jesus to humanity, and the emphasis rested on giving rather than receiving. In a social context, the custom signified a bond between giver and receiver and again stressed giving over receiving presents. Within the family and among friends, gift rituals strengthened such important, intangible qualities as amity, affection, appreciation, generosity, and mutual dependence, qualities that held no monetary value in the world of commerce. Rather, they expressed a moral economy that encoded relationships that were the most cherished and basic and, at the same time, the most vulnerable.

Each of the family members took part in the ritual in ways that revealed cultural assumptions and hierarchies. Much of the burden fell on the mother, who more often than not shopped for or created the gifts and orchestrated the ceremonies of giving. Husbands, probably because of their role as breadwinners and their absence from the everyday workings of the home, seemed inclined to bestow gifts more sentimental, less practical, and frequently more expensive than the hand-embroidered slippers wives often gave them. George Templeton Strong, after resolving to be "parsimonious" and spend no more than 20 dollars on his wife, became "inflamed" by a $200 cameo brooch displayed in the window of Tiffany's. With little hesitation, he went inside and bought it with money he had withdrawn that morning to pay bills.

Parents, of course, usually gave much more to their children than they received. Advice literature encouraged responsible parents to supply their children with toys. "One of the first duties of a genuinely Christian parent is, to show a generous sympathy with the plays of his children; providing playthings and means of play, giving them play-things," Horace Bushnell asserted. Christmas offered an appropriate time to present these treats and diversions. Money also made an instructive gift for children. One woman who grew up in Ohio at the beginning of the nineteenth century remembered that each of the children in her family always received a gold piece, but they were never allowed to spend it. "It had to go right into the bank," she said.

THE CHRISTMAS TREE

Just as Santa's visit and opening gifts marked the moment of the Christmas holiday, the Christmas tree demarcated the span and locale of the celebration. The tantalizing array of trinkets, toys, and mementos tied to its branches, and weightier treasures stowed beneath an imposingly decorated tree, created a powerful icon of the emerging American Christmas. The first accounts of a Christmas tree, a vestige of the evergreens Romans used at winter to symbolize regeneration, date to the German Reformation, after which the practice spread northward to Scandinavia. In England, Prince Albert, a German, made a gift of a small Christmas tree to his wife Queen Victoria in the mid-nineteenth century, reputedly marking the tree's first appearance in England. The custom spread easily and quickly in America. Charles Haswell remembered that as a teen in the 1830s he braved "a very stormy and wet night" to go to Brooklyn, where a number of immigrant German families had settled, to see their "custom of dressing a 'Christmas Tree.'"

Harriet Martineau had predicted the popularity of Christmas trees as early as 1832, when she noted that she had "little doubt" they would "become one of the most flourishing exotics of New England." An affluent urban class, which had grown fond of traveling, delighted in the Christmas trees they saw in Europe. Anna and George Ticknor toured Germany in 1835, where on Christmas Eve they had been dazzled by an evergreen alight with candles, the first they had seen. Two years later, they held a party at their home in Boston. Mrs. Henry Wadsworth Longfellow, who attended, wrote in her diary that the Ticknors had "a beautiful Christmas tree decorated with presents from one relation to another." It was the first she had seen and she "was as much excited as the children when the folding doors opened and the pyramid of lights sparkled from the dark boughs of a lofty pine."

Before long, small Christmas tree markets began to spring up in town squares. Sunday schools (and only later, often with protest, churches proper) began to set up Christmas trees and hand out candies to children. Magazines and books, increasingly available, also familiarized Americans with details of Christmas trees and the rituals attending them. In 1851, when her "children had such a number of gifts," Mahala Eggleston, who lived on Learmont Plantation near Vicksburg, "made a Christmas tree for them." She had learned about them "from some of the German stories" she had been reading. "Mother, Aunt and Liz came down to see it; all said it was something new to them," she wrote in her diary. *Godey's Lady's Book* especially helped define the tree's place in the

A young boy marvels at the wonders of a Christmas tree. Courtesy of Corbis.

American home Christmas. In 1850, it published in its December issue the first widely circulated picture of an small evergreen, decorated and atop a table, surrounded by a family.

The reasons for the tree's popularity were not hard to discern. Candies, toys, and candles transformed it into a fanciful vision of delight that dispelled the gloom of winter. At the same time, it expressed perfectly the age's romanticism that made nature a metaphor for moral ideals. The tree's symmetry and perpetual green when all outside was barren reflected beauty, order, and life in God-

Illustration of a traditional Victorian family Christmas, first appearing in *Godey's Lady's Book,* December 1850. Courtesy of the Library of Congress.

created nature. Its impressive presence in the parlor attested to the importance of the home Christmas holiday, creating a proper setting for secular, domestic, and even sacred holiday rituals.

This was especially so in the industrializing North. Yet the new aspects of the holiday—Santa's visits, a tree in the parlor, gifts wrapped in paper and string—were beginning to overlay southern traditions also. The conclusion of the Civil War hastened the expansion of this new Christmas tableau. Christmas possessed potent resources for grappling with issues of absence, discord, misunderstanding, forgiveness, and regeneration. It beckoned men and women past earthly travail into an idealized domestic haven that was neither particularly northern nor southern in its origins or biases. Moreover, it created a way of creating common bonds and traditions to bind the nation together. "In a day of general change," the editor of *Harper's* wrote, "we sigh for conservative elements and wonder how we may more closely attach the country to its best hopes and traditions."

AN OLD-FASHIONED CHRISTMAS

"We have saved out of the past nearly all that was good in it," wrote Charles Dudley Warner in 1884, "and the revived Christmas of our time is no doubt better than the old." The holiday, with its sentimentality and broad religious allusions, emerged against the dramatic backdrop and tragic needs of the Civil War. The democratization of American Christianity, and particularly the softening of Calvinist attitudes against Christmas, invited wider participation. Urbanization, mechanization, the double force of emancipation and massive immigration, and the power of commerce and industry, which were transforming American life at an ever-increasing rate, challenged old values and left the comfort of constancy behind. Faced with the dizzying realities and dislocations of modern life, culturally powerful Americans exercised a rising enthusiasm for premodern ceremonies and rituals through which they hoped to assert their position and values. They longed to find in them not salvation and substance, but an alternative to the vagueness of liberal Protestantism and the sterility of scientific truth. Adding to the basic form established before the Civil War, these well-educated and comfortably middle-class and wealthy Americans embraced, embellished, and expanded the scope of Christmas that had taken its beginning forms in the early part of the century, interpreting the holiday as a moment of simpler times when spirituality and community had flourished. All these elements helped fix Christmas on the national calendar.

A number of states, beginning in the 1830s, had made Christmas an official state holiday. By 1865, 31 states and territories had officially recognized Christmas as a legal holiday. and in 1870, the federal government declared Christmas a national holiday. These laws, the federal one included, suspended government services and bank transactions not only for Christmas, but New Year's, July 4, and a few other holidays. Thus, the "legalization" of Christmas had more to do with a declaration of a uniform set of days that confirmed American cultural norms than it did in specifically singling out Christmas.

Nevertheless, by the 1880s Americans had secured Christmas as a national holiday. They had culled bits and pieces of customs from the past, originated new traditions, and placed upon the entire holiday a meaning and order fit for their own times. They had, in effect, reinvented Christmas. They sent Christmas cards, decorated evergreen trees, caroled, hung Christmas stockings, and exchanged gifts, constructing for themselves and the nation a collage of ritual. Thus, during the Gilded Age, the silhouette of Christmas sharpened into the festival we associate with an "old-fashioned" Christmas. This Christmas fostered widened and more amorphous senses of community, ones that went beyond the confines of the front parlor, but also ones often more ethereal and spiritual than physical. Singing together at church, a shared attitude about how to approach the poor (especially as the gap between wealth and poverty expanded), or sending Christmas greetings rather than making a traditional house call created a feeling of belonging despite the disruptions of modern life.

Singing Christmas songs created, literally, a harmony, a sound and sentiment that contrasted with the noise of progress. Carols had once been an integral part of Christmas throughout Europe, but they were often bawdy, and certainly secular. Early in the nineteenth century, however, several Englishman began to revive carols and caroling, publishing books of notes and words. Americans borrowed from this growing repertoire, but by mid-century had also begun to write their own carols, among them "It Came Upon a Midnight Clear," "We Three Kings of Orient Are," and "I Heard the Bells on Christmas Day." Simply arranged and heartily sung, the American carols straight-forwardly interpreted religious and human sentiment. They transcended time and change (in much the same way that Americans envisioned Christmas itself) and characteristically avoided the earthly issues of revelry or poverty that characterized earlier music.

As to poverty and the poor, Charles Dickens's *A Christmas Carol* (1842), the story of Scrooge's visit to the Cratchit home on Christmas Eve, provided the paradigm for the moral attitude and obligation that Americans adopted at Christmas time. "Dickens," noted the *New York Times* in 1863, "brings the old Christmas into the present out of bygone centuries and remote manor houses, into the living rooms of the very poor of to-day." Yet, *A Christmas Carol* articulated the essence of Christmas in strikingly new terms. Rather than invoking nostalgia for a lost Christmas, this one found a suitable interface between rich and poor. Scrooge did not help all of his employees as a result of the visits from the Christmas ghosts, but only Bob Cratchit, who had shown himself and his family to be respectable albeit poor, and therefore worthy of Scrooge's apparent generosity. As important, it was the redemption of wealthy old Scrooge through his interaction with the Cratchits that made the "carol philosophy" so powerful.

Yet another way in which Americans maintained a sense of connection was through Christmas cards. Holiday cards were an almost entirely new idea, one that came to fruition when Louis Prang, a German-born immigrant, perfected multicolor lithography. The first cards he printed were small business advertisements, but by 1875, he had begun printing larger ones with Christmas motifs, intended to decorate homes and Christmas trees. These he regarded as small works of art, affordable to anyone. Soon his company was producing millions

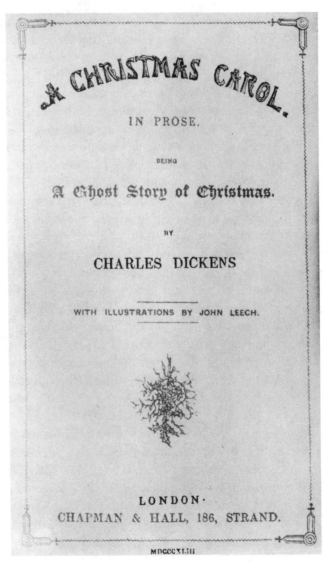

A Christmas Carol by Charles Dickens, 1843. © Brown Brothers.

of beautifully colored cards with seasonal messages. Americans adopted these with the same zeal they did other Christmas traditions and sent them out across the nation with stamps that cost a mere penny. "[W]ornout from choosing gifts" for old friends and school mates, one writer noted, "we usually fall back on Christmas cards, which constitute one of the most precious and at the same time inexpensive contributions of these latter days to the neglected cause of sentiment." Prang's Christmas card business flourished, but other manufacturers, particularly in Germany, soon entered the market, supplying cheaper, poorly printed cards. The advent in the mid-1890s of novel, less-expensive postcards accelerated the frenzy of sending holiday greetings. Disappointed in his attempts to provide a democratic art form, Prang sold his business and turned to manufacturing art supplies for school children.

Even as more and more Americans entered into the community of Christmas keepers, the elements that had first made the holiday popular continued to thrive, modified by technology and time. The Christmas tree, for example, remained central to the family Christmas. By 1900, one American in five was estimated to have one, but the preference grew for taller, more fully branched trees. The ornaments also stayed, but more elaborate glass ones, hand blown and silvered inside to make them shiny, began to appear beside the homey popcorn strings, candied fruits, and toys. In 1880, a salesman coaxed F. W. Woolworth to put the first few boxes of imported ornaments on the counter of his 5 cent store, where, to his surprise, they sold almost immediately. Within 10 years, Woolworth was importing nearly all of the glass balls produced in the German cottage industries of Thuringia. These as well as other mass-produced trim and tinsel dressed the trees more elaborately each year. Lights remained essential. A proper Christmas tree might hold hundreds of wax candles, briefly lit in an awesome display (and stashed behind it, a bucket of water and a blanket as safety precautions against fire). A number of inventors put their talents toward creating stable candle holders, but the real solution to the fire hazard, of course, was electricity. In 1882, in New York City, the vice president of the newly formed Edison Electric boasted of being the first to add electric lights (the small bulbs hand blown and hand-wired) to his tree. Soon after, in Reading, Pennsylvania, "bighearted Robert H. Coleman and his many employees," enjoyed a 25-foot tree lit with "220 two-candle power electric lamps. . . . A dynamo run by water-power in the basement of the building," reported the local paper, supplied electricity for it.

Shopping did not abate, nor did the gift-giving that resulted from it. By the 1880s, the new department stores stocked not just single items, but vast arrays of goods in all price ranges and qualities in artful displays. Their windows and atria, dressed in grand and festive seasonal themes, attracted sightseers as well as buyers. In the 1870s, these emporiums "often outdid the churches in religious adornment and symbolism, with pipe organs, choirs, religious paintings and banners, [and] statues of saints and angels." In this way, one historian argued, stores bathed "consumption in the reflected glory of Christianity." Lured by the opulence and guided by new and more descriptive advertising, women made lengthening gift lists and set out to search for the appropriate token for the maid, the doorman, the close friend, and their own children and families. Stores, competing for business, increasingly offered to deliver the presents to the household free of charge, wrapped in distinctively decorated papers, and tied with a colorful bow. For many, the pace and work of the holiday seemed to be reaching a point where it had become almost as troublesome as the everyday world from which it supposedly offered refuge. As one man put it in 1899, "Somehow or other Christmas…doesn't allow you any rest, what with one thing and another, I feel as if I had just returned from a tour on foot to the Rocky Mountains."

Whatever complaints adults may have had, they still welcomed Santa Claus. Dressed in his fur-trimmed suit and carrying a sleigh full of toys, he had traveled a long way since the early nineteenth century, when representations of him had depended mainly upon associations with Belznickel, St. Nicholas, Father Christmas, and related folk figures. Even Clement Moore's enormously popular "An Account of a Visit from St. Nicholas," which provided the "right jolly old elf" with "eight tiny reindeer," at first circulated only in a relatively narrow social setting. Yet by the Civil War, a more uniform visual perception of Santa, in which he was portrayed as increasingly human, taller and more robust, but at the same time possessing supernatural power, emerged. In 1881, Thomas Nast, the exceptional political cartoonist for *Harper's Weekly*, drew what became somewhat of an official portrait of him. He showed Santa as a cheerful, apple-cheeked old fellow wreathed in holly. He cradled a long-stemmed pipe in one hand; the other rested lightly on his generously rotund middle, enabling him to hold a wooden horse, a doll, and other playthings in the crook of his arm. Through the imaginations of a number of adults, among them Nast, Louisa May Alcott, and Katherine Lee Bates, Santa acquired ledgers to record children's conduct, a home at the North Pole, elves, and by some accounts, a Mrs. Santa.

Santa's credibility as an American folk hero depended on his role as a highly successful manufacturer and distributor of toys, placing him in the pantheon of America's captains of industry. He even looked like them, with his fur coat, full girth, and beard. He commanded a large work force of hardworking and dependable elf labor, who, seemingly without the help of modern machinery, built toys for good boys and girls. Elves, along with ghosts and fairies, were staples of Victorian literature. These North Pole elves, though, were not unlike immigrants working in the nation's sweatshops. Unassimilated and undifferentiated by personal name or character, their existence made manifest a maxim that hard work and a cheerful attitude benefited all. *Godey's* implicitly made the point in 1873, in an illustration titled "The Workshop of Santa Claus." It showed Santa encircled by toys and elves, but the accompanying editorial pointed out that the dolls, boats, tops, and toy soldiers were really made by foreigners who were "very poor."

Yet any analogies that might be drawn between Santa's work and late nineteenth-century capitalism lay enmeshed in paradox, for, in significant ways, Santa Claus also represented values at odds with the system. With his antiquated sled-and-reindeer transportation, this old, secular saint recalled idyllic earlier times in which competition, progress, prosperity, and efficiency mattered little. Whereas industrialists might grow wealthy from the innocence and naiveté of the populace, Santa gave his wealth to the most innocent and naive

Thomas Nast "invented" the popular image of Santa Claus in his illustration, "Merry Old Santa Claus," first appearing in *Harper's Weekly,* 1881. Courtesy of the Library of Congress.

of all—the children. As a philanthropist and quasi-religious figure, Santa Claus was a robber baron in reverse.

The Santa legend at once celebrated and critiqued the realities of the Gilded Age, speaking to the culture's ambivalence toward its material wealth. Santa mediated between spiritual and material worlds, a symbolic figure through which to experience, discuss, and criticize a culture beset and exhilarated by modernity. In a Protestant culture that traditionally looked upon visual representations of God, Jesus, and saints with great suspicion, this transition was significant. A letter to the Philadelphia *Lutheran* (December 22, 1881) came directly to the point of concern when it cautioned, "do not substitute for the Babe of Bethlehem, the figure of a Santa Claus." Yet, how was one to understand the miraculous in an age of Darwin? One little girl, an evangelical magazine reported in 1906, was told that Santa did not exist. A few days later she refused to attend Sabbath school, reasoning, "Likely as not this Jesus Christ business will turn out just like Santa Claus."

Unquestionably, Frank Church, editor of the *New York Sun,* provided the most persuasive, and best-known, discourse on the spiritual meaning of Santa. A letter from one Virginia O'Hanlon, written in 1897, asked the plain question, "Is there a Santa Claus?" "Yes, Virginia," Church replied, "there is a Santa Claus." His reasoning proved an exposition on belief itself. "Virginia, your little friends are wrong," he wrote. "They have been affected by the skepticism of a skeptical age. They do not believe except they see." Without Santa, he argued, "There would be no childlike faith then, no poetry, no romance to make tolerable this existence.... Nobody sees Santa Claus, but that is no sign that there is no Santa Claus." He concluded with an indirect but by no means weak assault on positivism and science. "The most real things in the world are those that neither children nor men can see.... Nobody can conceive or imagine all the wonders there are unseen and unseeable in the world."

THE TWENTIETH CENTURY AND THE PUBLIC CHRISTMAS

By the time Frank Church announced definitively that Santa existed, Americans had come to associate a distinct set of rituals, expectations, and attitudes with Christmas. City leaders reflected the acceptance by beginning to place Christmas trees in public squares each December. New York, apparently, erected the first in 1912. In 1923, President Calvin Coolidge began the tradition of an annual National Christmas Tree lighting ceremony. Although in time they abandoned their churchly guises, stores nevertheless continued to undergo marvelous alteration at holiday time, becoming strikingly "other" public places. During the 1940s, Chicago's Marshall Field and Company, competing for the attention of holiday crowds, transformed its huge department store into "a glittering fairyland...[with] the world's most gorgeous Christmas tree, [and] a brilliant pageantry." Decorated for Christmas, a city in all its public and commercial aspects transmuted into an environment quite different from what it was throughout the rest of the year. The altered context caused people who entered the shared holiday ambience to feel and act differently than they did at other times. In sum, public spaces at Christmas became an arena for exchanges of goodwill, cheerful greetings, and benign purpose. This representation of Christmas coincided with progressive assertions of citizens' obligation to harmony, faith, family, and civic unity—the qualities believed necessary to keep the nation healthy and prosperous. As one writer put it, Christmas became a community festival that "fostered a sympathetic spirit of brotherhood, as all classes of citizens voice good will and loyalty to their common city and country." Thus, what had once been seen as a domestic holiday with a relatively circumscribed public dimension now had a full civic and secular stage on which to be enacted.

To be sure, the appearance of people enjoying Christmas together fulfilled an expectation that in Christmas lay a key to social peace, a goal grown more important as immigration rates rose higher and higher in the late nineteenth and early decades of the twentieth century and as the population became more diverse. A "Contributor" to the *Atlantic* reported in 1930 that she and her family had "for years gone on Christmas Eve to midnight Mass. To be among hundreds of people of all colors and races, of all walks of life, who are drawn together by a common emotion, a common faith, is to be at once in harmony with the Christmas mood." She likened her experience to "that of a foreigner visiting a strange land," one "with which my own land has never been at war, toward which I have inherited no bitterness, no fear, no strong emotions of any kind." For her, beginning Christmas in a church had a way of dissolving what Walter Lippman called the "acids of modernity" that had broken life into an array of inharmonious elements.

For Americans who were not Christians or who did not celebrate Christmas, however, the holiday posed a serious dilemma. The public discussion about whether Jews should keep Christmas illustrated a central point about the public as well as religious significance of the celebration. One attitude, expressed by Rabbi Judah L. Magnes in 1903, held that Jews should neither fear nor reject the holiday. Christmas might even help them strengthen their own beliefs, he argued. He supported his point by noting that while many Jews protested, others "silently bring in the trees and the lights" into their homes. A Rabbi Schulman took an opposing view, objecting particularly to the Christmas entertainment in public schools and to the Christology that was part of it.

As Christmas became more ingrained in the general culture and as the first generations of American-born Jews faced choices concerning acculturation, the question of celebrating Christmas remained unsolved. In a 1939 airing of the issue in *Christian Century*, Rabbi Louis Witt asserted that Jews should keep Christmas, arguing that Christians had become more liberal and now emphasized the "universal humanness" of Jesus's teaching rather than a particular spiritual belief. Witt also thought that the "friendliness and good will" of Christmas made it nearly irresistible to anyone, including Jews. "After all," he pointed out, "the Jew is only human." Celebrating the holiday did not ordain that he was "thereby drawn by even the breadth of a hair nearer to the worship of an ecclesiastical Christ." A Jew keeping Christmas meant only that he met Christians on common ground, a strategy that protected him and other American Jews from being ostracized from a culture that had befriended them. The *Century's* Christian editor sided with Witt, focusing on keeping Christmas as a sign of being an American, not on its Christian meaning. For Americans, Jew and Christian, living in "a world of tolerance, of political liberalism, of democracy," he wrote, "it is not fair…to cherish a religious faith which provides a sanction for racial or cultural or any other form of separatism."

It was not the assumed pluralism of a publicly celebrated Christmas alone that expanded the meaning of Christmas, but the exigencies of market-driven economies. As Christmas had become more and more a secular and community celebration, the holiday's long and well-planned shopping season insured that one of its most important and noticeable attributes would be its power to generate sales. This fact led Congress, in 1941, to set Thanksgiving Day on the fourth Thursday of November. The act unified national practice and established an advantage of generally insuring more shopping days between Thanksgiving and December 25. Indeed, retail stores realized a significant portion of their yearly profits during the Christmas season. Many industries, especially those associated with the production and sale of luxury goods, and the consumer economy in general, relied on December sales to carry them through the year. Newspapers, magazines, radio, television, and, late in the twentieth century, Internet businesses, thrived on December revenues, dazzling consumers with a seemingly unlimited wealth of choice.

By the late twentieth century, Christmas had grown into a costly holiday. In 1998, Americans spent more than $160 billion on presents, about $700 per person. Add to this the expense of sending five billion Christmas cards, letters, and packages in December, and of transportation for those nearly 50 million Americans who traveled over the holidays. The economics of Christmas reached much farther, though. Japan, China, and other non-Christian nations have been adopting Christmas rituals, adapting the consumer aspects to fit within their own cultures. They have also profited. In the first nine months of 1997, for example, China exported artificial Christmas trees, ornaments, and lights worth in excess of $450 million, plus 10 times the stuffed toys and dolls that were made in America in 1995.

The increased economic importance of Christmas drew into sharper focus the oft-voiced notion that the sacred meanings, both religious and domestic, of the "old-fashioned" Christmas had correspondingly diminished. Thus, the perceived war between material and spiritual ends, made evident when the Roman Catholic Church declared the Feast of the Nativity, remained still apparent late in the twentieth century. Christmas "nowadays persists like an onset of shingles," columnist Russell Baker wrote in 1976. "You spend a month getting ready for it and two weeks getting over it.… If Scrooge…had started dreaming on November 25 and spent the next four weeks being subjected to desperate sales clerks and electronically amplified 'Jingle Bells,' he would probably have stopped at the Cratchits' on that fateful evening only long enough to smash Tiny Tim's little crutch." His sentiments had not changed appreciably from nearly a century earlier when the *New York Tribune* stated that Christmas needed "to be dematerialized."

Advertisers learned to mitigate this tension, often invoking the sentimental traits associated with the holiday—which helped to enhance profit. Coca-Cola's Santa ads provide a good example. During the 1930s, Coke wanted to find a way to sell its soft drinks in the winter and to expand its market to children. The answer was to show Santa refreshing himself with a Coke as he made his Christmas Eve rounds. This version of Santa Claus, which quickly become the standard, featured him in a red coat that was exactly the color of the patented red on the Coke label. The new ads did not direct anyone to buy or even to drink the product. They only showed that Santa, who brought Christmas, liked it.

Advertising strategies such as these embraced and complicated the dialectic between spiritual and material, even as the populace maintained a belief that they were sharply distinct. Public perception tended to hold that Christmas had become overly commercial. In almost direct contrast, movies, books, songs, and seasonal television shows elaborated a message that emphasized innocence, hope, charity, and community, all of which minimized the significance of commerce and goods. By the second half of the twentieth century, the annual rerunning of familiar holiday images and programs had become themselves a nostalgic ritual for many Americans. *Rudolph the Red-Nosed Reindeer, Miracle on 34th Street, A Charlie Brown Christmas, How the Grinch Stole Christmas, The Nightmare Before Christmas,* and other twentieth century tales invoked the Christmas that commented on American life itself, often suggesting to Americans that they retained, at heart, a goodness and decency untainted by money.

The first significant index of the increasingly mass-media character of Christmas in the twentieth century could be found, appropriately enough, in an advertising gimmick. In 1939, Montgomery Ward distributed free to its customers nearly two and a half million copies of *Rudolph the Red-Nosed Reindeer,* a story written by its ad department. The well-behaved young reindeer, whose nose was "red as a beet!," always obeyed his parents, comforting himself with the knowledge that on judgment day, which after all is what Christmas is for children, Santa would bring him as many gifts as the "happier, handsomer reindeer who teased him." On a particularly foggy Christmas Eve, sometime past midnight, Santa stopped at Rudolph's home and upon entering his bedroom was relieved to have his way lit by the dim glow of the sleeping deer's nose. The rest, as the story goes, is "history."

While Rudolph's good fortune indicated the trajectory of Christmas in the twentieth century toward mass marketing and an increased emphasis on children, the music and visual media streamlined, consolidated, and revised the holiday to match modern American life. Appealingly sentimental, "White Christmas," written by Irving Berlin, was introduced in the movie *Holiday Inn*

The cover from the sheet music to "Rudolph the Red-Nosed Reindeer," by Johnny Marks, 1949. © Culver Pictures.

(1942), in which Bing Crosby sang, on December 24, that he was "dreaming of a White Christmas" just like those he "used to know." Crosby's description of glistening treetops and "sleigh bells in the snow" joined the nostalgia intrinsic to the American holiday to the wistful longings of a nation entrenched in World War II. The combination imbued "White Christmas" with an intensified yearning that made the song a classic, selling over 30 million copies, the "world's all-time top-selling and most widely recorded song." At approximately the same time, two movies became Christmas standards. Emblematic of many Christmas stories, Frank Capra's *It's a Wonderful Life* (1946) created the holiday as a symbol for some essential quality believed to have been lost—in this case, a vital connection to community and family. The movie examined the life of a small-town business man (played by James Stewart) who, although he had always worked hard, believed that he had failed. On Christmas Eve, he attempted suicide only to be saved by his guardian angel, who revealed to him what would have happened if, as he wished, he had never been born. Saved, the man returned home to find that the entire hometown had come to his aid.

In yet another 1940s era movie, Valentine Davies's *Miracle on 34th Street* (1947) reaffirmed values similar to those middle-class progressives sought to insure at the turn of the century. Setting a "real" Santa amid the commerce and competition of New York City, *Miracle* confirmed the relevance of faith, imagination, cooperation, and traditional family structure in a modern age of rationality. Macy's personnel director, Doris Walker, the story ran, hired Kris Kringle to be the store's Santa even though he insisted he really was Santa Claus. His behavior further alarmed her when, convinced that Christmas had degenerated into "pure commercialism," Kris persuaded the owners of rivals Macy's and Gimble's that they would profit by referring customers to each other. The friendship that formed between her daughter Susan, "a rather serious child of

Still from the popular holiday classic, *It's a Wonderful Life,* 1946. Courtesy of Photofest.

six," and Kris made Walker even more wary of the store Santa. Walker, a single mother, had raised Susan to hold a hard-nosed belief in "utter realism and truth" (to Kringle, mother and daughter "were but unhappy products of their times"). Kringle's behavior ultimately led Macy's psychologist to send him to Bellevue mental ward. Only the New York Supreme Court could declare him sane—and the real Santa. The prospect looked bleak until Gayley, a lawyer and close friend of Walker and Susan, offered to help; he dragged a bulky U.S. mail sack into the courtroom and emptied its hundreds of letters addressed to Santa Claus. Faced with the irrefutable logic that the federal government would never try to deliver mail to an imposter or a fantasy, the judge found Kris Kringle quite sane. He was, indeed, Santa. In the end, *Miracle on 34th Street* rejected modern notions of rationality and female independence. It validated values it treated as their opposites: sentiment, love, family, and faith. Walker, taking a cue from her daughter, began to like Kris Kringle and also decided to give up her career at Macy's. She married Fred Gayley (after some matchmaking on Kringle's part) and therefore could provide a decent home for Susan.

However, a closer look at Kris Kringle reveals a Santa Claus less powerful than any of his forebears. In the nineteenth century, he might have swept in from some uncharted region in the north to shower toys on children. In the twentieth century, as an aging eccentric with few friends, Santa had little more than 30 dollars in his pocket and needed the Macy's job. He could only suggest to mothers where to shop for the gifts that would bring joy to their children. Repeatedly, he resorted to charm and cunning to accomplish his goals. Nor did he promote a belief in Santa per se. Instead he preached that exercising faith and imagination was good practice in and of itself. When Susan Walker confided in Kringle that her Christmas wish was for a real home and, implicitly, a real mother and a real father, Kringle helped set the stage for making her dream come true, but he lacked the magic to guarantee that it would happen.

While *Miracle on 34th Street* pictured a Santa humanized and in decline, it also portrayed a child possessed of a guileless potency. Young Susan Walker rescued her mother from the work world and gave her renewed domestic purpose—which neither Gayley nor Kringle could accomplish. Indeed, the very existence of Santa depended on a child's authentication. When Virginia O'Hanlon had raised the question of Santa's reality some 40 years earlier, Frank Church, a big-city news editor, an adult, vouched for Santa's truth: "Yes, Virginia, there is a Santa Claus." Now, a child performed the feat. That a child should exercise such power was a new theme of Christmas. Christmas stories throughout the nineteenth century portrayed adults as mediators of happiness and faith. In "An Account of a Visit from St. Nicholas," for example, a father watched over Santa's gift deliveries while his children stayed "sleeping all snug in their beds." In *A Christmas Carol*, despite the strong image of crippled Tiny Tim, Bob Cratchit and Scrooge, the men of the story, controlled the tale. Later in the century, women, particularly mothers, played central roles in Christmas dramas. In Willa Cather's "The Burglar's Christmas"(1896), for instance, the mother welcomed home her prodigal son on the holiday.

The culture's reliance on children as producers and bearers of Christmas spirit found one of its strongest statements in a children's book by Dr. Seuss (Theodore Geisel), *How the Grinch Stole Christmas* (1957) (a television version, directed by Chuck Jones and narrated by Boris Karloff, first appeared in 1966). Totally imaginary, it did not fuss with traditional humanitarian themes, expositions of miracles, or even the more conventional debates over the holiday's commercialism and materialism. It suggested instead that even the tangible, secular components of Christmas—trees, wreaths, mistletoe, bells, lights, gifts, roast beast, and ornaments (the Whos' Christmas has no Christian symbols)—were not necessary to the holiday. Thus, this vastly popular twentieth-century Christmas fable constructed a version of the modern Christmas in which the essence of the holiday lay wholly in its "spirit," and not in any of its material trappings.

The story itself gives a twist to Scrooge in *A Christmas Carol* and the narrative style a nod to "An Account of a Visit from St. Nicholas." The old and crotchety Grinch who lived just north of Who-ville so hated Christmas that he conceived the "wonderful, awful idea!" of stealing Christmas from the residents of the town. Dressed as Santa (and his dog Max outfitted with antlers), he slid down the chimney of the first Who house and systematically stuffed all the holiday presents—

Pop guns! And bicycles! Roller skates! Drums!
Checkerboards! Tricycles! Popcorn! And plums!

—into a sack and stole their food "quick as a flash." As he reached for the Christmas tree, however, he noticed "little Cindy-Lou Who, who was not more than two" quietly watching. Undeterred, he continued on his mission to ruin Christmas. On Christmas morning, anticipating how quiet and unhappy the Whos will be, the Grinch heard instead "every Who down in Who-ville…singing! Without any presents at all!" This puzzled him, until he comprehended that,

Maybe Christmas doesn't come from a store.
Maybe Christmas…perhaps…means a little bit more!

Upon this discovery, the Grinch's heart tripled in size, enabling him to sit at the head of the whole Who-ville holiday feast. The Whos, it turned out, understood Christmas all along, a truth grasped when one reads the Who-ville drama through the eyes of Cindy-Lou. As with Susan Walker, young Rudolph, and other small heroes of twentieth-century Christmas tales, her untainted faith and true-hearted goodness enabled her to trust that, no matter what happened, there would be a Christmas. And she was proved right; even the Grinch ended up celebrating it.

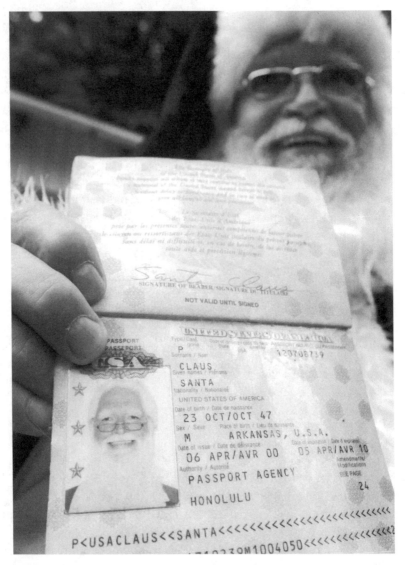

Santa Claus of Washington State shows his passport at the annual Santa Claus convention in Copenhagen, Denmark, Monday, July 25, 2005. © AP / Wide World Photos.

Youth's understanding of Christmas has become the culture's defining resistance to its equally held faith that the holiday has been overrun by crass commercialism. It follows, then, that when Christmas was not the central theme or even a minor one in a movie story line, directors, screenwriters, and others further codified and compacted the fragmented reminders of the holiday to convey an effective expression of American morality and faith in traditional values. An extraordinary number of top-grossing motion pictures released in recent years at least mention Christmas or flash a Christmas icon—usually a fleeting cameo of a Christmas tree or a string of holiday lights—regardless of the movie's actual theme. The reminder of the holiday establishes the essential "other" that summarizes almost instantaneously the beliefs of Susan Walker, Rudolph, Cindy-Lou, and a redeemed Grinch. In the Christmas celebration reside all goodness, kindness, hope, sacrifice, and tranquility. It stands as the all-purpose gauge against which the greed, violence, selfishness, and dishonesty of the late twentieth century can be measured.

In 1993, Tim Burton made more explicit the boundaries that demarcated the time, space, and rituals of Christmas. In *The Nightmare Before Christmas,* Jack the Pumpkin King discovered the pathway to Santa Claus's duchy of Christmas. Inspired by the liveliness and good humor of its citizens, Jack returned to his gloomy world of Halloween, where he constructed a sleigh from a coffin, busied his fellow haunters with making toys, and sent several small pranksters to kidnap Santa Claus himself. Jack's plan was to experience the joy of Christmas and at the same time to give Santa a much needed break. Of course he failed miserably. The toys he delivered scared the little children and alarmed their parents. Santa's Christmas kingdom, Jack learned when he and his sleigh were gunned from the sky, was not a permeable world. But some good did result. Contact with Christmas revitalized the realm of Halloween keepers and Jack found in his own domain a girl to love.

CHRISTMAS INTO THE TWENTY-FIRST CENTURY

To a large extent, Christmas is what Kris Kringle, in *Miracle on 34th Street,* called "a state of mind." It is a broadly inclusive notion that expanded throughout the twentieth century in tandem with commerce and continues into the twenty-first. The combination has allowed Christmas to maintain a prominent place on the American calendar. At the same time, its ambiguous meanings and uses within the culture continue to render it vulnerable to ongoing reinterpretations and borrowings—the same processes that generated the domestic form of the holiday as it emerged in the antebellum years. Changes in concepts of private and public, a declining portion of the population claiming to be Christian, a rise in multiculturalism as a national value, and the significant expansion of consumer-driven economies in previously more traditional cultures outside America, have changed the holiday in subtle but important ways.

For example, changes to Christmas have resulted from greater American emphasis on cultural diversity. In the 1960s and 1970s, minority groups increasingly claimed rights to celebrate their own beliefs, sometimes in place of Christmas and sometimes alongside. Hanukkah, the Festival of Lights, a traditional but minor Jewish holiday, took on a higher profile after the founding of Israel in 1948. In the United States, its observance has continued to increase, providing both a symbol of Jewish identity and, since the eight-day festival usually occurs in December and has developed a gift-giving component, a counterweight to Christmas. Kwanzaa, another December holiday, celebrates African American and pan-African unity. American Maulana Karenga created the seven-day celebration of "traditional African values of family, community responsibility, commerce, and self-improvement" in 1966, as an expression of black consciousness. Kwanzaa has since spread throughout the world; an estimated 18 million now annually affirm its Seven Guiding Principles. These are but two examples of ways in which the keeping of Christmas has come to share, rather than claim with near exclusivity, in the expression of American identity.

This widened sense of the holiday season comports with demographic trends and a series of Christmas-related church-and-state legal opinions. Between 1990 and 2001, the proportion of the population classified "Christian" dropped from 86 percent to 77 percent, while "none of the above" has grown significantly. This changing religious demography has been reflected in an increased sensitivity to Christmas displays in public places. Some claim that a Nativity Scene, a school choir singing "Silent Night," or, most recently, a store employee greeting a customer with "Merry Christmas" conflicts with personal beliefs and practices of non-Christians and nonobservers. The heightened tension has resulted in a number of lawsuits concerning the Establishment Clause of the First Amendment, some of which have ascended to the Supreme Court. Yet courts have not set a clear standard. At most, the Court seems to have put a "stronger emphasis on the context in which Christmas symbols are placed than on the symbols themselves." The implication is that a single crèche in a city park may be unconstitutional, but if "plastic reindeer," Santa, and other secular symbols are displayed with it, the scene transforms from religious to a secular tableau and will probably be allowed.

The evolving pluralism of the American holiday season, replete with the most enduring of popular Christmas artifacts and symbols, has taken on an international dimension. Some regard this as a specimen of cultural imperialism or the result of the globalization of the marketplace. Following World War II, for instance, as occupied Japan became a trading partner with the Western world, it began to adopt a secular version of Christmas. Holiday lights and gifts began to appear side by side with eastern traditions and belief but seemingly offered little real religious or cultural competition. In fact, American-type Christmas celebrations may be characteristic of nations as they modernize trade and seek new and wider domestic markets. In most cases, Santa Claus, a god of materialism, reigns, but as important, each nation's dominant culture adjusts its new holiday to its own ways. For example, secular Christmas images have begun to appear seasonally in China's big city stores, but within the context of Chinese life, holly and Santa take on a slightly altered meaning and look. The same can be said of the holiday as it emerges in other lands. A recent television image showed Iraqi street hawkers wearing Santa hats. The red and white hats evoked Christmas, but not precisely the Christmas that Americans know.

At each turn, the expansion of Christmas has raised questions about its profanation, secularization, and commercialization. While some groups periodically fight to "put Christ back in Christmas," others stress its more pluralistic values of peace on earth and good will toward all. Perhaps it is this very tension that keeps the holiday woven tightly into the fabric of American culture.

FURTHER READING

Marling, Karol Anne. *Merry Christmas!: Celebrating America's Greatest Holiday.* Cambridge, Mass.: Harvard University Press, 2000.

Miles, Clement A. *Christmas in Ritual and Tradition: Christian and Pagan,* 2nd. ed. Detroit, Mich.: Omnigraphics, 1913.

Nissenbaum, Steven. *The Battle for Christmas.* New York: Alfred A. Knopf, 1996.

Restad, Penne. *Christmas in America, A History.* New York: Oxford University Press, 1995.

Schmidt, Leigh Eric. *Consumer Rites: The Buying and Selling of American Holidays.* Princeton, N.J.: Princeton University Press, 1995.

Penne Restad

KWANZAA

- Kwanzaa is observed during the week of December 26–January 1.

- The first Kwanzaa was observed in 1966.

- Maulana Karenga, born Ronald McKinley Everett, originated Kwanzaa from a parsed-down version of the Zulu harvest festival Umkhosi as a Black Power alternative to Christmas.

- Kwanzaa comes from the Swahili word *kwanza* meaning first, as in "first fruits." Karenga capitalized the word and added an additional "a".

- On the sixth day of Kwanzaa weeklong festivities culminate in one grand feast called the Karamu.

- During the 1970s community-based organizations such as the EAST organization in New York, the Institute for Positive Education in Chicago, and the Urban Survival Training Institute in Philadelphia introduced Kwanzaa to African Americans in their respective cities.

- Kwanzaa in the late 1960s, 1970s, and early 1980s is the story about a community of people that collectively decide to challenge the hegemony of Christmas and stake out new areas for the Black Power movement.

- In the 1990s, white-owned companies and retail stores recognized Kwanzaa's commercial potential, pointing to a new direction in late twentieth-century capitalism: the marketing and merchandising of race, multiculturalism, and diversity via racial and ethnic holidays.

KWANZAA

If there ever existed any doubt about how high the political stakes were for the generation that lived through the 1960s and 1970s, then consider this statement by Basir Mchawi, an activist of the time: "It's time that we as Black People with Black families put down crazy cracker celebrations for something that is for us. Think about it: Easter, Thanksgiving, Passover, Chanukah, X-Mas, Columbus, George Washington, Independence Day, on and on.... Zillions of white holidays and lily white images—but nothing for us. Think about all of the negative effects of all these so-called holidays." Mchawi's observation is noteworthy for several reasons: first, it identified American culture as a source of discrimination, placing it alongside other forms of oppression; second, it underscored what some believed to be the absence of a viable set of black holiday traditions in American society; and last, the statement issued a clarion call to African Americans to do something about it. The quotation above encapsulates the historical context out of which Kwanzaa emerges—ferociously oppositional, unswervingly forthright, and doggedly determined to set a new cultural and political agenda.

To understand Kwanzaa is to comprehend the magnitude of the "African" revolution. Not the one necessarily waged in the streets and hinterlands of Algiers, Guinea, or Zanzibar, but a slightly different African revolution. This African revolution was as fierce and determined, and arguably as violent, as those waged throughout the so-called Third World. However, what was to be gained in this revolution was not land or political independence, but perhaps a more valuable and important commodity—the mind. This African revolution was a diasporic cultural war fought inside the African American psyche. The revolution waged inside the minds of black Americans would complete the revolution for civil rights that paralleled it, placing black Americans within a diaspora freedom struggle and a broader cultural awakening. But to believe this psychological and culture war required no munitions was to not know its complexity. Instead of guns or sophisticated military machinery, *Africa* itself became the arsenal of choice for black Americans. The arsenal consisted of the continent—its history, its languages, its people, its ceremonies, clothing, and mannerisms. African Americans weaponized African culture, using it both as a defense against the onslaught of cultural white supremacy and a new source of pride and freedom in blackness. As a product of this revolution, Kwanzaa was part of a broader strategy to redefine the totality of the black American experience from the standpoint of acquiring black consciousness. By attempting to discard the oppressor's culture, black Americans stood poised to replace it with their own understanding of who they were in the world: no longer Negroes, but blacks, and not only black, but African.

But no matter how much black Americans turned toward Africa, they could not escape the reality of their American nationality. Simply, the United States and its institutions would not allow them to. Kwanzaa would transcend the boundaries of black community, institutional, and familial spaces, reaching the larger U.S. society. For many outside of black America, Kwanzaa cohered well with corporate visions of marketing and advertising, multiculturalists' visions of inclusion and diversity, and religious visions of shared values. The evolving nature of race relations in the post–Civil Rights and Black Power eras placed Kwanzaa in an ironic position in regard to where the holiday ended up. By the late 1980s and early 1990s, Kwanzaa had become a part of mainstream American culture, no longer the exclusive property of black cultural nationalists or the wider African American population. The acceleration of consumer capitalism in the second half of the twentieth century, especially the last two decades, meant that not even cultural militancy of Kwanzaa's sort would remain free of the market and mainstream institutions. It would not take long for Kwanzaa, which included an invented Africa, essentialized notions of race, and rabid critiques of Christmas, to be transformed by corporate America to sell massproduced consumer goods and services in its name.

Concomitant with the corporate appropriation of black cultural expression, the multiculturalism and identity politics that swept the nation in the 1980s and 1990s greatly contributed to the holiday's appeal in American public culture. The multicultural milieu contributed mightily to Kwanzaa's shift from a provincial black nationalist cultural holiday to a more identifiable crosscommunity celebration. The nationalist language of the early Kwanzaa centered profoundly on concepts of power, liberation, and revolution. One generation later, cultural institutions like museums, religious bodies, and educational institutions, as well as the media and the federal government, advanced Kwanzaa in the name of diversity, recognition, inclusion, and goodwill. As a racial cultural holiday associated thoroughly with African Americans, Kwanzaa fit snugly into the new discourse on multiculturalism. Hence, this essay will explore two different Kwanzaas, or two moments in Kwanzaa's history. The first is the black nationalist Kwanzaa created by Maulana Karenga and promoted by black nationalists and other African Americans. The second charts the separation of the "nationalist" or "Black Power" Kwanzaa from its community and group origins and explores what I call the "multicultural" Kwanzaa.

MAULANA KARENGA AND THE FIRST KWANZAA

Maulana Karenga was born Ronald McKinley Everett on July 14, 1941 in Parsonburg, Maryland, near the southern Delaware border. Leaving behind his rural upbringing and the strict parenting of a Baptist preacher, Everett followed two older brothers who moved separately to Los Angeles in the early 1950s. Matt, the eldest of the Everett brothers, worked in the U.S. military as a merchant marine and was stationed in southern California. Chestyn, the second eldest, relocated to Los Angeles to pursue a career in the arts as an actor, writer, and painter. Young Ron Everett desired to attend college on the west coast, specifically the University of California at Los Angeles (UCLA). Two years after graduating from high school at the age of 16 he would get his chance to relocate. Trading in life in rural Parsonburg, Maryland for sunny California in 1959 not only represented a major geographical uprooting, but a foray into national and world politics, specifically issues pertaining to African Americans and the continent of Africa.

The creation of Kwanzaa in 1966 and Everett's quest to turn black America's attention to Africa had its roots some seven years before, when Everett enrolled at Los Angeles City College (LACC) in the fall of 1959 and transferred to UCLA in 1962. In his first year at LACC, Everett became the first black student body president while engaging in student activism on campus. When Everett transferred to UCLA on a language scholarship in 1962, he joined a campus that was already familiar with stoking the flames of racial and radical protests with Bruin chapters of the NAACP, CORE, the American Civil Liberties Union (ACLU), the Eugene Debs Club, the Student Peace Union, and the Young Socialist Alliance. The Nation of Islam also made its presence known on the campus of UCLA when its national representative, Malcolm X, spoke to the students in December 1962. The Afro-American Association—a Bay Area group that focused on black culture, pride, and history—was founded in 1962 and likewise identified UCLA as a site of protest. The organization's leader, Don Warden, spoke on campus two weeks after Malcolm X delivered his speech, with Everett in attendance. As a black student campus leader on the front lines of planning and meeting invited speakers, Everett consulted with both Malcolm and Warden. Everett decided to forego an invitation by Malcolm to join the Nation of Islam and instead forged alliances with the more cultural-oriented and less religious-focused Afro-American Association, becoming its Los Angeles and UCLA representative. Exactly one year after Warden delivered his message of cultural revitalization, Everett had undergone a name change, appearing as Ron Karenga of the Afro-American Association on a December 1963 UCLA panel entitled "Solution to the Negro Revolt." If 1963 represented the year Ron Everett, the "Negro," transformed himself into Ron Karenga, the "black nationalist," then campus politics was only part of the impetus.

Other reasons for Karenga's transformation were the African independence movement, the study of African languages, and courses in African Studies at UCLA. Decolonization had a profound effect on Karenga's thinking, much more than the civil rights movement in the United States. He identified the quest for political power as the central road toward freedom and liberation for Africans on the continent. "I said we need power," Karenga recalled, "and I'm identifying with the independence movement in Africa, that's a defining moment for me, this rise of Africa." Karenga read voraciously about African independence and black social movements in general: Jomo Kenyatta's *Facing Mount Kenya,* Kwame Nkrumah's *Africa Must Unite,* Marcus Garvey's *Philosophy and Opinions of Marcus Garvey,* Leopold Senghor's *African Socialism,* and Frantz Fanon's *The Wretched of the Earth.* UCLA proved that there was no better place to study African history, culture, and politics. In a bit of self-promotion that was not off the mark, the *Daily Bruin* reported in 1963 that "Africa is now the object of intensified study at UCLA through its African Studies Center. UCLA now offers a wider range of subjects dealing with Africa than any other university in the country."

Karenga took advantage of UCLA's offerings on Africa, taking classes with Dr. Bonaface Obichere, whom Karenga saw as the "premier African historian;" Councill Taylor, an anthropologist whose specialty was African ethnology; Dr. A. C. Jordan, who Karenga says "reinforced my interest in Zulu"; and William Welmers in a course on Ibo. Karenga was autodidactic, constantly checking Swahili books out of the library and getting "headaches trying to learn it all at once." Many of Karenga's professors are no longer living, but the few that remain from the early 1960s remember him well. Professor Sylvester Whitaker taught the upper division political science course on the "Politics of Africa." The course covered events from precolonial African traditional systems to the scramble for Africa in the nineteenth century, and ending with independence. Remembering Karenga as "very bright," Whitaker also recalled Karenga being a vocal student who was quick to challenge interpretations from the assigned material. Professor Michael Lofchie had Karenga in his "Governments and Politics of East Africa" course in 1964. As the semester progressed, the constant challenges by Karenga made it "more and more clear that our views did not coincide," says Lofchie, who also remembered Karenga coming into his office to discuss Kenya nationalism wearing a Jomo Kenyatta t-shirt and challenging the dominant interpretation of Kenyatta as argued by the Carl G. Rosberg and later John Nottingham book, *Myth of Mau Mau: Nationalism in Kenya.* Karenga's reveling in African history and culture, challenging historical interpretations and professors, and his love of African languages, was leading him to his own formulations. Karenga's proactive engagement with a plethora of different African subject matter helped him construct the holiday Kwanzaa in 1966 and also contributed to his evolution as a premier theorist of the Black Power Movement.

Black Power as a national social movement was in its early stages of articulation when the first official week of Kwanzaa commenced in December 1966. Six months earlier, Stokely Carmichael and others attempted to define to the nation what Black Power truly meant. Only weeks removed from the Meredith March against Fear, the media and civil rights leaders would not wait for a clear analysis and definition of Black Power from Carmichael and other theorists of the concept. Critics seized the moment and offered versions of the term immediately at odds with its major proponents. But if confusion abounded about what Black Power truly meant, no such national bewilderment dictated how Black Power should manifest itself during the Christmas holiday season. That is because no one anticipated Black Power's complexity and the kind of cultural work it would perform on behalf of African Americans. Certainly, no one envisioned Black Power's challenge to the traditional year-end holiday season and its bold reworking of the American calendar by Maulana Karenga and his cultural nationalist organization known as Us.

On December 25, 1965, three months after the founding of the Us Organization, Samuel Carr-Damu, one of the original members, visited Karenga's home to present his daughter with a black doll for Christmas. Karenga rejected the gift, stating that Us members should not celebrate Christmas. Since the entire rank-and-file of Us recognized some form of Christianity and were life-long celebrants of Christmas, the potential elimination of the holiday immediately posed a serious problem for the organization, especially those with young children. The urgency of questioning and perhaps substituting Christmas meant the future of Christmas in the organization would have to include an additional year-end celebration at the very least. It is not entirely clear in what manner the Us Organization celebrated or dealt with the issue of Christmas in 1965, but Karenga spent much of the following year researching African cultural practices, trying to find a suitable alternative for Christmas in 1966. Karenga scoured books on African history and culture, noticing the ubiquity of festivity and gaiety on the African continent around agricultural and harvest celebrations.

The search for the cultural alternative to Christmas meant returning to the source, or as Karenga became fond of saying, "going back to black." Going back to black was Karenga's idea of returning to what he understood as African tradition, an idea similarly postulated by Guinea President Sekou Toure called "re-

Africanization." While reading books on Zulu culture in South Africa, Karenga came across one particular harvest festival known as Umkhosi. Umkhosi was one of many first fruit or harvest ceremonies practiced in the Natal and Zulu-land regions of South Africa. The culmination of the harvest in Natal and Zulu regions usually occurred during the end of the year and at the beginning of the next, prompting the people in these areas to stop their daily activities and partake in an agricultural celebration. There were many ritual elements in the Umkhosi ceremony. But Karenga excluded components of the Zulu custom unfeasible in an American setting, instead focusing on ancestor veneration, feasting, ingathering of villagers, and the festival's appearance at year's end. Taking the name kwanza, meaning "first" in the original Swahili from "first fruits," Karenga capitalized the word "kwanza" and added an additional "a," using it to describe a new year-end holiday for his organization and for black Americans. "Kwanzaa then became for US and Black people," Karenga said, "a time and week of the gathering-in of ourselves rather than the agricultural harvests of our ancestors." Now armed with the building blocks of an "authentically" African tradition, Karenga instituted the new seven-day holiday (December 26 to January 1) for the Us Organization and black America. Only time would tell how well Kwanzaa would be received by African Americans and the rest of society.

In celebration of the Kwanzaa holiday, Sduduzo Ka Mbili performs a traditional Zulu warrior dance, December 23, 2003, at the Museum of Natural History in New York City. © Spencer Platt / Getty Images.

Traditional Kwanzaa candles. Courtesy of Getty Images / PhotoDisc.

On December 31, 1966, approximately 50 people packed a house near Washington Street and Tenth Avenue in Los Angeles to celebrate the end of the first Kwanzaa week. Smaller gatherings within the Us Organization had occurred during the five prior days, but on the sixth day of Kwanzaa, weeklong festivities culminated in one grand feast called the Karamu. Most Us Organization members attended, including Karenga and the top leadership. During the first Kwanzaa Karamu, Us members invited family and friends, and even found themselves among nonmembers who had heard about the celebration by word of mouth. The people who filed inside the home that evening experienced a celebration in two parts. From approximately early evening until 12 A.M., the first half of the Kwanzaa Karamu was administered with traditional Africa in mind. Us members wore colorful African dashikis and bubas. Men and women bowed and embraced, using Swahili terms to greet one another. The candles on a modified Jewish menorah were lit accompanied by the definition of the seven principles of Kwanzaa: Umoja—unity; Kujichagulia—self-determination; Ujima—collective work and responsibility; Ujamaa—cooperative economics; Nia—purpose; Kuumba—creativity; Imani—faith. For children, emphasis was placed on African storytelling and various skits on how to select a king. Adults sat on the floor and ate food with their hands. As the first half of the festivities came to a close, the second part of the Karamu commenced around 12 A.M.

If six to midnight represented an attempt to reconnect with a lost African past, then 12 A.M. to daybreak meant returning to the American present. Twelve A.M. until dawn encompassed the African American portion of the celebration. The early morning hours of January 1, 1967 were mainly reserved for adults as Us members and nonmembers alike drank and danced to the latest black music. James Brown blared from the stereo as Karamu attendees took to the floor. After officiating the first half of the Karamu, Karenga let the spirit of the moment engulf him as he danced to the music. Elizabeth Campbell, a nine- year-old girl who was allowed to witness some of the adult phase of the Karamu, recalls seeing Karenga that night:

> During the celebration, I saw for myself what made Ron Karenga special. I must have been 9 years old, old enough to take an interest in what was going on around me. I was used to seeing Karenga lecturing from a podium, looking so stern in his black clothes and dark-rimmed glasses. But now he was on the dance floor, enjoying himself with everyone else. I was surprised to see someone so serious—a big shot down with the folks and having a good time.

Young Elizabeth Campbell was the daughter of W. D. Campbell—an Us sympathizer who wanted his child to experience what the Karamu had to offer culturally. A second but older non-Us member recalled arriving by chance at the same inaugural Kwanzaa Karamu. Unlike young Elizabeth Campbell, who took notice of the adult phase of the feast, Iya Afin was enthralled by the first half ceremonies, remembering how the event transformed her life:

> I met some people in my apartment building who invited me to a feast. The feast took place at the US organizational meeting house in Los Angeles in 1967. They were celebrating a feast…known as Kwanzaa. The music, the food, the clothes, my people, I was entranced and captivated. For the first time in my life I felt at home in my own skin. I was listening to my people's music and dancing to my people's drums. At last I had a culture of my own. I felt a connection to my ancestors so strong that everything I had ever experienced in my whole life came back to me and I was changed forever.

While traveling on the East Coast in 1968 preparing for the Black Political Convention in Newark and the National Conference on Black Power in Philadelphia, Karenga promoted these major gatherings along with the little-known Kwanzaa. Attempting to raise awareness about the new holiday,

Karenga stressed the importance of embracing cultural alternatives in a speech at Howard University. He ask the black student body to consider exchanging longstanding family traditions based on European culture for something more culturally substantive: "If we ask people not to celebrate Christmas then we must be prepared to give them an alternative...so we did some research and found a Zulu custom where people came together for about a week around the first of the new year." In introducing this Zulu-inspired custom, Karenga did not mean for blacks to completely erase their Euro-American cultural traditions, but to recognize there existed a black cultural tradition beyond the strictures of American society.

Holiday, festival, and ritual promotion inside and outside of Us went hand-in-hand with radical group formations and political protest. When Karenga put his graduate studies on hold at UCLA in the summer of 1965 to organize blacks after the Watts rebellion, he took his role as activist very seriously. He often interacted with the likes of local NAACP, CORE, and SNCC members as well as newer black organizations on the streets of South Central Los Angeles. But Karenga's brand of activism did not stop at community advocacy and politics. Karenga's politics included holiday promotion. Promoting Kwanzaa and other black rituals was his form of political activism. Karenga was known to conduct meetings with various organizations in the Los Angeles Black Congress only to return to the hekalu (Us's headquarters translated as temple) later in the day to officiate an arusi—a wedding ceremony, or an akika—the nationalization and naming ceremony for children. From the hekalu it was on to a black denominational church to officiate a maziko (funeral) for a fallen comrade. But holiday and ritual promotion also meant organizing large public ceremonies in South Los Angeles like the Watts Summer Festival, annual Malcolm X birthday and assassination commemorations, and Uhura (freedom) Day rallies commemorating those who lost their lives in the Watts rebellion.

Interestingly, Us's first public appearance in southern California was not organized around activities in radical umbrella groups like the Temporary Alliance of Local Organizations (TALO) or the Black Congress. Instead Us appeared publicly for the first time during the inaugural Malcolm X observance in Los Angeles. Named for the Swahili word meaning sacrifice—Dhabihu—the day of Malcolm X's assassination or "martyrdom" proved the most promising out of all of Us's new holidays. The first Dhabihu brought 200 people on February 20, 1966 to the Garden of Prayer Church. With Malcolm's widow, Betty Shabazz, unable to attend, most of the local black nationalist organizations came together to pay tribute to Malcolm, who was assassinated one year earlier. Speeches were given praising Malcolm's legacy, and strident commentary promised to keep his work alive. Additionally, candles were lit and relit honoring Malcolm's memory. Confident about the success of the first Dhabihu, Karenga informed the audience, "this is going to be one of many holidays we are going to substitute for those celebrated by Euro-Americans." Though filled with much certainty about reprioritizing the calendar on behalf of African Americans, Karenga's remarks about a major Malcolm X holiday in subsequent years proved premature. Instead, Kwanzaa would become one of the most visible, if not celebrated, Black Power holidays, eventually outlasting the movement that gave it birth.

BLACK POWER AND THE EARLY PROMOTION OF KWANZAA

Although Kwanzaa began as an organizational observance in December of 1966, the holiday quickly gained currency among the wider Black Power community and some nonpoliticized blacks tied to neighborhood institutions. When Karenga met a series of political and personal misfortunes beginning with the UCLA shootout involving the Black Panthers in 1969 and his imprisonment for assault in 1971, the Us Organization fell apart. But Kwanzaa survived the political infighting, rising above internecine organizational battles and transcending both Maulana Karenga and the Us Organization. Kwanzaa's appeal beyond Karenga and Us was due to Black Power's growing political and cultural capital, which resonated with more African Americans as the years passed. For the outsider to Black Power, finding Kwanzaa in the late 1960s and early 1970s could be very hard. But for those who reveled in Black Power as a way of life, Kwanzaa was ubiquitous. Every December Kwanzaa could be located in black neighborhood institutions and Black Power places of gathering like community centers, schools, black museums, and the streets. Hence, if Karenga and Us gave life to Kwanzaa, then Black Power and the urban black neighborhood public sphere legitimized and sustained the holiday throughout the 1970s and 1980s before it assumed its multicultural character.

Community-based organizations such as the EAST organization in New York, the Institute for Positive Education in Chicago, and the Urban Survival Training Institute in Philadelphia introduced Kwanzaa in their respective cities. Many of these groups were Black Power advocates formerly tied to Amiri Baraka's Congress of African People (CAP)—the most influential black nationalist organization in the early 1970s. Some of these groups existed solely to promote Kwanzaa. Most of them, however, tied Kwanzaa to the larger process of controlling black neighborhoods. The men and women in community-based nationalist and nonnationalist organizations believed in creating their own schools, community centers, and publishing houses, reflecting their own Black Power politics. For them, Kwanzaa was just one in a series of activities that validated their struggle for institutional independence and cultural autonomy. Promoting Kwanzaa was an extension of building an independent school, a community center, or participating in Third World political struggles.

In Brooklyn, New York, home to one of the largest black populations in United States, the EAST organization labored diligently to get the word out about Kwanzaa. "If you know something about Kwanza already, spread the word," wrote Basir Mchawi of the EAST; "our greatest communications vehicle is our mouths." For the EAST, no single place proved more appropriate than another for the introduction of Kwanzaa. Members believed Kwanzaa could be held just about anywhere: "Support and initiate Kwanza programs in your community, at day care centers, schools, community centers, your home, etc." All African Americans should "try to make Kwanza a household word."

The EAST organization was typical of many community-based Black Power organizations in the business of promoting Kwanzaa. First, its physical presence on 10 Claver Place, up the block from busy Fulton Street, placed it in a strategic location to reach a large number of black people on a daily basis. Secondly, the EAST headquarters conducted simultaneous activities throughout the year: political rallies for black domestic and pan-African causes, the education of black children enrolled in their independent school—the Uhura Sasa School, and after-school programming and recreation for neighborhood youth. Lastly, the EAST headquarters, like other community-based sites, represented a clearinghouse for political and cultural information related to black people. Thus, the EAST organization in Brooklyn, New York became the site for all things representing African consciousness and Black Power. Anyone who lived in the neighborhood or walked by every December knew that 10 Claver Place was Kwanzaa's place of residence. As the founder of the EAST organization, Jitu Weusi, remembered proudly, "in 1970, the EAST...adopted Kwanzaa...and thus became the first institution east of the Hudson River to practice and observe Kwanzaa."

Promoting Kwanzaa on the streets of black Brooklyn in the 1970s meant challenging the popularity of Christmas within the black community. EAST publications during the month of December were filled with articles about blacks and Christmas, often chastising African Americans for over-consuming during the holiday season: "Now you fool where do you think you're going? Just come back here...sit down and let us put some sense in your head.... There are over $400 worth of outstanding bills which you still have from last year, including Christmas." The EAST felt that Christmas shopping for blacks was akin to slavery, extolling African Americans to "break the chains." "Once again, its time for us to PLAY THE FOOL.... MAS-X SEASON is here, better known as XMAS. The time for us to sigh, buy, cry, grin, and PURCHASE, purchase, PURCHASE! All for the hippie-dippey Christ and his OLD new year. TAKE THE CHAINS OFF YOUR BRAIN BLACK PEOPLE!!!" The EAST annually called for a boycott from Christmas shopping and asked African Americans to consider the cultural alternative to the main holiday tradition, admonishing: "As the holiday season approaches us again, when our monies are most likely at an all time low, we Afrikans had better seriously consider the alternative to the

Christmas rip off—Kwanza." Understanding the generational politics in black families where most members were wedded to the traditional Christmas season, the EAST cautioned black parents, "if you can't handle Kwanza, give it to your children. The young folks will love you for it and respect you more than Santa." The EAST summed up their feelings about Christmas and the new Kwanzaa holiday: "Kill Santa Claus, relive Kwanza, bring forth the cultural revolution."

Public announcements every December notwithstanding, Kwanzaa promotion in black neighborhoods manifested in large public events such as Kwanzaa parades, pre-Kwanzaa workshops, concerts, and large community feasts. In 1974, the EAST moved their normal Kwanzaa activities from their headquarters on 10 Claver Place to accommodate a larger crowd. After a children's Kwanzaa festival on December 20, and the follow-up family Kwanzaa activities from December 26 through December 29, the EAST reported that on December 31 "over 1,000 Brothers and Sisters...participated in...activities held at the Sumner Avenue Armory." By moving to a larger site, the EAST was able to commission nationally known artists, dramatists, and musicians such as poet Sonia Sanchez, musician Lonnie Liston Smith, and actors from the National Black Theater to help promote Kwanzaa at its 1974 celebration. The EAST reminded those unable to attend: "If you missed Kwanza '74, we'll be back when Kwanza lands again. Be sure you catch it this year. Kwanza '75 will be a sure nuff smoka."

While the EAST made Kwanzaa an annual ceremonial event in Brooklyn, other institutions promoted Kwanzaa in different parts of New York City. One of the earliest groups to sponsor public Kwanzaa celebrations was a social service agency called the Harlem Commonwealth Council located on 125th Street. The Harlem Commonwealth Council typically held annual Kwanzaa festivities at the Studio Museum in Harlem and area public schools. In December of 1971, the Harlem Council assembled 50 elementary students at the Studio Museum from Public School 68 to teach them about the new holiday. To enliven and embolden the message of roots, identity, and African cultural connection, as well as to reduce the generational gap between the messenger and the students, the council commissioned a 16- year-old ordained minister and director of the National Youth Movement named Al Sharpton to educate the students about Kwanzaa. The young, "heavy set" Sharpton, as the *New York Times* described him, wore an African dashiki and opened his talk by explaining to the students, "today you're going to learn something about Kwanza." In the trademark raspy voice he would become known for as an adult, Sharpton went on to explain in the simplest of terms the holiday's connections with the African past, telling the students, ranging from seven to nine years old, that Kwanzaa is "a spiritual ceremony" and that "harvesting...is traditional in Africa." After Sharpton provided a lesson on Kwanzaa's material symbols and the correct way to annunciate the holiday's Swahili terminology, the students were provided gifts, and seven of them were chosen to light candles on the kinara. The following year in

1972, the council gathered 300 more students at the Studio Museum to hear another lecture on Kwanzaa.

While solo organizational efforts were common among groups like the EAST, coalition-led Kwanzaas were a major feature of year-end holiday ceremonies in some cities. In 1971, the Confederation of Pan-African Organizations formed purposely to stage citywide Kwanzaa galas in Chicago. Haki Madhubuti and a few others had been performing Kwanzaa ceremonies in their organizations since the late 1960s, but the confederation recruited a broad cross-section of Chicago black nationalists to further popularize the holiday: Madhubuti and the Institute of Positive Education; Hannibal Afrik and the Shule Ya Watoto; Musa Kenyatta and the Republic of New Africa; Ife Jogunosimi and Mansong Kulubally of the Black Body; the United Africans for One Motherland International (UFOMI); the Chicago chapter of the Provisional Government; and Conrad Worrill—educator, columnist, and later the Chicago chair of the National Black United Front.

One of the most significant developments to come out of the Chicago Confederation was the Karamu Ya Imani—a community feast meaning "feast of faith." Proposed by Hannibal Afrik as a community-wide promotional and educational campaign, the first Karamu Ya Imani was held at the Ridgeland Club on January 1, 1973. Typically, children performed in the early afternoon. During the evening, the ritual phase for adults was held. Evening activities included pouring libations to the ancestors, lighting candles, and making commitments for the New Year. As was customary, food was prepared by volunteers, delivered, and placed in the center of the room for consumption. The 200-person gathering included much of the Chicago nationalist community but also a steady stream of apolitical blacks from the south and west side of Chicago. Black cultural nationalists also represented visually, appearing in colorful African clothing while ordinary blacks wore jeans, slacks, suits, and dresses. Remarks about the significance of embracing "African" culture were made by Hannibal Afrik and Haki Madhubuti, both of whom reiterated how important it was to instill a new set of values in African Americans, particularly black children. All speakers agreed to the efficacy of the Karamu Ya Imani and promised the confederation would institutionalize Kwanzaa in the windy city by holding the Feast of Faith annually.

In the years following 1971, an increasing number of participants forced the Confederation of Pan-African Organizations to move the Karamu Ya Imani to different locations in Chicago: the Viking Temple, the YMCA, the South Shore Cultural Center, the DuSable Museum, and the Packing House on 49th and Wabash. The growth of the Feast meant that more blacks in Chicago had come to embrace Kwanzaa, but there also existed a down side. By late 1978, the confederation found it increasingly hard to finance the Karamu Ya Imani, resulting in the dissolution of the Confederation of Pan-African Organizations. In 1980, however, a few of the original organizations in the confederation along with a number of newer groups reorganized as the African Community of Chicago and continued the tradition of the Karamu Ya Imani in the new decade.

In Washington, D.C., the same spirit of cooperation existed among Kwanzaa organizations united to promote the new Black Power holiday. Again, the black cultural nationalist community took the lead in the Kwanzaa publicity campaign. The first Kwanzaa gathering in the District was held at the home of local activist Sister Woody (Nia Kuumba) in 1970. Wider public festivities soon spread to the black independent school, Ujamaa Shule, under the direction of Baba El Senzengalkulu Zulu, and to Black Power houses of worship like the Temple of the Black Messiah and the Union Temple Baptist Church pastored by the Reverend Willie Wilson. The Museum of African Art under the educational direction of Amina Dickerson, the Reverend Ishakamusa Barashango, Ayo Handy, the D.C. Kwanzaa Committee, the Watoto Shule, and the United Black Community were also instrumental in introducing Kwanzaa in the 1970s. Many of these groups and institutions sponsored coordinated public Kwanzaa celebrations at their respective locations, making the holiday an annual event in the nation's capital.

But to understand Kwanzaa's reach during its Black Power period one only had to look at the wide range of black people that embraced the holiday. Ideas about Black Power usually conjure up images of wild-eyed radicals confronting established authority on the urban streets, never white-collar professionals who equally furthered the cause of Black Power politics. But the planning committee for Anacostia Museum's first Kwanzaa celebration in 1973 suggest otherwise. Included in the black museum's first Kwanzaa was Lawrence Boone, principle of Orr Elementary School, Jacqueline Williams, principle of Malcolm X Elementary School, Cynthia Wade, music teacher in the D.C. Public Schools, and Calvin Lockridge, instructor at Federal City College (University of the District of Columbia). That same year actresses Marla Gibbs and Esther Rolle of the very popular television sitcoms *The Jeffersons* and *Good Times* respectively started the Kwanzaa Foundation in Los Angeles—a charity organization based on Kwanzaa's seven principles that provided gifts to inner-city black youth during the holiday season. And five years later in 1978, Community School District 7 in the Bronx brought together an eclectic number of black and Puerto Rican professionals that annually held Kwanzaa activities for their students through the Black Student Advancement in Standard English Language program (BASEL).

The sheer number of community organizations and institutions promoting Kwanzaa underscored the holiday's ties to the Black Power movement and the larger black neighborhood public sphere—a counter-public peopled by political activists, cultural workers, ministers, educators, and others bent on changing the way the larger African American community understood culture, holidays, and themselves. Creating and sustaining a black holiday ultimately meant capturing the avenues and spaces of publicity: not only the calendar, but community centers, museums, schools, armories, churches, the airwaves, and even the streets. African Americans were empowered both by Kwanzaa and the public spaces the holiday occupied every December. The story of the public Kwanzaa in the late 1960s, 1970s, and early 1980s is not a story of a single individual, but a narrative about a community of people that collectively decided to challenge the hegemony of Christmas and stake out new areas for the Black Power movement. Kwanzaa was a product of a broad-based social movement that was national in scope but local in character.

FROM BLACK POWER TO CORPORATE AND MULTICULTURAL MARKETING

As Kwanzaa began to turn over to newer organizations and adherents by the late 1980s, the holiday's commercial potential loomed as a threat for the Black Power community. But the commercialization and the selling of Kwanzaa proved complicated given the various entities involved in the merchandising of the holiday. Some black nationalists saw the economic realm as a way to promote Kwanzaa to the black public as well as to create a sustainable black entrepreneurialism. These activists who had been part of the Black Power movement invited major corporations to take part in annual commercial/promotional campaigns, merging black entrepreneurship with white commercialism. Others resisted partnering with white business interests, underscoring Kwanzaa's sanctity and reverence as an anticommercial holiday and seeing the commodification of Kwanzaa as a major threat to black cultural productivity. What is fascinating about the appropriation of Kwanzaa is that the story appears more complex than simply a case of blacks and whites on opposite sides of the commercial divide.

The attempt to keep Kwanzaa pure and protected from commercial activity was a futile exercise from the beginning. Certainly by the late 1980s and early 1990s, the black holiday that came one day after Christmas proved too irresistible for white corporations, such as Hallmark, Inc. and General Motors. After two decades of controlling the Kwanzaa market exclusively, black businesses and entrepreneurs began to lose their grip in the very small market niche the holiday afforded them. In the 1990s, white-owned companies and retail stores suddenly recognized the holiday's commercial potential. As *Ebony* magazine noted in 2000, "Kwanzaa, the 34-year old holiday focusing on African American families, communities, and culture has proved to be far more than a fad. Its popularity has expanded enough to attract attention from the nation's biggest retailers. In short, the selling of Kwanzaa is becoming big business." This newfound recognition by big business not only signaled an awakening of Kwanzaa's commercial potential, but pointed to a new direction in late twentieth-century capitalism: the marketing and merchandising of race, multiculturalism, and diversity via racial and ethnic holidays.

The presence of white-owned corporations in racial markets like Kwanzaa underscored the confluence of multiculturalism and commodification in the last two decades of the twentieth century. As America buried the political vocabulary of the 1960s and 1970s—freedom, rights, power, revolution— multiculturalism of the 1980s and 1990s rested on the notions of inclusion, diversity, and recognition. The rise of multiculturalism in the 1980s opened up spaces to people of color in the American public sphere, making African Americans, Latinos, and Asian Americans politically, culturally, and economically visible. Multiculturalism's emphasis on the importance of race and ethnicity turned votes into a political commodity for politicians running for office. Likewise, multiculturalism made race and ethnicity an economic commodity for merchants, retailers, and corporations. It is not surprising that ethnic and racial customs, particularly annual calendar events, have become major occasions for buying and selling in the last 20 years. Even more than the standard American holidays like Christmas and Thanksgiving, racial and ethnic festivities enable corporations to penetrate specialized markets. Racial holiday markets like Kwanzaa not only provide companies a chance to increase profits, but to engage in the politics of public relations by peddling the ideas of diversity, inclusion, and recognition to the communities they serve in the marketplace.

But the marketplace was not only the purview of economic actors. Cultural institutions, such as churches and museums, also partook in ethnic and racial consumption by making Kwanzaa a standard year-end activity to bring more black bodies through the door. In the name of diversity and goodwill, major white cultural institutions discovered many tangibles in Kwanzaa: the holiday's ability to diversify annual programming that catered previously to an overwhelmingly white audience; its potential to augment the museum and church-attending public; and its ability to recast the museum, the church, and the school as racially and ethnically inclusive institutions. All of these desires are self-serving marketplace values often attributed to profit-making commercial entities. However, the fact that the end game is not profit for museums, churches, and schools does not hide the absence of marketplace and consumption behavioral intent. On the contrary, these cultural institutions often have a bigger stake in promoting identity-based marketing and consumption designed to both remake internal institutional politics in the realm of public relations while promoting the broader goal of diversity and inclusion of racial and ethnic minorities in society. What this ultimately meant was that Kwanzaa as commodity seemed understood by all involved: black nationalist, small black entrepreneur, black advertising copywriter, black greeting-card maker, Afrocentric boutique, white corporation, white bank, white museum, white church, Jewish synagogue, suburban white school, white media, and the United States Postal Service. What this also meant was that Kwanzaa's growing visibility in late twentieth-century American public culture appeared endemically tied to the marketplace decision-making and appropriation of corporate and cultural institutions.

Prior to the advent of multicultural marketing and Kwanzaa's discovery by big business and mainstream cultural institutions, the holiday's fourth principle, *ujaama,* promoted the idea of black entrepreneurialism between black producer and consumer. Building off of earlier twentieth-century "Buy Black" campaigns, Kwanzaa became the latest chapter in the history of race-based nationalist economics as a new key phrase was introduced in the 1960s called "cooperative economics." The cooperative economic thrust of black entrepreneurialism initially revolved solely around Kwanzaa-related products that could be marketed and sold: the holiday's ceremonial symbols like its candleholder (kinara), greeting cards, calendars, bumper stickers, and children's books. The business of kinara production existed on a small scale and was controlled by Black Power organizations and some black craftsmen. The craftsmen, many of them furniture makers and carpenters, lent their efforts to an industry void of any apparent contours or defining features. Black Power organizations like the Congress of African People (CAP) commissioned black craftsmen in the creation and production of Kwanzaa's most important ceremonial item, the kinara. As more African Americans embraced Kwanzaa each year, market demand increased for key Kwanzaa items. Therefore, it was imperative for black entrepreneurs to strategically place themselves in a position to supply this nascent market. They did. From the point of creation, distribution, and final sale, the Kwanzaa market and holiday merchandise was handled by Black Power groups, local boutiques, black bookstores, and small mail-order businesses owned by blacks.

A 1973 Congress of African People (CAP) report explained how the Black Power organization produced Kwanzaa ceremonial items and who would make the final determination on how the symbols should look. "Man is casting kinara with seven principles on it," an internal report noted, and "will send to Imamu Baraka before going into production.... Imanu Baraka needs to see models of everything and prices." The man in the memorandum is never identified by name or occupation, but it can be safely assumed that the individual, probably a skilled wood craftsman, was commissioned by CAP and entrusted to create a design acceptable to Baraka and his organization. The same report determined where and how Kwanzaa Kits would be delivered to individuals and merchants in the African American community: "Camden will be the distribution center." Local CAP-affiliated organizations would have vinara and kits available for the African American community, but "orders will be filled in Camden" for wholesalers and at "retail to people with no local CAP office." To eliminate confusion and difficulty in obtaining Kwanzaa ceremonial items, and to ensure proper distribution and pricing, it was important for the national distribution center in Camden, New Jersey to be in sync with local merchants, organizations, and people, as the same memo noted: "must get whole financial setup between local and national...can be done as soon as [we] have whole cost on items." Indeed, CAP went a step further by setting prices for individual items and full ceremonial kits. As part of the Kwanzaa Kit, individual vinara (candleholders) were priced at $5.50 a piece, the vikombe (unity cups) at $1.88, the mikeka (mats) at $1.40, and the mishumma (candles) at $.70. CAP also offered Kwanzaa greeting cards at $1.05 apiece and a Kwanzaa kitabu (a how-to-perform Kwanzaa pamphlet) at $.15. The price for the Kwanzaa Kit totaled $10.68, but CAP set the retail price at $17.50, making a gross profit of $6.82 per kit. CAP also turned a profit on individual vinara, pricing them separately from the kit at $11.00 apiece, knowing that as the single most important ceremonial item and the costliest to manufacture, many celebrants would only seek to buy Kwanzaa's candleholder and make do without other key symbols.

Kwanzaa Arts, a small business that began in Los Angeles in the 1970s, typified early Kwanzaa entrepreneurial efforts. Kwanzaa Arts began when three original celebrants of the holiday came together to promote Kwanzaa by marketing a free catalog containing various items. The catalog items included an "I Love Kwanzaa" bumper sticker, a Kwanzaa pin to wear on clothing, and magazine articles about the holiday. To publicize the holiday, Kwanzaa Arts advertised their catalog in major black newspapers.

The main purpose of the free catalog was to tap into the untested market of Kwanzaa greeting cards. Every item in the catalog, including the bumper stickers and pins, were free, except the Kwanzaa greeting cards. Kwanzaa Arts would use the greeting cards to economically capitalize on the holiday's relative obscurity by couching the catalog in the language of holiday promotion. Created by a young graphic artist and painter named Bernard Hoyes, Kwanzaa Arts issued a test card in 1975, showing the profile of a black woman with an Afro hairstyle, inset with a smaller black man's face staring straight ahead. Next to the man's face and behind the woman's image is a kinara, an ear of corn that symbolizes the harvest, and a talisimu—an Us Organization symbol. Encasing the entire image on the front of the card is the phrase "Happy Kwanzaa," with the Nguzo Saba and a brief description of Kwanzaa inside. Following the test card in 1975, Hoyes and Kwanzaa Arts released seven different greeting cards in 1977 corresponding to the seven principles. The seven cards amounted to a full package offered by Kwanzaa Arts. Sold mainly in 5″ × 9″ and 6″ × 9″, each card included the seven principles inside with an image on the front corresponding to one principle. These full-color cards were sold as a set, encased in black heavy paper with gold foil on the cover of the containing package. In black newspaper advertisements, Kwanzaa Arts directed its greeting cards to the black buying public with its yearly pitch: "At last you can celebrate this unique Afro-American Holiday by sending creatively designed Kwanzaa cards and matching envelopes. Satisfaction guaranteed...mail your order now to Kwanzaa Arts."

Kwanzaa Arts also attempted to make their cards available to a wider audience, but most major white distributors refused to market the card, citing the "esoteric" nature of the cards' images. Instead, Kwanzaa Arts sold their greeting cards directly to black bookstores in Los Angeles, Atlanta, and Brooklyn, New York, which readily promoted them to annual celebrants and newcomers to the holiday. According to Kwanzaa Arts founder Ngoma Ali, black schoolteachers purchased and used them as teaching tools in the classroom. Despite some interest, Kwanzaa Arts never sold the greeting card package beyond its first printing. In fact, it took six years to sell the initial production of 1,200, underscoring the difficulties of black distribution channels and how small the Kwanzaa market was in the mid- and late 1970s.

Kwanzaa Arts did not exist mainly to make a profit, which is why the company never tended to its bottom line. Kwanzaa Arts' purpose centered on the promotion of Kwanzaa while simultaneously remaining commercially hopeful that money could be made from the holiday. In most small business enterprises involving Kwanzaa in the 1970s, promotion and profit often overlapped. As Bernard Hoyes explained, "what I was trying to do was to market the whole idea of Kwanzaa from a utilitarian point of view. Kwanzaa wasn't going to be mass-distributed unless you put it in a form to be mass-distributed." Hoyes made promotion synonymous with profit, recognizing that Kwanzaa could also gain a following through economic enterprise and "not just in diatribes of political thought." Other Kwanzaa promotional/commercial start-ups thought similarly, appearing in other cities like Baltimore and marketing comparable items. One advertisement announced that "Kwanzaa Unlimited is proudly offering 3 authentic Kwanzaa celebration pins to be worn or given as gifts during the holiday season for just $9.99."

The 1980s witnessed greater involvement in the Kwanzaa market by other black entrepreneurs, especially those possessing more financial resources. More financial resources usually meant better-made goods and wider distribution networks. But a larger market that had the capabilities of producing meaningful profits also signaled the entry of white-owned companies in the Kwanzaa market. Black greeting card companies with staff, artists, and overhead emerged in the 1970s and began producing Kwanzaa cards in the early 1980s. Filling the void from an absence of greeting cards that reflected African Americans as a people, black companies such as Broom Designs, L'Image Graphics, Carole Joy Creations, and Love, Auntie Cheryl Greetings served an untapped market in racial and ethnic greeting cards. But as black greeting-card companies attempted to establish themselves in their own specialized racial market, Hallmark, Gibson, and American Greetings decided to partner with small black card companies to discern the growing demand for black greeting cards and the market's potential. Hallmark first test-marketed black greeting cards in 1987 by allowing a few black companies to sell their cards in Hallmark stores and in chain supermarkets contracted to sell the Hallmark brand name. Initially, Hallmark said it was not interested in producing the cards, only desiring to make them available to their black customer base. The response from black consumers for these black-inflected greeting cards, however, changed Hallmark's strategy. Black artist Synthia St. James's cards were tested and reproduced by Hallmark after the Jewish-owned card company EthnoGraphics used James's designs for its Kwanzaa cards. Hallmark also tested cards by motivational speaker and author Iyanla Vanzant, and several other artists. From 1987 to 1990, Hallmark used black greeting-card companies and black creative consultants to establish a new product—greetings cards that appealed directly to the African American community for all occasions throughout the year. These black cards were contracted exclusively under Hallmark's signature line Mahogany. Similarly, Love, Auntie Cheryl Greetings, Inc. obtained a licensing agreement from white-owned American Greetings Corporation, only to be dropped a few years later after American began its own line of black cards. Desiring to become the "black Hallmark," Love, Auntie Cheryl Greetings produced only for American, which caused the small company to fold after American Greetings terminated their relationship. In a similar arrangement, Recycled Papers—another major white-owned greeting card company—acquired L'Image Graphics—one of the most successful black greeting card companies since its founding in 1983.

Placing unlimited resources in the area of multicultural card production has been a formula used by Hallmark, Gibson, American, and Recycled Papers to reduce competition and put small black greeting-card manufacturers out of business. Kwanzaa represented only one in a series of racial and ethnic holidays merchandized by these corporations. In large white companies, the area of multicultural card production included extensive research on communities of color, uncovering population statistics and disposable incomes. Ethnic business centers were established to aid ongoing research. In-house production teams made up of black artists, designers, and writers tracked the latest trends in all areas of the media, as Hallmark's Melissa Bolden explained:

> I keep up with the latest publications, television programs, and retail catalogs targeted to our customer, and I love to immerse myself in cities where the African-American population is high. It helps me get outside of my own black experience because as with all cultures, there is a wide range of styles, forms of language, and attitudes that mainstream Americans sometimes overlook.

This kind of effort has allowed Hallmark to produce 800 cards related to the black experience, ranging from holidays, historical personalities, everyday occasions, and birthdays. Beginning with one Kwanzaa card in 1992, Hallmark annually produced 10 different cards for Kwanzaa by the end of the decade. Already controlling nearly 80 percent of the general greeting card market with Gibson, American, and Recycled, Hallmark's entry and steady progress in racial card production made the existence of black companies producing Kwanzaa cards nearly impossible.

Similarly, the struggle of black entrepreneurs to maintain their stake in the Kwanzaa market even existed at the level of street vending. Commercial street vending placed black entrepreneurs and consumers in direct contact with one another. But to move street vending beyond the level of a few individual entrepreneurs, black commercial expositions known as Kwanzaa Fests arose with major corporate underwriting. Kwanzaa expositions provided black producers greater access to black consumers, but the expositions also afforded corporate institutions a degree of public visibility in a show of community support and potential profit. The presence of huge corporate logos in close proximity to black entrepreneurs selling Afrocentric clothing represented a major turning point for both late twentieth-century capitalism and black nationalist economic enterprise.

Since 1981, Kwanzaa expositions occurred annually in Oakland, Chicago, and St. Louis. New York City, however, had always staged the largest Kwanzaa exposition containing the most black entrepreneurs, consumers, and corporate sponsors. In 1981, Jose Ferrer and Malik Ahmed, two long-time community activists who worked for the social service agency, the New York Urban Coalition, persuaded the organization to use Kwanzaa as a vehicle for community uplift. Ferrer and Ahmed created an idea similar to Kwanzaa Arts, in which Kwanzaa and its principles could be promoted via commercial enterprise rather than through political pronouncements. Ferrer and Ahmed shied away from proselytizing the holiday's principles to African Americans and instead pitched the idea of promoting Kwanzaa via economics. After moving around from location to location during the early to mid-1980s, Ferrer was able to partner with the *New York Daily News,* procure corporate underwriters with deeper pockets, and secure the Jacob Javits Center—a more permanent location in downtown Manhattan. Kwanzaa Fest's major sponsors included General Motors, Kraft Foods, Fleet Bank, Chase Manhattan Bank, Phillip Morris, AT&T, Anheuser-Busch, and electronic giant, Circuit City. These corporate sponsors underwrote the fest throughout the late 1980s and 1990s, paying overhead costs that could not be met solely through admissions fees. This corporate revenue stream not only increased attendance every December, but placed the fest on a more permanent financial footing, freeing Ferrer from the need to invest his own money with "no guarantee that it's going to come back."

Paying the bills gave corporate America an entry into the market of black consumers via Kwanzaa. For instance, during the annual Kwanzaa Fest, Heineken Beer used some of Kwanzaa's principles in a full page advertisement, citing: "Unity, Purpose, Creativity, Faith—Heineken is proud to celebrate Kwanzaa and everything that it stands for." Chase Manhattan Bank began issuing Kwanzaa checks in 1996. Anheuser-Busch and Seaman's furniture announced, "May the spirit of Kwanzaa be enjoyed by your family throughout the year." And a group of supermarkets and food producers, including White Rose, Chef Boyardee, Pepsi-Cola, Gerber, Nabisco, Met and Pioneer issued a collective statement: "We salute Kwanzaa, the unique American holiday that pays tribute to the rich cultural roots of Americans of African ancestry. The following companies and products support the seven principles, Nguzo Saba." For supporting the Kwanzaa Fest, the consortium of supermarkets and food companies "hope [black consumers] consider including [these products] in [their] traditional Kwanzaa meal planning and gathering of family and friends." Though BET and Carver Federal Savings Bank, two black-operated businesses, advertised in Ferrer's *Daily News* supplement, they never became corporate sponsors. In the 20-year history of the fest, Golden Krust Bakery was the only black company that ever paid enough to become a major sponsor.

While sponsor logos graced all areas of the Jacob Javits Convention Center, the small black entrepreneur always stood at the center of attention. Streams of people, mainly African American consumers, strolled six aisles of carnival and consumption, passing by African art, jewelry, cosmetics, books, and an occasional dance performance. Nearly 300 black businesses had a chance to pitch their products to the 30,000 people that passed through the aisles of the convention during the annual four-day event. Music blasted from the resident radio station WBLS-FM; children's plays were performed; and Nguzo Saba award tributes were given to influential people in the black and white community. Ferrer saw the fest as a mixture of festivity and black economic self-sufficiency, a confluence, as he called it, of education, culture, and commerce:

> There is direct correlation between education, culture, and commerce. These relationships have allowed other groups to succeed despite obstacles, in an often hostile environment. Many groups have used their culture as a means for economic growth and as a way to establish vibrant, comparatively self-sufficient communities. There's no logical reason why we shouldn't be the beneficiaries of our own economic might. The concept of black economic self-sufficiency is not new. Great leaders like Marcus and the Honorable Elijah Muhammad advocated it generations ago. The beauty of Kwanzaa…is that it addresses all of the components necessary to empower a people—economics, culture, and spirituality. Kwanzaa Fest is our small way of helping to bring about that reality.

Viewing the fest as a form of black economic self-sufficiency, as Ferrer did, only captures part of the story. The fest was also a prime example of business colonization. American companies were not only sellers of goods and services at the fest; they were sponsors of the festival, providers of culture, and facilitators of community relations. Corporate partnerships of the fest legitimized Kwanzaa and its racial politics for the mainstream American public. At the same time, the racial politics of corporate-sponsored Kwanzaas compromised the Black Power holiday. By the late 1980s, Kwanzaa was beginning to resemble the official culture it was created to subvert. Although the Kwanzaa Fest represented one of the largest examples of black American *Ujamaa,* it also had become one of the biggest corporate takeovers of black cultural expression in the United States. As Leslie Savan pointed out in another context: it is a pity "how easily an idea, deed, or image can become part of the sponsored world." This encroachment into racialized markets, however, could only have happened with black and brown cooperation.

The corporate reliance on black and brown entrepreneurs as points of entry into new racial and ethnic markets was part of a growing trend in multicultural merchandising and marketing, a phenomenon unheard of prior to the 1980s. Ethnic marketing agencies like Multicultural Marketing Resources, Inc., the Chisholm-Mingo Group, Cultural Access, Graham Gregory Bozell, and Mosaica facilitated corporate access to communities of color and race-specific cultural productions like Kwanzaa. These groups existed in order to put corporations like AT&T, Hallmark, and General Motors in touch with ethnic consumers. A company profile of the Chisholm-Mingo Group, one of the oldest black marketing firms, explains that its aim is to help corporate entities "leverage their ethnic roots and expertise by creating a pre-emptive emotional bond between the consumer and the client's products and services." The emphasis on emotional bonding with a particular product is designed to establish the company brand as a top purchase choice for the targeted community.

Attempts to create bonds between consumers of color and white-owned corporations can be potentially explosive, especially if the corporations (such as those of tobacco and alcohol) had histories of using aggressive marketing techniques that led to past charges of exploitation and discrimination. But the new multicultural marketers found ways around this problem, suggesting to their corporate clients that the way to build healthy relationships with ethnic communities is by engaging in public relations rather than marketing. Public relations, or what is sometimes referred to as corporate image advertising, proved important. According to a *Black Enterprise* magazine study, "some of the earliest campaigns commissioned were intended to strengthen the image of corporate clients in the black community." Lisa Skriloff, president of Multicultural Marketing Resources, echoed *Black Enterprise*'s assessment but in a slightly different way, surmising that the "essence of good marketing... is tying into something that is important to the consumer." By promoting and sponsoring Kwanzaa, other ethnic celebrations, and community affairs programs, corporations seek to establish a presence in communities of color that pay bigger dividends in the long run. The *New York Times* noted the McDonald's Corporation's use of this public relations technique in relation to Kwanzaa: "the McDonald's Corporation is running Kwanzaa ads created by Caroline Jones, Inc... that do not show a single Big Mac. The message is not so much about French fries and burgers as it is to show the company as understanding and respecting African-Americans' sense of family and community. One commercial... shows families in festive settings, including a choir performing to a jubilant congregation."

Multicultural Marketing Inc., the Chisholm-Mingo Group, and others have peddled the idea of ethnic difference to big business, making them see the advantages of marketing celebrations originating from communities of color: "Certainly there are opportunities where marketers reach to the general market, whether it's President's [sic] Day sales or a seasonal holiday shopping opportunity," says Lisa Skriloff. "It is the smart marketers who are looking for opportunities that are not overexploited and where they can cut through the clutter." Some marketers of color see their role as educating uninformed corporate clients about untapped racial and ethnic markets. Caroline Jones, a former partner in the Chisholm Group before branching out on her own, remembered: "most clients are not organized to look at the black consumer market in any long-term way, so we have to do it for them. And we want to do it. If we don't do it...we won't have a client."

Cultural institutions, like museums and churches, also know what it is not to have certain clients. In an age of diminishing returns and the difficulty of maintaining support from the federal government, museums have moved toward a more corporate and consumption-based model of marketing. Perhaps more than corporations, cultural institutions have made diversity and inclusion their primary aim by using cultural productions outside of their normal constituency to attract people of color. Andrea Ellis, a representative from the Kansas City Museum, echoed sentiments similar to marketer Caroline Jones, albeit in a different institutional context, when she said that the museum "wants to represent, as much as we can, the entire community with the holidays that are celebrated.... Kwanzaa is a culture we wanted to be sure we didn't miss out on."

As a legitimate part of the year-end festive season in museum corridors, Kwanzaa had indeed arrived in the name of diversity and goodwill. The 1990s was the decade Kwanzaa rose to the level of other traditional celebrations in visibility, if not in stature. As the *Age* reported in 1994, "Thanksgiving is a distant memory, the Hanukah menorahs have been put away, and the Christmas trees are destined to become recycled mulch. On America's crowded festive calendar that means one more thing: time to deck the halls for Kwanzaa." Kwanzaa was part of a growing movement toward holiday multiculturalism, oftentimes appearing alongside more traditional celebrations as well as less familiar ones. In 1989, the Chicago Public Library Cultural Center conducted four holiday ceremonies in the month of December that included Kwanzaa, Hanukkah, Christmas, and the Feast of Babaluaiye. In 1993, the Children's Museum in Tampa, Florida offered its own holiday cornucopia by staging Kwanzaa, Hanukkah, the Mexican celebration of Las Posadas, and the Swedish celebration of St. Lucia. In 1995, the Oakland Museum of California presented its annual "Winterfest: A Celebration of Family Tradition," which included Kwanzaa, Hanukkah, Italian American Christmas, Japanese American New Year, and Las Posadas. Kwanzaa and the other celebrations were couched in the language of diversity and cultural recognition, as well as history, as the Smithsonian stated: "Though different, all of the holidays mean more than just swapping gifts. They put people back in touch with their family heritage, teaching them about their forefathers. The Smithsonian knows this, that's why it's kicking off a six-day 'Holiday Celebration' to show how Christmas, Hanukkah, Kwanzaa, and the New Year are celebrated in America." Kwanzaa's elevation in status not only suggested the holiday had arrived, but that museums had also changed too by "opening themselves up to use by diverse communities," and showcasing cultures, "which would previously not have been thought 'museum-worthy.'"

While some black houses of worship still assessed Kwanzaa's value to their own congregations, other white churches saw Kwanzaa as a way to bring people together. For white religious institutions, Kwanzaa could be everyone's holiday. This form of holiday multiculturalism bore itself out in a variety of white religious denominations. In 1998, the First Unitarian Universalist Church in Detroit staged a single worship service that included most of the year-end holidays. "We recognize the Solstice, Hanukkah, Christmas, and Kwanzaa," interning Pastor Jean Darling stated. "We feel we have to do this.... It's best to be inclusive of everyone's customs and beliefs rather than choosing to celebrate one tradition over the others." The themes of holiday diversity and inclusion also manifested in Sacramento's Church of Scientology during the 1999 holiday season. Kwanzaa was one of several holidays featured in an event entitled "The Festival of Friends." The Festival was designed to "create increased understanding and affinity between people who make up the richly diverse Sacramento community." The Church of Scientology used different ethnic foods, stories, and art as part of its "Festival of Friends." In a similar holiday gala, the Emmanuel Presbyterian Church in Albuquerque, New Mexico determined that music would better suffice in creating a greater understanding between the races. From 1999 to 2001, Emmanuel Presbyterian Church commissioned De Profundis, a white a cappella men's choir to sing the music of Advent, Christmas, Hanukkah, and Kwanzaa in "genres ranging from the Gregorian Chant to a 12-part 'Harambee' [Kwanzaa]."

CONCLUSION

Kwanzaa's journey from a Los Angeles feast in 1966 to a 12-part "Harambee" inside a Presbyterian church in 1999 underscores how far the holiday has traveled in its brief history. But what Kwanzaa's historical trajectory also shows is the limits of Black Power as a social movement. Although the holiday now exists comfortably in white museums, churches, and schools, Kwanzaa's early history was part of a broader quest for African American well-being, a period that called for greater resources and power in the form of jobs, housing, education, and political representation. This politics of equality that sat at the heart of the Black Power movement went part and parcel with the companion struggle for cultural recognition. That struggle meant unabashedly calling for the redistribution of wealth while simultaneously privileging a new sense of blackness through cultural practices. By the 1980s, the connection between the social politics of equality and the cultural politics of recognition was decoupled with the demise of the Black Power movement. Kwanzaa, now orphaned in many ways, was left without the foundation that sustained it during its early period. The death of Black Power made it easier for Kwanzaa to be claimed by big capital and new pluralist-based movements like multiculturalism.

The rise of multiculturalism in the 1980s and 1990s built on and shared Black Power's concern for cultural recognition but not its drive for equality of resources and condition. Multiculturalism's drive to support new pluralist claims for group differentiation rested mainly on the visibility of minority cultures in the larger American public sphere. Easily and rather quickly, Kwanzaa found salience and utility within multiculturalism's brand of pluralism that stressed ethnic identity and diversity in American society. This is not to suggest that multiculturalism lacked political aims. It is to suggest that the manifestations of multiculturalism centered more on the symbolic—assessable emblems from racial and ethnic minorities like holidays—rather than substantive alterations in the material conditions of black Americans or people of color.

Despite multiculturalism's failure to adequately address the social politics of equality, the movement proved indispensable to Kwanzaa's growth since the late 1980s. Corporations, some who looked for new ways to make a profit, and others who saw Kwanzaa as a mechanism for good public relations, embraced Kwanzaa in the name of diversity. Mainstream museums, churches, and schools equally found Kwanzaa valuable for reasons of diversity, inclusion, and better community relations. Without America's fixation with diversity, and its determination to show that it had become a more inclusive society, Kwanzaa would have remained in the spaces of the black public sphere: community centers, black museums, independent schools, neighborhood streets, and the private sphere—in the home.

FURTHER READING

Brown, Scot. *Fighting For US: Maulana Karenga, the US Organization, and Black Cultural Nationalism.* New York: New York University Press, 2003.

Halter, Marilyn. *Shopping for Identity: The Marketing of Ethnicity.* New York: Schocken Books, 2000.

Karenga, Maulana. *Kwanzaa: A Celebration of Family, Community, and Culture.* Los Angeles: University of Sankore Press, 1998.

Mchawi, Basir. "Which Way Kwanza." *Black News* (December 1975): 8.

Pleck, Elizabeth. "Kwanzaa: The Making of a Black Nationalist Tradition, 1966–1990." *Journal of American Ethnic History* 20 (Summer 2001): 3–28.

Weems, Robert. *Desegregating the Dollar: African-American Consumerism in the Twentieth Century.* New York: New York University Press, 1998.

Keith A. Mayes

From New Year's Eve to First Night

"The joyous occasion known as New Year's Eve," the Charleston Office of Cultural Affairs lately lamented, "has in recent decades become for most people either a non-event or just another party, indistinguishable from others, memorable only for the change of a single digit and perhaps a noteworthy hangover." Over the last three decades, civic organizations have touted alternative "First Night" celebrations as the antidote to the loss of meaning and customary excesses surrounding the advent of each new year.

Ushering in the new year with special observances was ancient practice in Europe, especially when, under the older Julian calendar, the year began with the spring equinox in late March—which made perfect sense in an agrarian world. During the late Middle Ages, most of Europe switched to the Gregorian calendar system used today, although England and its American colonies did not accept the Gregorian calendar until the mid-eighteenth century. New Year's Day—that is, January 1—became a part of the midwinter cycle of festivities running from Christmas to Twelfth Night (January 6).

In English colonial America where the Protestant faith predominated, the midwinter festive cycle, and all holidays recalling Catholic Europe, were generally suppressed but never eliminated. New Year's Day, unassociated as it was with any particular saint, became a focus for winter observances in the English colonies, in which there were few holidays of any sort. European societies had developed two, concurrent festive styles, genteel and popular, to welcome the new year, and American colonists reflected these styles in their own observances.

For the common sort, the day frequently invoked traditional practices of social inversion and moral license. As Leigh Eric Schmidt observed in *Consumer Rites:*

The Buying and Selling of American Holidays (1995), the customary method of ushering in the new year involved "noisy revelry, openhanded eating, and bibulous drinking." In 1766 the *Virginia Almanack* recommended that all "should feast and sing, and merry be," and that the day should be marked by "strong ale, good fires, & noble cheer." As with Twelfth Night celebrations in England, a certain permissible level of misrule was expected, with the poor visiting the homes of the well-off to demand tokens of largesse, usually food and drink. In American seaport towns, containing the largest urban populations and little in the way of police, the misrule could get out of hand. Young celebrants occasionally ruled the night streets in noisy vandalism, even defying law and order by chasing off the night watchmen. Their favorite targets were the homes of the wealthy, where they crashed the New Year parties of the upper crust and tore down fences and gates—symbolic as well as physical boundaries between the social classes.

Those whose homes were invaded were trying to mark the occasion with genteel gatherings for the fashionable sort and with sometimes exotic gift exchanges. Today's Christmas-time gift-giving in part descends from ancient traditions of making offerings for a propitious new year. Even the lower sort in the early eighteenth century exchanged small tokens—cakes, fruit, spices—by way of "beginning well" the coming year. The gentry, however, could set themselves apart from the *hoi polloi* with the sort of gift-giving only they could sustain. One newspaper in 1770 carried an advertisement for "Proper presents to and from Ladies and Gentlemen at this season." These included, for the ladies, "Necklaces, lockets . . . silver plated tea urns and teapots," and for men, "dress swords [and] pocket pistols." Either gender might expect snuffboxes, toothpick cases, silk stockings, backgammon tables, and chess sets. The well-heeled might also bestow gifts on their servants or laborers. As Leigh Schmidt argues, New Year's gifts from the gentry were "not only about the mutualities of friendship, but also about the maintenance of hierarchies through benefaction & patronage."

Thus by 1800, on New Year's Day "misrule reigned without, ceremony & fashion within." The better sort might, and did, deplore the depredations going on outside, or sometimes inside, their homes, but there was little they could do about it. Besides the dedicated drinking and evening parties that characterized New Year's time, however, there was another, more personal practice associated with the occasion. Even American Puritans, no friends of midwinter festivities, considered the beginning of the year an appropriate time for introspection, as surviving diaries demonstrate. It was an occasion for considering the state of one's soul, the course of one's life, and ways to improve both. The modern "New Year's resolution" recalls the devout rededications to Christian devotion and practice of former times, the key to which was moderation in all things and a curb on self-indulgence. The typical modern New Year's resolution to lose weight recalls this tradition: atonement for holiday-season extravagance, and a well-meaning determination to live better.

New Year's seems always to have embraced "a curious mixture of excess and self-improvement." Frequent attempts to "civilize" the holiday have historically met with very limited success. Women were often at the forefront of these campaigns to rein in the (mostly male) excesses associated with the day. Throughout the eighteenth and nineteenth centuries, women tended to avoid public festive occasions, understandably distancing themselves from, as Schmidt describes them, "the riotous street carnivals in which rowdy male celebrants fired guns, banged kettles, fought, drank, and pillaged." Women assumed prominent roles in the reform movements of the nineteenth century, in which controlling alcohol consumption was perhaps highest on the agenda. As the genteel parties of New Year's percolated down to the growing middle class, the women who oversaw these occasions increasingly served coffee or other nonalcoholic beverages instead of punch. They also stressed more practical and edifying gift-giving, even bringing children into the act, for whom improving books were considered the best presents.

In the late twentieth century, a significant alternative appeared to the annual round of office parties, binge drinking, and consequent spike in tragic auto accidents. In 1976, a group of Boston artists initiated a city-wide New Year's Eve arts event pitched at family groups. Dubbed "First Night," the event expanded rapidly, as businesses, performing artists, and city officials recognized the civic and commercial advantages of attracting to the downtown area a segment of the population largely alienated from the holiday observances. Success bred imitators: in 2005 First Night celebrations were held in more than 200 cities in the United States and Canada. Promoters of First Night especially assert its community-building qualities. In Charleston, South Carolina, the night is "an opportunity for every Charlestonian woman, man, and child to rejoice in the common bond of community and the arts." For Monterey, California, the event has "a mission to bring families together and unite our community in all its diversity through the visual and performing arts." And in Pittsburgh, which adopted First Night celebrations in 1995, sponsors see it as "a wonderful way for people to come together and ring in the New Year in a festive, non-alcoholic atmosphere." The new urban extravaganzas freely draw on elements associated with other holidays; Pittsburgh's offers "something for everyone—from children's activities to performances by nationally known musicians to a fireworks finale." Even in these family-friendly celebrations, noise is still an important element for properly welcoming the new year.

A spokesperson for the Charleston Office of Cultural Affairs, whose lament began this essay, sees in First Night an opportunity for the restorative powers of civic ritual:

> One of the less happy trends that has accompanied the many accomplishments of the 20th century has been in the drastic loss of ritual in our lives. Once a potent source of inspiration, spiritual renewal, and community, ritual has mostly been overwhelmed by the cacophony of modern commercialism.

Setting aside the obvious ironies of combating "the cacophony of modern commercialism" with the undeniable commercialism of First Night, implicit in the writer's modern Jeremiad is a belief in the restoration of stressed, beleaguered communities through the medium of reanimating, communal ritual. It is a position perfectly consistent with the anthropological theories of Victor Turner and Clifford Geertz.

BIBLIOGRAPHY

"Abolish Columbus Day and Re-name it." *Petition to U.S. Congress, State and Local Elected Officials*. www.petitiononline.com/fadoct/petition.html.

Adams, David Wallace. *Education for Extinction: American Indians and the Boarding School Experience, 1875–1928*. Lawrence: University Press of Kansas, 1995.

Afin, Iya, and Ayobunmi Sangode. *Rites of Passage: Psychology of Female Power*. Brooklyn, NY: Athelia Henrietta Press, 1999.

"African-American Business Exchange Presents Holiday Expo and Kwanzaa Celebration." *The Sun Reporter* (November 23, 1995): S2.

Afrik, Baba Hannibal, and Conrad Worrill. "The History, Origin, and Development of Kwanzaa in the City of Chicago." Unpublished manuscript, November 26, 1999.

Albanese, Catherine. "Requiem for Memorial Day: Dissent in the Redeemer Nation." *American Quarterly* 26, no. 4: 386–98.

Almeida, L. D. "From Danny Boy to Bono. The Irish in New York City, 1945–85." PhD Thesis, New York University, 1996.

Americanus, Sylvanus [Samuel Nevill], ed. "The History of the Northern Continent of America." *The New American Magazine*. Woodbridge, N.J., 1 (January 1758).

Ames, Nathaniel. *An astronomical diary, or, An almanack for the year of our Lord Christ, 1738: … Calculated for the meridian of Boston in New-England, whose lat. 42 deg. 25 min. north / By Nathanael Ames*. Boston: John Draper, 1737.

Ancelet, Barry. "Capitaine, voyage ton flag:" *The Traditional Cajun Country Mardi Gras*. Lafayette: Center For Louisiana Studies, 1989.

Anderson, Benedict. *Imagined Communities: Reflections on the Origins and Spread of Nationalism*. London: Verso, 1991.

Applebaum, Diana Karter. *Thanksgiving: An American Holiday, An American History*. New York: Facts on File, 1984.

Art in the United States Capitol. Washington, D.C.: United States Government Printing Office, 1978.

Ashton, Dianne, and Rebecca Gratz. *Women and Judaism in Antebellum America.* Detroit, Mich.: Wayne State University Press, 1997.

Atkins, Gary L. *Gay Seattle: Stories of Exile and Belonging.* Seattle: University of Washington Press, 2003.

Badger, Reid. *The Great American Fair: The World's Columbian Exposition and American Culture.* Chicago: Nelson Hall, 1979.

Baraka, Amiri. *Autobiography of LeRoi Jones.* Chicago: Lawrence Hill Books, 1984.

———. "Why I Changed My Ideology: Black Nationalism and the Social Revolution." *Black World* (July 1975): 30–42.

Barashango, Ishakamusa. *Afrikan People and European Holidays: A Mental Genocide.* Silver Springs, Md.: Fourth Dynasty Publishing, 1979.

Bates-Rudd, Rhonda. "Celebrating Heritage and the Holidays: This is a Holy Time of the Year for Many Churches with Celebrations Lasting Well into the New Year." *Detroit News,* December 23, 1998.

Bazant, Micah, and Dara Silverman. "Love and Justice in Times of War Haggadah Zine." http://colours.mahost.org/events/haggadah.html.

Belchem, John. "Nationalism, Republicanism and Exile: Irish Emigrants and the Revolutions of 1848." *Past and Present* 146 (1995): 103–35.

Bell, Daryl. "Kwanzaa Expo '94." *Philadelphia Tribune,* November 8, 1994.

Bell, W. J. Jr. "The Federal Processions of 1788." *The New-York Historical Society Quarterly* 46 (1962): 5–39.

Bigelow, William Frederick. "A Day for Mothers." *Good Housekeeping* 110 (May, 1940): 4.

———. "Mother's Day." *Good Housekeeping* 92 (May, 1931): 4.

Bin Gorion, Micha Joseph, ed. *Mimekor Yisrael, Classical Jewish Folktales.* Trans. I. M. Lask. Bloomington: Indiana University Press, 1976.

Bingham, Caleb. *The American Preceptor, Being a New Selection of Lessons for Reading and Speaking, Designed for the Use of Schools.* Boston: Manning & Loring for Hall, 1794.

"The Birthday of General Lee." *Confederate Veteran,* February 1905.

Bishop, Patrick. *The Irish Empire.* London: Boxtree, 1999.

"Black Muslim Indicts Whites for Prejudice." *UCLA Daily Bruin,* March 25, 1963.

"Black People and the X-MAS Ripoff." *Black News,* December 1976.

"Blame Capitalism for Prejudice." *UCLA Daily Bruin,* October 24, 1963.

Blight, David W. *Race and Reunion: The Civil War in American Memory.* Cambridge, Mass.: Belknap Press of Harvard University Press, 2001.

Bodnar, John. *Remaking America: Public Memory, Commemoration and Patriotism in the Twentieth Century.* Princeton, N.J.: Princeton University Press, 1992.

Bogart, Michele H. *Public Sculpture and the Civic Ideal in New York City, 1890–1930.* Chicago: University of Chicago Press, 1989.

Bolt, Richard A. "A New Use for Mother's Day." *American Journal of Public Health* 21 (April, 1931): 438–41.

Borden, Timothy G. "Labor's Day: Public Commemoration and Toledo's Working Class." *Northwest Ohio Quarterly* 70 (Winter/Spring 1998): 4–27.

Bowers, Lula II. Interview, Works Progress Administration Federal Writers' Project, June 26, 1938, Library of Congress.

Brainerd, Cephas, and Eveline Warner Brainerd, eds. *The New England Society Orations: Addresses Sermons and Poems Delivered Before The New England Society in the City of New York 1820–1885.* New York: The Century Co., 1901.

Brattle, William. *An Almanack of the coelestiall motions, aspects and eclipses, &c. for the year of our Lord God, MDCXCIV. … Calculated for the meridian of Boston in N.E. 69. deg. 20. min. to the westward of London, & 42. deg. 30 min. north latitude, but may indifferently serve the most part of New-England / By Philo-Mathemat.* Boston: B. Green, 1694.

Brown, Scot. *Fighting for US: Maulana Karenga, the US Organization, and Black Cultural Nationalism.* New York: New York University Press, 2003.

Buck, Paul H. *The Road to Reunion, 1865–1900.* Boston: Little, Brown & Co., 1937.

Burke, Charles T. *The Silver Key: The Charitable Irish Society of Boston.* Watertown, Mass., 1972. Unpublished manuscript, John J. Burns Library, Boston College, Boston.

Burrows, Edwin G., and M. Wallace, *Gotham: A History of New York to 1898.* New York: Oxford University Press, 1999.

Bush, George W. "Columbus Day, 2003 by the President of the United States of America: A Proclamation," October 12, 2003; www.whitehouse.gov/news/releases/2003/10/20031012.

Bushman, Claudia L. *America Discovers Columbus: How An Italian Explorer Became An American Hero.* Hanover, N.H.: University Press of New England, 1992.

———. "The Appropriation of a Founder." *Capitol Dome* 40 (Summer 2003).

Butler, John Sibley. *Entrepreneurship and Self-Help Among Black Americans.* Albany: State University of New York Press, 1991.

Butterfield, L.H., Wendell D. Garrett, and Marjorie E. Sprague, eds. *The Adams Family Correspondence.* Cambridge, Mass.: Atheneum Press, 1963.

Byron, Reginald. *Irish America.* Oxford: Oxford University Press, 1999.

Callahan, Alice Anne. *The Osage Ceremonial Dance In-Lon-Schka.* Norman: University of Oklahoma Press, 1990.

Campbell, Barbara. "Harlem Pupils Get Early Start on Kwanza." *New York Times,* December 20, 1972.

Canedy, Dana. "Companies View Ethnic Holidays Like Kwanzaa and Three Kings Day as a Way to Reach a Niche." *New York Times,* December 30, 1998.

Carmichael, Stokely. *Stokely Speaks: Black Power Back to Pan-Africanism.* New York: Random House, 1965.

Carmichael, Stokely, and Charles Hamilton. *Black Power.* New York: Vintage, 1967.

Carroll, Pam. "Celebrating an African Companion to Christmas." *Washington Post,* December 24, 1987.

Carson, Clay. "A Talk with Ron Karenga, Watts Black Nationalist." *Los Angeles Free Press,* September 2, 1966.

Carter, David. *Stonewall: The Riots that Sparked the Gay Revolution.* New York: St. Martin's, 2004.

Carter, Kevin Leonard. "A 'Festival of Friends': Black Culture Night Held at Church of Scientology." *Sacramento Observer,* January 6, 1999.

"Celebrate 'Winterfest' at Museum." *Oakland Post,* November 22, 1995.

"The Celebration of Lee's Natal Day." *Confederate Veteran,* February 1901.

Chartrand, Rene, and Richard Hook (Illustrator). *The Mexican Adventure 1861–67.* London: Osprey Press, 1994.

Cherry, Conrad. "Two American Sacred Ceremonies: Their Implication for the Study of Religion in America." *American Quarterly* 21, no. 4: 739–54.

"The Chisholm-Mingo Group: Linking Advertisers to Urban Markets." *Multicultural Marketing Profiles, November/December 1997.* www.inforesources.com/test/news/profiles.

"Christmas Nigger." *Black News,* November 15, 1969.

Christofferson, Bill. *The Man From Clear Lake: Earth Day Founder Gaylord Nelson.* Madison: University of Wisconsin Press, 2004.

Clark, Dennis. *Hibernia America: The Irish and Regional Cultures.* New York: Greenwood Press, 1986.

Clark, Sandra Sageser. "Whirlwind Whistle Stops." *Michigan History Magazine* 77 (November/December 1993): 47–49.

Cohen, Shaul. *Planting Nature: Trees and the Manipulation of Environmental Stewardship in America.* Berkeley: University of California Press, 2004.

Cohn, William H. "A National Celebration: The Fourth of July in American History." *Cultures* 3, no. 1 (1976): 141–56.

Coleman, Kenneth. *The American Revolution in Georgia, 1763–1789.* Athens: University of Georgia Press, 1958.

The Columbian Souvenir Album: A Memento of the World's Fair. Boston: The Art Souvenir Company, 1892.

"Columbus Day." Miami-Dade County Public Schools. www.patriotism.org/columbus_day.

Columbus in the Capitol: Commemorative Quincentenary Edition, 102d Congress, 2d Session, H. Doc. 102–319. Washington, D.C.: U.S. Government Printing Office, 1992.

"Columnists Line up to Back Marchers in Parade Dispute." *The Advocate,* April 23, 1991.

"Confederate Flags Wave as Riley Celebrates Confederate Monument." *The Associated Press,* April 26, 2004.

"Confederate Heritage Groups Take Aim at Riley Holiday Plan." *Chattanooga Times Free Press,* February 23, 2004.

"Confederate Soldiers Honored for Defending Homes and Freedom." *Birmingham News,* April 26, 2004.

"A Conversation with Jose Ferrer: Kwanzaa Fest's Founder Talks About the Making of the World's Largest Kwanzaa Celebration." *Kwanzaa Fest '98 (Daily News),* December 1998.

Cooper, William J. *Jefferson Davis, American.* New York: Vintage Books, 2000.

Copeland, Nancy. "Novelist Baldwin Talks About Racial Problem." *UCLA Daily Bruin,* May 13, 1963.

"CORE Picket Lines Draw 25 from UCLA." *UCLA Daily Bruin,* June 14, 1963.

Costen, Melva. *African American Christian Worship.* Nashville, Tenn.: Abingdon Press, 1993.

Coulter, E. Morton. *The Journal of William Stephens, 1741–1743, II.* Athens: University of Georgia Press, 1958.

Count, Earl W. *4,000 Years of Christmas: A Gift of the Ages.* Berkeley, Calif.: Ulysses Press, 2000.

Coursey, D. G. "The New Yam Festival Among the Ewe." *Ghana Notes and Queries* (December 1968): 18–23.

Cox, Karen L. *Dixie's Daughters: The United Daughters of the Confederacy and the Preservation of Confederate Culture.* Gainesville: University Press of Florida, 2003.

Craven, Wesley Frank. *The Legend of the Founding Fathers.* New York: New York University Press, 1956.

Cressy, David. *Bonfires and Bells: National Memory and the Protestant Calendar in Elizabethan and Stuart England.* Berkeley: University of California Press, 1989.

Crimmins, John D. *Irish American Historical Miscellany: Relating to New York City and Vicinity Together with Much Interesting Material Relative to Other Parts of the Country.* New York: The author, 1905.

———. *St. Patrick's Day: Its Early Celebrations in New York and Other American Places, 1737–1845.* New York: The author, 1902.

Cummings, Judith. "City Blacks Begin Fete of Kwanzaa." *New York Times,* December 27, 1973.

Cunningham, Henry Winchester, ed. "Diary of the Rev. Samuel Checkley, 1735." In *Publications of the Colonial Society of Massachusetts, XII, Transactions, 1908–1909.*

Dalmais, Irénée, Pierre Jounel, and Aimé Martimort. *The Liturgy and Time.* Vol. 4. *The Church at Prayer.* Trans. Matthew O'Connell. Collegeville, Minn.: The Liturgical Press, 1986.

"Davidson's 'Rebels' Win War in Just Two Hours." *Charlotte Observer,* May 10, 1953.

Davies, Horton. *Worship and Theology in England From Andrewes to Baxter and Fox, 1603–1690.* Princeton, N.J.: Princeton University Press, 1975.

———. *The Worship of the American Puritans, 1629–1730.* New York: Peter Lang, 1990.

Davies, Richard O. *America's Obsession: Sports and Society Since 1945.* Belmont, Calif.: Wadsworth Publishing, 1994.

Davies, Wallace Evan. *Patriotism on Parade: The Story of the Veterans and Hereditary Organisations in America, 1783–1900.* Cambridge, Mass.: Harvard University Press, 1955.

Davila, Arlena. *Latinos, Inc.: The Marketing and Making of a People.* Berkeley: University of California Press, 2001.

Davis, Susan G. *Parades and Power: Street Theatre in Nineteenth-Century Philadelphia.* Berkeley: University of California Press, 1986.

"Day for Gray Honors South's Struggle; Newcomers Know Little about Holiday." *The Atlanta Journal-Constitution,* April 24, 2004.

De Lancey, Edward F. "Columbian Celebration of 1792, The First in the United States." *The Magazine of American History* 29 (January 1893).

"De Profundis-The A Capella Men's Choir of Albuquerque." www.unm.edu/~shapiro/music/deprofundis.

Dean, Bennett Wayne. *Mardi Gras, Mobile's Illogical Whoopdedo.* Mobile, Ala.: Adams Press, 1971.

Debs, Eugene. "The Significance of Labor Day." *The Arena* 14 (October 1895): 303–7.

"Decoration Day." *Harper's Weekly,* June 6, 1874.

Deloria, Philip J. *Playing Indian.* New Haven, Conn.: Yale University Press, 1998.

Denning, Michael. *The Cultural Front: The Laboring of American Culture in the Twentieth Century.* New York: Verso, 1996.

Dennis, Matthew. *Red, White, and Blue Letter Days: An American Calendar.* Ithaca, N.Y.: Cornell University Press, 2002.

"Dia de las Culturas." *COCORI Complete Costa Rica.* www.cocori.com/library/crinfo/columb.htm.

Diary of John Leach, 1757–1758. Massachusetts Historical Society.

Dickey, John Marcus. *Christopher Columbus and His Monument, Columbia.* Chicago: Rand, McNally & Co., 1892.

Diner, Hasia R. "The Most Irish City in the Union: The Era of Great Migration, 1844–77." In *The New York Irish,* ed. Ronald Bayor and Timothy Meagher. Baltimore, Md.: Johns Hopkins University Press, 1996.

Douglas, George William, ed. *The American Book of Days,* 2nd ed. New York: H. W. Wilson and Company, 1948.

Douglass, Frederick. *Autobiographies,* ed. Lewis Henry Gates Jr. New York: Library of America, 1994.

———. *Life and Times of Frederick Douglass Written by Himself.* Hartford Conn.: Park Publishing, 1881.

———. "There was a Right Side in the Late War: An Address Delivered in New York, New York, on 30 May 1878." In *The Frederick Douglass Papers,* Ser. 1: *Speeches, Debates, and Interviews*. Vol. 4, 480–92, ed. John W. Blassingame and John R. McKivigan. New Haven, Conn.: Yale University Press, 1991.

Duberman, Martin. *Stonewall*. New York: Dutton, 1993.

DuCille, Ann. *Skin Trade*. Cambridge, Mass.: Harvard University Press, 1996.

Dyson, Michael Eric. *I May Not Get There with You: The True Martin Luther King, Jr.* New York: Free Press, 2000.

Eastman, Susan. "Museum Offers Children a Cultural Look at Holiday." *St. Petersburg Times,* December 6, 1993.

Eisen, Arnold M. *Rethinking Modern Judaism*. Chicago: University of Chicago Press, 1998.

"11th Annual African American Holiday Expo and Kwanzaa." *Oakland Post,* November 26, 1995: 4.

Eliot, Jonathan. *Historical Sketches of the Ten Miles Square Forming the District of Columbia*. Washington, D.C.: J. Eliot Jr., 1830.

Ellis, John B. *The Sights and Secrets of the National Capital: A Work Descriptive of Washington City in All Its Various Phases*. Chicago: Jones, Junkin & Co., 1869.

Everett, Ron. "Student Body Veep Explains School Role." *Los Angeles Collegian,* December 6, 1960.

Fabre, Genevieve. "Pinkster Festival, 1766–1811: An African-American Celebration." In *Feasts and Celebrations in North American Ethnic Communities,* ed. R. A. Gutiérraz and Genevieve Fabre, 13–28. Albuquerque: University of New Mexico Press, 1995.

Fast Facts About Mahogany Cards. www.pressroom.hallmark.com;

Ferrer, Jose. "Flexing Our Economic Muscle." *Kwanzaa Magazine (Daily News),* December 1997.

Fields, Mamie Garvin, with Karen Fields. *Lemon Swamp and Other Places: A Carolina Memoir*. New York: Free Press, 1983.

The Fifty-Ninth Annual Report of the Commissioner of Indian Affairs to the Secretary of the Interior. Washington, D.C., 1890.

"First Annual Memorial Staged for Malcolm X." *Los Angeles Sentinel,* March 3, 1966.

First and Second Books of Maccabees. *Oxford Study Bible with the Apocrypha*. New York: Oxford University Press, 1992.

Fish, Stanley. "Boutique Multiculturalism." In *Multiculturalism and American Democracy,* ed. Arthur Melzer, Jerry Weinberger, and M. Richard Zinman. Lawrence: University Press of Kansas, 1998.

Fliegelman, Jay. *Declaring Independence: Jefferson, Natural Language, and the Culture of Performance*. Stanford, Calif.: Stanford University Press, 1993.

Flippen, J. Brooks. *Nixon and the Environment*. Albuquerque: University of New Mexico Press, 2000.

Foner, Philip S. *May Day: A Short History of the International Workers' Holiday, 1886–1986*. New York: International Publishers, 1986.

———, ed. *We, the Other People: Alternative Declarations of Independence by Labor Groups, Farmers, Women's Rights Advocates, Socialists, and Blacks, 1829–1975*. Urbana: University of Illinois Press, 1976.

Foner, Philip S., and Robert James Branham, eds. *Lift Every Voice: African American Oratory, 1787–1900*. Tuscaloosa: University of Alabama Press, 1998.

Forbes, Esther. *Paul Revere and the World He Lived In*. Boston: Houghton Mifflin Co., 1942.

Force, Peter, ed. *American Archives*. 5th series, 3 vols. Washington, D.C.: 1848–53.

"Forty UCLA Students Join Sit-In." *UCLA Daily Bruin,* November 11, 1963.

Foster, Gaines. *Ghosts of the Confederacy: Defeat, the Lost Cause, and the Emergence of the New South, 1865–1913.* New York: Oxford University Press, 1987.

Frank, Thomas. "Why Johnny Can't Dissent." In *Commodify Your Dissent: Salvos from the Baffler,* ed. Thomas Frank and Matt Weiland. New York: Norton, 1997.

Fraser, Nancy. "From Redistribution to Recognition?: Dilemmas of Justice in a 'Post-Socialist' Age." In *Theorizing Multiculturalism,* ed. Cynthia Willet. Oxford: Blackwell Publishers, 1998.

Fried, Richard M. *The Russians are Coming! The Russians are Coming! Pageantry and Patriotism in Cold-War America.* New York: Oxford University Press, 1998.

Friedman, Monroe. *Consumer Boycotts: Effecting Change Through the Marketplace and the Media.* London: Routledge, 1999.

Frothingham, Richard Jr. *The History of Charlestown, Massachusetts.* Salem, Mass.: Higginson Book Co., 1989.

Gallagher, Gary L. *Lee and His Generals in War and Memory.* Baton Rouge: Louisiana State University Press, 1998.

Garcia, James. *Cinco de Mayo: A Mexican Holiday About Unity and Pride.* Chanhassen, Minn.: The Child's World, 2003.

Geffen, David. *American Heritage Haggadah: The Passover Experience.* New York: Gefen Publishing House, 1992.

"A General Decoration Day." *Confederate Veteran,* September 1907, 392.

Gerstle, Gary. *Working-Class Americanism: The Politics of Labor in a Textile City, 1914–1960.* Princeton, N.J.: Princeton University Press, 2002.

Gildrie, Richard P. "The Ceremonial Puritan Days of Humiliation and Thanksgiving." *New England Historical and Genealogical Register* 136 (Jan. 1982): 3–16.

Gilje, Paul A. *The Road to Mobocracy: Popular Disorder in New York City, 1763–1834.* Chapel Hill: University of North Carolina Press, 1987.

Gillespie, Mary. "Spiritual Values to Receive a Special Seasonal Tribute." *Chicago Sun-Times,* December 1, 1989.

Gillis, John R., ed. *Commemorations: The Politics of National Identity.* Princeton, N.J.: Princeton University Press, 1994.

———. *A World of their Own Making: Myth, Ritual, and the Quest for Family Values.* New York: Basic Books, 1996.

"Gilmore Seeks 2nd Holiday on the Friday Before King's." *Washington Post,* January 20, 2000.

Glatzer, Nahum N. *The Schocken Passover Haggadah.* New York: Schocken Books, 1996.

Gnojewski, Carol. *Cinco de Mayo: Celebrating Hispanic Pride.* Berkeley Heights, N.J.: Enslow Publishers, 2002.

Goizueta, Roberto. *Caminemos con Jesús: Toward a Hispanic/Latino Theology of Accompaniment.* Maryknoll, N.Y.: Orbis Books, 1995.

Gomes, Peter J. *The Pilgrim Society 1820–1970.* Plymouth, Mass.: The Pilgrim Society, 1971.

Grand Army of the Republic. *The National Memorial Day: A Record of Ceremonies over the Graves of the Union Soldiers, May 29–30, 1869,* compiled by E.F.M. Faehtz. Washington, D.C.: Headquarters, Grand Army of the Republic, 1870.

Gravely, William B. "The Dialect of Double-Consciousness in Black American Freedom Celebrations, 1808–1863." *Journal of Negro History* 67 (Winter 1982): 302–17.

The Great Columbus Day Farce: Why Columbus Day should NOT be a Celebrated Holiday. http://cs.nmu.edu/~Ihanson/PowderKeg/PK7/Columbus.html.

Green, Fletcher M. "Listen to the Eagle Scream." *North Carolina Historical Review* 31, nos. 3–4 (1954), 295–320, 529–49.

Greenberg, Cheryl. *Or Does it Explode: Black Harlem in the Great Depression.* New York: Oxford University Press, 1991.

Grimes, Ronald L. *Beginnings in Ritual Studies.* Washington, D.C.: University Press of America, 1982.

Grossman, Jonathan. "Who Is the Father of Labor Day?" *Labor History* 14 (Fall 1973): 612–23.

Halter, Marilyn. *Shopping for Identity: The Marketing of Ethnicity.* New York: Schocken Books, 2000.

Haltigan, James. *The Irish in the American Revolution and their Early Influence in the Colonies.* Washington D.C.: Patrick Haltigan, 1908.

Harlan, Louis. "Booker T. Washington and the National Negro Business League." In *Booker T. Washington in Perspective: Essays of Louis Harlan,* ed. Raymond W. Smock. Jackson: University of Mississippi Press, 1988.

Harris, Zoe, and Suzanne Williams. *Piñatas and Smiling Skeletons: Celebrating Mexican Festivals.* Berkeley, Calif.: Pacific View Press, 1998.

Harrison, Don. "Panelists Ponder Integration." *UCLA Daily Bruin,* December 13, 1963.

Hatch, Jane M., ed. *The American Book of Days,* 3rd ed. New York: H. W. Wilson and Company, 1978.

Hausen, Karin. "Mother's Day in the Weimar Republic." In *When Biology Became Destiny: Women in Weimar and Nazi Germany,* ed. Renate Bridenthal, Atina Grossman, and Marion Kaplan, 131–52. New York: Monthly Review Press, 1984.

Haverty-Stacke, Donna Truglio. "Constructing Radical America: A Cultural and Social History of May Day in New York City and Chicago, 1867–1945." Ph.D. diss., Cornell University, 2003.

Hayes, Denis. *The Official Earth Day Guide to Planet Repair.* Washington, D.C.: Island Press, 2000.

Haynes, Lemuel. "Liberty Further Extended: Or Free Thoughts on the Illegality of Slave-keeping" (1776). In *Major Problems in the Era of the American Revolution, 1760–1791,* ed. Richard D. Brown, 309–10. Boston: Houghton-Mifflin, 1992.

Heinze, Andrew. *Adapting to Abundance: Jewish Immigrants, Mass Consumption and the Search for American Identity.* New York: Columbia University Press, 1992.

Hertzberg, Hazel H. *The Search for an American Indian Identity: Modern Pan Indian Movements.* Syracuse, N.Y.: Syracuse University Press, 1971.

Higham, John. *Strangers in the Land: Patterns of American Nativism, 1860–1925.* New Brunswick, N.J.: Rutgers University Press, 2002.

A History of the Origins of Memorial Day as Adopted by the Ladies' Memorial Association of Columbus, Georgia, and Presented to the Lizzie Rutherford Chapter of the Daughters of the Confederacy. Columbus, Ga.: T. Gilbert, 1868.

Hobsbawm, Eric. "Introduction: Inventing Traditions," in *The Invention of Tradition,* ed. Eric Hobsbawm and Terrence Ranger. Cambridge: University of Cambridge Press, 1983, 1–14.

Hochbruck, Wolfgang. "'I Ask for Justice': Native American Fourth of July Orations." In *The Fourth of July: Political Oratory and Literary Relations, 1776–1876,* ed. Paul Goetsch and Gerd Hurm, 155–65. Tübingen, Germany: G. Narr, 1992.

Holi, Melvin G., and Paul M. Green. *Chicago: A View From City Hall.* Chicago: Arcadia Press, 1999.

Holland, Jack. *The American Connection: U.S. Guns, Money, and Influence in Northern Ireland.* New York: Viking, 1987.

Holm, Tom. *Strong Hearts, Wounded Souls: Native American Veterans of the Vietnam War.* Austin: University of Texas Press, 1996.

Hopko, Thomas. *Worship.* Vol. 2. *The Orthodox Faith: An Elementary Handbook on the Orthodox Church.* New York: The Orthodox Church in America, 1972.

Horsford, Victoria. "Golden Krust Bakery: A Recipe for Success—First African-American Business to be a Kwanzaa Fest Sponsor." *Kwanzaa Magazine* (*Daily News*), December 1997.

Hough, Franklin B. *Proclamations For Thanksgiving.* Albany, N.Y.: Munsell & Rowland, 1858.

Hunt, Richard P. "The First Labor Day." *American Heritage* 33, no. 5 (1982): 109–12.

Hunter, Charlayne. "Spirit of Kwanza—Time of Giving: Harlem Pupils Told of Ritual Celebrating Harvest." *New York Times,* December 24, 1971.

Hurvitz, Rabbi Mark. *A Growing Haggadah.* www.davka.org/what/haggadah/.

Hyman, Paula. *Gender and Jewish Assimilation in Modern Jewish History.* Seattle: University of Washington Press, 1995.

Indigenous Peoples' Literature. www.Indians.org/welker/columbu1.html.

"In Perspective: Karenga's Mission is for Posterity." *The Hilltop,* January 5, 1968.

Irving, Washington. *The Life and Voyages of Christopher Columbus.* 2 vols. New York: George P. Putnam, 1850.

Jamal, Hakim. "Celebration Planned for Malcolm X." *Los Angeles Sentinel,* May 16, 1968.

Javersak, David T. "Labor Day in Wheeling." *Upper Ohio Valley Historical Review* 9, no. 1 (1979): 31–35.

Johnson, Elmer Douglas. "A Frenchman Visits Charleston in 1777." *South Carolina Historical and Genealogical Magazine* 52, no. 2 (April 1951): 89.

Johnson, James P. "How Mother Got Her Day." *American Heritage* 30 (April, 1979): 14–21.

Jones, Howard Mumford. *O Strange New World; American Culture: The Formative Years.* New York: The Viking Press, 1952.

Jones, Kathleen W. "Mother's Day: The Creation, Promotion, and Meaning of a New Holiday in the Progressive Era." *Texas Studies in Literature and Language* 22 (Summer 1980): 175–96.

Joselit, Jenna Weissman. *The Wonders of America: Reinventing Jewish Culture, 1880–1950.* New York: Hill and Wang, 2002.

Joyce, William L. *Editors and Ethnicity: A History of the Irish-American Press, 1848–1883.* New York: Arno Press, 1976.

Junod, Henri A. *The Life of a South African Tribe.* Vol. 2. New Hyde Park, N.Y.: University Books, 1966.

Kachun, Mitch. "'A Beacon to Oppressed Peoples Everywhere': Major Richard R. Wright Sr., National Freedom Day, and the Rhetoric of Freedom in the 1940s." *Pennsylvania Magazine of History and Biography* 128 (2004): 279–306.

———. *Festivals of Freedom: Memory and Meaning in African American Emancipation Celebrations, 1808–1915.* Amherst: University of Massachusetts Press, 2003.

Kane, Thomas. *The Dancing Church around the World.* 2 DVDs. Cambridge, Mass.: Tomaso Production, 2004.

Kanner, Bernice. *The Super Bowl of Advertising: How the Commercials Won the Game.* Princeton, N.J.: Bloomberg Press, 2004.

Karenga, M. Ron. "Kwanzaa: Concepts and Functions." *Black Collegian,* December/January 1979: 127–28.

———. *Kwanzaa: Origin, Concepts, Practice.* Inglewood, Calif.: Kawaida Publications, 1977.

Karenga, Maulana. *Kwanzaa: A Celebration of Family, Community, and Culture.* Los Angeles: University of Sankore Press, 1998.

Kasinitz, Philip. "New York Equalize You? Change and Continuity in Brooklyn's Labor Day Carnival." In *Carnival: Culture in Action-The Trinidad Experience,* ed. M. C. Riggio. New York: Routledge, 2004.

Kazin, Michael, and Stephen J. Ross. "America's Labor Day: The Dilemma of a Worker's Celebration." *Journal of American History* 78, no. 4 (March 1992): 1294–323.

Keller, Mike. "Everett Wins: VP Defeats AS Treasurer, Record Crowd Turns Out To Support New AS Prexy." *Los Angeles Collegian,* January 13, 1961: 1.

Kelly, M. C. "Forty Shades of Green: Conflicts over Community among the New York Irish, 1860–1920." Unpublished Ph.D. thesis, Syracuse University, 1997.

Kelton, Jane Gladden. "New York City St Patrick's Day Parade: Invention of Contention and Consensus." *Drama Review* 29, no. 3 (Fall 1985): 93–105.

Kilroe, Edwin P. *Saint Tammany and the Origin of the Society of Tammany or Columbian Order in the City of New York.* New York: M. B. Brown, 1913.

Kinser, Samuel. *Carnival American Style: Mardi Gras at New Orleans and Mobile.* Chicago: University of Chicago Press, 1990.

Kovic, Ron. *Born on the Fourth of July.* New York: McGraw-Hill, 1976.

Krauze, Enrique. *Mexico: Biography of Power.* New York: Harper and Collins, 1997.

Krige, Eileen Jensen. *The Social System of the Zulus.* Pietermaritzburg, South Africa: Shuter and Shooter, 1965.

Kwanzaa 2000 Facts. www.pressroom.hallmark.com.

"Kwanzaa Becomes $700 Million Business." *Ebony,* December 2000: 42.

"Kwanza in Brooklyn." *Black News,* January 31, 1975: 2.

Lamb, Yanick Rice. "Sentimental Returns: Black Owned Greeting Card Companies Meet Special Challenges to Get Their Share of the Holiday's Profit." *Black Enterprise,* December 1989: 79–80, 82.

Lindahl, Carl, and Carolyn Ware. *Cajun Mardi Gras Masks.* Jackson: University Press of Mississippi, 1997.

Lipkis, Andy, and Kate Lipkis. *The Simple Act of Planting a Tree: A Citizen Forester's Guide to Healing Your Neighborhood, Your City, and Your World.* Los Angeles: Tarcher Publishing, 1990.

Litwicki, Ellen M. *America's Public Holidays, 1865–1920.* Washington, D.C.: Smithsonian Institution Press, 2000.

Lorini, Alessandra. "Public Rituals and the Cultural Making of the New York African-American Community." In *Feasts and Celebrations in North American Ethnic Communities,* ed. R. A. Gutiérraz and Genevieve Fabre, 29–46. Albuquerque: University of New Mexico Press, 1995.

Love, William DeLoss. *Fast and Thanksgiving Days of New England.* Boston: Houghton, Mifflin, 1895.

Lowery, Linda. *Earth Day.* Minneapolis, Minn.: Carolrhoda Books, 1991.

Lyman, Henry. "Speech of Henry Lyman: Our Fourth of July." *Southern Workman,* August 16, 1887.

MacDonald, Sharon, and Gordon Fyfe, eds. *Theorizing Museums: Representing Identity and Diversity in a Changing World.* Oxford: Blackwell Publishers, 1996.

Madhubuti, Haki. *Kwanzaa*. Chicago: Third World Press, 1972.

Maier, Pauline. *American Scripture: Making the Declaration of Independence*. New York: Alfred A. Knopf, 1997.

Malone, Russ. *Irish America*. New York: Hippocrene Books, 1994.

Marchand, Roland. *Creating the Corporate Soul: The Rise of Public Relations and Corporate Imagery*. Berkeley: University of California Press, 1998.

Marling, Karal Anne. *Merry Christmas!: Celebrating America's Greatest Holiday*. Cambridge, Mass.: Harvard University Press, 2000.

Mason-Draffen, Carrie. "In Kwanzaa, Two Festive Traditions." *New York Times,* December 24, 1986.

Matthews, Albert. "The Term 'Pilgrim Fathers' and Early Celebrations of Forefathers' Day." *Transactions of the Colonial Society of Massachusetts* 17 (1915): 292–391.

Mauldin, Barbara, ed. *Carnaval!* Seattle: University of Washington Press, 2004.

McCarthy, J. P. "St Patrick's War." *National Review* 45, no. 7 (April 12, 1993): 26.

McClester, Cedric. "Editor's Comments," and "Kwanzaa: A Cultural Reaffirmation." *Kwanzaa Magazine* (1984–1985): 6, 13.

McConville, Brendan. "Pope's Day Revisited, 'Popular' Culture Reconsidered." In *Explorations in Early American Culture* 4 (2000): 258–80.

Mchawi, Basir. "Kwanzaa, By Any Means Necessary." *Black News* (December 1976): 6–8.

———. "Which Way Kwanza." *Black News* (December 1975): 8.

McMahon, Eileen. *What Parish Are You From? A Chicago Irish Community and Race Relations*. Lexington: University Press of Kentucky, 1995.

McNamara, Brooks. *Day of Jubilee: The Great Age of Public Celebrations in New York, 1789–1909*. New Brunswick, N.J.: Rutgers University Press, 1997.

Meier, August. *Negro Thought in America, 1880–1915*. Ann Arbor: University of Michigan Press, 1988.

"Memorial Day." *Confederate Veteran,* January 1893: 21.

"Memorial Day—Its Origin." *Confederate Veteran,* May 1893: 149.

"A Merry Little Kwanzaa Does Its Share For 'Christmas Creep.'" *The Age,* December 28, 1994.

Meyer, Eugene L. "Kwanzaa Reaffirms Roots, Holiday Lets Americans Honor African Heritage." *Washington Post,* December 26, 1986.

Meyer, Michael A. *Response to Modernity: A History of the Reform Movement in Judaism*. New York: Oxford University Press, 1988.

Miles, Clement A. *Christmas in Ritual and Tradition: Christian and Pagan*. 2nd. ed. Detroit, Mich.: Omnigraphics, 1990.

"Military Crosses Given at Memorial Day Services." *Charlotte Observer,* May 10, 1955.

Mishler, Paul C. *Raising Reds: The Young Pioneers, Radical Summer Camps, and Communist Political Culture in the United States*. New York: Columbia University Press, 1999.

Mitchell, Reid. *All on a Mardi Gras Day*. Cambridge, Mass.: Harvard University Press, 1995.

Morgan, T. J. *Fifty-Ninth Annual Report of the Commissioner of Indian Affairs to the Secretary of the Interior, 1890*. Washington, D.C.: Government Printing Office, 1890.

Morison, Samuel Eliot. *The Pilgrim Fathers Their Significance in History*. Concord, N.H.: Society of Mayflower Descendants in the State of New Hampshire, 1937.

Morris, Glenn, and Russell Means. "Why Autonomous AIM Opposes Columbus Day and Columbus Day Parades." *American Indian Movement*. www.dickshovel.com/colum.html.

"Mother's Day, Inc." *Time* 31 (May 16, 1938): 17–18.

"Mr. Davis's Birthday." *Confederate Veteran* (May 1905).

"Mr. Davis's Birthday a Legal Holiday." *Confederate Veteran,* October 1904: 477.

Nadell, Pamela S., ed. *American Jewish Women's History.* New York: New York University Press, 2003.

Nardone, Richard. *The Story of the Christian Year.* New York: Paulist Press, 1991.

"Negro Cry: 'Black Power!'—What Does it Mean?" *U.S. News & World Report,* July 11, 1966.

Nelson, Bruce C. *Beyond the Martyrs: A Social History of Chicago's Anarchists, 1870–1900.* New Brunswick, N.J.: Rutgers University Press, 1988.

Nettl, Bruno. *Blackfoot Musical Thought: Comparative Perspective.* Champaign: University of Illinois Press, 1989.

Newman, Simon P. *Parades and the Politics of the Street: Festive Culture in the Early American Republic.* Philadelphia: University of Pennsylvania Press, 1997.

Nissenbaum, Stephen. *The Battle For Christmas.* New York: Alfred A. Knopf, 1996.

Nobleman, Marc Tyler. *Earth Day.* Minneapolis, Minn.: Compass Point Books, 2004.

Nye, David. *Image Worlds: Corporate Identities at General Electric, 1890–1920.* Cambridge, Mass.: MIT Press, 1985.

Nyerere, Julius K. "Ujamma—The Basis of African Socialism." In *Ujamaa—Essays on Socialism.* New York: Oxford University Press, 1968.

"Observance Set for Malcolm X." *Los Angeles Sentinel,* February 3, 1966.

Oelschlaeger, Max, ed. *After Earth Day: Continuing the Conservation Effort.* Denton: University of North Texas Press, 1992.

Official Souvenir Programme, New York Columbian Celebration, October 8th to 15th, 1892. New York: Brentano's in Union Square, 1892.

O'Hanlon, Ray. *The New Irish Americans.* Boulder: Colo.: Roberts Rinehart Publishers, 1998.

O'Leary, Cecilia Elizabeth. *To Die For: The Paradox of American Patriotism.* Princeton, N.J.: Princeton University Press, 1999.

"One Country, Two Sides, Many Remembered." *Knoxville New-Sentinel,* May 20, 2004.

"The Origin of the Ladies Memorial Associations." Rutherford Scrapbooks. Vol. 41. Eleanor S. Brockenbrough Library, The Museum of the Confederacy, Richmond, Virginia.

"The Origins of Memorial Day." Department of Veterans Affairs, Office of Public Affairs. www1.va.gov/pubaff/mday/mdayorig.htm.

Palacios, Argentina. *Viva Mexico! A Story of Benito Juarez and Cinco de Mayo.* Orlando, Fla.: Steck-Vaughn, 1992.

Panaccione, Andrea, ed. *May Day Celebration.* Venice, Italy: Marsilio Editori, 1988.

———. *The Memory of May Day: An Iconographic History of the Origins and Implanting of a Workers' Holiday.* Venice, Italy: Marsilio Editori, 1989.

Patterson, Michelle Wick. "'Real Indian Songs': The Society of American Indians and the Use of Native Culture as a Means of Reform." *American Indian Quarterly* 26, no. 1 (Winter 2002): 44–65.

Pencak, William. *For God and Country: The American Legion, 1919–1941.* Boston: Northeastern University Press, 1989.

Perrier, Hubert, and Michel Cordillot. "The Origins of May Day: The American Connection." In *In the Shadow of the Statue of Liberty,* ed. Marianne Debouzy. Saint-Denis, France: Presses Universitaires de Vincennes, 1988.

Pettegrew, John. "'The Soldiers' Faith': Turn-of-the-Century Memory of the Civil War and the Emergence of Modern American Nationalism." *Journal of Contemporary History* 31, no. 1: 49–73.

Petuchowski, Jakob J. "The Magnification of Chanukah: Afterthoughts on a Festival." *Commentary,* January 1960.

Pharo, Eugene. "This Mother's Day Business." *American Mercury* 41 (May, 1937): 60–67.

Piehler, G. Kurt. *Remembering War the American Way.* Washington, D.C.: Smithsonian Institution Press, 1995.

Plant, Rebecca Jo. "The Repeal of Mother Love; Momism and the Reconstruction of Motherhood in Philip Wylie's America." Ph.D. diss. Johns Hopkins University, 2002.

Pleck, Elizabeth. *Celebrating the Family: Ethnicity, Consumer Culture, and Family Rituals.* Cambridge, Mass.: Harvard University Press, 2000.

———. "Kwanzaa: The Making of a Black Nationalist Tradition, 1966–1990." *Journal of American Ethnic History* 20 (Summer 2001): 3–28.

Pollard, Vic. "Clean Ghetto Is Issue for Negro, Warden Asserts." *UCLA Daily Bruin,* December 10, 1962.

Pope, S. W. *Patriotic Games: Sporting Traditions in the American Imagination, 1876—1926.* New York: Oxford University Press, 1997.

Powers, William K. *Indians of the Northern Plains.* New York: G. P. Putnam's Sons, 1971.

———. "Plains Indian Music and Dance." In *Anthropology on the Great Plains,* ed. W. Raymond Wood and Margot Liberty. Lincoln: University of Nebraska Press, 1981.

———. *War Dance: Plains Indian Musical Performance.* Tucson: University of Arizona Press, 1990.

Quarterly Journal of the Society of American Indians. 1913–1915.

"Quotations for Columbus Day." *Welcome to The Quote Garden!* www.quotegarden.com/columbus-day.html.

Rader, Benjamin. *In Its Own Image: How Television Has Transformed Sports.* New York: Free Press, 1984.

Raspberry, William. "America's Black Island Faces Depopulation, Not Integration." *Register-Guard* [Eugene, Ore.], July 4, 1997.

Raynal, Abbe [Guillaume Thomas Francois]. *A Philosophical and Political History of the Settlements and Trade of the Europeans in the East and West Indies.* 6 vols. Trans. J. O. Justamond, F.R.S. Dublin: John Exshaw, 1784.

"Records of the Old Colony Club." *Proceedings of the Massachusetts Historical Society,* 3 (1888): 382–444.

"Red Letter Days in Dixie." *Confederate Veteran,* February 1904, 78.

Restad, Penne. *Christmas in America: A History.* New York: Oxford University Press, 1995.

Ridge, John T. *The St Patrick's Day Parade in New York.* New York: St Patrick's Day Committee, 1988.

Ridley, Jasper. *Maximillian and Juarez.* London: Phoenix Press, 2001.

Rigal, Laura. "'Raising the Roof': Authors, Spectators and Artisans in the Grand Federal Procession of 1788." *Theatre Journal* 48, no. 3 (October 1996): 253–57.

Rizzo, Margaret Schmitz. "Museum Teaches Kwanzaa Values Through Celebration." *Kansas City Star,* December 24, 1998.

Robertson, William. *History of America.* Vols. 8–10 of *The Works of William Robertson with a Sketch of his Life and Writings.* London: Thomas Tegg, 1824.

Rogers, Nicholas. *Halloween: From Pagan Ritual to Party Night.* New York: Oxford University Press, 2002.

Rosenbaum, Claudine. "Smithsonian Takes a Look at Holiday Diversity." *Washington Times,* December 24, 1992.

Rossman, Marlene L. *Multicultural Marketing: Selling to a Diverse America.* New York: AMACOM, 1994.

Rothman, Hal K. *The Greening of a Nation? Environmentalism in the United States Since 1945*. Fort Worth, Tex.: Harcourt Brace, 1998.

"Rules and Regulations for the Government of the Parade." Issued by the St. Patrick's Day Parade and Celebration Committee. Copy in the Donald O'Callaghan Papers, box 6, folder 5, American Irish Historical Society, New York.

Rushkoff, Douglas. "The Open Source Haggadah Project. www.opensourcehaggadah.org/.

Ryan, Mary P. *Civic Wars: Democracy and Public Life in the American City during the Nineteenth Century*. Berkeley: University of California Press, 1997.

Sale, Kirkpatrick. *Conquest of Paradise: Christopher Columbus and the Columbian Legacy*. New York: Knopf, 1990.

Samuels, Gail. *Enduring Roots: Encounters With Trees, History, and the American Landscape*. New Brunswick, N.J.: Rutgers University Press, 1999.

Santino, Jack. *All Around the Year: Holidays and Celebrations in American Life*. Urbana and Champaign: University of Illinois Press, 1994.

———. *The Hallowed Eve: Dimensions of Culture in a Calendar Festival in Northern Ireland*. Lexington: The University Press of Kentucky, 1998.

———, ed. *Halloween and Other Festivals of Death and Life*. Knoxville: The University of Tennessee Press, 1996.

Sargent, Edward D. "Alternative Festival, 'Kwanzaa' Celebrates Spirit of Community and Heritage." *Washington Post*, December 25, 1980.

Sarna, Jonathan. *American Judaism*. New Haven, Conn.: Yale University Press, 2004.

Savage, Kirk. "The Politics of Memory: Black Emancipation and the Civil War Monument." In *Commemorations: The Politics of National Identity*, ed. John R. Gillis, 127–49. Princeton, N.J.: Princeton University Press, 1994.

Schauffler, Robert Haven, ed. *The Days We Celebrate*. New York: Dodd, Mead, 1940.

———. *Memorial Day (Decoration Day): Its Celebration, Spirit, and Significance as Related in Prose and Verse, with a Non-Sectional Anthology*. New York: Moffat, Yard and Company, 1911.

Schiffman, Lawrence. *From Texts to Traditions: A History of Second Temple and Rabbinic Judaism*. Hoboken, N.J.: KTAV, 1991.

Schiller, Herbert I. *Culture, Inc.: The Corporate Takeover of Public Expression*. New York: Oxford University Press, 1989.

Schisgall, Oscar. "The Bitter Author of Mother's Day." *Reader's Digest* 76 (May 1960): 64–66.

Schmidt, Leigh Eric. *Consumer Rites: The Buying and Selling of American Holidays*. Princeton, N.J.: Princeton University Press, 1995.

———. "The Easter Parade: Piety, Fashion, and Display. *Religion and American Culture* 4 (Summer 1994): 135–64.

———. "Piety, Commercialism, Activism: The Uses of Mother's Day." *Religion On-line*. www.religion-online.org/showarticle.asp?title=173.

Schreiber, Alfred L. *Multicultural Marketing: Selling to a New America*. Lincolnwood, Ill.: NTC Business Books, 2001.

Schwartz, Dona. *Contesting the Super Bowl*. New York: Routledge, 1998.

Schwartz, Seth. *Imperialism and Jewish Society, 200 B.C.E. to 640 C.E.* Princeton, N. J.: Princeton University Press, 2003.

"Scituate and Barnstable Church Records." *The New England Historical and Genealogical Register* 10 (Boston: 1856): 37–43.

"The Second Annual Kwanzaa Celebration of Community School District 7 [1979]." Kwanzaa Vertical Files, Schomburg Library.

Seymour, Susan. "Gifts that Say 'We Love You, Mom!'" *Better Homes and Gardens* 21 (May, 1943): 14.

Shabaka, Segun. "Kwanza." *Black News,* December 1975: 16.

———. "Symbols of Kwanza." *Black News,* December 1975: 16.

Shaw, David. "'Negro A Monster Stripped of His Culture'-Malcolm X." *UCLA Daily Bruin,* November 29, 1962.

Shaw, Peter. *American Patriots and the Rituals of Revolution.* Cambridge, Mass.: Harvard University Press, 1981.

Shea, John Gilmary. "Pope-Day in America." Paper read before the United States Catholic Historical Society, January 19, 1888. Library of Congress Broadsides.

Shields, Thomas J. "The 'Tip of the Iceberg' in a Southern Suburban County: The Fight for a Martin Luther King, Jr., Holiday." *Journal of Black Studies* 33, no. 4: 499–519.

Shulman, Jeffrey. *Gaylord Nelson: A Day for the Earth.* Frederick, Md.: Twenty-first Century Books, 1992.

Shurtleff, Nathaniel B., ed. *Records of The Governor and Company of the Massachusetts Bay in New England.* Boston: B. White, 1853–1854.

Sigler, Elinor. "Journalist Raps Negro Leaders." *UCLA Daily Bruin,* March 27, 1963.

Silber, Nina. *The Romance of Reunion: Northerners and the South, 1865–1900.* Chapel Hill: University of North Carolina Press, 1993.

Silverstein, Alan. *Alternatives to Assimilation: The Response of Reform Judaism to American Culture, 1840–1930.* Hanover, N.H.: Published for Brandeis University Press, 1994.

Skinner, Charles R. *Arbor Day Manual: An Aid in Preparing Programs for Arbor Day Exercises.* Freeport, N.Y.: Books for Libraries, 1977.

Smikle, Ken. "The Image Makers: Black Ad Agencies Use Diversified Services and General Market Accounts to Further Their Growth." *Black Enterprise,* December 1985.

Smith, Michael P. *Mardi Gras Indians.* Gretna, La.: Pelican Press, 1994.

Smith, Mike. "Celebrating the Worker." *Michigan History Magazine* 85 (September/October 2001): 44–53.

Softky, Elizabeth. "A Kwanzaa Memory: Growing Up with Dr. Karenga." *Washington Post,* December 20, 1995.

South End Forever and North End Forever: Extraordinary Verses on Pope-Night, Or, a Commemoration of the Fifth of November, giving a History of the Attempt, made by the Papists, to blow up the King and Parliament, A.D. 1588. Together with some Account of the Pope himself, and his Wife JOAN; with several other Things worthy of notice, too tedious to mention. Boston, 1768. Broadside 36, no. 28. Massachusetts Historical Society.

Spillman, Lyn. *Nation and Commemoration: Creating National Identities in the United States and Australia.* Cambridge: Cambridge University Press, 1997.

Spitzer, Nicholas. "Mardi Gras in L'Anse de 'Prien Noir: A Creole Community Performance in Rural French Louisiana." In *Creoles of Color of the Gulf South,* ed. James Dormon. Knoxville: University of Tennessee Press, 1996.

Springer, Haskell. *Washington Irving: A Reference Guide.* Boston: G.K. Hall and Co., 1976.

Starosta, William J. "A National Holiday for Dr. King? Qualitative Content Analysis of Arguments Carried in the Washington Post and New York Times." *Journal of Black Studies* 18, no. 3: 358–78.

"State to Honor Rebels' Dead." *Charlotte Observer,* May 6, 1962.

Stefoff, Rebecca. *The American Environmental Movement.* New York: Facts on File, 1995.

Stein, Marc. *City of Sisterly and Brotherly Loves: Lesbian and Gay Philadelphia, 1945–1972.* Chicago: University of Chicago Press, 2000.

Stevens, Joann. "A Lifestyle Called Kwanzaa, Black Maryland Families Celebrate a Week of Ceremonies That Reflect Age-Old African Traditions." *Washington Post,* December 27, 1979.

Stokes, Isaac Newton Phelps. *The Iconography of Manhattan Island, 1498–1909.* Vol. 4. New York: Oak Knoll, 1998.

Strassfeld, Michael. *The Jewish Holidays: A Guide and Commentary.* Philadelphia: Harper and Row, 1985.

Summerhill, Stephen J., and John Alexander Williams. *Sinking Columbus: Contested History, Cultural Politics, and Mythmaking during the Quincentenary.* Gainesville: University Press of Florida, 2000.

Sweet, Leonard. "The Fourth of July and Black Americans in the Nineteenth Century: Northern Leadership Opinion with the Context of the Black Experience." *Journal of Negro History* 61 (July 1976): 256–75.

Teal, Donn. *The Gay Militants.* New York: Stein and Day, 1971.

Thacher, James. *History of the Town of Plymouth.* Boston: Marsh, Capen & Lyon, 1835.

"Thanksgiving Day in New York up to Date." *Harper's Weekly,* November 28, 1891: 950.

Toure, Sekou. *Toward Full Re-Africanization.* Paris: Presence Africaine, 1959.

Travers, Len. *Celebrating the Fourth: Independence Day and the Rites of Nationalism in the Early Republic.* Amherst: University of Massachusetts Press, 1997.

Troupe, Quincy. "Festival Welcomes Uhuru Militants." *Los Angeles Free Press,* August 18, 1967.

Tyler, Bruce. "The Rise and Decline of the Watts Summer Festival, 1965–1986." *American Studies* 31 (1990): 61–81.

"UCLA Tops Africa Study." *UCLA Daily Bruin,* July 30, 1963.

Van DeBurg, William, ed. *Modern Black Nationalism: From Marcus Garvey to Louis Farrakhan.* New York: New York University Press, 1997.

Vartanian, Pershing. "The Puritan as Symbol in American Thought: A Study of the New England Societies 1820–1920." Ph.D. Diss, University of Michigan, 1971.

Vecoli, Rudolph J. "Primo Maggio: May Day Observances Among Italian Immigrant Workers, 1890–1920." *Labor's Heritage* 7, no. 4 (1996): 28–41.

Verter, Bradford. "Interracial Festivity and Power in Antebellum New York: The Case of Pinkster." *Journal of Urban History* 28 (2002): 398–428.

"Virginia's Tribute to Jefferson Davis." *Confederate Veteran,* May 1900: 216.

Waldstreicher, David. *In the Midst of Perpetual Fetes: The Making of American Nationalism, 1776–1820.* Chapel Hill: University of North Carolina Press, 1997.

Walker, C. Irvine. "Correct Estimate of Jeff Davis." *Confederate Veteran,* October 1908: 476.

Warner, Michael. *The Letters of the Republic: Publication and the Public Sphere in Eighteenth-Century America.* Cambridge, Mass.: Harvard University Press, 1990.

"Warner Wants to Meet Confederate Advocates." *Richmond Times-Dispatch,* January 19, 2002.

Warren, Charles. "Fourth of July Myths." *The William and Mary Quarterly,* 3d ser., 2, no. 3 (July 1945): 237–72.

Watts, Theodore F. *The First Labor Day Parade, Tuesday, September 5, 1882: Media Mirrors to Labor's Icons.* Silver Spring, Md.: Phoenix Rising, 1983.

Way, William. *History of the New England Society of Charleston, South Carolina, 1819–1919.* Charleston, S.C.: Published by the Society, 1920.

Weems, Robert. *Desegregating the Dollar: African-American Consumerism in the Twentieth Century.* New York: New York University Press, 1998.

Weiser, Francis X. *Handbook of Christian Feasts and Customs: The Year of the Lord in Liturgy and Folklore.* New York: Harcourt, Brace and World, 1952.

Weiss, Don, with Chuck Day. *The Making of the Super Bowl: The Inside Story of the World's Greatest Sporting Event.* New York: McGraw-Hill, 2003.

"What is Kwanzaa?: Thirty-Two Years After Its Creation, the Holiday Remains Misunderstood by Many." *Kwanzaa Fest '98* (*Caribbean Life*), December 1998: 7.

"What Mother's Day Means," *Parents' Magazine* 17 (May 1942): 49.

Whigham-Desir, Majorie. "Boom in Black Greeting Cards." *Black Enterprise,* December 1995: 104.

White, Shane. "'It was a proud day': African Americans, Festivals, and Parades in the North, 1741–1834." *Journal of American History* 81 (1994): 13–50.

Whites, LeeAnn. *The Civil War As a Crisis in Gender: Augusta, Georgia, 1860–1890.* Athens: University of Georgia Press, 1995.

Wiggins, William H. Jr. *O Freedom! Afro-American Emancipation Celebrations.* Knoxville: University of Tennessee Press, 1987.

Williams, Clarence G., ed. *Reflections of the Dream, 1975–1994: Twenty Years of Celebrating the Life of Dr. Martin Luther King, Jr. at the Massachusetts Institute of Technology.* Cambridge, Mass.: MIT Press, 1996.

Williams, Michael. *Americans and Their Forests: A Historical Geography.* Cambridge: Cambridge University Press, 1992.

Williamson, D. Todd. *Liturgies of the Triduum.* 3 videocassettes. Chicago: Liturgy Training Publications, 1999.

Williamson, Mary L. *The Life of Robert E. Lee.* Richmond, Va.: B. F. Johnson, 1895.

Willis, Susan. "I Want the Black One: Being Different—Is There a Place for Afro-American Culture in Commodity Culture." In *Cultural Remix: Theories of Politics and the Popular,* ed. Erica Carter, James Donald, and Judith Squires. London: Lawrence and Wishart, 1995.

Wilson, Charles Reagan. *Baptized in Blood: The Religion of the Lost Cause, 1865–1920.* Athens: University of Georgia Press, 1980.

Wilson, Woodrow. "An Armistice Day Statement." In *The Papers of Woodrow Wilson.* Vol. 64: 7, ed. Arthur S. Link. Princeton, N.J.: Princeton University Press, 1966.

Winslow, Edward. "Good News From New England." In *A Library of American Puritan Writings: The Seventeenth Century.* Vol. 9. *Histories and Narratives.* New York: AMS Press, 1986.

Winsor, Justin. *Christopher Columbus and How He Received and Imparted the Spirit of Discovery.* Boston: Houghton, Mifflin and Company, 1891.

Wolfe, Howard H. *Mothers Day and the Mothers Day Church.* Privately printed, 1962.

Wolfson, Ron. *Hanukkah: The Family Guide to Spiritual Celebration.* 2nd ed. Woodstock, Vt.: Jewish Lights Publishing, 2002.

Wright, Louis B., and Marion Tinling, eds. *The Secret Diary of William Byrd of Westover 1709–1712.* Richmond, Va.: The Dietz Press, 1941.

The Writings and Speeches of Daniel Webster. 18 vols. Boston: Little, Brown, & Co., 1903.

Yoder, Jacob E. *The Fire of Liberty in Their Hearts: The Diary of Jacob E. Yoder of the Freedmen's Bureau School, Lynchburg, Virginia, 1866–1870,* ed. Samuel L. Horst. Richmond, Va.: The Library of Virginia, 1996.

Young, Alexander. *Chronicles of the First Planters of The Colony of Massachusetts Bay, From 1623 to 1636.* Boston: Charles C. Little and James Brown, 1846.

———. *Chronicles of the Pilgrim Fathers of the Colony of Plymouth.* Boston: Charles C. Little and James Brown, 1841.

Zelizer, Viviana A. "Multiple Markets: Multiple Cultures." In *Diversity and Its Discontents,* ed. Neil J. Smelser and Jeffrey C. Alexander. Princeton, N.J.: Princeton University Press, 1999.

INDEX

ABOUT THE EDITOR
AND THE CONTRIBUTORS

LEN TRAVERS is associate professor of history at the University of Massachusetts at Dartmouth. He is the author of *Celebrating the Fourth: Independence Day and the Rites of Nationalism in the Early Republic* (1997) and "The Paradox of 'Nationalist' Festivals: The Case of Palmetto Day in Antebellum Charleston," in William Pencak, Matthew Dennis, and Simon P. Newman, eds., *Riot and Revelry in Early America* (2002).

DARYL ADAIR is a senior lecturer in humanities at the University of Canberra, Australia. He has written on various aspects of Irish, Australian, and diaspora history, and also on sports history and tourism. His main publications include (with Wray Vamplew) *Sport in Australian History* (1997), (with Mike Cronin) *The Wearing of the Green: A History of St Patrick's Day* (2002); and (with Brent Ritchie) *Sport Tourism* (2004).

DIANNE ASHTON is professor of religion and director of the American Studies Program at Rowan University. Dr. Ashton is the author of *Rebecca Gratz: Women and Judaism in Antebellum America* (1997), which was recommended by the New Jersey Council for the Humanities; *Jewish Life in Pennsylvania* (1998); and coeditor of *Four Centuries of Jewish Women's Spirituality* (1992). Her essays on American Jewish history have appeared in more than a dozen scholarly collections and in several encyclopedias. She currently sits on the boards of the Philadelphia Jewish Archives Center, the Jewish Women's Archive, and the Executive Council of the Academic Advisory Board of the American Jewish Historical Society.

James W. Baker served from 1976 to 2001 as director of research, vice president of museum operations, and senior historian at Plimoth Plantation in Plymouth, Massachusetts, helping to establish the outdoor museum's innovative first-person role-playing interpretation method in 1978. His publications include "Haunted by the Pilgrims," in *The Art and Mystery of Historical Archaeology: Essays in Honor Of James Deetz* (1992); "Thanksgiving Then and Now," in *Thanksgiving Cookery,* ed. Elizabeth Brabb (1994); and *Plimoth Plantation: Fifty Years of Living History* (1997). He has also given numerous presentations on the symbolic role of the Pilgrims in American culture. He is now curator at the Alden House Historic Site in Duxbury, Massachusetts.

Claudia L. Bushman teaches American studies at Columbia University. She considers herself a social historian and has written 10 books including *America Discovers Columbus: How an Italian Explorer Became an American Hero* (1992). The real genesis for her interest in holidays, however, came from her years as executive director of the Delaware Heritage Commission, a state agency that celebrates events. She was privileged to commemorate the creation and ratification of the Constitution of the United States, which elevated Delaware to "The First State" with such events as the recreation of the journey of Delaware delegates to the Annapolis Convention and The Great Bicentennial Ladybug Launch.

Clayborne Carson is professor of history and director of the King Papers Project at Stanford University. As editor of King's papers, he has published numerous works including *The Autobiography of Martin Luther King, Jr.* (1998) and 5 volumes of a projected 14-volume edition of *The Papers of Martin Luther King, Jr.* He is also coauthor of *African American Lives: The Struggle for Freedom* (2005).

Shaul Cohen is Associate Professor of Geography and Co-Director of the Peace Studies Program at the University of Oregon. His teaching focus is Human Geography, especially topics related to the interface between environment, politics, and culture. He is the author of *Planting Nature: Trees and the Manipulation of Environmental Stewardship in America* (2004), in which he critically examines the political and cultural aspects of tree planting campaigns around the world. His forthcoming *Doing Dirty Work: Land, Labor, and the Ungrounding of America,* will explore broader questions of alienation and people's relationship with nature in the modern age.

Karen L. Cox is the director of public history at the University of North Carolina at Charlotte. Her book *Dixie's Daughters: The United Daughters of the Confederacy and the Preservation of Confederate Culture* (2003) won the Julia Cherry Spruill Prize for the best work published in southern women's history. She is currently researching a book on Confederate culture.

Mike Cronin is academic director of the Centre for Irish Programmes for Boston College in Dublin, Ireland. He has written widely on aspects of Irish history, and also sports history. His main publications include: *The Blueshirts and Irish Politics* (1997), *Sport and Nationalism in Ireland* (1999), *A History of Ireland* (2001), and (with Daryl Adair) *The Wearing of the Green: A History of St Patrick' Day* (2002).

MATTHEW DENNIS is professor of history at the University of Oregon. He is the author of *Red, White, and Blue Letter Days: An American Calendar* (2002), *Cultivating a Landscape of Peace: Iroquois-European Encounters in 17th-Century America* (1993), and co-editor of *Riot and Revelry in Early America* (2002). He is currently working on a book, *Bones: Memory and Mortal Remains in America*, and is the general editor of *The Encyclopedia of World Holidays and Celebrations: A Country-by-Country Guide* to be published by Facts On File in spring of 2006.

MARK S. DYRESON is associate professor of kinesiology and affiliate professor of history at Penn State University. He is the author of *Making the American Team: Sport, Culture and the Olympic Experience* (1998) and of numerous articles on the subject of sport and culture.

J. BROOKS FLIPPEN received his Ph.D. from the University of Maryland and is presently professor of history at Southeastern Oklahoma State University. He is the author of *Nixon and the Environment* (2000) and a forthcoming biography of the environmentalist Russell E. Train.

DONNA T. HAVERTY-STACKE is assistant professor of history at Hunter College, City University of New York. She received her Ph.D. in History from Cornell University (2003), Master of Letters in Modern History from Oxford University (1997) and B.A. in American Studies from Georgetown University (1994). Her article, "'Boys Are the Backbone of Our Nation': The Cultural Politics of Youth Parades in Urban America," appeared in Volume 29 of *Prospects: An Annual of American Cultural Studies*. Haverty-Stacke is currently preparing a book-length study titled, "Constructing Radical America: May Day in New York City and Chicago, 1867–1960."

LOUIS M. HOLSCHER is professor and chair of Mexican American studies at San Jose State University, and has taught a wide variety of courses in sociology, criminal justice, and Chicano studies at a number of universities in North America. He has also worked for the Arizona Court of Appeals and as a staff attorney for the Federal Court of Appeals in San Francisco. Holscher has over 30 publications on Chicano music and popular culture, race and ethnic relations, crime, and criminal justice. Outside academia, he has worked for the United Farm Workers Union as a boycott coordinator and is a major collector of Chicano, soul, and blues music.

PETER HOPSICKER earned his Ph.D. in Sport History and Sport Philosophy from the Pennsylvania State University. He has presented several papers at the

North American Society for Sport History (NASSH) and the International Association for the Philosophy of Sport (IAPS) Conferences. Hopsicker is currently assistant professor of kinesiology at Penn State Altoona.

KATHLEEN W. JONES is associate professor of history at Virginia Tech. She is the author of *Taming the Troublesome Child; American Families, Child Guidance, and the Limits of Psychiatric Authority* (1999) and an article on the history of Mother's Day.

MITCH KACHUN teaches in the History Department at Western Michigan University, specializing in African American history, public commemorations, and historical memory. He is author of *Festivals of Freedom: Memory and Meaning in African American Emancipation Celebrations, 1808–1915* (2003), and coeditor, with William L. Andrews, of *The Curse of Caste; or, the Slave Bride* (forthcoming), a previously unpublished 1865 novel by Julia C. Collins, a largely unknown African American woman writer.

SAMUEL KINSER is director of the Center for Research in Festive Culture and Presidential Research Professor (history, emeritus) at Northern Illinois University. He is currently completing *Crazy by Convention: From Mardi Gras to Halloween, American Festivities and the Carnivalesque* (2006). Recent publications include "Amerindian Masking in Trinidad's Carnival" (with H. Bellour), in *Culture in Action*, ed. M. C. Riggio (2004) and "Paratextual Paradise and the Devilish Arts of Printing," in *Paratext, the Fuzzy Edges of Literature*, ed. C. Dauven, Carla Davven-van Knippenberg, Daan den Hergst Jelle Koopmans, Lisa Kuitert (2004).

J. STANLEY LEMONS is professor of history at Rhode Island College. His general specialty is America cultural history, and he has publications in women's history, African-American history, American religious history, and popular culture. Among his most recent books are *FIRST: The History of the First Baptist Church in America* (2001) and *The Elect: Rhode Island's Women Legislators, 1922–1990* (2001).

ELLEN M. LITWICKI is associate professor and chair of history at State University of New York–Fredonia. She is the author of *America's Public Holidays, 1865–1920* (2000) and is currently working on a cultural history of American domestic gift giving.

KEITH A. MAYES is currently an assistant professor in the Department of African American and African Studies at the University of Minnesota, Twin Cities. He is currently working on a manuscript entitled *Alternative Observances: Kwanzaa and the Making of the Black Holiday Tradition*.

BRENDAN MCCONVILLE is professor of history at Boston University. He is completing a book entitled *The King's Three Faces: The Rise and Fall of Royal America, 1688–1776* and is at work on a volume on the American Revolution.

ERIKA MEITNER is the Morgenstern Graduate Fellow in Jewish Studies at the University of Virginia, where she received her M.F.A. in poetry, and is currently pursuing a Ph.D. in religious studies. Her first collection of poems, *Inventory at the All-Night Drugstore,* was published by Anhinga Press in 2003, and her most recent articles about Judaism and material culture are forthcoming in *The Practice of American Sacred Space* (2006), and *Cool Jewz: Contemporary Jewish Identity in Popular Culture* (2006).

BRUCE T. MORRILL, a Jesuit priest in the Roman Catholic Church, is associate professor and graduate program director in the Theology Department at Boston College. He has lectured widely in the United States and Europe and regularly publishes articles and reviews in various theological journals. His books include *Anamnesis as Dangerous Memory: Political and Liturgical Theology in Dialogue* (2000).

G. KURT PIEHLER is associate professor of history and director of the Center for the Study of War and Society at the University of Tennessee, Knoxville. He is the author of *Remembering War and the American* (1995), coeditor of *Major Problems in American Military History* (1999), and consulting editor for the *Oxford Companion to American Military History* (1999). He was the founding director (1994–1998) of the Rutgers Oral History Archives of World War II, which supplied the material for his 1997 televised lecture "The War That Transformed a Generation" for the History Channel.

WILLIAM K. POWERS has a Ph.D. in anthropology from the University of Pennsylvania. He is presently editor and publisher of Lakota Books and the author of over 20 books and monographs on Plains Indian culture, including *Oglala Religion* (1982), *Yuwipi* (1984), *Sacred Language* (1992), and the history of powwow, *War Dance* (1990). He lives in New Jersey and New Orleans.

PENNE RESTAD is a senior lecturer in American history at the University of Texas at Austin. She is the author of *Christmas in America: A History* (1995).

NICOLAS G. ROSENTHAL is a postdoctoral fellow at the University of California Humanities Research Institute, Irvine. His work, which focuses on race and ethnicity, the American West, and American Indian history, has appeared in several anthologies and journals, including the *Pacific Historical Review* and the *Western Historical Quarterly.* Currently, he is revising his doctoral dissertation, a twentieth-century history of American Indians and the Los Angeles metropolitan area.

JACK SANTINO is a professor of folklore and popular culture at Bowling Green State University. He has been president of the American Folklore Society and editor of the *Journal of American Folklore.* He has published extensively in occupational folklore and more recently in ritual, festival, and celebration. He is the author of several scholarly articles, ethnographic films, and books, including

Signs of War and Peace: Social Conflict and the Public Use of Symbols in Northern Ireland (2001).

TIMOTHY STEWART-WINTER is a graduate of Swarthmore College and a doctoral student in the Department of History at the University of Chicago. His research interests include gender, sexuality, and urbanism in the United States in the post-World War II period.